A Trout In The Milk

Profiles In Prosecution

Mel Harmon

authorHOUSE®

AuthorHouse™
1663 Liberty Drive
Bloomington, IN 47403
www.authorhouse.com
Phone: 1-800-839-8640

First published by AuthorHouse   5/17/2011

ISBN: 978-1-4567-6745-7 (sc)
ISBN: 978-1-4567-6744-0 (hc)
ISBN: 978-1-4567-6746-4 (e)

Library of Congress Control Number: 2011907418

Printed in the United States of America

AUTHOR'S NOTE

"Good judgment comes from experience. And where does experience come from? Experience comes from bad judgment." (Mark Twain)

Well —– **good judgment**, or shall we say COMMON SENSE, is either **innate** or **acquired**. *Innate* IF it traces back to a <u>life</u> <u>before</u> <u>life</u> **OR** to the composite experience of a person's <u>ancestral</u> <u>lineage</u> – AND *acquired* IF it traces back to a person's composite experience in <u>mortality</u>.

Consensus may be hard to achieve with respect to **origin.** However, I'd say there is an undeniable FACT regarding that which <u>is</u> a **palpable reality** – COMMON SENSE <u>**isn't**</u> so common. The fact is, so called COMMON SENSE is an extremely **<u>uncommon</u> <u>commodity</u>** – a *classic* MISNOMER! Criminals <u>PROVE</u> the **un-<u>commonality</u>** of common sense. If they had <u>it</u> there wouldn't be any need for Prosecutors. Those characters who are LIFERS in the SLAMMER can certainly attest to **the Experience** *BAD* <u>judgment</u> brings. Show me a Murder that makes sense! GOOD JUDGMENT is a damned hard trait to come by.

I'm the son of a dairyman. I discuss <u>experiences</u> from my life growing up on The Farm in **Part One.** Those happy days are a time of frugality and hard work – of simplicity – of gratitude and love. A time when *judgment* is molded.

The Farmer became a Lawyer. **Part Two** is a discussion of <u>experiences</u> from my career in The Courtroom. I <u>haven't</u> utilized *actual Transcripts* of Court Proceedings as a factual basis for my remarks. Obviously, if an author isn't using Court Transcripts, he <u>can't</u> offer verbatim recitations. I've used *case outlines* and *memory*. Both sources are subject to human fallibility, though my *outlines* were meticulously prepared. The precursor of Prosecutorial **tongue sweat** is <u>sweating fingers</u>. As for my *memory* – well, it's certainly flawed. However, many things are etched into my psyche. Please be advised that <u>names</u> have often been *deliberately* changed. Moreover, my text is fact *blended* with fiction – to a certain extent. I've used logical inference and some creative imagination to fill in <u>details</u> that shortfalls in memory and the inability to be a fly on the wall have failed to provide. Accordingly, the book contains a generous mix of literary license.

I can **truthfully** say I <u>never</u> had an agenda during my career, nor did I act from ulterior motive. I diligently tried to *see* things as they *are*. I <u>never</u> personally knew the parties, nor the witnesses, nor the Victims or their families. I had <u>no</u> *personal* interest in the outcome of <u>any</u> case.

I'm **not** a racist. I <u>believe</u> in the brotherhood and equality of *all* human beings. **<u>Each</u>** of us is spiritually begotten by an Eternal Father in Heaven. I'm not preaching when I say this, I'm explaining **my** *personal* moral and spiritual *values*. They are the seed bed of my character and of my motivation.

I <u>don't</u> pretend to be a <u>wise</u> man, but I'd like to believe I've acted wisely with a modicum of consistency. I'm <u>not</u> a promoter of "snake oil" schemes. <u>Not</u> a Prosecutor programed to believe my service changed the nature of things. I'm just saying I tried to be fair –– ONE case at a time.

Respectfully,
Mel Harmon

PREFACE

"Some circumstantial evidence is very strong, as when you find a trout in the milk." (Henry David Thoreau, *Journal. November 11, 1854*)

There are two great branches of evidence in a Criminal Case. They are **direct evidence** and **circumstantial evidence**. The meaning of direct evidence is as plain as the nose on your face. A first grader can easily grasp the concept. Whatever a person perceives with any of his physical senses is <u>direct</u> <u>evidence</u>. *Seeing* a nose on a face is direct evidence that the face has a nose. *Seeing* a dead body is direct evidence that the person is dead. If you *see* a crime happen that is direct evidence. And if you *smell* it or *touch* it or *taste* it or *hear* it as it happens – that is also *direct evidence*. <u>Everything else</u> is *circumstantial*. Therefore, the meaning of circumstantial evidence is easily comprehended and just as easily categorized. There's no need to ever be confused about the meaning of circumstantial evidence again. *If it isn't direct evidence it's circumstantial evidence*! And since we know the plain-as-the-nose-on-your-face definition of direct evidence, we know exactly what evidence is circumstantial. It's as easy as falling off a log. Which will be <u>circumstantial</u> <u>evidence</u> IF the witness testifying against you does not see you fall, but does see you sitting on your posterior next to the wobbly log dusting off your pants.

Further, it may surprise quite a few people to learn that circumstantial evidence is *not* qualitatively inferior to direct evidence. I repeat, circumstantial evidence is *not*, per se, entitled to *less* weight than direct evidence. This seminal concept of criminal evidence, as I understand it, rests upon an unequivocal premise: *both* direct and circumstantial evidence, IF firmly established, are entitled to be given the **same** amount of <u>weight</u> – subject, of course, to the vagaries of evidence <u>credibility</u>.

The fact is: a *confession* is circumstantial evidence. Likewise, *fingerprint* and *bullet* and *DNA* evidence are <u>circumstantial</u>. Most evidence in criminal cases <u>is</u> circumstantial.

I'm very fond of Henry David Thoreau's classic example of circumstantial evidence. I've used it hundreds of times during Summation. It became my signature explanation of <u>circumstantial</u> <u>evidence</u>. Thoreau states, "Some circumstantial evidence is *very* strong, as when you find A TROUT IN THE MILK." (ibid. – emphasis added)

I grew up on a dairy farm. I know the importance of having a herd of cows that achieves high-volume milk production. The more milk the cows make the more money the farmer makes. And although we never resorted to such measures at Harmon Farm, [Would I admit it if we did?] I fully appreciate this stubborn reality. <u>Some</u> dairy farmers *might* be profoundly tempted to increase their milk supply by dipping the milk can into a stream of water. Which, of course, is how the slippery trout in Thoreau's analogy got into the milk. Nobody saw the farmer lower his milk can into the stream, but we can be absolutely **positive** he did.

Why? Well, the trout didn't spontaneously generate in a can of milk. The natural habitat of a cutthroat trout is *not* performing deft figure eights in a foaming vessel of fresh, warm milk. The fat cutthroat didn't come from the cow's udder, she's a milk maker not a trout maker. Her udder *isn't* a fish hatchery, trust me on this one. So, since the squiggly cutthroat didn't come from the cow's udder, it *had* to come from the farmer's stream of water. Hence, Thoreau's astute observation of record has withstood the passage of time. "Some circumstantial evidence is very strong, as when you find a trout in the milk."(ibid.)We didn't see it happen, but the circumstances are so compelling we **know** it <u>did</u> happen! The finned scrapper getting his <u>first</u> taste of milk is <u>**irrefutable**</u> evidence of dairy farmer duplicity!

The CIRCUMSTANCE EVIDENCE in many criminal cases is compelling **proof** of criminal defendant complicity!

CONTENTS

PART ONE

By The Sweat Of My Brow

"In the sweat of thy face shalt thou eat bread, till thou return
unto the ground; for out of it wast thou taken: for dust thou
art, and unto dust shalt thou return."(*Holy Bible*, Genesis 3:19)

There's A House I Know By Heart

"There's a house whose rooms I know by heart
Where I read my books and got a loving start.
Where trees grew tall and children played in shade.
Where dreams were dreamt and memories made.
Where we heard Bible stories and did as we were told.
Where four children grew up and their parents grew old.
Where the value of work and sweat each child did learn ––
Where once was joy for which my heart does yearn."
(Anonymous – adapted)

Chapter 1

I'm the son of a farmer. When I was two years old my father and mother moved into a four room adobe farmhouse. The year was 1940 –– a time of simplicity and frugality. We had kerosene lamps for lighting, a coal burning stove for heating, and a wood burning stove for cooking, There was no central heating nor cooling system – we had no electricity. We lived without much money, without a telephone, without a television, without a washing machine, and without running water. We only had a battery powered radio, and our culinary water had to be hauled from town in a large metal barrel.

One day the water barrel slipped and mashed one of Dad's thumbs. It looked like a fleshy appendage of bloody pulp after the accident. I was terrified! The sight of the mushy thumb remains etched in my mind to this day. Recovery is painfully slow. And sometime during the healing process my father, blessed with innate common sense, acquires a greater appreciation for thumbs. He decides that two healthy thumbs are a very valuable commodity. Therefore, once he is physically able – necessity being the mother of invention, he builds a cistern on a nearby hillside. Then, with the confluence of a crudely constructed water pipe system, town water poured into the cistern from a 500 gallon tank secured in a wooden frame that slides in and out of the bed of our pickup truck, and the law of gravity – we have some running culinary water at our farmhouse. And Dad doesn't have any more mashed thumbs, though an occasional scaly lizard does find its way into our water supply.

Actually, there is running irrigation water just a few rods east of the house. A large irrigation canal fed by river water borders our farmland for half a mile. It carries irrigation water for hundreds of acres under cultivation throughout the Fields. The Canal is wide and deep and the current swift. Several years before the smashed thumb incident, and only a few months after we'd moved to the farm, I chose to do some exploring, so I've been told. Mom has recited the story on many occasions. What follows is a reasonable facsimile of her various accounts of the event.

I am playing on the back doorstep of our farmhouse, when I decide to shake things up by embarking on a summer stroll – solo . My quest will take me about a quarter mile along the narrow west bank of The Canal in search of my Father. So, I scamper through the small, lateral irrigation ditch immediately south of the house, which is empty. Then, I make a beeline for the Big Ditch – the Fields Canal. My objective is soon attained.

I pause at the brink of the waterway, peer into the depths of the roily water, and hang a hard right. Childish instinct choosing to toddle along the razor thin footpath that threads its way through thick brush along The Canal. Hoping the primitive path leads to my Daddy. Thereafter, short, unsteady, tipsy step after step I persistently trudge through the thick underbrush along the edge of the swift moving water. Separated from the channel of the stream by a scant twelve inches of bank. One carelessly discarded farm implement, one slip, one stumble, one misstep, or one slight cave-in along the path I trod would have caused me to splash unseen into a certain watery grave – sweeping me miles downstream in the turbid water and out of the mortal lives of two loving parents.

But it didn't happen. It's been said,"God protects babies and fools."

(George Bernard Shaw) I'm living proof of the veracity of the renowned playwrights flippant remark. Heaven protected me that pivotal day long ago when a baby boy foolishly strays from his Mother's safe haven and tries to find his Daddy all by himself.

Words cannot adequately describe the reaction of my dear Mother when she notices her little toddler in striped coveralls is missing. I believe my Mother's worst nightmare has always been that one of her children would fall into the murky waters of the big irrigation ditch and drown.

She runs around the outside of the farmhouse, and seeing no sign of me, she dashes to The Canal. Breathlessly staring upstream and downstream as a fervent prayer forms in her pounding heart. "Dear God, no – no – no! Not my precious baby. Please don't let him be in the water. Please. Please. It will kill me if *I've* let him fall into the water!" However, she still sees nothing. There is no sign of the curly, tousled little head of hair. As quickly as a blink of the eye, it seems, he is gone.

My Mother can see my Father working in the second field south of the farmhouse. She begins running and stumbling along the narrow ditch bank toward him. The rough brush scratches her legs and the palms of her hands are abraded by smother weed, Johnson grass, sunflowers, and clods each time she falls. The heavy growth of foliage along The Canal shields the intrepid little toddler from her view. Tearfully, panic-stricken she screams my Father's name, "Elmer –– Elmer –– Elmer, help me! Melvin's gone. Melvin's gone. I'm afraid he's fallen into The Canal. Dear God, help me! Help us!"

Who can fully grasp the anguish of a mother who fears she has lost her little two year old, the first-born of her womb, into a treacherous current of deep running water? That little one who is the object of her loving care each day from the time the sun rises until the sun sets – and into the night. My Mother's fright becomes hysteria. The delirium makes it hard for her to see or think and breathe. She is crazy with grief and misgiving. How is it possible *she* has allowed this to happen? How can *she* ever forgive herself?

Finally, her screams, her frenzied gestures, and her desperate dash along the canal bank catch Dad's attention. He drops his shovel and runs along the ditch toward her. She's so distraught he's been unable to fully understand the situation. But he has heard her cries concerning "Melvin" and fears the worst. His heart aches. Tears stream down his face as he plows through the brush.

Then suddenly, in a heartbeat, darkness turns to light. The foolish toddler and the frantic father meet. He sees me as I see him, and I scamper into his open arms. SAFE – in the loving grasp of my Daddy. My Mother is about fifty feet away. When she sees my Father scoop me into his arms, she sees an answer to heart-felt prayer and senses the nearness of the Lord. She's lifted into brilliant blessed rays of happiness again. It's as though a son has been reborn. *Her truth* is redemption, self-forgiveness, and the chance to be a more vigilant mother. Black depression is dispersed and boundless joy envelopes her soul.

The relief is immediate and immense. Everything around her evolves into a golden haze. She loses strength in her legs, her eyelids flutter, and she collapses in a heap on the ground. My Precious Mother FAINTS! The beauty of life renewed, hers and mine, is a sacred remembrance.

My *first* actual <u>mortal memory</u> is of a black pickup truck rack. What this particular pickup truck is to"pickup"are pigs going to market. So, more precisely stated **the rack** is really a black-pigs-going-to-market-rack for the family's black Ford truck. A brood of ill fated pigs raised on our farm is scheduled to make an unsolicited one-way trip to California. These porkers are probably content to reside in the squalor of our pig digs for the remainder of their natural lives. They undoubtedly have no interest in making a cramped trip to the Golden State in the bed of a pickup. But Dad has a different plan in the late summer of 1942.

The presence of pigs on the farm isn't prompted by an altruistic view of swine. The pigpen domain is the stinkiest spot on our property. The pigs are only tolerated because Dad loves pork <u>and</u> he believes we can sell those we don't eat for a profit when they achieve marketable size. Furthermore, Dad's oldest brother lives in Glendale, California. Therefore, a trip to the coast will provide us with an opportunity, as the expression goes, "To kill two birds with one stone." Rather, it gives us an excuse to roam. We can visit our relatives <u>and</u> *kill* six pigs with *one* trip from home.

My Father painstakingly constructs the pig rack, and even though my youthful skills as a painter are seriously deficient, Mom and me proudly paint **the rack** a gleaming black to match the color of the pickup truck. No self-respecting farm family can travel to California without being color-coordinated. After several coats of pain have been applied, **the rack** reposes for a time in the yard about thirty feet west of the farmhouse. There the shiny black pig rig can dry and be displayed. The town road is a single, narrow dirt lane that winds just a few feet north of the house. The eye-catching black rack is a visible monument for all to see. The Harmons intend to take their pigs to the slaughterhouse themselves.

When the big day arrives, we manage to coax our little herd of pork-chops-on-the-hoof up the chute to the height of the pickup bed. From that level the squealing bristly mammals are prodded into the bed of the truck. I remember how they slid and sprawled and sh––t as their hooves made contact with the slick metal surface.

And then we were off to L.A. –– Dad and Mom and me. There wasn't any Disneyland yet, the Magic Kingdom is a decade and a half into the future. Nevertheless, the excitement we felt, as we embarked on this grand adventure with our cargo of six, was euphoric. These farm folks were livin large! Though I do recall feeling a slight lump in my throat as we headed west on the dirt Fields Road. This is my first trip away from the security of our snug little adobe house.

We didn't do any sightseeing. We drove straight toward the market. It isn't easy, even when you have a shiny new black rack, to travel nearly 400 miles with six *homesick* pigs in a pickup bed. Well, maybe it isn't homesickness but a form of *seasickness* that is the problem. I only know those six pigs pooped a lot. Every time we make a turn there is a palpable sway to the entire pickup as the porkers <u>slide</u> and <u>scramble</u> from one side of the bed to the other. It makes steering difficult for Dad, and of course, the smell becomes incredibly noxious! Traveling down the busy highway we leave an unmistakable aroma in the air, and an unmistakable trail of litter spattered on the road – from muck seepage through the end gate of the old Ford.

To say we were not adept at driving in a big city is a gross understatement! All three of us are intimidated by the size of Los Angeles, California. Even the pig-squealing moves up a few decibels in intensity as we chug and shimmy through the streets of L.A. Perhaps, the piglets sense the slaughterhouse lays at the end of the journey – awful in it implication for them.

We don't know the way to the slaughter yard, of course. Our foray through the city consists of a series of turnoffs to frantically study the big city map, which to us is practically indecipherable, a lot of backtracking, and a host of directions solicited from people who clearly don't know any more about Los Angeles than we do. Our entire venture into the bowels of L.A.'s meat packing district could have been a primer in how <u>not</u> to traverse the byways of a big city. It's a pitiful exhibition of how to go in ever expanding circles without meaning to.

Obviously, farm-folks on the move in a large city don't want to have an accident. Well —— we did! I don't really know if "the accident" is precipitated by Dad's inexperience with metropolitan driving, the confusion of being lost in the maze of Los Angeles streets, the embarrassment created by the noise and smell of our little Ford pig-transport —— whose newly painted black rack has lost its sheen, the distraction of six skidding pigs, the spectacle of curious on-lookers gawking at every intersection —— or *fate*. I only know we did have a bump-in.

As we lumbered through one of those seemingly endless big city intersections, we broadside a yellow Cadillac driven by a fancy big-city dame. The event catapults us into a tizzy. I don't have a clue who the lady was – we didn't wait around to get her name. It could have been Greta Garbo for all we knew, or some other Hollywood legend.

My Father quickly hops out to survey the damage to our pickup. It is minimal. There wasn't much velocity behind the impact. After all, I did say we were "lumbering" through the intersection at the time of the collision. And a cursory head-count of the porker-six did not suggest any fatalities – only a mucky melee! So, Dad gets back into the cab, puts the ole stick shift into a grinding reverse, and we go traipsing off into the big-city-maze.

I don't know how extensive the damage was to the Cadillac – we didn't wait around to do a crash-damage inventory. I don't know if the police were called – we didn't wait around to share pertinent facts with the gendarmes. And **we** didn't contact any coppers about the situation after we'd left the scene neither. Too flustered to think straight was our excuse, I suppose.

We do turn to look "ere...[we] drove out of sight," and the big-city cookie has extricated herself from her vehicle. (Clement Clarke Moore, *Twas the night before Christmas Poem*, adaptation) She is standing in the intersection shaking her fist, and probably shouting expletives.

Only the good Lord knows what she's saying, but her body language didn't look friendly, and I'm going to guess she's launching a slew of unsavory epithets in our direction. However, it's all to no avail. The mishap is behind us. The pig farmers in the piggie-van from hicksville are going, going —— gone!

Eventually, we do find the Los Angeles stockyards. There we unmercifully unload the slaughterhouse-six. We hated [Ha!] to part company with our stinky companions, but Dad's wallet is plumper when we leave, and that is ample solace for the emotional trauma of leaving our soon-to-be- pork-chops behind. Though, had the six prime porkers had their say so, they surely would have oinked a dour, "**We** <u>definitely</u> do mind being left behind."

We stayed the night in Glendale with Uncle Irvin, Aunt Winnie, and my cousin Mary. I still remember how friendly they were. Aunt Winnie was charming and sweet and hospitable. She seemed especially anxious to make us feel welcome and to attend to all our needs. Uncle Irvin was very nice too, but in a somewhat more reserved manner. Mary was several years older, and much more grownup and sophisticated than me. We didn't have much in common then – except for the same last name. She tried to engage me in youthful conversation, but I could only shyly drop my head and fidget my fingers.

Later that night, lying all alone on an unfamiliar bed in a dark bedroom in a strange house far away from our farmland, I recall crying inconsolably. We'd experienced a very eventful day. Perhaps, a little too exciting for a country boy. Many thoughts were cascading through my mind. It isn't always pleasant being away from home. It's a little scary, and I yearned for the comfort and security of customary surroundings. Lonely for the little adobe house I **knew** by heart. "Mid pleasures and palaces we may roam, Be it ever so humble, there's no place like home." (Adapted from American actor and dramatist John Howard Payne's 1823 opera, *Clari, Maid of Milan*)

My Mother heard me and came to offer sweet condolence. She cradled me in her arms. Laid by me on Aunt Winnie's fluffy bed, and told me a story about a boy with a motorcycle. We'd seen motorcycle riders on the road earlier as we'd driven along the highway to California.

I don't remember anymore about the story. I've never had a motorcycle. I've never wanted a motorcycle. I've never ridden a motorcycle. And I wasn't very interested in motorcycles that distant night in Glendale, California. But I do remember that my dearest mother was able to quiet my sobbing and dry my tears and make me feel <u>less</u> lonely. She did it with a hug and a kiss and a story. It is the <u>first</u> of many stories I have remembrance of Mom telling me. I'd love to have her tell me the story again, but she is gone *<u>for now</u>*.

Christmastime was magical at our adobe farmhouse. Seated by the soothing warmth of our coal burning stove, my Mother lifted my imagination into orbit with tales of reindeer and Santa Claus, elves and toys, the bright Star over Bethlehem – and Baby Jesus.

My first recollection of Christmas morning is being held in the strong arms of my Father, gazing in wonderment at a model train set, complete with an engine, two cars, and a caboose, chugging around a circular track on our kitchen floor. A colorfully lighted Christmas tree illuminated the clanking choo-choo. I had no idea such amazing toys existed. I was told that Santa brought it from the North Pole. That he brings toys to nice boys and girls all over the world at Christmastime, but that the <u>greatest</u> gift of Christmas is the **gift** of God's Only Begotten Son.

Of course, the world is a big place. Santa needs lots of helpers in his workshop to make toys for the whole world. The way it was explained to me, these helpers are called *elves*. One of the most important elves is *Tippy Toes*. He's the chief elf of the Santa Claus intelligence apparatus. The name is a <u>derivative</u> of tiptoe. He's quiet and stealthy. Presumably, moving about with his weight on the balls of his feet and his heels off the ground. He secretly comes around in the weeks before Christmas to find out whose being naughty or nice. He reports his findings to the Main Man at the North Pole. The concept of *Tippy Toes* worries me as a youngster. I think about him a lot. I certainly don't want to be left off the North Pole Christmas gift list.

One cold, windy December night, while I sat at our kitchen table looking outside, I see Santa's snoopy elf eyeballing me through the frosty window. He just peers at me for a few moments, taking my measure, and *poof*–– he vanishes. It is an eloquent testimonial to the power of suggestion and to Mom's power of persuasion. She'd made me a true believer. For those who are curious, *Tippy Toes* is a dead ringer for Micky Mouse.

> "How beautiful is youth! how bright it gleams
> With its illusions, aspirations, dreams!
> Book of Beginnings, Story without End,
> Each maid a heroine, and each man a friend."
> (Henry Wadsworth Longfellow, *Morituri Salutamus*,
> The Complete Poetical Works of Longfellow, 1922, p.311)

Farm life was hard, but it was good. Life on a farm is "Rich in saving common-sense..." (Alfred, Lord Tennyson, *Ode on the Death of the Duke*

of Wellington [1852] Stanza 4) It's a matter of establishing fundamental priorities. We were short on cash, but we weren't short on love. There was an abundance of <u>love</u> on the farm! I've lived for many years on this earth now, but life has never been better, nor have the seasons been more blessed, than they were during those early days in our little adobe house. We faced the future fearlessly, because we faced the future with faith and love – and each other.

Over time my three sisters joined us to sweeten the mix. After the third little girl appeared on the scene, the four room adobe farmhouse was expanded to seven rooms and given a white stucco face-lift. It is simply a matter of common sense! A large kitchen, a bathroom, and the girls' bedroom were added.

Book of Beginnings, Story without End. (Longfellow, ibid.) A child likes to play, and in the natural order of things – he has playmates. However, back in the 1940s the Harmons didn't have neighbors. Furthermore, I was four and a half years old before my first Sister came along. So, playtime for me is often solitary time. I have playthings, but they aren't of the human kind.

I would sit on the back doorstep of our farmhouse with my tortoiseshell *Kitten*. A cat with yellowish brown mottled or clouded coloring that resembled a turtle's shell. I'd tug his whiskers and tickle him, talk to him and reason with him, rub his belly and listen to him purr for hours. He'd stretch himself across my lap and I imagined if I petted him <u>long</u> enough, he would miraculously change into a little boy. Someone I could play with.

We had a pile of discarded bricks on red sand west of the house. I'd take my toys outside. Then sit in the sand and make fields, fences, and sheds for my trucks, tractor, and farm implements. It wasn't uncommon for me to lift bricks off the red dirt and have large yellow *Scorpions* scurry into view. They were very aggressive, and they'd rush out from under the bricks prepared to do battle. Their lobsterlike pincers exposed and their jointed stingers curved up and menacing behind them. It was an impressive display. They were quick, fearless – and poisonous.

I'd scamper away from my yellow protagonists, and manage to avoid being stung. But my Sister Ilene received a Scorpion sting on her foot while she was playing on the front porch. Scorpions aren't very friendly playthings.

I didn't appreciate having to share my farm terrain with a variety of desert *Snakes* neither. Like the scorpions, certain snakes seemed hell-bent on projecting themselves into my childhood games. I gotta say, I have a phobia for snakes! I was born with it, but having them as frequent companions on my playground turf didn't help matters. During my youthful years I saw them almost daily. They seemed to enjoy hanging out in the rocks, cactus, yucca, chaparral, sagebrush, cow corrals, ditch banks, hay fields, and cane fields as much as I enjoyed hiking in those venues.

The chief offenders I remember on the farm were the California Kingsnake, Gopher snakes, and Red Racers. Curiously, I have no memory of ever seeing a rattlesnake on our land, though they are indigenous to this area.

The Kingsnake comes in many varieties. I'm told, the generic <u>kingsnake</u> label references their taste for eating other snakes on occasion. A Kingsnake isn't poisonous, though that news would be academic to whatever he's eating. The scarlet kingsnake is often confused with coral snakes – which of course, do have lethal venom. There's a saying: "If red touches black, it's okay for Jack. But if red touches yellow, Jack's a dead fellow."

The California Kingsnake is black with between twenty to forty five white bands or stripes. It's rather docile around humans, grows to three or four feet and, supposedly, is popular as a pet – though I wouldn't know anything about making a snake a pet. If I'm walking through an alfalfa field, and have a close encounter with a kingsnake, I'm going to practically jump out of my shoes. It always been that way – whether I've been seven or seventy.

The Gopher snake is a large and powerful snake. It kills its prey by constriction. Sometimes it reaches six feet in length. Not surprisingly, it eats rabbits, lizards, <u>gophers</u>, and other rodents. The desert food chain is a lot about who eats what and what eats who. The Gopher snake's skin pattern is similar to a rattlesnake, and it is sometimes mistaken for a rattler. The slithering nemesis of gophers may be yellowish or cream colored and have brown or reddish blotches along the back. The books I've read tell me he's a "gentle and easygoing snake." But I've never handled one.

However, may the record reflect and I want a standing objection, the *Red Racer* is easily my most vexing ophidian experience on the farm. He is Coluber Constrictor. A dryland Boa. His habitat is cactus and yucca scrub and, it seems, <u>wherever</u> a farm boy chooses to walk. He's quick, as the name implies, and he has a nasty disposition.

The Red Racer gets as long as six feet, has a slender whip-like body, and a coloration that varies from gray to tan to pink with black crossbars present on the neck. As the Racer ages, it takes on a more distinct reddish appearance. Its diet consists of lizards, small snakes, mice and birds. He's the fastest snake in the desert, and glides across the ground at speeds up to 7 mph. Further, he's mean tempered, and though he's not poisonous, his bite can tear the flesh. This snake shouldn't be handled by amateurs. He's a fellow who should definitely be avoided.

Oh my, therein lies the problem. These long limbless reptiles seemed to be everywhere when I was young. In my mind, they used a tag team approach with the kid from the house. They laid in wait, hanging out under nearby yuccas until I made an appearance, and then one or more of these lightning fast rascals would dart out to intercept me. Let me simply say, when you're five <u>and</u> you're at ground zero <u>and</u> your top speed has been clocked at less than six miles per hour <u>and</u> there's a Red Devil coming lickety-split in your direction at 7 MPH – you're sweating bullets. You're wondering why you came out of the farmhouse. You're wondering what tree or fence or wagon you can climb. You're wishing you were packing heat or hand grenades or that you had a machete to cut these ole boys into ribbons.

Fortuitously, the Red Runners never caught me in their sharp fangs, though I suppose they could have. Perhaps, they never really wanted to catch me. It's like this was a game to the Racers, that they just wanted to <u>torment</u> me. They were aggressive only to a point. When I ran from them they ran toward me. Yet, when I stood my ground with a menacing stick or lobbed rocks in their direction, they'd hold their ground. Then go zipping on their merry way.

The bottom line is: I may have been solitary, but not so desperate for friends I'd be willing to fraternize with pugnacious Red Racers.

It goes beyond our beef with the occasional *Lizard* that bathed in our cistern drinking water. Yes, they're creatures of the Almighty, but I found them a little creepy too. They're reptiles, for gosh sakes. Also, they're sooooo jittery. They scramble into nearby bushes, sprint across your path, and around your feet. Making you think they're going to climb on your shoe – and go north. Sometimes they do!

My Father's experience is a case in point. I didn't see it happen, but he's told me the story a number of times, and I've noticed he shudders each time he does. I believe that's a compelling indicia of reliability in this instance. Dad didn't often shudder.

He was getting ready to irrigate, and is walking along the weedy bank of a headwater ditch in the good old summertime when it happens. Once the water is actually turned on the field, Dad will be wearing irrigation boots. But he's wearing high-top work shoes and carries a shovel over one shoulder at the time of the incident. The shovel's a powerful tool, but it will be useless against the impending incursion. It will be man versus lizard.

Dad plants his right foot on the ground, without warning a lizard darts out from the shade of a clump of smother weed, and climbs on his shoe. My Father is startled. He's not great enamored of lizards, and he's certainly not too keen about giving a lizard a ride on his work shoe. He drops the shovel, lifts his leg, and tries to shake the speedy invader off. The ploy backfires. The already distraught lizard doesn't want to take a nose dive into the hot crusty dirt, so he crawls up the shoe and ducks under the bottom of Dad's right trouser leg. Hell fires! That's the last place a sweaty farmer wants a flaky lizard. Worse still, the speedy reptile doesn't stop at his ankle. He quickly does a circular reconnaissance of the immediate area of entrapment and scampers upward. Which, given his vertical momentum, seems to be the only option available.

Hey, we have a problem here. Lizards have sharp teeth and they bite. This rambunctious fellow is in an extremely delicate location where he can inflict some serious damage. My Father is now dancing a jig and sweating profusely. Fools and lizards rush in where angels fear to tread. The impulsive lizard has rushed in but he can't find the way out. Further, Dad's bouncing about is scaring the bejeebers out of his uninvited guest – who thinks he's on a slippery slide and is desperately using the braille system in an effort to find something to grab.

Luckily for the two principals, since the Lizard is already inside, Dad has <u>loose</u> fitting clothes. After what seems like an eternity to my Father, the four leggety reptilian pushes past the crotch and hotfoots his way across the waistline. Suddenly, four sets of little claws are tweaking a farmer's belly. The sensation is maddening. Dad tries to trap the little guy with his hands, but the jittery lizard scuttles up his chest, exits the collar of his shirt, and clambers on to Dad's neck.

Finally, a breath of fresh air for the brazen reptile with the indomitable climbing technique.

My Father attempts to swat the trespasser off his neck, but the irascible lizard eludes his swipe. Crawls across his face, under the brim of his straw hat, and swiftly emerges on top of Dad's head. Ah-ha. The intrepid intruder has reached the pinnacle. He's conquered the human mountain. Gone as far north as he can go. He's gone all the way – the feisty little lizard has scored. It's a great exhibition of broken field running, or should we say – perpendicular scrambling.

However, it's over as quickly as it began. Dad flips the hat off his head, and deftly flicks the high flying lizard back to earth. A lizard is like a cat it seems. The lizard lands on his feet and darts back to the shade and safety of smother weeds.

Chastened and wiser, I'd say, and far less likely to scamper across a man's shoe again. The shortest distant between two points is a straight line, but the safest distance between two points for a lizard is often going to be a circular line. He doesn't go over the shoe he goes around it!

My Father is shaken, but unharmed. However, he could **never** talk about the lizard that crawled under his clothes from the right pants leg to the top of his head without <u>shuddering</u>!

Dad didn't get the name, rank, and serial number of the fast moving reptile, but from his cursory description I'd say it was a Western Whiptail lizard, a.k.a. Cnemidephorus Tigris. The Western Whiptail has black and white to brownish orange scales and parallel stripes down its dorsal side. Thus, coloration probably explains Tigris and Whiptail refers to the lizard's long tail that resembles a whip. I guess my Father is lucky, his ears could have taken a whipping while the C. Tigris perched on his head. Curiously, this species of lizard is rather shy – until it panics.

Another way a lonely farm boy can choose to pass time is harassing *Doodlebugs*. It's much more pleasant than walking around, stepping over, and <u>running</u> from poisonous scorpions, desert snakes and Whiptail lizards. The Doodlebug name is descriptive of a variety of insects, especially the larva of ant lions. The bugs I dealt with were about half the size of one of my little-boy pinkies. There were many small Doodlebug craters outside the picket fence in front of our adobe farmhouse. They didn't go unnoticed. I'd scoop up handfuls of sand, and go from hole to hole, sifting dirt slowly into Doodlebug pits. Actually, not a very polite way to greet a colony of Doodlebugs. They'd come churning up to the surface, expecting to feast on hapless morsels that had fallen into their carefully engineered sand traps, only to be inundated by a five year old's <u>sandy</u> showers. A double barreled setback for the Doodlebugs: no lunch and peepers full of grit. If the Doodlebugs had been conversant in English, I'd have been the target of some thorough chastisement. Of course, I never hurt them, I just teased them. They were my *insect* playthings. And I did feed them on occasion. I'd drop miniature black ants into their holes.

Charming characters such as scorpions, snakes, and lizards kept me inside a good deal during my early years. Within the walls of the house whose rooms I know by heart, it's a world of *tinker-toys, tops, train sets, Lincoln logs, dominoes, checkers, cards games, crayons, coloring books, marbles, and MOM.* I diligently labored over my childhood toys with a passion born of an industrious nature and innate curiosity. I liked to build things, take things apart, draw things, color things, listen to things, watch things spin, and watch things fall over. It wasn't very cool in the summer and not very warm in the winter, but our wonderful farmhouse shielded us from nature's extremes and from my adversaries on the outside.

Dad worked in the fields from early morning until dark. He'd come inside for breakfast and dinner – our afternoon meal. He'd eat supper after his working day was over. During the first years when my Father was busy farming, it would be just my Mother and me in the house. She **read** to me a lot. She taught me about the magic of Christmas and she taught me about the magic of *books*. She taught me about the magic of farm *sounds* and *beauty* and the miracle of being *alive*.

I loved to sit on my Mother's lap and listen to stories from the Holy Bible. She read almost every day to me from a book of Bible stories. Her repetitious accounts of *Noah* and the ark, of Jonah in the belly of a great fish for three days and three nights, of *David* slaying Goliath with his sling, of the love of *Jacob*, who worked fourteen years for the hand of Rachel in marriage, of *Joseph* being sold into Egypt by his brothers, of *Moses* hearing God speak from a burning bush, receiving the Ten Commandments, and parting the Red Sea, of *Samson* being shorn of his hair and his strength by Delilah, of *Elijah* calling down fire from heaven to thwart the prophets of Baal, of *Daniel* being spared in the lion's den, of *Shadrach, Meshach, and Abed-nego* refusing to kneel before a gold image and their survival in a fiery furnace, of *Angels* heralding the birth of the *Baby Jesus* in a Bethlehem stable, of the Sermon on the Mount, for "strait is the gate, and narrow is the way, which leadeth unto **life**,"(Matthew 7:14) of the Samaritan woman by the well and the **living water** of *JESUS*, of the <u>parables</u> of the Good

Samaritan and the Prodigal Son, of *JESUS* walking on water, turning water into wine, feeding the multitude of over five thousand with five loaves of bread and two fish, raising Lazarus from the dead, of the triumphant entry of *JESUS* into Jerusalem riding on the back of a humble donkey, of the misguided treachery of *Judas Iscariot* in betraying *JESUS* with a kiss, of the preeminently sacred implications of Gethsemane and Golgotha and the Empty Tomb, the appearance of *JESUS* to *Saul* on the road to Damascus, of *king Agrippa* telling *Paul* his testimony **almost** persuaded him to be a Christian, (Acts 26:28) and the prophetic eloquence of the Apostle John in the Book of Revelation.

These wonderful stories made a tremendous impression on the heart and mind of a young boy. The images the words created and the morals they taught were a powerful influence in my formative years.

> "Who can mistake great thoughts?
> They seize upon the mind; arrest and search,
> And shake it; bow the tall soul as by wind;
> Rush over it like a river over reeds."
> (Philip James Bailey, *Festus*)

But my Mother gave me light from many lamps. She read children's stories frequently from Mother Goose Nursery Rhymes, The Little Red Hen, Brer Rabbit, Alice in Wonderland, Through the Looking Glass, Cinderella, Jack and the Bean Stock, Pinocchio, The Gingerbread Man, Tales of Peter Rabbit, Goldilocks and the Three Bears, Snow White and Rose Red, Rumpelstiltskin, Snow White and the Seven Dwarfs, The Three Little Pigs, Hansel and Gretel, The Wizard of Oz, The Old Lady Who Lived in a Shoe, and others. These delightful stories sent my imagination flying away on joyful wings of fancy.

After I learned to read, my Mother was free to devote her reading time to my sisters. The adorable little girls with curly locks joined our family enclave over a fourteen year span. The ability to read was a tremendous resource for filling my hours of solitude. I became a farm boy bookworm. Spending many exciting hours interfacing with the adventure heroes in the books I read. Each became my friend and confidante and inspiration. I read and reread and read again such classics as Robin Hood, Treasure Island, Kidnaped, Black Beauty, Gulliver's Travels, Alice in Wonderland, The Tales of Uncle Remus, The Little Shepard of Kingdom Come, The

Adventures of Tom Sawyer, Adventures of Huckleberry Finn, The Black Stallion books, the Hardy Boys mysteries, and many others.

There is magic in words. However, it's always important to remember who is saying the words, and why he's saying them. That helps a reader put the magic into context. Especially, if the declarant is *Humpty Dumpty*. I don't think the following quotation requires an explanation:

> "When I use a word," Humpty Dumpty said
> in rather a scornful tone, "it means just what
> I choose it to mean——neither more nor less."
> (Lewis Carroll, *Through the Looking Glass*)

Bathing was a work in progress on the farm. We always had an abundance of water in the irrigation Canal – that is, when it wasn't being cleaned or repaired. But my mother wasn't ever keen about using the so-called "river bloat" for bathing purposes. It's inherently suspect in her mind, which is to say, there is positively no way of knowing at a given moment in time how many livestock have done their business in the water upstream. Of course, water could always be heated on the metal flattop of the kitchen stove, but boiling doesn't change the color nor odor of the water, or eliminate the floating debris that seemed endemic to open flowing canal water that flows through stock yards.

Obviously, in the days when all we had for bathing was town water hauled in the ole water barrel, given my Mother's predilection against using river water as bathing water, family baths were few and far between. Such a situation can be tolerated, to an extent, in the cooler months of the year. However, during the sultry heat of the good old summertime, sans air conditioning and effective deodorants, the circumstances of personal hygiene inside our house were challenging – to say the least. A farm is a place that makes lots of *sweat*!

When we did bathe, we did the honors in a small galvanized steel #3 tub. I'm speaking of a round container approximately twenty four inches in diameter and about sixteen inches high. And I ain't talkin about a private bath. I'm speaking of a #3 placed in the middle of the kitchen floor, filled with water warmed on the kitchen stove for a birthday suit dousing in the presence of whomever happens to be in the house. Listen, a farm boy in the forties can't be a prude, because it's hard to be inconspicuous in a <u>four</u>

room adobe house sudsing yourself up au naturel in about seven inches of soapy water.

I've already documented the mashed thumb that led to running water from a hillside cistern. That salient reality makes bathing a weekly ritual. However, the bathroom came later. We used an outhouse for our personal needs. So, the #3 tub continues to be a fixture on the kitchen floor until my third little sis makes her debut. Every Saturday evening Mom uses a bucket to pour stove-heated water to the desired level in the humble #3 bathing receptacle and sets a bar of soap in a dish on the floor – even if we claim we don't need a bath yet. Then, one at a time, the children share the bath water. Generally, Mom and Dad wait until after we've retired for the night to do their bathing.

Naturally, the foreign particulate in the irrigation canal didn't keep farm folks from using it as a combination swimming pool and bath tub during the <u>summer</u> months. If we wanted to go swimming in the canal we'd say, "Let's go hit the ditch." That said, we'd all laugh, put on our suits and go take a dip. Swimming was a refreshing break from the summer heat.

My Father took full advantage of the running water just east of the farmhouse when the weather was warm. That's where he took daily baths. Every night after dark, Dad would take the short stroll to the canal with three things – a towel, a bar of soap, and a change of underwear. Under the cover of nighttime darkness, he never bothered to take a swimsuit!

Incidently, Dad continued to use his nocturnal "hit the ditch" modus operandi long after the farmhouse had been expanded to include a bathroom with a nice porcelain tub.

I loved the *sounds* of farm life from our farmhouse. This was greatly facilitated by our need to have fresh air circulating through the house during mild seasons. There are two outside doors. Each has a screen door in addition to a solid wood door. We also have screens on the windows. The size of the house is conducive to hearing what happens inside and the screens are conducive to hearing most of what happens outside.

There is a cacophony of *sound* to be heard from the house where dreams were dreamt and memories made. Discordant – though symphonic in its melodious score. A daily conundrum of complexity and simplicity that offers soothing refrain and sweet sustenance to the spirit.

I'm thinking of the *sounds* of the past now – remembering. My mind hurdles the intervening years and sees faint images of my youth. I <u>see</u> my Mother's soft face and <u>hear</u> her voice. I'm sitting on her lap. She's **reading** to me – tenderly, lovingly. Her words are spoken with a benevolence that sinks deep into my heart.

I <u>see</u> my Mother's hands. She's playing the piano. We haven't had it long. Dad has sold a prize bull to buy a piano. He does it to humor Mom and he wants his children to be pianists. Some might say that's an interesting tactic for a farmer, He undoubtedly needs <u>farmhands</u> more than he needs piano players. But Dad loves music, and he's planning for the future. He wants to be able to spend cold winter nights in our farmhouse enjoying music. The strategy works. All four of his children, including yours truly, learn to play the piano.

Mom loves the piano and she especially enjoys musical arrangements for the piano by Eddy Duchin. Although my Mother didn't receive many formal lessons as a little girl, she has passed many pleasant hours at the keyboard since her childhood. One of my first recollections, after the purchase of our family piano, is <u>hearing</u> the poignant *sounds* of my Mother's rendition of the classic old tune, "Memories." She is playing from a book of Eddy Duchin adaptations with such a sense of rhythm and feeling and beauty, that in the hundreds of times I've played the same arrangement, I always attempt to mimic her style.

But my Father's love for piano music has to take a back seat to his love for the mellow *sounds* of another instrument. Dad's first musical love is the melodic, brassy bell *tones* of the **trumpet.** He buys me a trumpet when I'm in the 5th grade. He doesn't have to sell a prize bull to get it neither. He pays twenty five dollars – cash on the barrel head. It's a silver horn the school bus driver's son played when he was in school.

It's not easy to play a trumpet. A boy has to place the mouthpiece on his lips just right and blow into the mouthpiece just right to make *trumpet sounds* come out the other end. Becoming a trumpeter takes lots of practice, an abundance of breath expelled from the lungs, a good embouchure, three well lubricated valves, and strong lips. An aspiring trumpet player doesn't just wake up one morning and discover he's an expert. Playing well requires a measure of dedication and time.

I did my best to learn how to play – for my Dad and for me. I also love the mellifluous *sounds* of the trumpet. After I acquired a smidgen of skill, my oldest little sister accompanied me on the piano while I practiced. We had glorious times together, and provided trumpet and piano music in the farmhouse on many cold winter nights, and during every other season of the fleeting years of our youth – for others in the family.

However, there is one scary night when the dominant *sound* has nothing to do with a trumpet or a piano. The twenty five dollar silver beginner horn has been relegated to musty closet duty, and I've got my left fingers wrapped around the valves of a shiny gold lacquered instrument. I've been tooting trumpet for five school years, and I'm a second year teen with significant mouthpiece lip puckering and horn blowing time under my belt.

It's a sultry summer evening in 1953. The two tall elms that frame our front gate have begun to flutter in sudden stiff gusts of wind. A thunderstorm is blowing toward the farm. The *sound* of thunder can be intermittently heard in the distance. Flashes of lightning are starting to illuminate the dark sky. The impending tempest is lifting dirt into the air and propelling it against the west side of the farmhouse. The *sounds* of gritty grains of red sand and tiny pebbles impacting the vinyl siding of our recently enlarged house are like the pelting rat-a-tat of small BBs.

A white picket fence parallels the front of the house where dreams were dreamt and memories made. It's situated just north of the tall elm trees. My Father often uses one of the trees for shade while he works on machinery parts. On this particular evening, Dad has pulled the tractor and a piece of farm equipment up to the picket fence for lubrication and repairs. He has his grease gun and his tools laid out on the ground in front of the fence. He's just begun to adjust a part on the side delivery rake.

Inside the house, my nine year old sister sits at the piano plunking the keys. I'm standing in the middle of the living room about five feet away from my young accompanist, the mouthpiece of the trumpet is pressed firmly to my lips, and I'm holding the golden horn straight out from my body. We're playing the first verse of a trumpet solo.

It happens quickly – without warning. There is a blinding flash of bright light, and almost simultaneously, an extremely loud BANG occurs. It *sounds* like an explosion – shaking the entire house. But there's no detonation. This is a natural phenomenon. It's a BOLT OF LIGHTNING – an **atmospheric** event! An area directly around my trumpet is immediately enveloped in an evanescent glow. But the bolt of electrical energy has not struck the farmhouse nor the trumpet, it has zig-zagged into a power pole box about thirty feet away from the house. My little sister and I are unharmed by any rogue discharge of electric current. The trumpet has not acted as an ad hoc lightning rod.

Outside under the elm, the wrench Dad has in his hand radiates an incandescent light and shocks him. However, he is not directly struck by the bolt nor injured by the shock.

It's an awesome display of the power of nature which leaves our family emotionally shaken for the remainder of the night. Dad's equipment repairing and my trumpet playing come to a screeching halt. Instead, family members solemnly gather inside our blessed farmhouse in a spirit of gratitude and love for each other – and for **Him** who is The Master of ocean and earth and skies. The *sounds* and *emotions* of the night are never forgotten. It's the evening lightning became an uninvited guest in our front yard, and we felt momentarily surrounded by raw electric current.

Though the incident has given me cause to wonder. Was the lightning bolt an act of divine intervention triggered by the Lord's heavenly chagrin over my trumpet playing or was it a heavenly exclamation point?

Whatever! A Mother knows how to ease jittery nerves. She has the perfect recipe to ease family tension. Mom makes popcorn and hot cocoa. Then we all sleep like babies.

We were living during *radio's golden era*, And the squawk box is a treasure trove of home entertainment. No television. No video games. No home projector. No family movies. BUT we did have a *radio*. BP (Before Power) it's battery powered, AP (After Power) it's electrical, and we acquired a *phonograph*. When we aren't playing the trumpet or the piano, the smooth *sounds* of such luminaries as Vaughn Monroe, Dinah Shore, Bing Crosby, Judy Garland, Nat King Cole, Frank Sinatra, Billy Holiday, Elvis Presley, Peggy Lee, Sammy Davis Jr., Sarah Vaughn, Billy Eckstine, Frankie Laine, Mahalia Jackson, Johnnie Ray, Dinah Washington, Louis "Satchmo" Armstrong, Jo Stafford, Al Jolson, Ella Fitzgerald, Perry Como, and other crooners are primary mediums of *sound* in our farmhouse.

The *radio* is an ear candy dispenser. A wellspring of music, merriment, intrigue, inspiration, news, boxing – and baseball! *Radio* carries us across the whole spectrum of moods. If I wanted a break from the daily humdrum, some thrills 'n chills and goose bumps, I could turn the *radio* dial. For example, I could tune in to "The Shadow." A legendary *radio* drama that gives me a rash of goose bumps from the moment the moderator speaks the memorable words, "Who knows what evil lurks in the hearts of men?

Heh – heh – heh – heh – heh – heh – heh. The Shadow knows –– " After my chill meter is activated, a scary mystery unfolds.

Please understand, The Shadow *sounds* spooky, but he's a crime buster –– and The Shadow is no garden variety run-of-the-mill protagonist. He defies laws of gravity, speaks every language, unravels any sinister code, becomes invisible when circumstances demand, clouds and confuses the minds of his adversaries. A righteous result is inexorable from the beginning. After The Shadow exhibits his invincibility by bringing the bad guy to his knees, the show ends with a chilling reminder: "The weed of crime bears bitter fruit. Crime does not pay! The Shadow knows –– heh – heh – heh – heh – heh – heh."

And both sobered and heartened by images portrayed in *sound*, I resolve at the end of each program that I will **never** commit a crime! The Shadow is a **tough** customer for criminals!

Furthermore, The Shadow has confederates. There are other potent crime busters on the *radio*. Two other notable crime fighters live in my memory. They are both well schooled in their craft – and gentlemen, as the titles of their shows denote.

"Mr. Chameleon." is a match for any crook. He"s a master of disguise. A famous and dreaded police detective to those who break the laws, who employs disguises to track down killers. He has a different disguise and a different case to crack each week, and he <u>always</u> brings his man to justice.

That is comforting to a boy on the farm. It gets lonely on occasion, and doing chores on dark nights at the corrals often gave me the shivers. I'd feel like evil eyes might be peering at me, that someone in the darkness could be waiting to pounce. The hair, so to speak, on the back of my neck would stick up. And I'd wish I was back at the farmhouse, or that someone had my back. Someone like, say, Mr. Chameleon.

"Mr. Keen, Tracer of Lost Persons" is a really sharp fellow. The criminal minds of kidnappers are incapable of coping with the perspicacity of Mr. Keen as he tracks down missing persons. He's a sure-fire bloodhound. Keen perception and shrewdness give Mr. Keen the upper hand. He <u>sees</u> clues left by abductors on the trail and <u>sees</u> past their clumsy efforts to conceal the whereabouts of their victims. Mr. Keen is a winner, and when he wins, bad guys lose.

It's a moral principle I wanted to adopt. I decided early in life that I wanted to be a winner – a law and order type of guy!

There were other crime dramas broadcast over the airwaves. Shows such as, "The Adventures of Philip Marlowe," "Yours Truly, Johnny Dollar," "Murder and Mr. Malone," "Perry Mason," "Dragnet," "The General Mills Radio Adventure Theater Gangbusters," "This is Your FBI," and of course, "Mr. District Attorney."

If romance is a listeners thing, and my Mother fancied it, *radio* had a full slate of programs describing the unsteady flight of Cupid's amatory arrows. "Our Gal Sunday," The Romance of Helen Trent," "The Guiding Light," "Amanda of Honeymoon Hill," "Stella Dallas," "This is Nora Drake," and "John's Other Wife" are a few of the *radio* soap operas that explored the heart throbs, heart flights, and heartbreaks of love's shifting landscape.

I watched a lot of this stuff as a kid. I watched because my Mother watched. I'm a romantic. Perhaps, some of this has its antecedent in those early days when the *sound* of *radio* soaps is a fixture in the farmhouse. Love and learn is a premise my mother and I extracted from the soaps when *radio* was king.

Each episode of Our Gal Sunday began with an opening statement. I must have heard it a hundred times, at least. Over time it got burned into my beans, but that was then. Presently, I had to go to the internet for the precise verbiage: "Once again, we present Our Gal Sunday, the story of an orphan girl named Sunday from the little mining town of Silver Creek, Colorado, who in young womanhood married England's richest, most handsome lord, Lord Henry Brinthrope. The story that asks the question: Can this girl from the little mining town in the west find happiness as the wife of a wealthy and titled Englishman?"

Whether Sunday finds happiness seemed to be in jeopardy during every episode, but the *listening* audience seems to be happy. It's a five day a week rendition of compelling tales of romance that stays on the air for two decades with *listeners* by the millions.

Helen Trent's love life is more of the same. The program begins: "And now, The Romance of Helen Trent, the real life drama of Helen Trent, who when life mocks her, breaks her hopes, dashes her against the rocks of despair, fights back bravely, successfully, to prove what so many women long to prove, that because a woman is thirty five or more, romance in life need not be over, that romance can begin at thirty five."

In other words, the hope for true love should flourish inside a woman's breast regardless of her age. Hey, that concept packs quite a wallop and has widespread appeal in the ranks of the female population.

There were 7,222 episodes of the program. During that time frame it's intriguing that Helen <u>never</u> marries and <u>remains</u> thirty five years old throughout the airing of the show, though she does have a constant boyfriend. Really, they have a very long courtship.

Incidently, the <u>soap</u> <u>opera</u> tag stems from sponsorship of these radio dramas by large soap companies. Contemporary television soaps trace <u>their</u> origin to the *golden epoch of radio.*

An <u>ear</u> candy dispenser. A wellspring of music, merriment, intrigue, inspiration, news, boxing – and baseball! If a *listener* wants to levitate, there's nothing quite like *listening* to beautiful well played music to lift the spirit. There were oodles of musical <u>programs</u> on the *radio* in the forties and fifties.

For instance, "The Sammy Kaye Show," the elegant piano styling of "The Eddy Duchin Show," "The NBC Symphony Orchestra" conducted by maestro Arturo Toscanini, the legendary "Al Jolson Show," "The Guy Lombardo Show," featuring the Royal Canadians band, and "The Spike Jones Show," featuring the City Slickers band. Spike specializes in performing satirical arrangements of popular songs. Ballads and classical works receiving the Jones version were punctuated by gunshots, whistles, cowbells, and ridiculous vocals.

Also, "Your Hit Parade," which offers the most popular and best selling songs of the week, "The Original Amateur Hour" which determines order of appearance by spinning a wheel, and has the audience vote for a winner by phone or post cards, "The Bell Telephone Hour" which showcases the best in classical and Broadway music, the "Kraft Music Hall" and the "Philco Radio Time" that are both a blending of music/variety featuring Bing Crosby, " "The Dinah Shore Show," a variety show that highlights personal hits and music of its star, and "The Kate Smith Hour," a variety show offering music, comedy, and drama with new talent guests and appearances by top personalities of films and theater. Kate is a big girl. She weighs 235 pounds at thirty, but is unfazed. She entitles her 1938 autobiography, *Living in a Great Big Way.* She once observed, "I'm big, and I sing, and boy, when I sing, I sing all over." Kate Smith is best known for her rendition of "God Bless America."

If a *listener* wanted comic relief, a panoply of programing tickled the funny bones of those within earshot. So, we weren't stuck with a lot of quiet time in the farmhouse to worry about the deprivations of farm life, unless that was our choice. It wasn't! We yuked it up nightly as we *listened* to *radio* humor."The [George] Burns and [Gracie] Allen Show" is a comedy/sitcom. "The Bob Hope Show" is a rich mixture of comedy and variety. "Archie Andrews" is a comic book series – a syndicated comic strip in animation."The Edgar Bergen – Charlie McCarthy Show" is comedy. Edgar's a ventriloquist and Charlie's a dummy, but on the air it's often hard to tell who's the actual dummy. "The Phil Harris – Alice Faye Show" is a comedy, and she more than holds her own against him. "The Jack Benny Program" is comedy based. Jack plays the role of a chronic tightwad, and <u>insists</u> on remaining thirty nine despite his chronological age. "The Red Skelton Show" is classic humor. His comedy skits are some of the best ever. "Amos 'n' Andy" features weekly situation comedy, "Fibber McGee and Molly" is one of the longest running comedies in the history of classic radio in the U.S. Then there's "Our Miss Brooks," and her brand of American situation comedy made it seem like she belonged to everyone. Eve Arden plays an English Teacher at a fictional High School.

And we're not done yet. There are *quiz* shows, *prize* giveaway shows, *western* shoot-em-ups, *gossip* columns, *newscasts*, and *religious* programing. *Radio* gave farm families a well rounded diet of life – media style.

We had "Professor Quiz," *radio's* first true quiz show. Later,"The Quiz Kids" provide audience participation for over a decade of broadcasting. Questions are submitted by *listeners*, and answered by a panel of five children. "Queen For A Day" helps usher in big prize giveaway shows and is a forerunner of modern reality television. "Arthur Godfrey's Talent Scouts" is a major hit. Talent Scouts bring discoveries to programs to showcase their talents. The winner of each show is determined by an audience applause meter.

"The Lone Ranger"rides *radio's* open range. A masked Texas Ranger gallops around the Old West blowing away injustice – with the aid of his laconic, resourceful sidekick Tonto. When a show ends, the audience hears a triumphant, "Hi-yo, Silver, away," as the masked wonder rides his horse toward the setting sun. Really, that's good stuff to a farm belt kid.

"The Roy Rogers Show" is a component of *radio* fare in the fifties. The so-called "King of the Cowboys" sits tall in the saddle in *radio* land on his golden palomino Trigger. The "Singing Cowboy" Gene Autry is the only celebrity to have five stars on the Hollywood Walk of Fame. He's a *radio* personality too. Not to be outdone, the "Red Ryder Series" also regularly sweetens the mix of *radio* cowboy stories aired in the farmhouse.

Louella Parsons, an American gossip and Hollywood columnist, lifts celebrity tattletales to an art form with her *radio* chit-chat. It makes pithy grist for suppertime small talk, but it's not informative about things that matter.

Fortunately, there **are** programs that provide coverage of current events that do matter. The forties and fifties are pivotal times that will affect generations. There is *radio* news of the catastrophic carnage of World War II that ends with the defeat of the Axis Powers on the battlefield. The war in the Pacific ending only after atomic bombs have been dropped on Hiroshima and Nagasaki.

Sadly, coming quickly on the heels of an end to the hot war is the cold war. We *hear* of the partitioning of Germany and the city of Berlin, the Soviet Union imposing an Iron Curtain over eastern Europe that enslaves millions, and the clear and present danger of nuclear holocaust between east and west. The World holds its breath as an uneasy nuclear standoff ensues. It's a world in turmoil as the free world vies with the world of dictatorship for the hearts of mankind. China falls to communism and all of southeast Asia appear to be in jeopardy. The situation is frightening to a boy on the farm – and to his parents. We're anxious to gather any tidbits we can from the world stage.

When we go to the movies a <u>news</u> reel segment precedes the featured attraction on the silver screen, but we don't go to the movies often. Our primary <u>source</u> of news is still the *radio*. The times dictate our priorities. We need factual information during these turbulent years. Our *radio* is a prized possession. It's an <u>ear</u> candy dispenser, but in the act of dispensing vital <u>news</u> it's much more.

Broadcast journalists keep us connected. I remember three men who are particularly newsworthy! Lowell Thomas presented and commented on the news for four decades. His signature sign-on is "Good evening, everybody," and his sign-off is "So long, until tomorrow." It seemed like he was speaking directly to us. Edward R. Murrow is an American icon. Recognized by his peers as a <u>great</u> broadcast journalist because of his integrity in delivering his <u>news</u> stories. He first came to prominence with a series of *radio news* broadcasts during World War II. Millions of *listeners* in the United States and Canada tuned in for Ed Murrow"s reporting. Bob Trout is best known for his work before and during the Second World War. He's known as the "Iron Man of Radio" for his fortitude, composure, ab lib skills, and elocution. The *voices* of Lowell and Ed and "The Troutster" are welcome guests in our farmhouse!

Nor are the gods of *radio* unmindful of our spiritual needs. The "Old Fashioned Revival Hour" is a weekly Sunday broadcast."Happy Half Hour With the Bible"from the Bethel Baptist Church is a regular in the forties and fifties. Part of the Sunday menu is "Music and the Spoken Word," featuring the Mormon Tabernacle Choir. A 360 voice organization that was founded in 1847, <u>one</u> month after the first company of Pioneers entered the Salt Lake Valley. It has been on the air since 1929, making it the longest running *radio* broadcast in America. Initially, the organ, choir, and announcer shared a single microphone that was attached to the ceiling of the Tabernacle. The announcer stood on a ladder in order to speak into the mike. "The Lutheran Hour"is a long-running Christian outreach program. Billy Graham's Evangelistic Association broadcasts the"Hour of Decision." The original broadcast aired November 5, 1950. Religious programing helps us face the uncertainties of the day.

Radio is a wellspring of music, merriment, intrigue, news, inspiration, **boxing** – and **baseball**! Boxing nights are full of fireworks. Pabst Blue Ribbon bouts are every Wednesday. The Gillette Cavalcade of Sports officially began in 1942. It covers a variety of sports, but is primarily remembered by Dad and me for its focus on Friday night <u>boxing</u> at Madison Square Garden from the mid forties through the fifties. Every great boxer of the era, that is, Rocky Marciano, Sugar Ray Robinson, Gene Fullmer, Archie Moore, Rocky Graziano, Willie Pep, Rex Layne, and many others appeared on one or more broadcasts.

Gillette's theme song was the "Look sharp/Be Sharp March." Wednesday and Friday nights the farmer and the farm boy may not have looked real sharp, but we *listened* sharp. Our <u>ears</u> were held close to the *radio* so we could absorb the full fury of the bouts from bell to bell.

And –– baseball. They played a lot of <u>daytime</u> Major League baseball during the late forties and fifties, and the Boys of Summer brightened my summer days on the farm. I lived and breathed baseball, as the expression goes. Though the <u>living</u> part is necessarily vicarious. I never played on a baseball team. And the <u>breathing</u> baseball part has to take the modus of buying a baseball and *smelling* the stretched, handstitched, white **cowhide** that covers it. I didn't get to big league ballparks as a kid neither. We're still talking *radio*, right.

What I'm really trying to convey is the love of a **fan** for baseball. An affinity that seems innate, and it's not a passing whim. I began to follow Major League baseball in 1949, and I've been a devotee ever since. My team is the Cleveland Indians. I've charted their seasons for <u>sixty</u> years, and they've never won the World Series during those six decades. They did win it all in 1948, beating the Boston Braves in six games. That's why I chose them as my team the <u>next</u> year. I thought I was picking a winner – jumping on a bandwagon, but my premise has been false. It's a Mel Harmon hypothesis chockablock full of high hopes in April with high hopes dashed in October – for <u>sixty</u> seasons of baseball.

But I've stuck with the Tribe. Whatever I am not, it can't be said I'm not loyal. A one-woman man for forty nine years of marriage, and a one-team man for sixty years of World Series futility. And I didn't simply dip my foot into the water, I got into baseball all over – being especially hardcore as a preteen and as a teenager. I knew every player's team. I knew player positions, pitching records, earned run averages, batting averages, runs batted in, home runs, and the career stats of all the stars of the game. These guys are bigger than life – my heroes!

The Mutual Network carried a *Game of the Day* throughout most of the fifties baseball seasons. An unforgettable *sound* in our farmhouse during the fifties is the *sound* of baseball on the *radio*. The typical scenario has me laying on the living floor at mid day with my ear next to the *radio*. While my father takes his afternoon nap, I'm *listening* to the crack of bats against baseballs [What are the odds of hitting a <u>round</u> baseball **squarely** in the sweet spot with a <u>round</u> bat?] and the chatter of hotdog venders and the roar of the crowd and Dizzy Dean singing *Wabash Cannonball* between late innings.

The announcers are my heros too. They're like family members. Their colorful commentaries trigger a daily flood of baseball fantasy in my mind. Al Helfer does broadcasts from 1950 – 54, Dizzy Dean is 1951-52, Bud Blattner for 1952 and 54, and Bob Fulton for 1954. Incidentally, the Indians played in the 1954 World Series. They had a season record of 111 wins and 43 losses, but their stellar year is meaningless in the Series. The New York Giants swept them in four straight games. Aargh! I lost five bucks to Jeb Blake on that one – at a time when five bucks is really BIG.

Why so much fuss over the squawk box? Well, *radio* was our **ear** to the outside world. It would be difficult to exaggerate the importance of *radio* in our lives. It molded our minds, steadied our hearts, and gave solace to our souls. During the golden era of *radio*, the transmission of *sound* messages played a positive role in making our farm life golden too!

Discordant – though symphonic in its melodious score. From our farmhouse we <u>heard</u> *sounds* from all seasons and *sounds* from a broad spectrum of God's amazing creatures.

I remember wintery blasts against the eaves of the house. Howling **wind** has a distinctive *sound* to youthful ears. It happened frequently through the years, but I usually associate the wrathful *sound* with winter months. The prolonged wail of gusting wind around the corners of the farmhouse is not unlike shrill tones of season's greetings from a feisty, out of tune, December trumpeter. But he's not a happy bugler. His summons is brash and full of rage. Filling chilly nights with blustery moans – as though an upset stomach prompts the plaintive din blown through his horn, or like he's angry with his wife, or hell bent on mobilizing subterranean demons from the bowels of the earth beneath our house.

The rushing wind arrives in alternating waves. Surging helter-skelter as it comes. Furious is followed by furtive, and every stage is irrepressible, penetrating, and eerie. The bugler mutes his horn, as the bellow of wind dies down – and then removes the mute – sending melancholy notes blaring into a shrieking thrust of wind along the undersides of overhanging roof, and into the solemn darkness – swirling <u>and</u> straight lining. Eventually, blowing past at last. A wintery gale is a whiner – a grouch – an old, disheartened, jilted, wayward warrior <u>homeward</u> bound. But where is home? He seems unable to find it. Always coming back in due course – still looking!

They can be heard inside the farmhouse on balmy days when windows are open and young children are outside shouting. It's a favorite pastime on the farm. We get a kick out of yelling at a mountain, That's right. We'd <u>verbally</u> fling things at a hill, and it slavishly throws them back at us verbatim – without a stutter, nor a lisp, or a trace of botched memory. The transmission from the butte back to us is a perfect replication because it's an **echo**. It's the repetition of *sound* by reflection of sound waves. Secondary *sound* produced when loud speech or other loud noise deflects off the solid mass of a large, steep hillside.

But please be advised, it's not just any large hill. It's the same rocky ridge from which out cistern was excavated, and it's got smarts. I'm sure it could be multi-lingual with proper priming, yet I've only heard it speak English. Further, it's a good sport and indefatigable. Whether the hour is daytime or nighttime, and regardless of the time of year, there is no pouting nor silent treatment. Our hillside companion is always willing to talk trash. Hurling the same goofy words back that we've dispatched. An echo can be an earful.

God's amazing **creatures** don't do echos, but that doesn't diminish their contribution to nature's high definition *sound* system. The lusty, inconsonant honking of migratory Canadian geese, as their classic V-pattern flight over the farmhouse signals a change in seasons, is a nostalgic natural high. I'm referring to their altitude and to a poignant *sound* that can't be replicated.

Winter nights bring *sounds* of the collective *yapping* of packs of lonely, hungry coyotes to the farmhouse. The ravenous *howls*, visions of chicken gizzard dancing in coyote heads, usually begin far away on the east mountain in early evening, but get much closer as nighttime deepens. Coyotes are reclusive. They're not a threat to humans, but they pose a definite threat to a farmer's chicken population. A chicken who wants to see the morning light better sleep in the henhouse with one eye cracked open – if coyotes are on the prowl. Otherwise, a deadly night raid will seriously reduce egg production and make the issue of a chicken becoming a fryer for Sunday Dinner a moot point.

We didn't mess with frog legs on the farm. That would have been borderline sacrilegious. We wanted to enhance the frog population, not curtail it. We ate pork and beef and venison. We didn't eat frogs, we *listened* to frogs, and allowed them to gorge on pesky insects to their heart's content. No *sound* of summer evenings is more explicit in my mind than the rambunctious rivet – rivet – rivet of country frogs in nearby irrigation ditches. The little, smooth-skinned amphibians, with legs honed for hopping, compose exquisite daily ditch-bottom choral offerings during dinner hour. Their resonant croaking is restful and edifying.

Meanwhile, male crickets add their own special tweets of summer evening orchestration to the *sound* portfolio.

The *sounds* of many other creatures dot the days of our farm lives. There are Chinese ring-necked pheasants, plying their trademark clarion crow from damp hayfields at mid morning, and doves, quail, killdeer, and meowing cats and whining brats (mostly me) – and owls and cows and woodpeckers.

The mention of birds often triggers thoughts of song birds. Many birds offer melodic calls. However, woodpeckers have a bizarre acoustical skill. Their beaks produce a trademark *sound*. Woodpeckers are devoted snare drummers by nature. They make *sounds* by striking their beaks against wood – tap, tap, tap, tap, tap, ad infinitum. These guys use beaks in wood like men making manholes in asphalt use jack hammers. Now, that is a dizzying, brain rattling, jaw-tiring regimen.

Woodpeckers have an amazing work ethic. Their boundless energy, single-minded focus, passionate determination, and drilling expertise seem to be genetic. "Born to drill baby. Drill baby drill!" Yet penetrating a slab of wood with a beak is a daunting assignment, even for a veteran woodpecker.

They'd peck away at the northeast corner of the house immediately below the eave for hours each morning, studying, listening, searching for juicy termites and other plump insects hanging out in the weathered boards. While we're eating breakfast they're looking for breakfast. A tag team of **hard hat** feathered vertebrates. Part of the bird kingdom labor force – blue collar workers. Card-packing members of the United Pecker Workers of America. Even though the woodpeckers have **hard beaks** not hard hats.

The seasonal woodpeckers at our place are both alarm clocks and sources of breakfast rap music. They try to make the Harmons rappers with their rhythmic tap, tap, tap, but we aren't blessed with rhythm. Though once, I honestly think I saw Dad, over a hearty breakfast of scrambled eggs and bacon and toast, inadvertently tapping his foot to a persistent, woodpecker sunrise cadence.

The boy who will be a Lawyer can learn from the woodpecker approach to its task: <u>Know</u> your board [the case] and <u>tenaciously</u> <u>bore</u> your board [passionately prosecute the case].

And there are other memorable *sounds*. Here comes Santa Claus right down Harmon farm lane, much to a child's delight. He'd come calling every Christmas Eve with bells jingling on his red Santa jacket, knock on the front door, come in while emitting a bevy of Ho–Ho–Ho's, and pass out little brown bags full of freshly popped corn and other goodies. Then he'd proclaim a rousing, "Merry Christmas," and depart as rapidly as he'd arrived. Jingling – jingling – jingling as he went his merry way.

We also have Dad's affable *tone* and the wondrous twinkle in his eyes as he tenderly greets me – after I've done something that pleases him: "Hello sunshine" or "Hi moonbeam." Contrasted on rare occasions, by the sonorous *sound* of Mom's firm voice when she has good cause to be <u>angry</u> with me. Especially, when she's pursued me to the yard, finds a switch, and uses it on my legs. The stinging *sound* of switch to shins isn't linked to specific seasons, but it certainly leaves its mark – on my skin and my memory.

The *sounds* of farm life are myriad. There are *sounds* of raindrops on rooftops and of newborn calves weakly *bleating*, of roosters *crowing* and tractor engines *putting*, of choppers *chopping* hay and cow's hooves *clacking* across milk house floors, of stanchions being *locked* into place and the *pulsating* squish – squoosh – squish of milking machines collecting their frothy white fluid from cow udders. Plus, the runny sh–t *splattering* into a drainage gutter, the *guttural* swear words as cow tails intended for swatting flies swat my Father instead, the fitful *snoring* as Dad sleeps off the fatigue of his previous day – and radio *music*. Dad has this theory that *music* calms <u>and</u> motivates his cows. Calm cows aren't kicking nor sh–ting cows. We don't need hobbles for calm cows. Motivated cows are high producing cows. It's a no-brainer if Dad's premise is correct. Bigger raw-milk volume makes bigger paychecks.

Learning to be a good *listener* on the farm served me well in the courtroom. Being *hard of listening* doesn't bode well for those who want to be successful farmers or effective lawyers.

The farming life piqued my sense of *smell* as well. Farmland scents ranged across the wide sweep of sensory experience. The examples that follow are <u>each</u> uniquely pungent: the aromas of freshly baked bread and newly mown hay, whiffs of bacon frying and freshly brewed hot coffee, warm steaming silage on a cold winter day and warm steaming loose cow manure, the palpable stench of mucky pigpens <u>anytime</u> and the odoriferous smell of skunk pee on <u>anything</u>, the sizzling gamy scent of cooking venison and the hot cinnamon piquancy of baking pie cookies, the pristine pink fragrance of a Queen Elizabeth rose in May and the aromatic simmer of apricot jam being poured into canning bottles, a foul smelling cow carcass being pulled east of the canal and brackish malodorous red flood water rising to the top of canal banks, the hazy pall of smoke from burnt toast in the kitchen and the fresh damp aroma of sage during morning strolls on nearby hillsides, being down-wind from cow piles ground into greenish dry dust in the barnyard, the putrid odor of the outhouse, and the bitting fumes of fuel oil exhaust as a tractor is steered over land being disced prior to fall planting, the heat of eye-smarting, wind driven smoke at outdoor wiener roasts and the permeating aroma of succulent turkeys – stuffed with homemade dressing, roasting in cookers on Thanksgiving Days, the aromatic gastronomic stimulation of dried beans simmering on a stove burner and the faint scent of sour milk that lingers inside a milk barn even though it is hosed down and scrubbed on a daily basis, the fetid smell of frying fish and the reeking **sweat** of bodies and **sweaty** clothing.

SWEAT that is not induced by a case of nerves nor a breaking fever, but sweat conceived by honorable <u>hard</u> <u>labor</u> under intense summer sun. Therapeutic sweat, freely flowing through open pores. Lubricating sunburnt skin. Therapeutic because of what it does to body and mind!

Parents should teach their children the incalculable value of hard work! I learned this powerful principle from my Father on our farmland and from my Mother in our farmhouse. **They** produced children. **They** lived productive lives. <u>He</u> produced crops and milk and paychecks. <u>She</u> provided nurturing and training and homemaking. **Together** <u>they</u> provided an environment for growth – spiritually and temporally. **Their** lives were wet with honest sweat! **They** <u>believed</u>, and they taught us to believe, that there is NO SUBSTITUTE for **hard work**. No shortcuts. No freebie rides down easy street.

Dad <u>and</u> **Mom** demonstrated every day of <u>their</u> adult lives that anything is attainable if we are willing to work. By **their** words and **their** examples <u>they</u> gave us the fail-safe formula for success. A lead-pipe cinch which <u>ultimately</u> guarantees achievement. There is **no** proxy for measured, persistent, <u>blessed</u>, indefatigable labor. Work is the precursor of good fortune. The prerequisite to success!

"Is it hard or easy to get to heaven? Well, it's hard if you work at it easy, and it's <u>easy</u> if you **work** at it hard." (Albert Payne, University of Utah Institute of Religion) The principle has an infinite number of applications. Is it hard or easy to be a farmer's son? It's hard if you work at it easy, and it's <u>easy</u> if you **work** at it hard. Is it hard or easy to drive a tractor reasonably straight on a thirty acre piece of land? It's hard if you work at it easy, and it's <u>easy</u> if you **work** hard at setting your sight on a specific marker at the end of the field <u>and</u> on steady-handed steering toward the marker. Is it hard or easy in the heat of growing season to stack two hundred fifty 60 pound bales of hay on flatbed wagons to be hauled to the barn? It's hard if you work at it easy, and it's <u>easy</u> if you **work** at it hard. Which means *sweating* hard, and you'll definitely need a good pair of gloves. Is it hard or easy to get rid of gophers? It's hard if you work at it easy, and it's <u>easy</u> if you **work** at it hard. Which means never giving up. Being relentless. If you can't drown them by flooding their underground network with irrigation water, smoke them out. If smoke doesn't work, poison them. And if poison doesn't work, try trapping them. Make them suffer. But if the traps come up empty, hire a damned bulldozer and dig the bounders out of their holes.

Is it hard or easy to get through law school? It's hard if you work at it easy, and it's <u>easy</u> if you **study** at it hard Even in school The Law is a jealous mistress. Is it hard or easy to be a Trial Lawyer? NO, not if the Trial Lawyer **works hard** at his profession!

From four room adobe to seven room vinyl, and tons of living. Seventy one years and counting. Still with the strength to stand –– grand in simplicity and grace. <u>Anointed</u> by **the life that was** <u>and</u> **the sacred memory of loving relationships that were**. "There's a HOUSE whose rooms I know by heart... Where dreams were dreamt and memories made." (ibid.) A precious, nurturing friend – where values were infused that will never fade.

THE PASSIONATE SENSE OF WHAT MIGHT BE

"If I were to wish for anything, I should not wish for
wealth and power, but for the passionate sense of
what might be, for the eye, which ever young and
ardent, sees the possible. Pleasure disappoints,
possibility never. And what wine is so fragrant,
what so sparkling, so intoxicating, as possibility."
(Soren Kierkegaard)

Chapter 2

A month after I became a first grader a school bus began to pick up students
in the fields. The bus stop was on the fields road about fifty yards north
of our farmhouse. It was exciting for a six year old to ride a bus to school.
However, the school district conducted split sessions for first graders that
year. The advent of school bus privileges for field-ites doubled the length of
my school days. My afternoon sessions morphed into a.m. <u>and</u> p.m.

I wasn't crazy about the arrangement at first, but expanded schooling
was a big bonus over the long haul. I needed, no – I required a good start
in the educational process. Solitary farm boy life and genetic shyness made
socializing in a redbrick schoolhouse a challenging proposition. <u>Long</u>
days under the diligent tutelage of my teacher gradually brought me out
of my shell. Even in the first grade, I believe I began to sense life's infinite
possibilities!

I remember that first morning. I arrived on the bus and went straight
to my classroom. I recall being the first person to arrive, and I was terrified.
Students were to sit at tables placed around the room. But I didn't know

where to sit or where to stand or what to do with myself. I didn't know another soul in the school, except for my teacher, and she hadn't arrived yet. So, I just stood by the front door and nervously twiddled my thumbs. I felt really awkward. Very out of place, extremely self conscious, and incredibly apprehensive. Sort of like a fish out of water – or a trout in the milk. I felt like my little high top shoes were going to burn holes in the floor as I waited.

It seemed like an eternity. It wasn't. The teacher arrived about ten minutes later. She greeted me warmly, escorted me to my table, and to the chair assigned to me. I sat down and waited some more – still feeling awkward and out of place. Gradually, other students began to enter. But that didn't ease my nervousness. The others settled in at various tables around the classroom, but over in my corner, it continued to be just my table and me. As each child came in, he or she would immediately spy the new kid. We'd lock eyes, they'd look away, go to their seats, sit down, and then unabashedly stare at me. Or so it seemed.

I felt like the loneliest little guy in the world. I began to fervently wish I could become invisible, or run out of there, or harass doodlebugs, or –– that somebody would sit down at my table. Several minutes later someone did. His name is Dowel.

He smiled, introduced himself, and began to talk nonstop. Interspersing his words with soft laughter. We bonded immediately, and I quickly relaxed. Dowel was a godsend. **What a difference** Dowel made! **What a difference** any rational individual **can** make – if only they will!

Suddenly, I felt like I belonged in the classroom. I sensed the possibilities wrapped up in morning sessions at school. Presto! My awkwardness and self consciousness and apprehension disappeared. When others joined Dowel and I at the table it wasn't a problem. I'd already made a connection with someone in the class. I had a friend. After sixty four years, I remain in Dowel's debt for his simple acts of kindness and friendship on my first morning in first grade.

The school bus ride wasn't short. We traveled approximately 22 miles each way. Factoring distance and stops into the equation, that translated into about fifty minutes of bus time going to school and about the same amount of bus time going home. That's close to 100 minutes X 5 of bus time every week.

Things tend to get a little unruly, much to the chagrin of drivers, when school kids are confined to a bus for 8 1/3 hours per week. **Idle** time for a bunch of kids is <u>incompatible</u> with their nature. Consequently, there were plenty of paper airplanes and spit balls launched, seat changes, singing in the round – with mind numbing monotony, arguing, wrestling, tag games, and on rare occasions, a few stalwart souls trying to study. Bus drivers adopted various rules and strategies in an effort to cope with the disciplinary problems. However, spit balls continued to fly, arm wrestling and head locks stayed fashionable, while dashing for different seats and on-going tag games still held sway.

The most effective deterrent involved an unscheduled stop on the itinerary. The bus route included an 8 1/2 mile – 20 minute loop. Therefore, students were given the option of getting off the bus at the beginning of the loop for some playtime. The idea being: sail your airplanes, fly your kites, throw your footballs, propel your spit balls, wrestle, argue, play tag, play marbles, run like wild yahoos along washes and hillsides, use up your excess energy, and then re-board the bus at the site of disembarkment or at the next scheduled stop – about a half mile down the road.

Naturally, this type of procedure would be anathema in today's world, but this was 50-60 years past. We did things a lot different back in the days of yore. Nobody ever got seriously injured, nobody got sued, and kids like me had some good times outside the bus while it was making its loop.

My cousin taught me how to shoot marbles at the loop trail head, and I got to play cowboys and Indians on acres of chaparral forested, dusty, rocky terrain that I may never have set foot on – except for the unofficial bus stop that was a crown jewel of student management. Though the kids who disembarked, went on to school somewhat sweatier and somewhat dirtier than they were when they left home. Bus drivers benefitted from the practice, but moms had to deal with clothes and kids requiring a bit more detergence time.

But I didn't always get off the bus at the impromptu stop. Perhaps, I should have. Playing tag is considerably more risk free when a student isn't traveling in a moving conveyance. I'm in the third grade now, older but not wiser. I'm engaged in a very competitive game of tag with three others. Gene is it. Coincidentally, he's just boarded the bus. He and his sister got on about five minutes before the incident. We're only about a mile and a half <u>plus</u> two additional pickups from their house. A substitute driver named Jack is at the helm. He's already frazzled, which is perfectly understandable. Transporting a bus load of hooligans to school isn't any picnic. We've been pushing the envelope as far as we can since he's not the regular wheel guy.

This is why we dare play tag on the bus with reckless abandon. We're trying to take advantage of a sweet situation. However, there are times when sweetness turns sour, and a situation becomes uncontrollable. The bus is traveling about 35 mph and approaching a gradual turn in the gravel road. The other two players have scurried up the aisle to the front of the bus. Driver Jack seems oblivious to the tag competition. He's intent on steering the school bus down the road. "Please Lord, just get me to the schoolhouse on time."

Gene thinks he has me cornered. I dart to the back of the bus, with my back pressed against the emergency door. I'm poised to scramble to the left or the right, depending on Gene's mode of attack. He cooly surveys my position. He's ready to pounce forward and lay the big gotcha tag on me. He's sure he's got me trapped, hopelessly hemmed in. There is no possible escape route. But ole Gene is wrong. He's miscalculated. <u>Almost</u> anything is **possible**. Harmon does have a built-in escape hatch! How? Where? What? Why, the emergency door dummy.

As Gene lunges toward me and I push away in an effort to avoid his tag, something totally unexpected happens. The emergency door suddenly yields to the pressure against it – and, inexplicably, OPENS at 35 m.p.h.

The effect is dramatic. **Poof** –– and <u>two</u> who were in are <u>out</u>, as quickly as those who remain inside can say, "Boys overboard."

There's instantaneous bedlam on the bus. Poor Jack. Poor, substitute driver Jack. Unbelievable! He's a one-day fill in, and something like this happens on his watch. He probably can't expect too many future calls from the School District.

But enough said about Jack. What about the two boys overboard? Actually, it's primarily <u>poor</u> Gene. He goes out the door **face down**, and it's not a soft touch down. Gene learns the <u>hard</u> way that little boys really can't fly. His flight is a swan dive into the ground, with precious little hang-time. Ouch! The free fall is blunted only by his outstretched hands – and his nose.

Afterwards, he's got a bloody, pulpy nose that looks bent out of shape, and numerous scratches and abrasions on his hands and face. Driver Jack isn't into medical technician stuff. He takes one look at Gene and turns the bus around. We take Gene back home. It's a very short school day for Gene. He's back before his mother can finish her cup of hot postum.

I fared somewhat better. My departure from the bus is backwards. To this day, my recollection of the event is vivid. There's the sensation of a door opening, of momentary suspension in the air, and of hitting the road **hard**. Very hard. It jolts every inch of my frame and I must have bounced about six inches as I hit the gravel. My next impressions are dizziness and an inability to catch my breath. I'm rolling over and over and over on the ground like a spinning log, and the wind has been knocked out of me. I finally catch my breath, and begin to inhale gasping gulps of air, about the same time my body comes to a stop on the shoulder of the road. A cloud of dust rises from the accident scene.

I sit up and get back on my feet with some difficulty. My back is hurting between my shoulder blades, and I'm a little woozy. I've been thoroughly shaken, but luckily, there are no broken bones.

The crisis is past. Everyone gets back on the bus. Gene has to stay home, but I quietly continue my bus ride to school. Being a tight-lipped little guy, I purposely neglect to inform the teacher of my misfortune.

However, the walls seem to have ears. The word gets around as though it's an active agent in a process of osmosis. Of course, the active agents who spread the news of falling objects from a school bus are fellow students from the school bus. Jabber mouths who don't know when to keep their traps shut.

In time, the news gets to the school nurse. She isn't amused by my coverup. She shows up at our class around 11: 00 a.m. Confers briefly with my startled teacher, and then escorts me from the class room to the nurse's office. I'm asked some questions, told to remove my shirt, and a cursory examination is conducted. There is no evidence of serious injury. But a rash of small holes and big time smudging on the back of my shirt—and several large scratches on my back, provide irrefutable evidence of complicity in acts of tomfoolery on a school bus. Nevertheless, I'm given a mild reprimand and pronounced fit to go back to class.

As for the tag game, Gene never laid a hand on me. I suppose he has to be called the *loser by a nose*. A Trial Lawyer has to have a strong competitive edge to his personality and I've possessed that quality all my life. The emergency door caper is a case in point: the spirit of competition stirred in my bones as an eight year old third grader. A kid who'll risk falling out of a school bus moving 35 m.p.h. to avoid taking a tag is a fearless competitor!

School bus drivers can be characters. Driver # two gets a little quirky right before my eyes. We were sailing along one bright, heretofore, uneventful morning when a pheasant rooster darts into the path of the fast moving bus. Oh, hapless ring-necked fowl. It's the wrong place and the wrong time and the wrong reason to jaywalk. Let's break it down. Wrong place: a straight-of-way means greater torque – higher vehicular speed. Wrong time: a school day at 8:10 ante meridiem means a bus will be in the neighborhood. Wrong reason: Scooting when this fellow scoots means he's crazy. The mind of a pheasant rooster can't be read by me, but there is **no** good reason under God's blue heaven for a pheasant in its right mind to scurry into the axle length trajectory of a speeding bus! He's flat out inviting a wipe out.

To his credit, driver #two tries to avoid the pin-headed pheasant. He cranks the steering wheel to the left and the bus swerves sharply. But evasive action is ineffectual. The bus passes over the flighty bird and we all hear the tell-tale thud.

Driver #two brakes the bus to an abrupt stop, and those in the back of the bus give the rest of us the bad news. The ole pheasant has been conked hard on the noggin by some part of the school bus undercarriage, and it appears to be more than a slight concussion.

We all pile out of the bus. The woebegone bird is flopping around in the middle of the road, spattering blood with every flap. We simply stand behind the bus, momentarily stunned. There are no veterinarians in the crowd. It's too late anyway. The jaywalking pheasant is going – going – **gone**!

Mister #two tells us to get back on the bus. We need to hurry or we'll be late for school. He says he'll collect the remains and give the dead bird a decent burial. He promises he'll do right by our unfortunate feathered friend. Then, he collects a brown paper bag from behind the driver's seat, walks to the recently deceased, gently stashes the accident victim in the bag, and places the remains under his seat. This being preparatory, as we understood Chinese ring-neck pheasant *interment* procedures, to burial in some peaceful plot of sand.

The rest of the trip to school passes without incident. We go to our various classes, trying to focus on school lessons being taught by our teachers. Now, I can't speak for others so I'll keep this in the first person, all during the school day I couldn't get the accident completely out of my mind. Lingering, troubling me, brooding in the back of my mind were thoughts of the late inhabitant of the marshlands. I'd been on the bus that did the damage. Somehow, I felt a certain degree of responsibility.

Comfort came, however, when I'd flash back to Mister #two's assurance that he would give the plump bird a proper burial.

I need to explain something. I'm usually one of the first to get on the school bus in the morning, so I generally sit in the first seat behind and to the right of the driver. I typically sit in the same place on the way home. This habit is followed on the afternoon of the fowl-demise. This seating places me directly behind the bus glove compartment. A fact that's generally of no consequence – strictly a moot point. Who cares what's in the old glove compartment, probably just papers.

But it ain't a moot point on this trip home. It becomes a matter of genuine curiosity as bus wheels hit a deep washboard in the road. The bus lurches and bounces – and the glove compartment door pops wide open. Instantly, my eyes open really wide too. Inside the glove box, to my surprise and my chagrin, I see our late feathered friend snugly reposing in the compartment – without his feathers or his entrails or his head or his claws. And quicker than I could have said, "Plucked feathers," Mister Driver #two reaches over, slams the door shut, and glowers at me. His eyes and his expression say all that needs to be said. They say, "That's for your eyes only. Don't yap your mouth about something you might think you've seen that is none of your business."

But I knew what I'd seen. I recognized the duplicity of the driver. I'd seen the woebegone pheasant rooster inside the glove compartment all dressed out for Mister #two's evening meal. The impulsive bird wasn't buried in a nice place under the ground somewhere. He'd been decapitated, declawed, plucked, gutted, rubbed, washed, and tenderized for a deep fry. Two drumsticks and two thighs and a succulent white breast about to be dipped into boiling-hot grease at suppertime.

Perhaps, driver #2 meant well when he said he'd do right by our unfortunate feathered friend and give him a decent burial, but that was right after he'd had breakfast. Boy, were we naive! We believed Mister #2, but an empty stomach in the afternoon overpowered his *will* to keep the promise he'd made in the morning, and his *empathy* for a dead bird. There wouldn't be any interment service, #2 would only be serving fried pheasant to his palate and his belly.

Notwithstanding my childish distaste for accident exploitation, I **did** keep my mouth shut. I <u>never</u> told my fellow travelers what I'd seen in the glove box. However, I did notice a peculiar change in Mister #two's driving habits after *the incident*. Before the fatal accident, driver #2 always tried to <u>avoid</u> pheasants who fluttered into harms way, but afterwards – he always

43

TRIED TO HIT pheasants, even if they weren't in harms way. Pheasants could be running along the shoulder of the road, and Mister # 2 would sharply veer the bus toward the prey and make a beeline for the unsuspecting morsel, I mean – pheasant. Though to my percipient knowledge, #2 never bagged another pheasant rooster with his bus. However, his long suffering futility in the enterprise, didn't keep him from repeatedly trying. All of which conveys this nugget of truth, the pheasant driver #2 inadvertently mowed down must have tasted **damn** good!

Speaking of roosters, those of the chicken species were fearless foes in the barnyard. During my elementary school years we had <u>at</u> <u>least</u> three or four roosters running lose in the corral area. I don't know why, maybe they saw me as a nascent rival with the hen population, but the roosters seemed to take pleasure in picking on me. Which translates into **pecking** on me, whenever they got close enough.

I'd become familiar with a *bully factor* on the school grounds, and the roosters became *bullies of the barnyard* in my eyes. Their mode of operation bore similarity to my <u>red</u> <u>racer</u> adversaries. The cock roosters appeared to lay low until I got close to their rendevous site of choice, then they'd come scudding toward me just itching for a fight. If they managed to make it a close encounter they became airborne. I'm not particularly tall now, but in those faraway days I was extremely short. They'd come at me with feathers all ruffled up, and try to jump on my chest. Sometimes they succeeded. Or if they were really being sneaky, they'd scuttle up behind me and jump on my back.

It became a painful nuisance. A serious threat <u>every</u> time my chores took me close to the barn. Nobody likes to be pecked by stupid roosters. Their beak bites hurt, and their claws were sharp as needles. They'd scratch my skin though my shirts and my trouser legs. I'd lay awake at nights plotting defensive ploys and bloody revenge. These roosters were making me their plaything – their <u>pecking</u> bag. It wasn't amusing. Rooster play is **fowl play**, and I became very determined to extract a measure of comeuppance from these conniving birds.

I needed a solution bad, but short of an edict of extermination by my father, which wasn't practicable – we needed roosters to fertilize the hen's eggs – there weren't any viable answers. Obviously, it's tough for a little fellow to hold his own against barnyard bullies with razor sharp beaks and barbed claws. The challenge seemed insoluble. The irony of the tale is that my battle plan eventually comes from the <u>funny</u> <u>papers</u>. Really, where is the logic in a small fry getting the skinny on roosters from a zoology textbook or from the unedited works of Alfred Lord Tennyson?

Once I'd learned to read, I made it my practice to read the funny papers that appeared in our weekly newspaper. The paper was printed each Thursday, but we usually didn't retrieve the newspaper from the Post Office until Saturday evening. So, after we'd attended our church meetings on Sunday, reading my favorite comic strips became a Sabbath Day afternoon ritual.

Actually, my favorite funny strip isn't too funny. *Prince Valiant* is a gallant warrior. The funnies portray him as a heroic figure living in jolly old England in the days of Tennyson's King Arthur. He rubs shoulders with the knights of the round table, and engages in weekly **jousting** with insurgents of the kingdom. *Prince Valiant* is my hero. Herein lies inspiration for a strategy to neutralize the rowdy roosters.

A rooster insurgency schemes to usurp the strolling privileges of a little *prince of the homestead*. Dooming him to confinement in his adobe palace for the rest of his childhood days, as he perceives the dilemma.

I decide to take on my barnyard insurgents with the guile and courage of a medieval warrior. Assuming the regal persona of a *knight of the realm*. A sworn defender of the downtrodden and disrespected, the ambushed and clawed and pecked and disparaged. Namely: me! It becomes a matter of protecting my dignity, my personal honor, and my barnyard freedom. The cause is just and expedient.

I methodically choose my armor. My helmet is a thick beany cap from winters past, the breastplate a soiled corduroy jacket commandeered from a closet, two pairs of pants, stiff leather gloves, and cowboy boots. My sword Excaliber is a 2 inch by 5foot red slat from the silo fence. It gives me a sliver edged bludgeon to use on the combs of the cretin roosters.

Thus girded, I go forth to joust with the upstart fowl. They see me coming, bide their time, and allow me to advance deep into their domain – unmaligned. Then they mount a fierce charge, coming at the *solitary knight* from every direction. Beaks and claws bared. Wanting to scratch and prick and draw blood. A battle royal ensues. They cluster around me. They jump on my back and on my chest. But I resist their onslaught. They cannot penetrate my homespun armor, and I fight to shake off the rascally roosters as though I'm a company of ten lancers. Swinging my red slat sword in wide arches with reckless abandon. Frequently finding the mark on unprotected crowns of rooster topknots. Rooster blood streams across feathery faces and sprays outward to land on crusty cow piles and speckle nearby fences with outlandish red, dripping polka dots.

I cringe now, as I reflect upon the bloody spectacle, but please remember the stakes. This is a battle over turf, and my youthful determination refused to yield to the fowl insurgency of yesteryear. It didn't happen during this initial skirmish between the *knight-errant* and his rooster antagonists. The fact is: there were various encounters for several weeks. Each time I warded them off with my rustic armor, and beat them down and bloody with my makeshift sword of justice. Eventually, steadfast persistence and a bloodstained silo slat restored order to the barnyard *realm*.

I became *Lord and Master* over the rooster clan. They'd cower instead of charging, and scurry away when I came around. Holding their distance, casting furtive glances, respecting me from afar. <u>Remembering</u>, no doubt, their bloodied combs, battered flanks, and bruised cock egos. The punishment inflicted was severe, but it did deter! **Lesson learned**.

I've previously referenced the *bully factor* on playgrounds. I'm going to return to that subject. I experienced an educational, though painful, <u>run in</u> with an irksome bully that is quite memorable. I was in the fourth grade, a feisty little nine year old. Double B, that is *bully boy*, is a ninth or tenth grader. He's matriculating at a junior high school on the other side of the street from the elementary school. Enjoying easy access to our playground area, and Double B makes treks across the street with monotonous regularity during lunch hours. He thinks because he's begun to experiment with a razor he's a tough guy.

He rides the field school bus, and tries to rule the roost. Making the bus his personal fiefdom while we're on the road. His forays around the perimeter of our playground with two cronies are calculated. He's there to intimidate the field-ites without encroaching too far into the playground. Indulging in a clumsy form of psychological warfare: calling the field-ites out by name, making hand gestures that depict brute force, taunting, strutting, finger pointing and shouting verbal threats. Offering a preview of what he'll do on the way home.

Later on the school bus, Double B randomly torments four of us. He <u>slyly</u> pinches, pulls tufts of hair, tugs our ears, trips us, uses knuckle punches to make shoulder hickeys, steals marbles from our pockets, shoots us with spit balls, tightly twists our arms behind our backs until we've agreed he's the *bus boss*, and makes the ride home thoroughly miserable. Further, he promises to kick some ass if we rat on him.

Double B has tried to put us between a rock and a hard place. He's older. He's bigger. He's stronger. And it gives him a terrific rush to see four little fellows squirm. The bullying boosts his sense of identity in a way good grades will not. He says he's simply not the academic type.

However, the squirmees don't want their situation to be long-term. So, we have a meeting one morning before the school bell rings. Making a pact to turn the tables on *bully boy*, if we can. A conspiracy is born. The enterprise entails an element of surprise. At the first opportunity, away from the scrutiny of meddling school officials and a wimpy school bus driver, four co-conspirators plot to jump the tormentor and pummel him into submission. Forcing him to pledge a cessation of all further hostilities. We're thinking that **four on one** will win out, even when the four are half pints. Hmmmmmm. Good luck with that concept, Chaps.

We also enter into an oath of secrecy. No member of the foursome is to say anything about conspiring to obtain vigilante retribution. That said, we finalize the plan with hand shakes. The school bell rings, and we hurry to our respective classrooms. Confident that vindication lies ahead for the four would-be pugilists. *Bully boy's* pestering will soon be history. Unfortunately, the young accomplices will discover that the path of school boy thuggery is a slippery slope – and a painful one. Our cause may be just, but does the end justify our means?

I suppose my built-in sense of moral restraint made me wary. Causing me to reflect upon our schoolboy scheme. Frankly, the thought of roughing-it-up with *bully boy* was a little troublesome to me. I'd acquired a smidgen of experience in a teacher-supervised rumble. Once prior, another kid and myself went about 45 seconds on the playground with boxing gloves. We were given some space, and other students formed a ring around us about three feet deep. I almost got my block knocked off. This kid constantly peppered my face. Every time he threw a punch it landed on my nose or my forehead or my mouth. I'm lucky I didn't lose some teeth. As it was, I got a bad bloody nose and welts on my forehead. He really cleaned my clock. I'm don't think I hit my opponent a single time.

So, I thought about the plan to pummel *bully boy*, and our oath of secrecy. I'm wasn't in the habit of keeping secrets from my Mother. After several days, I decided to take her into my confidence. Therefore, I spilled the beans. I laid out the whole plot and the reasons behind it. Mom listened closely. When I'd finished she gave a little sigh and pulled me close. She didn't say a thing at first. Moments passed. Then she gave me a lingering hug and in substance whispered, "I've been bullied. I know how you feel, but you haven't been hurt. He's only doing this to get attention. Ignore him. Don't make a fuss. Don't give him the attention he wants. This young man won't have fun if you don't react to his pestering, and he'll stop doing it. But whatever happens, **do not** pick a fight. **Do not** be part of any plan to beat up on him. Stay out of it. You'll REGRET IT if you do! And there **is** something else I want you to do. **Be his friend**. What this boy needs are friends."

Good advice – as subsequent events teach me. Yet, I didn't heed her counsel. Not that I was hard of hearing. I heard what Mom said, but what I heard didn't sink in. My problem isn't being a nine year old with a physical handicap, I'm a nine year old with a concentration deficit. I'm *hard of listening*! And I had my three friends on the school bus to contend with, I'd entered into a pact to levy a portion of corporal punishment upon *bully boy*. Giving three others my word to be their accomplice. When push comes to shove I am unwilling to rescind my prior commitment. Therefore, the youthful foursome continue to bide their time until an opportunity arises to barge into a **four on one** with their nemesis.

It comes three days later on a Tuesday afternoon following school. The scenario seems tailor-made for a field road fight. The window of opportunity opens without foreknowledge. The field bus is pressed into service to transport additional junior high students home because their bus is in the shop. They are dropped off before the field bus begins its regular route. Thereafter, with *bully boy* and *the four* still on board the bus develops mechanical difficulties. Before it returns to town for a tummy tuck at the nearest garage, the driver lets student passengers out if they want to disembark. They may either walk home or wait on the country roadway to be picked up after the bus is fixed. And holy misalignment of the polar stars, ole *bully boy* and *the four* who wish to clean his plow are among those who choose to get off the bus.

The stage is set. Lights – camera – action! The principals, including yours truly, are off the bus together. It is after school hours at a remote spot away from the scrutiny of meddling school officials and a wimpy school bus driver. Also, the four half pint conspirators still have the will to rumble.

Five minutes later, while Double B's back is turned, we go trundling in for a **four on one** pile-on. But the blind-side offensive isn't effective. He's much larger than we are, and he beats off our initial thrust. I'm brusquely thrown down. I pick myself up and run at him again. Double B is on his feet, but two of my comrades are hanging on his back. I go in <u>low</u> hoping to cut his legs out from under him. He sees me coming and swings his foot forward. I stumble, and the metal tap on the heel of his shoe clips me in the middle of my forehead. It breaks the skin, burrowing a 2 inch long gash between my eyebrows and my hairline.

The force of the impact momentarily stuns me. Blood streams from the wound, and the injury has an immediate sobering effect upon all combatants. The adrenalin rush accompanying the initial offensive fizzles. Even *bully boy* seems chastened by the unexpected consequence. Instant calm settles on those present. Several handkerchiefs are offered to help me stifle the bleeding, and I hastily leave the scene. Walking a mile and a half to the farmhouse. Each step haunted by a belated recognition of the magnitude of our miscalculation, and by the awful, consuming dread I feel over an impending face-off with my Mother. The plot has been ill-conceived from the outset. We hadn't botched execution so much as we'd botched the conception of such a fiasco.

What's a hundred times worse, I have disobeyed the loving counsel of my Mother and my insubordination has been unbelievably stupid. I walk inside feeling like a doomed little dunce. The ugly, red gash on my forehead is a brazen badge of my disrespect and empty–headedness.

I stumble down the driveway to our house. My Mother's expression is one of shock and dismay when she spies the laceration on my forehead. She rushes to me, cradling me in her arms. Tearfully she exclaims, "Oh, my poor little man. I'm afraid this is going to leave a bad scar on your forehead. Let me clean you up, and put some disinfectant on the wound. What in the world happened, Melvin?"

I'm not able to get any words to come out. I merely drop my head and stare at the floor. Mom presses her inquiry again. More firmly – more insistent this time. "Tell me what happened, Melvin."

I don't have the gumption to tell her. I'm tongue-tied. Truly embarrassed. But she captures my gaze and holds it. I look pitiful. She's crying. Then, a light of comprehension flashes across her mind. Her expression changes from confusion to exasperation. She grips each of my shoulders with a hand, and implores: "NO, YOU DIDN'T. **I told you not to**! I told you that you'd regret it. Why, Melvin? Why? Are you proud of yourself, Little Man?"

My Mother hastily leads me to the bathroom. Where she tenderly uses cotton gauze and warm water to clean the surface of the wound. Then she applies rubbing alcohol to disinfect the laceration. Frankly, the treatment burnt like hell. Greatly enhancing the stinging pain in my forehead and a searing pain that engulfs my heart. I could only murmur apologetically. "I'm sorry, Mom. I should have listened better. You were right."

The fact is: a caring, responsible, loving mother is usually right! The slide from knight-errant in the barnyard to school boy thug on the fields road is an unnerving memory. The 2 inch gash burrowed into my skin by the metal tap on *bully boy's* heel leaves a scar on my forehead for several years. Reminding me, every time I looked in the mirror, of the fate that awaits wayward boys. Life's a game of hard knocks when a fourth grader makes bad decisions.

Oh, the passionate sense of possibilities. It **is** *possible* for a boy to always mind his parents, but the path of obedience is a wavering conundrum – a winding maize of temptation.

We milked dairy cows. Though my sisters tried to ride them on occasion. The typical result being an unceremonious trip to the middle of a manure pile. The income our farm produced came from raw milk and sugar beet seed. We milked cows and we harvested beet seed.

Cows have to be fed to make milk. Scattering hay along the mangers was one of my primary chores. During summer grazing I was herdsman-in-chief, responsible for getting our herd from barnyard to pasture. Sometimes the task was quite eventful. One time especially sticks in my mind. Probably, because each time I think of the experience I see cow hooves!

The pasturing venue in this instance is about three quarters of a mile from the farmhouse. We don't have many neighbors in the fields. However, the road the cows have to be herded along takes us past the residence of our closest neighbors. They're approximately half a mile from our house. The dirt road is a gentle slope from our corrals to the neighbors place. The road takes a ninety degree turn to the left when it intersects property of the other family.

They're nice people, and we have a very amicable relationship with them. However, there is one dry bone to pick. They always keep a dog. Some years they have **two** dogs. That salient fact is anathema to a dairy farmer who must regularly move a herd of 30-35 cows past the dog – or dogs, as the case may be.

Anyone possessing a rudimentary understanding of cows and dogs knows they often aren't compatible. Cows are cud-chewing bovines who enjoy lots of quiet down time. They like things peaceful and humdrum. They don't particularly care for the yap-yap-yapping of dogs, the seemingly boundless energy of a high strung dog, nor the intrinsic snoopiness of a dog. Whether they're ambling along a one lane rutted road to pasture or sleepily reclining in the dry manure digs of the barnyard.

Whereas dogs, on the other hand, receive brains genetically ingrained with the notion that a dog has **two** basic job descriptions: BARKING and CHASING COWS! A few exceptions exist, but generally speaking, cows and dogs are **not** a good mix. The intermingling of bovine and canine is almost guaranteed to send the cows into a tizzy.

Accordingly, every trip past the neighbor's place is an adventure *waiting* to happen. The cows come by twice a day. Going to pasture and coming from the pasture. And it's about the same time each day. Now, I don't know if the neighbor dog – or dogs, as circumstances arranged themselves, actually required sleep. I only know there was boisterous neighborhood yapping every time we went by.

I need to make an important disclosure. The herdsman-in-chief is **not** a shepherd! I'm talking dairy <u>cows</u> here, not sheep. I didn't walk in <u>front</u> with shepherd crook in hand leading my flock of sheep. Cows aren't typically amenable to being led. They have to be **herded**. That's a rear-guard action. An animal isn't herded from the front. A herdsman-in-chief does his job from behind the cows. He has to prod and push and holler, implore and throw rocks, and swing sticks at flanks and backsides – to get the herd where it's supposed to be.

This dynamic is particularly applicable as we approach and pass beyond the neighbor's pad. I think the engagements with us may have been the *high* points of every summer for the mutts. On the other hand, the nervous agitation that pervades each passing is probably the *low* point of every summer for the cows. Which explains, of course, why it was extremely hard for the herdsman to get his herd past the twice-daily doggie ambush.

Regardless of direction, the herd always became apprehensive within the last hundred yards prior to the encounter zone. However, except for a <u>single</u> skirmish on a specific sultry afternoon there was no serious incident. Simply a chronicle of annoying passage. Causing the herdsman to *sweat* a little harder to perform his duties.

But in the heat of the **dog** days of summer, there is a hot day when all hell breaks loose. It comes suddenly –– without a hint of thundering hooves. We're on the way home in the late afternoon. Traipsing and graining and milking and a flaky alfalfa supper await the herd. The stride of the herd is brisk until we approach the doggie check point. Instantly, I sense the wariness of the herd. Though I don't detect extraordinary apprehension.

I'm herdsman-in-chief. Naturally, I'm bringing up the rear – about 20 feet behind the procession. It's dusty walking behind them, I need to allow some space to facilitate oxygen intake. Yet, when the gait of the herd slows, I move in closer with a hefty stick. Prepared to lay some wood on the rumps of the laggards. The whole point in being herdsman is to maintain FORWARD **movement**. The last thing I want is dawdling cud chewers as we move through the area of canine harassment.

Unknown to me, a debacle awaits just down the road. And it's not going to be averted by laying wood on a few slowpokes. The problem lies in front. The issue is: what happens if the leaders of the herd, the pace-setters, get SERIOUSLY SPOOKED! Well actually, when that happens the *instinct of the herd* kicks in. Making the herdsman and his measly stick moot objects, as I learned from first hand experience.

The neighbor's dog – or dogs, as the <u>two</u> laying in wait will definitely demonstrate, are **not** tied down. They are free to roam and harass at their pleasure. Heeding the genetic call to bark and chase cows as we enter their sphere of influence. The tandem is in a frenzy on this particular day, and I can't say why. I can only speculate. Are they underfed? Have they been whipped into surly moods by the master's boots? Eaten extra-peppy dog biscuits? Swallowed rat poison? Chewed on too much loco weed? Ingested a ration of energy enhancers? Are they smarting from a losing tussle with a slew of skunks? Has the obnoxious stench of liquid secreted by skunk glands triggered a <u>two dog</u> hallucination at the sight of black and white cows? Or is it simply fate? **Whatever**, the bottom line is I got bushwhacked by STAMPEDING COWS acting like a herd of berserk buffalo.

And I do mean **whacked**. Time and time and time again. It was raining hooves. I didn't come to the pasture to round up the herd equipped with a crash helmet, though I needed one for protection against serious brain rattling. It turns out on this grim day, <u>**two** hyperactive dogs</u> are <u>too</u> much bark for domesticated bovine!

Both dogs abruptly rush with *delirious fury* into the path of the lead cows. Outdoing themselves in putting on the dog. Their incessant barking is deafening to the herd leaders. They shuffle backwards, cowering before the dual onslaught. Snarling, lips curled and teeth bared, **the <u>two</u>**

assailants nip at the ankles of a half dozen terrified herd leaders. The clamorous agitation of the **two** canine blows the herd leaders away. *Severely spooked* by the dual offensive, they do something my youthful mind has <u>never</u> imagined until this moment.

The leaders TURN, and like deranged want-a-be bison they come charging back the way they've come. The rest take their cue from the turn-coats. It happens so quickly I have **no** time to run to the shoulder of the road. A herd of befuddled, 1500 pound dairy cows comes THUNDERING TOWARD ME, bellowing, udders swaying, churning chunks of dirt before them, a surging tidal wave of mangy milk maids on the hoof. Many tons of beef in flight – to compound a solitary farm boy's tenuous plight.

Profuse thoughts flash across my mind at this instant, but the predominating point is an unspoken prayer, "Lord, I'm not much, but I'm all I've got. Please take them around me." My unarticulated plea is *partially* answered in the affirmative. **Some** of the stampeding cows do go around me, BUT – they <u>don't</u> all go around me. The incident creates considerable dust, which billows into the air. I begin to choke and debris flies towards me. The cusp of the stampede goes by, but an on-rushing cow bumps my right hip and I fall down.

It's all a blur after that, but a boy doesn't have to *see* cow hooves to know he's being clipped by hoofs. I'm **whacked** again and again in various places on my noggin, my shoulders, my legs, and my shoes. Then, as quickly as it began, the rampage ends.

I'm still alive, still conscious, but dazed and dusty and disheveled. I just sit there in the settling haze collecting my thoughts for a few minutes. During this process, I take cognizance of having survived the stampede intact. No bones are broken, my heart's beating, my lungs are respirating, and my brain's functioning – in a fashion that would be slow for some but is normal for me.

I have *probable cause* to feel a great debt of gratitude. It is a debt I can never fully pay, but <u>I</u> <u>can</u> live in *thanksgiving daily* – to Him who does **completely** answer every fervent prayer in His inimitable way. I *could have* taken ponderous, direct hits to my head from the horde of powerful animals. Knocking me senseless. Perhaps, fatally disabling brain function. COULD HAVE, but it <u>didn't</u> happen. I was struck numerous times, but <u>not</u> one blow devastated my existence. Praise to God from whom all blessings flow!

My boyish, <u>still</u> functioning mind recognizes the darkness of numbing goofiness that could have been, and humbly contemplates the passionate sense of what <u>still</u> might be. Rejoices in visionary eyes ever young and ardent – that **see possibility** in the awesome potential of every human life.

Reposing in the roadway of hoof pocked dirt, I dust myself off, get to my feet, collect the cows, and succeed in getting them <u>past</u> check point crazy-dogs this time. If at first a young herdsman doesn't succeed, then he should try again – and again if the situation calls for do-overs!

Pushing the cows forward, the youthful herdsman trudges up the sloping road home, *returns* the herd to the barnyard, and *reports* the experience to his Father. Saying, Dad **is displeased** is an understatement. He's livid. The matter is taken up with the owner of the offending dogs. He says his dogs stay, but promises to rein in the cow chasing. Thus, the dogs continue to offend by their barking (that's what dogs do), but maintain a considerably lower cow-chasing profile in all subsequent dog days of summer.

Without meaning to equate cows and people, I do offer a crude analogy I believe is pertinent. Just as **cows** going to pasture need a herdsman to get them past a gauntlet of barking dogs nipping at their ankles, so **witnesses** going to the Courthouse need a herdsman to get them past the procedures, fears, and dangers implicit in the *Courtroom gauntlet*. A Prosecutor is necessarily a herdsman.

IT IS <u>NEITHER</u> PLEASANT <u>NOR</u> EASY BEING A WITNESS IN A MURDER CASE! Experienced persons connected to the Criminal Justice System understand these truisms. This is why the Law gives a power of subpoena to Prosecuting Attorneys. If left to their own devices, very few witnesses would voluntarily show up in Court to testify **against** an accused killer. Even after service of subpoena, many persons must be virtually blindfolded, led, pushed, guided, enticed, cajoled, polygraphed, threatened with contempt, emotionally counseled, constantly reassured, babysat, telephoned, transported, and promised witness fees to get them into the Courtroom and on the Witness Stand.

Let's face it, being a witness is not a happy-go-lucky stroll along a beach. The bottom line is stark. If the Prosecutor is dealing with a percipient witness he's working with someone who *absolutely* **knows** the capabilities of the Defendant. A person who has *actually* **perceived** the murder with one or more of his physical senses. Such a witness **knows** this murderous character has already dispatched a living person or persons to the morgue. Therefore, he's highly apprehensive about putting <u>himself</u> in harms way. KILLERS typically don't want to get caught, and after they're caught they certainly don't want to be found guilty. Conviction means **severe** punishment. Life in the slammer or death in the execution chamber comes to mind. KILLERS tend to be disdainful toward those who abet their demise in Court. Witnesses see danger in cooperation. They fear **any** participation in the Prosecutorial process will put them on a potential hit-list. The stakes are huge in **murder trials**!

Witness will ask about the Courthouse venue. Who's going to be there? Will **HE** be in the Courtroom? Will **HIS** family and friends be among those who will hear my testimony and *see me*? The answer is YES. The Defendant **will** be in the Courtroom. It's **HIS** Trial. He has a RIGHT to confront the witnesses against him and he also has a constitutional RIGHT to a Trial that is public. His family and friends are entitled to be in the Courtroom **IF** they maintain appropriate judicial decorum.

So, witnesses have to be constantly assured that they'll be safe. They have to be told that bailiffs and corrections officers will be in the Courtroom. Further, numerous law enforcement officers can be immediately summoned if problems occur. Witnesses will be told to be *oblivious* to the persons present. Stay focused. Look straight ahead. When you're in the Courtroom look at the Court personnel and the Judge and the Prosecutor. The Defendant and his supporters will not hurt you. The entire Courthouse will be secure.

As I indicated four paragraphs above, a witness in a **murder case** has to be "virtually blindfolded." Emotional concerns must be addressed. Fears minimized. A Prosecutor becomes an unnatural blend of friend, confidante, babysitter, shrink, spiritual advisor, truth galvanizing poligrapher, phone buddy, an arm of the Court emphasizing Judicial powers of contempt, a taxi service, and yes — a sort of **herdsman**. Pushing, prodding, and imploring witnesses to experience the exquisite green pasture of the witness chair.

Of course witnesses will be nervous. It's only natural for them to be stressed out by the Courthouse occurrence. But imagine the alternative. Are we to turn communities over to the hooligan element? What happens if everyone opts out of cooperation with law enforcement? A free society can only be preserved by the full involvement of its members in important societal matters. NOTHING is more important than **law and order**. Communities MUST be **protected** from criminal acts. Every citizen has a sacred responsibility to do what they can. It **is** the price of citizenship! That is the nuts and bolts of the speech a Prosecutor gives each time he goes to the plate! He knows he's not going to hit a home run <u>without</u> **witnesses**.

Just as a dairy farmer knows he's not going to bring home checks to sustain his family without the cooperation of <u>every</u> cow in the herd.

Switching from a pair of sneak-attacking, turf-protecting **dogs**, I'd like to touch on the impact a sneak-attacking, imperialistic **nation** can have on a six year old. It's so true that many things are simply a matter of <u>perception</u>. Hence, the passionate sense of *what might be*, can bring the <u>passion</u> of **fear** front and center.

It is the first week in June, 1944. My first year in school is almost history. A fortiori, history is being made across the world. The war years are grim times. An aura of paranoia grips the country. The local school board, perhaps in response to urging by federal authorities, has decided to end the year with an exclamation point. The entire elementary school is summoned to the gymnasium for an "information" assembly.

Little first graders like me expect to be entertained not intimidated at assemblies. We anticipate tumbling acts, readings, music, dancing, treats, and a joyous sendoff into summer. What we get is a batch of **straight talk** – from the Principal and down through the ranks.

We're told the Japanese are making a last-ditch attempt to turn the war around. They plan to scare the American people into an anti war frenzy by sending *balloons* aloft that are loaded with powerful **bombs**. The balloons will be launched from sites under the control of imperial Japan with the expectation that prevailing air currents will carry them to the continental United States. There they will randomly descend to the ground and **explode**. Prompting the American population to insist that their leaders immediately sue for a cessation of all hostilities.

Whether this last-straw brain child born of desperation, has any feasibility or even the remotest chance of success, is unknown to me and my fellow grade school students. We don't get any sort of engineering nor armaments critique. We're just told it's <u>probably</u> going to happen. So, LOOK OUT!

The Principal and other purveyors of information concerning the *balloon threat* to the homeland repeatedly make and reiterate one seminal point. Wherever you go BE WATCHFUL! We <u>don't</u> know what these things will look like. We <u>don't</u> know where they'll land or when they'll

detonate. If you see anything *strange*, don't go up to it. Don't even think about touching it. STAY AWAY from it, and RUN in the opposite direction. Have a great summer vacation, but be safe and be CAREFUL!

Theoretically, the school assembly is a good idea, but **words of warning** must be carefully *crafted* for youngsters. Otherwise, summer is transformed into a perceptual nightmare.

The things we've been told really scare me. The warning is emphatic, but the nature of the menace is **non-specific**. Quote: "We don't know **what** these things will look like." Yeah, they spoke of balloons. But what *shape* will the balloons be, what *color* will they be, what *size* will they be, and what type of *hardware* will they be carrying?

I've been exposed to the endless grist mill of wartime propaganda churned out on radio news programs and movie theater new reels. That hype portrays the enemy as maniacal, scheming primates unworthy of the human race.

The effect of the "information" assembly upon a wimpy little farm fellow is predictable in such an atmosphere. I'm stunned by the disclosures. I passionately ponder the sense of *what might be* almost every waking minute and while I'm sleeping – I dream about it.

It's a state of being scared out of your wits, but not knowing what you're scared of. They said in the gymnasium if we saw "anything *strange*, don't go up to it. Don't even think about touching it. STAY AWAY from it, and RUN in the opposite direction." But what the hell does **strange** mean? A bush can be strange. Shooting stars framed in a dark sky can be strange. A full orange moon rising above a mountain can be strange. Discarded junk and building materials blown around by the wind can be strange. Old abandoned cars can be strange. Cactus blooms and weeds with tassels and hollowed out rocks and stray beach balls can be strange. Lots of things a little paranoid boy with a big imagination hasn't seen before **look** *strange*. The desert is littered with things that look strange to some. It's simply a matter of perception.

My summer of 1944 is miserable. The world was full of boggy men that year. I spent the whole summer looking UP for balloons coming down and looking AROUND for balloons already down. **Whatever** *balloons* were, because every where I looked I supposed I had *possible* **sightings**. The sense of *what might be* enemy *balloons* was all around me.

World War II ended the next year. When the war ended farm boy paranoia ended. No more hype. No more sightings. No more miserable summers. Only childhood memories of **bleak thoughts** about BALLOONS

WITH BOMBS that *might have been*. Though I had <u>recurring</u> dreams of Zeros strafing the farmland for at least a decade.

Christmas morning 1947 brought the rapturous *possibility* of giving my feet a little relief. A shiny new Schwin **bicycle** appeared next to the Christmas tree. Gracious. <u>A bike in the room</u>! It didn't assemble itself. It didn't pedal itself inside. It <u>wasn't</u> there on Christmas Eve when I went to bed. And there is the matter of that crayon scribbled letter I left by the milk and cookies.

Circumstantial evidence of a visit by Santa, but surely not plausible proof of a Santa Claus phenomenon beyond a reasonable doubt. More representative, I'd say, of a tangible testament of parental love. Although neither of the *possibilities*, Santa or my parents, bothered to resolve the twin problems of lack of pavement [we had none], and abundance of puncture burrs [we had thousands].

Never mind the negatives. I thought it was beautiful. The most spectacular riding-machine a farm boy could imagine. It made me feel quite grown-up to be the new <u>owner</u> of a bicycle. Not a tricycle, mind you. A <u>full-size</u> two-wheeled marvel without any hint of a third wheel, or of training wheels for that matter.

However, there is a catch 22 to bicycle ownership. Simply offering one's adoration to the bike is insufficient. You get it so you can ride it. It's disrespectful to a shiny-new Schwin not to ride it, and to parents who gave it to you so you could ride it. Loving parents whose procurement sacrifice is not inconsequential.

In my case, the *trick* is to simultaneously get my uncoordinated feet from the ground to the pedals while lifting my wiry little buns on to the seat. And to manage, <u>after</u> I'm in the *saddle*, to stretch my stubby legs far enough to rotate both pedals in sync with my feet. Thus, causing the bicycle chains to transmit power from the pedals to the wheels. Smartly propelling the <u>full size</u> two-wheeled marvel down the road. All of this being accomplished while maintaining a proper balance and deftly steering my front tire around sharp rocks, an assortment of pebbles, the ubiquitous puncture burrs, and hard to spy cactus needles that litter the path of the old farm road.

I knew I needed a <u>slope</u> to lower the challenge of my endeavor. There was such a slope in the road a short distance from the farmhouse. So, on a chilly early morning the day after Christmas, I pushed my spiffy Schwin beauty up the aforementioned slope in the road. I did it while Dad milked, and though I did not know it at the time – as my *angel Mother* anxiously watched. She became an eye-witness to my <u>hours</u> of travail and achievement.

Alas, *breaking-in* a new bicycle can be a lot like trying to ride a **bucking** *bronco* in a rodeo arena. Especially, when the arena sod consists of frost, red dirt, loose pebbles, and protruding slabs of **rock** partially buried in hard pack. Any <u>beginner</u> must be prepared to experience frequent falls, but they won't be soft-gel *touch* **downs** on this terrain. And possibly adding insult to injury, a reasonable expectation exists that <u>when</u> the little cowboy is *thrown*, the resulting tumble may be exacerbated by the big bike falling on him. It's not a simple task to *bronco-bust* a <u>full</u> <u>size</u> Schwin bike.

Yet, despite my physical liabilities, and the frosty, red dirt, pebble strewn, rock bumping course the bike has to crisscross, I **did**, after having the full prerequisite of "working at it hard" extracted from my pudgy little body, learn how to ride a bicycle.

I would push the bicycle up the slope. Struggle mightily to climb on. Go flying a few feet down the hill, and tip-over. This happened over and over again. Each time I fell on the hard ground it hurt bad. I acquired the bruises and blood and scrapes and scabs to prove it. The shiny *new* bike soon became a dusty, dented *new* bike. Recurring impressions prompted me to quit, to give up until I got bigger and older and better coordinated. But I didn't. I'd get up, brush myself off, pick up the bicycle, and awkwardly climb aboard again. Persisting in my mission to **tame** the two wheeled rough rider.

In later years, my Mother often referred to the <u>ordeal</u> she observed through the living room window that bright, cold day-after Christmas when I <u>initiated</u> my quest to become a cyclist. She would say, "Melvin, you have always been <u>determined</u>. If you <u>really</u> want to do something you do it! I have known this from the day I watched you learning how to ride your bicycle. I wanted to rush out of the house, hold you in my arms, and wipe away your tears. But I managed to resist my maternal instincts. It was difficult for me to show restraint, but I stood there for a long time watching you toil to stay upright.

"You must have tipped over fifty times. The repeated falls scraped your knuckles, bloodied your knees – and damaged your ego. Despite the frustration of short term failure, you refused to quit. You kept at it until <u>finally</u> you were able to *ride high* from the top of the hill to the bottom of the hill. There you crashed your bicycle, of course, but it was amazing progress.

"You got off the ground and, proudly, came running into the house to tell me what you'd accomplished. And you continued to *work* at riding your bicycle in the days that followed. It was <u>so</u> hard for you, but you did what you set out to do. You learned to ride a big bicycle!"

Yeeaaahh**hh!** Three cheers for the passionate sense of *what can be*. If a <u>two</u> wheeler *can be* conquered, why isn't a <u>one</u> wheeler within the realm of *possibility*? <u>Anything</u> *can be* conquered! Bring on the allegorical unicycle. Bring on the <u>Trial</u> <u>Work</u>. **IF** a farm boy can *ride high* down a slope why can't he *ramble* into the Courthouse? Strong core values, determination, confidence, lofty goals, and hard work *can* **transform** sod busters into crime busters.

Speaking of busting sod, money is always in short supply on the farm. We need to bust sod in a way that enhances family finances. Dad and Mom confer. They announce that we need a <u>third</u> cash crop to supplement the efforts of the dairy herd and the sugar beets. They've decided to plant three and a half acres of **cantaloupes**. A muskmelon with a hard ridged, warty rind and sweet orange meat. Our parents tell my little sis and me that cantaloupes may be the solution to our cash short-fall.

So it came to be, that the Harmons become cantaloupe farmers early one summer. My Father gets the old Farmall tractor primed, we shovel cow manure into a spreader, and take turns broadcasting natural green miracle grow over land being prepped for the cantaloupe patch. Dad plows the ground and I disk. Next, I drive the tractor across the land pulling a rectangular wooden level.

Leveling is dusty work, However, two exhilarating thoughts occupy my mind as I maneuver the tractor back and forth over the ground. I'm steering toward a vision that energizes each turn. I see truck loads of big round ripe cantaloupes as sweet as honey headed to market, and a pickup bed full of money headed to the bank. Yippee – a happy day is on the way. The farmin Harmon foursome will soon be <u>loaded</u> with melon money. Uuuuh, not really!

The field foreordained for cantaloupes is ready for planting in the first week of June. Early one gorgeously sunny morning the Harmons begin their cantaloupe cavalcade. Our entire family, consisting of Dad, Mom, my little sister, myself, and <u>two</u> gray cats both named "Smokey," gather at the top of the field.

I'll explain the name thing. Being a dairy farm, most folks assumed we had an abundant supply of milk to feed stray cats. Therefore, it became a fact of farm living for us to be the unsoliciting recipients of many of the community's excess felines. A good number of these cast-offs were smokey grays. So, not wanting to complicate matters unnecessarily, we just called them **all** "Smokey."

We divide into two work crews. Dad and Mom are the self appointed crew chiefs. They explained that we will work side-by-side on adjacent rows. They will wield the hoes. Carefully excavating small hills, just the right distance from the furrows to the top of the rows, for the cantaloupe seed to be dropped into. The task assigned my sister and me is to drop 3-4 seeds into <u>each</u> cantaloupe hill. Dad and Mom will then push a thin layer of soil over the seed with their hoes, and each will use a foot to pack the soil into place.

Once we understand our respective team roles, we commence the arduous chore of planting. Confident our efforts will reward us with a bounteous crop of melons. It takes us three long, *sweat-filled* days to complete the planting phase. We work from cow milking to cow milking, with naps and short lunch breaks in between.

We've worked the ground, fertilized the ground, and planted the ground. Now, it's time to <u>irrigate</u> the ground. Cantaloupes won't grow without precious, clear, cool, thirst-quenching, soil-soaking water. Water is inextricably involved in the creation of *life*. The scriptural allegory of "living water" is profound and true.

Carefully, Dad coaxes H2O down the rows. He wants to ease water down the furrows so seed won't wash away. Slow watering minimizes seed erosion and maximizes deep ground drenching. Moisture and warm sunshine cause swelling seed to germinate.

Several days later, cantaloupe sprouts begin their steady assent though the ground. Small green, double-button shoots emerge from the soil's soft womb. The miracle of life bursting though pliant seams in the soil. The field of green sprouts grow up and out. Almost overnight, it seemed, they became small vines of stems and glistening fuzzy leaves. The stems thicken, the leaves expand, and runners push outward like green tentacles groping the ground.

There is a so-called **<u>law</u> of the harvest**. What you sow is what you reap. Meaning: when *cantaloupe* seed is put inside the ground it won't be *tomato* plants that sprout on top of the ground. Seed determines species. HOWEVER, cantaloupe seed in the ground and cantaloupe plants on top of the ground are **not** a guarantee the Harmons will have truck loads of ripe cantaloupes motoring to market. Many **variables** exist between sprouting and harvesting.

But for a time, heaven smiles down on the cantaloupe farmers. Small, virile, wonderfully yellow blossoms begin to grace the vines. All over the field trailing vines create a constellation of brilliant yellow and green and promise!

More time passes. Other watering turns saturate the soil. Weeds are hoed. The blossoms dry and small oval-green cantaloupes appear. A medley of little melons form on vines across the entire field. Our excitement is not bounded by the four corners of our cantaloupe patch. It jettisons beyond the confines of our farm land. The size of daydreams growing in direct proportion to the size and number of growing melons. Carrying us into a fanciful dimension where streets are lined with gold, and dairy farmers with cantaloupe patches have pockets full of gold coins.

Each day the family takes stock of the progress of our burgeoning melons. More objective eyes may have viewed the melon vine peepshow about as exciting as watching flies fly. But in those good days, the daily inspection of our cash-on-the-vine cantaloupes was a whirl on a carousel, and the carnival doesn't come to town very often. Oh, the passionate sense of *what might be*. No wine is so fragrant nor sparkling nor intoxicating – as *dreams of possibility*.

Then gradually, with the passage of weeks, the embryonic cantaloupes grow into large, warty, green globes. The cantaloupe extravaganza appears to be moving past the back stretch, rounding the turn, and heading for home. Yet, farming is **not** an exact science. A serious obstacle will obstruct the finish line!

One cloudy day at the height of our optimism, I'm out in the patch melon gazing. Actually, this practice had become a favorite pastime of mine. I'm looking for the biggest, roundest cantaloupe in the field. What I see perched on top of one of our fledgling cantaloupes is the biggest, ugliest **bug** in the field.

There are many bugs on a farm. This is especially true in a field on a farm. Nevertheless, my inner sense immediately tells me there is something *ominous* about this single, gray-brown insect. It scampers down the melon to the vine's connecting umbilical stem, as I watch, and commences to chew. Sucking nutritive fluid from the hapless cantaloupe vine.

I didn't like this. So, that night at the supper table I report what I've seen to my parents. Dad utters an excited, "You did!" He and Mom then simultaneously exclaim, "That sounds like a **squash bug!**" And little sis squeals, "Oooh, I like to squash bugs with my feet!"

Dad interjects, "This is exactly what we want you to do. Squash bugs are a cantaloupe's worst enemy. **Squash bugs** kill cantaloupe vines!"

The next morning the whole family, including the two cats named Smokey, gather at the head of the cantaloupe patch. We have one objective: determine, if possible, whether I've actually seen a squash bug. Methodically, we search several rows of vines. Carefully bending over. Surveying individual plants. Lifting up the leaves and looking under them for bugs or pockets of bug eggs. Parents and two siblings have each taken a row.

It happens in a short time. What we didn't want to happen – *happens*. Mom lets out a disappointed gasp. She says, "I just saw one scurry across a vine. It **is** a squash bug." We all hurry to her side. Each of us peers intently into the bowels of a large cantaloupe vine with four to five good sized green melons growing from it.

We all see it. Identification confirmed! An "Anasa tristis" is on the vine. A mobile bug that utilizes piercing, needle-like, sucking mouthparts to drain plant juices from well established cantaloupe vines – causing them to wilt and die. The adult "Anasa tristis" is dark grayish brown in color. The edge of the body has alternating gold and brown spots in many instances. Fully developed bugs measure about one inch in length. Adults live an average of 75 to 130 days. This viability factor gives these rapidly multiplying *suckers* plenty of time to inflict a terrible toll on a patch of melons. Adult females deposit brownish-red eggs in large clusters on lower leaf surfaces. "Anasa tristis" targets cucumbers, squash, pumpkins, and melons. Of course, "Anasa tristis"is simply a highfalutin scientific name for ––– **SQUASH BUG!!** Sadly, squash bugs have invaded the hallowed domain of our cash-crop cantaloupes.

We search other vines for further evidence of squash bug infestation. Others are sighted, scurrying over our cantaloupes in a sinister samba. Primed and ready to launch a major offensive against our vulnerable melon crop.

The Harmons rendevous at the farmhouse. We quickly agree that these circumstances require a declaration of war. During the war council we agree to commit our time, our talents, our sacred resolve, and all our available resources – to stamp out the propagating squash bug population in the cantaloupe patch.

We adopt a four-fold plan of attack. First, we will implement my little sister's modus operandi. We will comb the vines, so to speak, and squash the bugs we see with out feet and our fingers. As Mom explains to sis and me, if a squash bug is positioned between the thumb and the index finger, it can be squashed lifeless in a flash.

Second, we will douse our vines and our greenie melons with Mom's home-brew concoction of vinegar and soap. She claims this potion has been passed down through several generations of her ancestry and that it has an amazing success rate. Mom says, "The vinegar odor will send most of the bugs scampering, and the ones who don't cut and run will eat the soap and die of lye poisoning."

Third, we will use commercial fertilizer to revitalize our cantaloupe crop. Dad believes super healthy cantaloupe vines will have maximum resistance to squash bug damage, and also vows to persuade the ever watchful water master to squeeze out a little extra water to irrigate our crop. He thinks the promise of a dozen ripe cantaloupes might be a winning argument with His Watership.

Fourth, we will immediately quarantine vines that become sickly from vampire-sucking squash bugs by extraction. It will be a form of surgical husbandry. Uprooting and burning all ailing plants.

For days we fan out across our precious cantaloupe reserve. Determinedly squashing squash bugs. Generously spraying vines with vinegar and soap. Fertilizing and profusely watering. Frantically uprooting and burning vines that have succumbed to the voracious appetites of the ubiquitous "Anasa tristis." Attempting to stem the bad bug nemesis is back-breaking work. The *sweat* rolls off our faces and down our backs as we labor under the glare of the mid summer sun. Our cause is an obsession.

No family could have worked harder to save a crop. Yet, the squash bugs are relentless. Despite our best efforts, the piles of wilting burning vines become larger every day. We're forced to supplement our four-fold war plan. We set bonfires in each corner of the field, and in places on the field where dying vines have been cleared away. However, the bug invaders seem oblivious to smoke in their eyes. We place rotting, damp boards around the field to attract marauding bugs. Hoping these bug-o-boards will collect hundreds of juice-sucking beasties under them. Making our task of squashing squash bugs more efficient. We dust our vines with DDT in a last-ditch ploy to exterminate the outlaw bugs with insecticide.

Nothing works. The hordes of bugs ravish our cantaloupe patch. It's apparent that vinegar and lye soap aren't very good deterrents under existing circumstances. The only things dying are melon vines. The bugs are like a tidal wave – inexorable, incessant. Resembling a plague sent from Biblical times.

We seek an act of divine intervention. Our prayers are transmitted nightly to heaven's lofty heights. We hope for a miracle to save our melons, but no glorious, airborne fleet of dive-bomber seagull squadrons sweeps intrepidly from the west coast to gorge on scads of gourmet "Anasa tristis"cuisine. Dad says the Lord must not like the flavor of cantaloupes. Mom suggests that the Lord is too busy saving souls to worry about saving three and a half acres of cantaloupes.

The crop is NOT saved. The swarm of squash bugs becomes catastrophic. Once they've acquired a taste for our melon vine julep their thirst is insatiable. They're like drunken grim reapers. Sucking the life from our dreams of a third cash crop.

All our hopes, all our planning, all our working, all our *sweating*, all our praying – ended in disaster! Our putative cantaloupe crop lay in ruins. What began as a field of dreams, becomes a field of carnage. A vast expanse of swarming, sucking, scurrying bugs and drooping, yellowing, dying cantaloupe vines. We probably harvested only eight to ten wilted, insipid tasting melons. They were hardly the right stuff to put pockets full of money in Harmon coveralls.

Ironically, the squash bug infestation lasts for years. Several subsequent generations of "Anasa tristis"were conceived on our farm. Presumably raised, primed, and groomed to ravish any future, though far less imposing, Harmon cantaloupe, cucumber and summer squash gardens.

Now, many years later, I'm in a reflective mood. Socrates said, "All learning is remembering." I believe him. I'm glad I still remember our ill-fated cantaloupe patch, and I'm sensing what the **memory** teaches me.

Had our dreams of a bountiful cantaloupe harvest been realized, the money would long since have been spent. The taste of the sweet juicy cantaloupes would have lost their savor. The remarkable family camaraderie of that summer would have faded into the conglomeration of other summers past in the manner of daily sunsets. The event would have been a mere *footnote* in those green growing years on the farm.

The **squash bug invasion** makes a tremendous difference. The bugs make the memories distinctive. The cantaloupe crop is just a hazy glitch in another growing season without the bugs. They give the **memory** substance, character, passion, and longevity. We <u>should</u> cherish our memories. We're inspired and instructed by our memories. We lose our identity without powers of recollection. Squandering the sense of what we are!

The squash bugs showed amazing tenacity. But the Harmons were also tenacious. That summer in the cantaloupe patch taught us about our strength as individuals and as a family. The squash bugs destroyed our cantaloupe vines. They did **not** destroy our spirit, our will to live, to dream, and to labor for good causes.

Mark Twain once said, "Good judgment comes from experience, and experience comes from bad judgment." The Harmons used bad judgment when they planted <u>too</u> many cantaloupes. Three and a half acres of melons was far more vines than we could manage <u>and</u> sufficiently protect. Yet, from the experience of losing the squash bug war we acquired better judgment.

We never planted three and a half acres of cantaloupes again! We learned to prioritize. We learned there are more important things in this life than cantaloupes – and greenbacks. We decided we didn't need another cash crop. Milk and beet seed were our money makers. At the end of the day –– at the end of a lifetime, the things that *matter most* <u>are</u> **family relationships!**

And so it was –– ONCE upon a cantaloupe.

A sugar beet is any plant of the genus *Beta* with an edible root. We didn't raise them to eat, however, we raised them for seed. And seed is acquired from the opposite end of the sugar beet plant. The sweet beets are planted in the fall and harvested the following summer. Fortunately, the sugar beet plant is **not** a magnet for the indomitable squash bug. Sugar beets seem to hold little attraction for the deadly nemesis of cantaloupe vines, nor would they be susceptible if they did. Sugar beets have a genetic immunity from the juice draining properties of the piercing, needle-like mouthparts of squash bugs.

The seeds are planted close together in long rows extending the length of the field under cultivation. A mature, vigorous patch of sugar beets grows to about six feet in height. Beet <u>seed</u> develops from flowering tassels forming at the top of the plants. The reproductive unit consists of small burrs capable of developing into another sugar beet.

A beet <u>seed</u> farmer allows his field to *go to seed*. When the <u>seed</u> burrs are full size, the beet plants are cut down with a mower, swath by swath, and stacked into **piles** to dry. The roots are left in the ground. The object of this phase of the operation is to harvest <u>seed</u>. Other farmers plant the beet <u>seed</u> we grow, and harvest the sweet roots that are processed, and refined into beet sugar. It's a two tiered operation to get sugar. First, the seed is made. Second, the seed that's made – makes the sugar. But I'm getting ahead of myself. That's up the road at the farm of somebody else.

There are *three keys* to success in beet <u>seed</u> business. Success being defined as converting *SWEAT* into a nice cash payoff. First, a good <u>contract</u>. Second, a good <u>yield</u>. Third, good <u>luck</u> getting dry threshed seed into the warehouse.

The *good contract* is probably the trickiest of the three. Why? Because this *key* **isn't** something the beet seed farmer can control. The <u>contract</u> is basically imposed by the company agent. The power of allotting acreage is totally within the auspice of his authority, and the <u>contract</u> designates the acreage that may be used in growing sugar beet seed *each* year. Unless a farmer has decent acreage he is predestined to have a small <u>yield</u> and, consequently, a small beet seed <u>check</u>. So, predestined by whom? Why the beet seed CZAR, naturally. He determines success or break-even or fizzle in the beet <u>seed</u> business from the get go. The beet farmer submits a bid, but it is the CZAR who rejects, modifies, or accepts the acreage bid.

We had a small farm. When you're small you don't carry much clout. Your influence is minimal. Your juice non-existent! It isn't surprising that my Father complained on a yearly basis about the size of the acreage quota we were assigned by the AGENT. But the problem <u>wasn't</u> confined to decisions of the AGENT. A significant part of the problem is COMPANY policy. No parcel of land could be planted for sugar beet seed on consecutive years. Beet land had to be *fallowed* for three years before sugar beets could be planted again. To explain, land is *fallowed* when it is plowed and harrowed and left unsown or uncultivated. Therefore, having a small farm complicates allotment decisions. The *fallowing* policy creates a challenging gerrymandering chore for small farmer bidding. His proposal is necessarily limited by the size of his <u>available</u> land, whether it's owned or rented. BIG is BETTER in the context of acreage allotment.

A beet seed farmer never knows the size of his <u>yield</u> until the *seed* is separated from the *chaff.* The dry piles of stalk, stems, leaves, and <u>seed</u> have to be **threshed**. Threshing requires a **thresher**.

Only a few people in the fields owned threshers. They hired out for custom work during the threshing season. A THRESHER is a large metal, dinosaur appearing apparatus, notable for its collection of pulleys, conveyor belts, clouds of dust, the clanking sound generated by its moving parts, and the use of a tractor as its power source. The hired THRESHER and its crew are positioned in convenient locations on the beet seed field. The *piles* of <u>dry</u> sugar beet plants that have gone to <u>seed</u> are carried to the thresher by *slips*, forked into the machine, the <u>seed</u> is separated from the chaff, and 90-100 lbs. of threshed <u>seed</u> is funneled through a spout into <u>each</u> coarse burlap bag – as the chaff is being blown out the back. A six inch needle threaded with twine is used to sew the tops of full bags of seed shut.

My typical role in the threshing enterprise is to ride a **workhorse**, harnessed to a *slip*, to provide muscle to <u>drag</u> *slips* across the field. The *slip* is loaded with plant parts and seed to be threshed, pulled along side the hopper for unloading, pulled back into the field for reloading – and so forth. We generally used two or three combinations of <u>horses</u> and <u>slips</u>.

A *slip* is a flat carrier designed to <u>slide</u> over the ground of a beet seed field. It has no wheels, and consists of approximately 8' x 12' slabs of plywood that are framed on the ends and sides by 2" x 4" boards that help minimize slippage of the beet seed cargo from the carrier.

Riding the big boned, broad chested, brownish-black **workhorses** or WORK PLUGS, as we preferred to call them, is an unforgettable experience. No saddles. No saddle blankets. Using only a bridle, we rode bareback. But there is plenty of padding for a rider's posterior. These old girls were well-fed and plump, especially around the rump. There's no sense of bone or rib cage as the rider bounces along, just rolling mounds of fat. Riding a WORK PLUG is a little like straddling a swaying burlap bag full of jell-O. I'm thinking liquorice.

WORK PLUGS only have two gaits. Despite trying as hard as we possibly could to mix things up, the old Plugs would offer just two speeds. They'd <u>walk</u>, very slowly paced, as though they're catching a snooze between each lazy step; and they'd <u>trot</u>, a very bouncy *four step*, while alternately lifting *each* diagonal pair of legs. The trotting effect is a steady as she goes jog, that sends the backside of a rider jiggling all over the crest of the plush beast moving in heavy hoofed four–four time. The primary issue isn't comfort, it's staying on your steed.

I'm not an equestrian expert, but my personal experience tells me that WORK PLUGS <u>really</u> enjoy trotting. They can keep it up for half a mile at least, without altering the neck-cricking rhythm of the clop – clop – clop – clop.

It's evidently their time to stretch and let <u>everything</u> hang out.

They didn't get to <u>trot</u> when they were hooked up to the *slips*, however, <u>trotting</u> did occur while we rode from the beet seed field to the barn. The big Plugs being inspired, no doubt, by thoughts of fresh, green, chewy stacks of baled hay and deep gulps of stale cistern water. Well, it was wet at least. Still refreshing to overheated **workhorses** on simmering summer afternoons

The <u>best</u> part of threshing beet seed **is** the unlikely dichotomy of riding WORK PLUGS –– and **fishing**. No, we didn't ride the big, hard-pulling, *four stepper* equestrians to fishing ponds during our down time. But on those occasions when stray cloudbursts came our way at threshing time, we **did** go fishing! Sugar beets can't be threshed if they're wet. Whenever it rained that meant threshing delays and it meant the entire threshing crew went off to the fishing relays. I love to fish. So, making an abrupt transformation from the *sweat* of a threshing field to the *cool* alpine splendor of a splashing trout stream is heaven sent. I'll never forget the rainy days on threshing days.

The problem with rain during threshing is protecting the <u>bagged</u> beet seed. Those 90-100 lb. bags of seed **have** to be kept DRY. The biggest issue facing the beet seed farmer is getting his seed into the warehouse without getting so much moisture inside bags of seed that they mildew. Rotten seed won't germinate. It is worthless for raising the sweet sugar roots that sweeten cereal bowls and sugary, buttery cinnamon rolls, etcetera. Therefore, any stacks of full seed bags must be securely covered with tarpaulins during inclement weather.

The quintessential time in <u>every</u> beet seed season is that *moment* when the <u>last</u> bag of DRY beet **seed** is safely stashed away inside the sugar beet warehouse. It is a day of celebration and dreams of dollar signs! The crop that began in the mind of my Father <u>now</u> graphically embodies **his** passionate sense of what might be – seed by seed/bag by bag. Incidentally, mature dry sugar beet <u>seed</u>, maybe a quarter of an inch in diameter, resembles miniature broccoli florets.

A good Dad knows how to spell. He knows that a father's **love** for his son is spelled T– I– M – E. My Father worked hard, but he liked to play hard too. He believed that no man is too wealthy or too destitute to play with his son. Probably, **fishing** was Dad's favorite form of play. Deep down, I think he felt if more parents focused on the truly consequential business of life, there would be a shortage of fishing poles in the world. I know fishing poles weren't scarce at <u>our</u> farmhouse.

I remember my first fishing trip. My Father, an uncle, and two cousins took me <u>stream</u> fishing when I was six or seven. We packed fishing gear, lunch, several cans of worms [fish bait – not our lunch], braved the threat of rattlesnakes, and got down to some serious trout fishing.

Pursuant to Dad's patient tutoring, and under his ever watchful eye, I tried to master the art of threading squiggly worms on hooks. It isn't an easy task, nor is it a pretty one – too much blood and guts. The fact is, worms don't like to be threaded on hooks and they break off a lot.

The next daunting challenge is getting my fishing line and my threaded bait into the swirling stream without getting snagged on tree branches above the water or rocks and roots below the water –– and scaring the ever-wary trout downstream.

My introduction to the fishing art is an amazing experience. No one fell into the creek. No one got bit by a rattlesnake. The trout seemed to relish the taste of our ugly worms. I managed to hook **ten** fish with Dad's help, <u>and</u>, FISHING succeeded in hooking me! Fishing is part of my Father's legacy. It has given me a treasure trove of memories, and plenty of fish fry dinners.

A **tractor** <u>seat</u> is a dandy vantage point on calm, clear days for viewing a wide expanse of the Garden of Earth and for probing the depths of a human soul. A boy can *see* far away, *dream* his dreams, and *think* insightfully on calm, clear days. Though the slightest breeze makes dust when land levels and disks are being dragged across dry ground. The spectacle is, therefore, often a <u>blend</u> of beauty, introspection, dust, and *sweat*. An opportunity to **contemplate** creation, chicks, chocolate, and catching a glimpse of who I am.

I possess a NATURAL affinity for Deity and Truth, for Brotherhood and the *seed* of Possibility that lies <u>within</u> each Child of God, for Nature and Beauty, for Human Dignity and Freedom, for Equality and Justice, for Family and Eternity, for Love and Remembrance. I'm a <u>naturalist</u>! Not from training, but a lover of <u>nature</u> and <u>truth</u> by innate propensity. The panoramic vistas and the solitary philosophical thoughts are nurturing hours, and I logged hundreds of hours in a tractor <u>seat</u> on the farm.

Not every day in a tractor <u>seat</u> is calm and clear, however. I didn't drive a contemporary tractor loaded with accessories. I steered the old Farmall. Nothing protects me from the elements. No cabin. No heater. No air conditioning. No radio. No power steering. In summertime, the blast furnace effect of hot wind billows a mass of dust into the air that settles on a floppy, straw hat brim, a *perspiring* face, and two sets of *sweaty* arms and grimy hands. While in the <u>late</u> autumn planting season, stiff, bone-chilling wind whips up clouds of dust that settle on a frigid face and coat and jeans and shivering hands gripping the steering wheel. On such days, a wide expanse of the Garden of Earth is hazy, and catching a glimpse of who I am is not the least philosophic. It's more a matter of trying to be sure I'm neither too hot nor too cold!

Obviously, a farm boy frequently works outside. His **eyes** are constantly bombarded by dust, hay leaves, and other particulate. As a result, I had chronic bloodshot eyes and red eyelids. The condition became a source of serious embarrassment to me in my teenage years.

My Mother takes me to see an eye doctor. He examines my eyes, and sagely concludes that they **are** <u>RED</u>. Ah ha, I knew it first! He says I have a *low grade infection*. He gives me some ointment to rub on my lids, and sends me back to my farm boy lifestyle, to-wit: a daily regimen of dust, hay leaves, and particulate.

The ointment doesn't solve the problem. It only highlights my red lids. Exactly what I didn't need. My eyes continue to absorb daily doses of irritants. It's a situation of cause and effect. The cause is particles of debris. The effect is red devil eyes, and it remains an issue for years. The doctor's medicine can't get it done, only **time** heals – eventually. The prescription for a cure is simple. The redneck has to move indoors. Once he's hanging out in the Courthouse instead of working the barnyard, his *low grade infection* subsides.

The notion of lawyering didn't cross my mind until the 10th grade. Actually, until my fifteenth year I never thought much about a career. I suppose I assumed I'd follow in Dad's footsteps. Like father like son. What's good for <u>my</u> Dad is good enough for me.

Our graduation service from Junior High School is right around the corner. The farm kid is on the program. Not because of scholarship, nor political genius, nor extraordinary talent. I'd run for student body president the previous year, and got trounced by a girl – though she **is** a lovely girl. So, when the class got together to choose a <u>class</u> president, they felt <u>sorry</u> for me. They made me president by acclamation.

Tenth graders are the graduating class. It's a longstanding tradition at our Junior High that the 10th grade class president is charged with the responsibility of offering a short welcoming <u>speech</u> on behalf of his class at graduation. I think that's the other reason these rascals picked me as Class Prez. The criteria for my political stature is two fold: **Pity** <u>and</u> their **Fear** of public speaking.

The week of graduation arrives. A rehearsal is scheduled. I open the practice with an *uptight* rendition of my remarks. The script is ill prepared and the speaking is tentative. The Principal monitors the practice. Afterward, he pulls me aside. He's <u>not</u> especially pleased. I'm informed that I have a slight *speech impediment*. Furthermore, my script is hardly scintillating. He's saying in a nutshell, "Don't embarrass me or my school. We'll have a large crowd. You've got to step it up to a higher level of performance."

He really hurt my feelings, but the point has been <u>bluntly</u> made. Graduation isn't for four days. I retool my script, and practice my *articulation* for about **ten** hours. What does a <u>determined</u> fifteen year old farm boy have to do after school except –– chores and practice? I practiced in front of my Mother, in front of the mirror, and outside in front of the echoing mountain that throws sound back at a declarant. That's the best I can do without a tape recorder.

The big evening arrives. I'm extremely nervous, but there is NO substitution for preparation. My *speech* is quite good considering I'm a Nervous-Melly kid from the sticks.

Several days later, I place my yearbook outside the Principal's office on a stack of annuals waiting to be signed by his Leadership. Returning in about thirty minutes to pick up my signed book.

I open the yearbook to the page N. R. has signed next to his picture with some trepidation. He's written, "Dear Melvyn: Being your teacher has been a genuine privilege; one of the things that makes teaching bearable. You have a fine mind and an excellent speaking voice. You would make a <u>good</u> **lawyer** – for that matter you will do well at anything you try. Accept my very best wishes. Newell R." (emphasis added)

I'm pleasantly surprised at the generosity of his words. This is a man I respect – in a sense he's someone I fear. He <u>is</u> THE MAN in Junior High. But I suppose <u>fear</u> and <u>respect</u> are kindred verbs in this circumstance.

The Principal is astute. His initial criticism has been a motivational ploy, and he <u>recognizes</u> the determined response of his student. The change between rehearsal and show-time is striking. The Principal's complimentary yearbook signing <u>reflects</u> his appreciation for those self-evident hours of practice that have lifted the level of my performance at the graduation program.

A motivational critique, a <u>single</u> yearbook autograph, a gentle career nudge, a few words of subtle nuance from a principal to his student, can make a HUGE difference. The comment about me making a <u>good</u> **lawyer** sort of takes my breath. It's the <u>power</u> of suggestion. It's a mind altering concept. A course-changer. I'm impressed by the idea. This view into a *world of possibility* sticks in my head. It's the passionate sense of *what might be* for a farm boy WILLING to **work**!

I become a member of **debating** teams in High School and Junior College. Devoting long hours late into the night in the preparation of my debate cases. DEBATE becomes my greatest *academic passion*. I enjoy the satisfaction of <u>research</u> that produces quotations in support of propositions I must advocate, and I'm exhilarated by the intensity of <u>argument</u> during debates.

It's excellent training for a future trial lawyer. A matter of going from the Schoolhouse to the Courthouse. SUMMATION is a form of Courtroom **debate**.

But, my lawyering career is SHOVEL-MADE, in a sense. Contemplating the *possibility* of something is one thing, actually <u>doing</u> it is a workhorse of a different color. I may have been tip-toeing towards the litigation trail, but there are specific circumstances on the farm that ultimately decide my fate. Lawyering gets traction in a **tractor seat** on blistering hot *sweaty* days – as our Farmall belches noxious exhaust fumes. Hardly a recipe for good respiratory health.

I <u>remember</u> days on my knees, with a HOE in stained hands, methodically pulling and hoeing **weeds** along exceedingly **long rows** of sugar beet seedlings. The <u>idea</u> of lawyering germinates with each **bead** of *sweat* that unrelentingly rolls off my face, sliding down my back in a steady stream, soaking my shirts, sapping my strength, and dampening my will for farming. I'm thinking on such occasions, "I must have oodles of very large pores. It's not cool to *sweat* so much!"

I have an epiphany of sorts in an **irrigation ditch**. The last one hundred feet at the end of the ditch has collected about nine inches of silt. We're scheduled to start a watering turn in three hours. The sediment has to be dug out in order to get a full stream of water to the far south side of the field. I'm alone with my **shovel**. The blade's too dull. The dirt's too deep. The sludge too packed. The task too large. The weather's too humid. The temperature must have been at least 115 degrees in the shade, and I'm laboring in unfiltered sunshine. I felt like a two-legged chunk of meat sizzling in an oven.

But as egregious as they are, the most demoralizing aspect of my job isn't connected to the *elements*. It's a *farmland issue*. There isn't enough bank left on either side of the ditch to hold the build-up of silt I'm *shoveling*. I strain to scoop a shovel-full of sediment from the ditch bottom and, about fifty percent of the time, it rolls back in the ditch when I attempt to toss it out of the ditch. Damn, that's as frustrating as hell!

Actually, the SHOVEL **is** a fitting symbol of farm life. Dad always kept his shovels sharp and shiny. He considered shovels to be **the** definitive farming hand tool. I stop to wipe my sweaty brow. A single impression recurs in my mind. It is emphatic in its clarity: "You don't want to be SHOVEL-BOUND for the rest of your life. SHOVELING makes *sweat*. You have a serious aversion to being *SWEATY*!"

The lawyering deal takes *root* in the **milk house**. We've gone from milking **eleven** cows under the barn shed with a generator powered De Laval Milker to **forty** cows in a milk house with electricity. Electrical power came to our farm in the early 1950s.We have stanchions in the milk room for handling six cows at a time, a silver set of electric Surge Milkers to magically, with the cooperation of our bovine guests, extract nature's premier beverage from cow udders – using teat cups and a calibrated pulsation process initiated by a vacuum pump. There is an adjoining grain room manger for scoops of rolled barley, **designed** to entice the old girls inside and keep them munching while they give up their warm, opaque, nutritious white fluid. The milking process always starts in a cow's head!

Obviously, *strategy* is a **key** to successful dairying. Grain-fed cows are relaxed cows, and as a general rule, relaxed cows are high producing cows. Yet, it is an incontrovertible fact of the dairy business that the best laid plans of a dairyman can go totally awry. Case in point: WHEN the power

GOES OFF in his high-tech **milk house** on a sultry summer evening. KA-CHING!

No POWER? That means <u>no</u> teat cup foursome on cow udders and <u>no</u> vacuum pump suctioning. Bring out the milk buckets boys. That means the milkers are the dairyman and his son. The milk has to be extracted by laborious hand pulling and finger squeezing. Ouch! Aching palms and stiff fingers.

No POWER? That's means <u>no</u> rhythmic squoosh–squish into hefty Surge Milker drums, only intermittent *hands on* squirts into farm milk buckets. It means cows pray the milkers <u>don't</u> have *rough* hands. It means a radical departure from an Actus Reus the herd is used to, and an equally radical herd departure from behavior the farmer is used to.

No POWER? That means the cows will be psyched out. It means the scoops of rolled barley in the manger won't make relaxed cows this evening. *Hand jobs* on teats will mean loose manure flying out bovine backsides, tails that generally swat flies will be swatting milkers. It means cows that don't often require restraint will be kicking the hell out of the milkers if their instincts aren't keen and their feet aren't agile. It means Dad saying, "Pass the hobbles, Son." It means hooves in buckets of milk and buckets upended. Milk likely seasoned with barnyard hoof droppings. It means anxious cows slipping and sliding as they back across a gutter full of runny cow piles and alfalfa–green splattered floors and walls.

No POWER? That means a severe drop in the amount of frothy white stuff collected from the **forty** four legs on hooves. It means milking will take 3 ½ hours instead of 1 ½ hours. It means any farmers passing by to turn water down the lateral irrigation ditch will probably hear swear words from our **milk house** they've never heard before. It means I'm going to be doing double and triple duty with the SCOOP SHOVEL. It's a dirty job, but a dairyman's son has to do it. Cows being milked BY HAND poop profusely. All that messy green goo has to be extricated from the milk room someway.

Like I said earlier, my legal career is SHOVEL-MADE, in a sense! Only a maniacal, masochistic farm-teen LIVES through an evening milking **forty** jittery, shittery cows WITHOUT **power**, and still visualizes himself being a milk man. Instead, he puts his SCOOP SHOVEL down, cautiously wipes *sweat* from his brow, <u>manure</u> *spatter* from his chin, and makes a solemn VOW!

I gave LIFE a lot of thought in the hay loft. The **barn** became the majestic centerpiece of our farming operation. We unloaded <u>wagons</u> of loose hay and baled hay by the hundreds into the barn. Before Dad purchases a baler, a derrick is used to get loose hay from wagons to the stack. A <u>cable</u> pulled by the tractor hoists a four-tined fork of hay to the top of the barn where it travels over pulleys along a derrick that spans the length of the barn. The fork is tripped when it's over the drop area and loose hay falls to the stack. The derrick fork grasps about one eighth of a load of hay, making this process significantly more expeditious than forking the hay from the wagon to the stack by hand.

A. T. B. [after the baler] we put the derrick fork into dry dock. It languishes in an old granary collecting dust and rust and cobwebs. But the **barn** stays active. Filled to the rafters with methodically stacked <u>baled</u> hay. The **barn** kept hay bales dry during inclement weather, the **barn shed** sheltered cows while they ate, and high in the cozy *seclusion* of the hay loft I found a place of refuge – of relaxation – of reflection – of remembrance.

There's one frightful moment I witness from the **barn** that I'll never forget. It <u>could</u> have changed everything! We'd just unloaded a wagon of baled hay. I'm sitting on the stack slightly above the level of the rafters. My father says he needs to repair the south barn eave. We have a large <u>tall</u> **barn**. Dairy cows are big alfalfa consumers. It takes a large <u>tall</u> **barn** full of hay to keep cow bellies full and cow udders tight.

Heavy wind has damaged the south eave, blowing boards from the edge of the roof. A sizable opening has left part of the haystack vulnerable to penetrating rainfall. Damp bales become rotten bales. There is a double barreled result. Rotten bales generate heat and heat creates a risk of *fire*. Further, the spoilage of rotten bales creates *unappealing* feed for the herd and hay that has *lost* its nutritive value.

The height of the **barn** is a complicating factor. We have no crane to lift my Father to the top, and our longest ladder is about <u>four</u> feet **too short**. Elevating him to the required level has to be *make-shift*. So, the empty wagon is left next to the **barn**. The wheels can't roll. The wagon remains hooked to the tractor – though it won't have optimal stability. It's going to rock slightly as weight shifts on the rack, and the margin for error is small with a high-rise project.

Dad recognizes the risk, but he has to fix the **barn**. He lifts our longest ladder on to the wagon rack, steps along the wagon tongue to the rack, carefully raises the ladder to an upright position on the rack, slides it forward about twelve inches into a shallow <u>rut</u>, and allows the *tip* of the ladder to rest against the <u>eave</u>. The *base* of the ladder being *mounted* on the wagon <u>rack</u>, albeit a very steep angle, due to the length of the ladder and the distance between the wagon and the top of the barn.

He then makes several cautious trips up and down the ladder. Boards, crowbar, hammer, and nails have to be <u>either</u> in his pocket, or resting on the edge of the barn roof that has withstood the wind's gusting fury. Finally, he's set.

Dad positions himself on a rung that allows him to be chest level with the top of the barn. I hold my breath. My gaze flashes from the roof he's repairing to the base of the ladder on the rack and on to the ground. It's a *long*, <u>long</u> **way** to the barnyard below! His perch seems precarious to me.

The project goes well for, say, ten minutes. Two boards have been partially nailed into place. My father has the crowbar in hand. He needs to pull a nail out of a stud at the apex. The nail is stubborn. One hand isn't getting the job done. He uses both hands on the crowbar, balancing himself on the ladder with his feet, and applies two-fisted pressure on the rusty, wayward, embedded nail. A final <u>tug</u> – and it's OUT.

Hooray —— oh **NO**! My emotions race quickly from inward cheer to inward dismay. The nail falls harmlessly to the wagon rack, but the backward tugging motion causes the ladder, so sharply angled, to swing away from the top of the **barn**. It's a horrifying moment. For an instant. For a split second. For a tantalizing milli-second twinkling. I **think** I'm about to see my Father <u>plunge</u> backwards on the ladder to the packed barnyard surface below. A broken back? Devastating head trauma? Internal injuries? Death? —— **NO family provider nor protector!**

The crisis ends as quickly as it began. My Father has excellent reflexes. He wasn't called "Flash Harmon" on the tennis court in his college days without some basis in fact. He's got a terrific backhand. Dad's <u>left</u> arm swings **in** as the ladder swings **out**. He's <u>not</u> two-handing the crowbar any more. Deftly, his firm <u>left</u> hand grabs a beam of the **barn** vertex, and he steadies his backward swing. The base of the ladder stays wedged in the wagon rack groove, the ladder is re-balanced against the eave, and my Dad – dear, dear Pops – comes down from his high-rise labor for a breather!

There are **no** words capable of describing my sense of relief. Our family has dodged a bullet, so to speak. I am spared the heavy weight of heartache. My gratitude is ineffable. I–am–flat–out–blown–away! *Tears* form in the eyes of one who has SEEN something **miraculous** from the hay loft.

My place of refuge in the **barn** is <u>sacred</u>. It's like a farm-made **cathedral**.

Like a one-boy Quaker worship hour. <u>Alone</u> with the rafters, the subtle influence of the Creator of heaven and earth, the fragrance of freshly baled hay, the sound of a barn roof that creaks in the breeze, the presence of an occasional field mouse, the soft clucking of contended hens scratching in the barnyard below, the putt-putt of a tractor in the distance, my books and a kaleidoscope of thoughts.

Looking north, I see puffy white clouds adrift in a sea of blue sky and the ever changing personality of the mountain that echos. Each dawning day brilliant rays of the rising sun, starting at the peak, make their golden descent down the face of Morning Gold Mountain. The contrast, between lines of sunshine and shadow, during this specular downward slide of golden light to the base of the hill is awesome. Yet in the afternoon, soaring hawks framed in summer blue, sun-bathed rocky ledges near the crest, and the caw–caw of high flying crows, create an equally exquisite horizon.

The north end of the **barn** is like a window to the world of God's creative prowess, and I have the privilege of sharing it –– and **being** part of it. A secluded place where my *daydreams* became my *benchmarks*.
"But there is a spirit in man: and the inspiration of the Almighty giveth them [memory]..." Excuse me –– "understanding." (Job 32:8) However, memory works closely with <u>understanding</u>. Without **memory** "<u>understanding</u>" isn't preserved!

Farm life is woven into the fabric of my being. Deep and instructive are its etchings on my memory. Spencer W. Kimball said, "When you look in the dictionary for the most important word, do you know what it is? It could be <u>remember</u>......**Remember** is the word." (*Circles of Exaltation.* Brigham Young University, 6/28/1968 – emphasis added)

I agree. A middle-size, inauspicious, uncomplicated, easy-to-spell, three syllable term **is** the dictionary's *preeminent* word. Think about it, what physical ailment most definitively robs an individual of his dignity and his quality of life? I believe the answer is Alzheimer's or some other severe form of dementia. When a man <u>loses</u> his mind he's lost almost everything. Without MEMORY we don't know <u>who</u> we are, or <u>what</u> we are. Those who <u>can't</u> remember or <u>won't</u> remember have lost the ability to retain knowledge and to enjoy a decent quality of life. Their existence is hollow – without substance, without appreciation, without reverence. If we're not REMEMBERING we're <u>not</u> **grateful**, and if we're ungrateful we're <u>not</u> **humble**.

I am *humbly grateful* to the wonderful PARENTS who **gave** me life —— and <u>taught</u> me HOW to live. [They}...gave me eyes, [they]...gave me ears; And humble cares, and delicate fears; A heart, the fountain of sweet tears; And love, and thought, and joy." (William Wordsworth, *The Sparrows' Nest*, Stanza 2)

The lawyering <u>deal</u> took *root* in the **milk house**. A trout in the milk? – NO, **not** at our dairy. <u>Hooves</u> in buckets of milk and buckets upended. Milk <u>seasoned</u> with barnyard hoof droppings. Anxious cows slipping and sliding as they back across a gutter full of <u>runny</u> cow piles and alfalfa-green splattered floors and walls. <u>Flies</u> in the milk, but **no** trout in the milk. More likely a turd in the milk, *circumstantial evidence* that the power went off at milking time. Though there IS a metaphorical trout with a <u>scoop</u> <u>shovel</u> in the **milk house**. IT'S ME!

Farm life is a stepping stone, a learning experience, a time of enrichment, a memory maker, an experiment in *sweat* – but it ISN'T me. I'm a <u>fish</u> out of water in the **milk room**. My <u>destiny</u> **is** in the Courtroom.

I'm a man of thought – of logic – of letters – of **summation**. PREFERRING cerebral *sweat*, finger *sweat* and tongue *sweat* to the **sweat of my brow**.

PART TWO

By The Strength Of My Jaw

"In my youth, said his father, I took to the law, And argued each case with my wife: And the muscular strength, which it gave to my jaw, Has lasted the rest of my life." (Lewis Carroll)

Direct Evidence Follies
At Freedom Park

There are **two** great branches of evidence in a Criminal Case, as I *said* earlier. They are **direct** evidence and **circumstantial** evidence. The meaning of direct evidence is as plain as the nose on your face. A first grader can easily grasp the concept. Whatever a person perceives with any of his physical senses **is** direct evidence. *Seeing* a nose on a face is direct evidence that the face has a nose. *Seeing* a dead body is direct evidence that the person is dead. If you *see* a CRIME happen that is direct evidence. And if you *smell* it or *touch* it or *taste* it or *hear* it as the CRIME happens – that is also direct evidence. EVERYTHING ELSE is circumstantial. Therefore, the meaning of circumstantial evidence is easily comprehended and just as easily categorized. There's no need to ever be confused about the meaning of circumstantial evidence again. IF IT **ISN'T** DIRECT EVIDENCE **IT'S** CIRCUMSTANTIAL EVIDENCE!

Chapter 3

"**Some** circumstantial evidence is **very** strong, as when you find a trout in the milk." (Henry David Thoreau, ibid., p.1 – emphasis added)

Listen up. I'm a figurative *trout in the milk* at the Courthouse. I–am–living– **circumstantial–proof**–of–an–incontestable–fact! IF a short, nondescript, sod busting refugee of the farm belt, once accused of having a speech impediment – a super shy, shovel-made law student so unnerved by the Socratic method he's awestruck – a poor note-taker who squeaks his way to a diploma by the grace of Gilbert's Outlines – an all-thumbs typist of bar exams who pecks his way to membership in the Nevada State Bar – a jobless outsider who travels to Las Vegas short on cash, connections, confidence, and <u>doesn't</u> know how to shepardize – a *dork in court* – THIS GUY, the heretofore described.

IF **HE** can become a PROSECUTOR **anybody** can become a Prosecutor. All a person has to do is **work hard**, be **hard nosed**, and be a **dynamic champion** of JUSTICE!

I <u>often</u> hear it said, by Defense Attorneys who have an interest in saying it and by News Commentators who are misinformed in saying it and by Lay Persons who are uninformed in saying it, that the CASE being presented is **ONLY** *circumstantial* – as though such a comment conveys a prescient insight into the **proof** of criminal cases. **NOT TRUE.** This notion **is** PALPABLE NONSENSE!

A proffer of <u>direct</u> <u>evidence</u> is NOT per se superior to *circumstantial*. A proffer of <u>circumstantial</u> <u>evidence</u> is NOT inherently inferior to <u>direct</u> <u>evidence</u>. The *circumstances* and *nature* and *source* of probative evidence <u>determine</u> its CREDIBILITY! **Weight** ascribed to criminal evidence must be predicated upon **specific** offers of proof, whether the evidence is <u>direct</u> or <u>circumstantial</u>. Such <u>decisions</u> can **ONLY** be made on a **case-by-case** basis. A criminal case is NOT a fungible. EVERY CASE <u>IS</u> UNIQUE.

Always be skeptical of generalities. Be skeptical of ANY evidence until it is **convincingly** established. This **is** the CORRECT mind set of a Prosecutor. **Don't** get *blown away* by numbers. **Don't** assume a case consisting ENTIRELY of <u>direct</u> <u>evidence</u> will AUTOMATICALLY have potent persuasive power with a Jury!

I <u>should</u> have been more of a <u>skeptic</u> with the **hand-over-case** Deputy

Doug gave me on a Friday before the Monday it went to Trial. It had **five**, count em, FIVE **eyewitnesses** who'd pointed incriminating index fingers at the Accused. An eyewitness, for those who have been raised in another galaxy, is a person who has *seen* the crime happen with his <u>own</u> TWO EYEBALLS. He's not getting this by word of mouth. **THIS** is someone who <u>knows</u> it happened and <u>knows</u> who

made it happen because HE SAW IT happen! Yeah, **THOSE** kind of witnesses. DIRECT EVIDENCE people. And Deputy Doug hands me a Friday afternoon <u>case file</u> that has FIVE of **THEM**. The **"case truth"** says this one is a lead pipe cinch! Ooooooh Dougie, you sandbagged me. You made it sound like a stroll in the park. IT ISN'T! This one is DIRECT EVIDENCE **follies** at the <u>park</u>, i.e., Freedom Park.

The NAME <u>should</u> have been a **red flag**. The Defendant's <u>first</u> **two** names are BENJAMIN FRANKLIN. Hey, wait a minute – whoa! BEN FRANKLIN! Isn't that the **famous** guy? <u>Inventor</u> of Franklin stoves, lightning rods, odometers, and bifocal glasses. <u>Public Official</u>? Postmaster of Philadelphia, deputy Postmaster General of the British North American Colonies, and Postmaster General under

the Continental Congress. <u>American Patriot</u>? An influential Founding Father. A Signer of the Declaration of Independence, quote: "We must all hang together, or assuredly we shall all hang separately."[*Independence Day, July 4, 1776*] Also a member of the Continental Congress, President of the Pennsylvania Constitutional Convention of 1776, Minister to France, a negotiator of the peace treaty with

Great Britain, a delegate at the 1787Constitutional Convention, and Signer of the U.S. Constitution. <u>Author</u> and <u>Philosopher</u>? He's the "...time is money" man [*Advice to a Young Tradesman*], along with other classics. To-wit: "He that goes a borrowing goes a sorrowing" [*Maxims prefixed to Poor Richard's Almanac*];

"Dost thou love life? Then do not squander time, for that is the stuff life is made of [ibid.]; and "Plough deep while sluggards sleep." [ibid.] <u>God Fearing Theist</u>? "There never was a good war or a bad peace." [*Letter to Josiah Quincy, September 11, 1773*] – "A Bible and a Newspaper in every house, a good School in every district –– all studied and appreciated as they merit –– are the principle support of virtue, morality, and civil liberty." [*Letter to the Ministry of France dated March 1778*] – "The longer I live, the more convincing proofs I see of this truth: 'that God governs in the affairs of men.' And if a sparrow cannot fall to the ground without his notice, is it probable that an empire can rise without his aid." [*June 28, 1787 – Constitutional Convention*] <u>Virtually</u> a <u>Saint</u>? Died in Philadelphia, Pennsylvania 4/17/1790 – interment in Christ Church Burial Ground.

Of course, in the heat of hectic weekend Trial preparation, I <u>didn't</u> *remember* all these things. **Too bad**. The Case against BEN FRANKLIN will be a whiffer at the plate! The founding-father **name** is STRIKE ONE – and the pitch count only gets worse. The Trial Jury <u>will</u> RING me up!

Enough said about Benjamin Franklin the American icon. The Defendant is simply a *regular Joe* Benjamin Franklin –– . He didn't come to court packaged with accolades. He's just plain ole Ben, and the **name** has nothing to do with the outcome. It's merely the outrageous <u>excuse</u> I use when I'm telling Courtroom war stories and trying to be funny.

THE PROBLEM IS **EVIDENTIARY**! We have a WORST CASE scenario here. Like man, this is a **strictly** DIRECT evidence case. I've got *eyewitnesses* but NO <u>corroboration</u>. It's THE EVIDENCE, silly.

The Crime occurs at Freedom Park on a Sunday evening. The park is crowded with people bent on capping the weekend with a blowout of folk music and binge drinking. It's not clear <u>how</u> or <u>why</u> the fracas starts. Things simmer for 30-45 minutes. Then heated words are exchanged, punches thrown, and one of the principals leaves the area. He reappears five minutes later with a <u>knife</u> in his right hand. <u>Races</u> up to the **victim**, <u>stabs</u> him *three* times in his <u>chest</u>, and <u>darts</u> into the cover of darkness and hundreds of other park guests. Neither the **knife** nor the **assailant** is apprehended at the scene. A 911 call is made, but the victim dies before paramedics arrive. Two of the stab wounds have penetrated his chest cavity, piercing his heart.

Las Vegas Metropolitan Police investigate the killing. FIVE persons say they have witnessed the stabbing. Detectives assemble a photographic lineup of ex-felons believed to frequent Freedom Park, sequester the <u>eyewitnesses</u>, and they *individually* view the photo display. *Three* of the five identify the Defendant. The other two are uncertain, and fail to make any photo ID. A week later the Defendant is arrested, invokes his right to a speedy Trial, and the Trial is set within sixty days of his arraignment.

It's hardly a piece of cake. Fifteen days before Trial, the Defense *files* notice of **alibi witnesses**. The Trial begins. The percipient witnesses testify, and the Case <u>seems</u> solid. Notwithstanding the inability of <u>two</u> of the five **eyeball witnesses** to pick the Defendant's photograph from the police photo lineup, ALL FIVE of the witnesses who *see* the crime, **positively**, according to their descriptions in Court, **identify** Benjamin Franklin –– as the <u>knife</u> wielding perpetrator at Freedom Park!

<u>Three</u> of the five are personal friends of the deceased. <u>One</u> of them is among those who selected the picture of the Defendant.

I'm not in a position to question the veracity of testimony offered under oath in this Case. I wasn't at Freedom Park during the stabbing. I don't know what happened, but I **do** know this. Being a witness in a Murder Trial is an ordeal. It's neither easy nor pleasant to testify in open court – and the call to testify is <u>not</u> risk free. Whoever did this has already demonstrated a proclivity for murder. **If the killer** is the person on Trial, an <u>identifying</u> witness **is** telling **him** *to– his– face* that **he's** a **murderer**, and putting himself at the mercy of the Criminal Justice System. Will the Defendant hold a grudge? Suppose he's <u>acquitted</u> and hits the street? WHAT THEN?

It's an <u>OPEN</u> COURT. Others hear the testimony. Others become aware of identifications and the <u>identity</u> of the identifiers. Suppose family or friends of the Defendant are among those present. <u>Identifying</u> witnesses have also told them *to– their–faces* that they **are** accusing the Defendant of **murder**. WHAT WILL THEY DO? Emotions skyrocket in a Murder Trial Courtroom –inside and beyond the rail. Tension often feels so palpable it could be sliced with a butcher knife.

The existence of FIVE in-court identifying witnesses is **not** a trifling factor in these proceedings. The IDENTIFYING FIVE appear to be formidable at first blush, but their *state of mind* at the time of the crime is in issue. They are subjected to intense scrutiny on cross examination. Are they *biased*? <u>Three</u> of the identifiers are personal friends of the deceased. What of the power of *suggestion*? They see the accused at counsel table. <u>Two</u> of the identifiers did **not** pick the Defendant's picture in the photo lineup. Were they *intoxicated*? The evidence establishes that <u>four</u> of the five had been drinking. Do they *know* the Defendant? No one knew him. What were the *lighting* conditions? A meteorologist testifies it would have been twilight at the time of the stabbing. Not optimal for *seeing*, but identification is possible. How *close* are they to the killer? The evidence varies from five feet to thirty five feet. How *long* do they see the assailant? <u>Two</u> of the five have several sightings. The other <u>three</u> see the attacker only at the time of the crime. How good is their *eyesight*? <u>Two</u> of the five were wearing glasses. The other <u>three</u> have not had recent eye examinations, but believe they see well. What are their powers of *perception* and *retention* and *expression*? Variable but average. *Demeanor* on the witness stand? Nervous, polite, and engaged.

There are <u>five</u>, but are they CREDIBLE? That is the ultimate issue. The FIVE are initially compelling , but cross examination creates cracks in their **eyeball identifications**. Questions are raised in the minds of the Jury. Perhaps, that wouldn't have mattered <u>had</u> <u>there</u> <u>been</u> **corroboration**.

Where oh where is the corroboration? A viable *eyewitness case* generally NEEDS **corroboration**. Corroborating evidence supports, strengthens, confirms, substantiates, and CONVINCES. Naturally, a Prosecutor can't choose the type of connecting evidence he'll have in a case. He can't turn a nob on an evidence machine and get it to spit out reams of **corroboration**. He's stuck with what the investigation gives him.

However, the DA's Office can choose which cases to prosecute. The commission of serious crimes does **not** spontaneously produce PROOF BEYOND A REASONABLE DOUBT. **Some crimes** are not provable and the **perpetrator of some crimes** is not identifiable. Some Case Submissions must be denied.

I'll suggest a few examples of corroboration:

1. Well, a **bloody** KNIFE with **bloody latent prints** would have been very nice. **Blood** matching the *victim* and **prints** matching the *Defendant*. Type AB blood, let's say, from a *victim* with AB blood, and the *Defendant's* right pinky fingerprint in blood from the KNIFE that **is** the MURDER WEAPON. Combine this convincing corroboration with the five eyewitness identifications and I've got a **dead-bang winner**! There probably isn't an objective Juror on the planet who wouldn't vote for conviction, even if his first two names are Benjamin Franklin. Likewise, there probably isn't an objective reader on the planet who wouldn't want to vote for conviction under **these** circumstances. Hey, guess what gang? The **bloody** KNIFE with **bloody latent prints** is CIRCUMSTANTIAL EVIDENCE! Remember, it's direct evidence if the crime is perceived by any of a witnesses' *physical senses*. EVERYTHING ELSE is **circumstantial**.

2. FLIGHT from the scene of the stabbing would have been wonderful. A killer **apprehended** by police as he FLEES from the crime venue **is** *going to be TOAST*, right? FLIGHT is CIRCUMSTANTIAL EVIDENCE of a consciousness of guilt. If someone who looks like the assailant and is dressed like the assailant is running away, it probably isn't **just** COINCIDENTAL. He'd better have a damn good excuse. Something like, "I'm *the* twin brother and I've got irrefutable proof I just parachuted from an alien space craft. I'm running to sound the alarm. The Martians are coming, the Martians are coming; it's "Independence Day" – again."

   That's a winner either way, isn't it? He's either got an ALIBI or he's INSANE!

3. I love A CONFESSION. Who better knows what happened than the fellow who made it happen? Whether <u>inculpatory</u> **words** of an accused are uttered at the time of arrest, at the station house, or at another location, the urge to purge guilt that produces an acknowledgment of complicity by the offender **is** high impact evidence. Assuming, the CONFESSION is voluntary and based on **fact**. The Constitution is not offended when guilty persons stub their toes by *foolishly* becoming loose-tongued about criminal conduct. Silence is golden to an accused. Conversely, silence is a **black hole** to the Prosecutor. Man, I certainly could have used a CONFESSION in the **<u>Direct</u> Evidence follies at Freedom Park**. Of course, such a phenomenon would have changed the <u>nature</u> of the **case evidence**. CONFESSIONS ARE <u>CIRCUMSTANTIAL</u>.

4. <u>Knows</u> the victim and has A BEEF with him. Evidence of a *pre-existing* relationship between Defendant BEN and the Victim <u>would</u> have been neat. When people have *known* each other before a crime, it raises a possibility that **bad blood** exists between them. That information may fill in a crucial blank: WHY did the Defendant do the crime? **Motive** isn't a necessary element of a crime, but Jurors like cases that have **evidence** of MOTIVE. The Trial Jury may need it to <u>convince</u> them the Defendant did the crime and deserves the time. Well Folks, here's a rather predictable news flash in light of where this narrative has been going. **Evidence of <u>motive</u>** is most assuredly CIRCUMSTANTIAL What a **<u>knife</u> <u>wielding</u> <u>killer</u>** thinks, *inside* the dark recess of his malevolent heart, is definitely <u>not</u> within the *purview* of an EYEWITNESS.

Only a CIRCUMSTANTIAL CASE? The next time you hear someone say this, a *stubborn truth* should come to mind. A Criminal Case that's **only** a DIRECT CASE may not be so hot neither. It isn't written in Statutory Law that *percipient witness* testimony is always **credible**, and it isn't chiseled in granite that *circumstantial evidence* is always **incredible**. **Only** a CIRCUMSTANTIAL CASE? Actually, the strongest evidence imaginable is circumstantial! *Fingerprint, bullet, DNA*, and *confession*evidence are <u>circumstantial</u>. *Most* evidence in criminal cases **is** circumstantial. Circumstances that *seem* COINCIDENTAL receive plenty of attention from skilled homicide investigators. They're <u>dubious</u> of chance, fluke, fortuity, happenstance, and simultaneity – maybe so, but probably <u>not</u>. The **laws** of *cause and effect* usually come into play. An astute Cop *Case Cracker* doesn't <u>really</u> believe in **coincidence**!

Whatever. The burden of proof in a Criminal Case is PROOF BEYOND A REASONABLE DOUBT. The bottom line is: WHATEVER gets a Prosecutor to that point is **his** *Holy Grail*!

Defendant Ben alleges an ALIBI. The *object of his quest* is the creation of REASONABLE DOUBT. An *alibi* is a <u>claim</u>, coupled with <u>supporting</u> evidence, that WHEN a **criminal act** takes place, the Accused is <u>somewhere</u> else.

There is a tavern half a mile from Freedom Park. Ben tells Police he **is** there when the killing occurs. SIX <u>separate</u> tavern goers confirm his contention. They are placed under subpoena. After the States rests, the Defendant's **alibi case** is presented. All SIX of the confirming witnesses testify. Defendant Ben doesn't testify. He's an ex-felon. The Defense chooses to keep this fact under wraps.

The tavern people aren't teetotalers. They're experiencing a little neighborhood camaraderie at a local watering hole. There aren't any abstinence advocates in this crowd. <u>B</u>ooze is flowing down gullets and streaming into blood vessels at the time of the stabbing. Hence, recollections are a bit too fuzzy to unequivocally establish Ben's ALIBI, and they are **not** coupled with <u>supporting</u> evidence. Yet, they muddy the water. Raising an additional specter of doubt regarding the **veracity** of the Freedom Park <u>Five</u>.

Ben's guys aren't perfect, but the perceptions of every <u>percipient</u> witness at the crime scene are flawed as well. The result isn't surprising. Deliberation lasts into the second day and –– BEN **WINS**! The Jury does NOT find proof beyond a reasonable doubt in the **direct evidence follies at Freedom Park**. God sometimes protects babies and fools. A Trial Jury unenthusiastically <u>protects</u> a Defendant with half a dozen *alibi* witnesses whose beaks have been dipped in the sauce and happens to be an ex-felon named Ben.

However, there's an intriguing post-script. An ironic affirmation to the *instincts* of a Trial Jury sworn to render a verdict of *equal* and *exact* **justice**. Three years later Law Enforcement discovers that the Freedom Park

Verdict <u>has</u> been TRUE. Their initial investigation had identified the WRONG perpetrator. The *fallibility* of a criminal case based **strictly** on <u>direct</u> <u>evidence</u> is undeniably demonstrated.

The Coppers are pursuing a separate investigation. Attempting to build a case against a drug dealer. They have a wired confidential informant working the streets. He engages in a conversation with the **target**. Verbiage between the two includes admissions with respect to the drug case <u>and</u> the Freedom Park stabbing. The **target** <u>acknowledges</u> he is the *knife wielding* Freedom Park SLAYER.

No pressure. No inducement. No entrapment. No setup by the informant. He knows nothing about the prior **murder**. It's a purely gratuitous **confession** made to *the wire*. Imprudent bravado of a brash KILLER, <u>belatedly</u> beating his chest in an effort to validate his status as someone really BIG AND BAD. The totality of circumstances gives the utterance an indicia of reliability. After all, **who** knows better what happened than the fellow who made it happen!

Some <u>circumstantial</u> <u>evidence</u> is very strong, as when you find a spontaneous **confession** *recorded* IN THE WIRE. Defendant Ben's prosecution has been based upon a false <u>premise</u>. The news is gratifying to me. A Prosecutor is a passionate champion of JUSTICE, **losing** is **winning** IF a blameless Defendant is exonerated! It's the ONLY time, to my knowledge, I went to **trial** against an INNOCENT MAN. Others were acquitted, but acquittal is **not** the equivalent of INNOCENCE.

The Ultimate Act Of Selfishness

"A word [or a bullet], once sent abroad, flies irrevocably."
(Horace)

Chapter 4

"The journey of a thousand miles <u>once</u> begins with a single step." (Chinese Proverb, emphasis added) My <u>journey</u> as a **Trial** Lawyer begins with *two* steps. They occur on consecutive weeks. Both are <u>robbery</u> cases. Each involves a single victim and a single robber. A fellow Deputy D.A. is assigned to *ride shotgun* for both outings. The Trials are straightforward and short, having uncomplicated facts and issues. Tailor-made for a rookie being spoon fed. The Office powers-that-be don't want me traumatized during my first trips to the trenches. Of course, <u>tailors</u> don't make **crimes,** and management level <u>prosecutors</u> don't design **crimes,** <u>robbers</u> MAKE **crimes** and **circumstances.**

It takes a day and a half to complete <u>each</u> Trial. To my immense satisfaction, both end in <u>conviction</u>. Praise the Lord and pass the rhetoric, I'm on my way!

Two months later the District Attorney introduces me to the big time. He selects me to be second chair **with <u>him</u>** in the Trial of a *double* MURDER case, transferred from Lyon County to Clark County, due to a Court-ordered change of venue. The crimes involve the killings of *two* Wyoming businessmen in northern Nevada. Both victims are shot to death. Killed in a *spat* of bullets. My Boss's invitation thrills me, humbles me, and unnerves me. I feel as though I'm *sweating* bullets.

The <u>engine</u> for the Crime is greed! There are *four* conspirators. <u>One</u> is a business **partner** of the victims. The Crime Venue is in Lyon County. Therefore, the Lyon County Sheriff's Department conducts the homicide investigation, a Special Prosecutor appointed by Lyon County drafts charging documents, and also manages certain procedural machinations preceding our Trial. Incredibly, total immunity is granted to a triggerman in return for Trial testimony. He is <u>not</u> the **partner**. Equally incredulous is the <u>acquittal</u> of a second triggerman in a Trial handled by Lyon County's Special Prosecutor.

Mr District Attorney, affectionately known as Pappy, and I are prosecuting Defendant Ted. Pappy gives me <u>two</u> Trial assignments. I am to conduct Direct Examination of the Medical Examiner. The M.E. has performed autopsy examinations upon the victims, and will offer opinions regarding their cause of death. Also, I am to offer the <u>Opening</u> Final Argument. Obviously, Pappy wants to present the STATE'S REBUTTAL

Trial begins. The Medical Examiner is the fifth witness. Methodical disclosure of the Victim Pathologies goes reasonably well. Both victims <u>were</u> healthy men. There are **no** significant findings of <u>disease</u> inside either body. **No disease**, but there is significant evidence of extraneous *antibodies* inside each corpse. There–are–BULLETS! Surely, it is inconceivable that any **foreign bodies** could be any more *opposed* or detrimental to the well being of living human beings than BULLET **fragments**.

A BULLET discharged through the barrel of a gun *flies irrevocably*. <u>Bullets</u> hurt people. <u>Bullets</u> make holes in people. <u>Bullets</u> penetrate skin and skulls and vital organs. The blunt burrowing trauma of <u>bullets</u> crashing into brains, hearts, lungs, vertebrae, and major arteries is devastating. <u>Bullets</u> KILL. <u>Bullets</u> tear people from loving companionship with families and friends. <u>Bullets</u> involuntarily pluck people from the joys and tribulations and ineffable experiences of mortal life – sending them hurdling beyond the veil. <u>Bullets</u> are irrevocable. <u>Bullets</u> fired into human bodies are EVIL! **Murder–is–despicable!**

The Medical Examiner tells a tale of TWO MURDERS. His testimony offers **proof** of CORPUS DELICTI, that is, the **body of the offense**. The human remains in the morgue are <u>each</u>, respectively, <u>bodies</u> of the crimes. What they are NOT is **proof** of WHO DID IT. **A dead man is <u>not</u> a TATTLETALE.**

The Medical Examiner describes the extent of injury and the presence of <u>bullet</u> projectiles in each body. He offers a series of crucial opinions. It is his opinion that **the deaths** were <u>not</u> the result of disease process nor natural cause. His opinion <u>is</u> that **the deaths** were <u>not</u> accidental and <u>not</u> self inflicted. His opinion <u>is</u> that **the deaths** are HOMICIDAL, i.e., **death by criminal agency**! And that **is** the **proof** of CORPUS DELICTI. Death by MEANS of criminal agency.

So, as is readily apparent, the Direct Examination of a Medical Examiner is extremely consequential in Murder Trial Proceedings. It is FOUNDATIONAL to **ALL** other evidence. A Murder CONVICTION <u>cannot</u> be obtained without a showing of corpus delicti.

However, <u>bullet</u> killings are <u>not</u> easily challenged by the Defense. My first-ever examination of a Medical Examiner isn't exemplary, but I get the job done. Pappy commends me for my examination, and I <u>thank</u> him for the honor of being his junior partner in a Murder Trial.

Evidence <u>connecting</u> Defendant Ted to the double murder is presented. The State rests. The Defense offers its evidence. Instructions are settled and read to the Trial Jury. FINAL ARGUMENT **begins**!

WOW! My first-ever SUMMATION to a Jury in a Murder Case. I'm so nervous I can't hold my hands steady. Lucky for me, I won't be taking notes of what I say. I walk stiffly to the lectern and take a deep breath. Every set of eyes in the Jury Box is **staring** expectantly at me. Waiting, waiting, waiting to see if anything profound will come out of the Kid's mouth, OR if he's got the balls to SAY anything.

I have an instantaneous flashback to a cartoon I've recently read. I'm seeing myself as the character portrayed in the funnies. **Lawyer** Throckmorton stands cowering before the Jury with a glazed, faraway look in his eyes. His hair is uncharacteristically SPIKED. Flying out in every conceivable direction, as though he's just put his finger in a light switch. He's dazed, befuddled, and delusional. Obviously, the bewildered gentleman has *cracked* under the stress of argument to the Jury. He mumbles tentatively, "WHO are these people and WHY are they staring at me like this?"

The reverie fades. I'm <u>not</u> delusional. I <u>know</u> **who** these people are and **why** they're staring at me. I pull myself together. There's work to be done. A case to argue. I'm stressed, but not oblivious. It's time to exercise my jaw.

My mouth opens. I make my argument. It's rather pedestrian really. Not polished. Not impassioned. Not confidently uttered. More or less what veterans expect from a rookie Prosecutor. I haven't yet envisioned the full PARAMETERS and POWER of **Summation**. That realization will come with time and repetition. But it's a start. The second chair Deputy doesn't *crack* under stress. He delivers his speech to the Jury. His jaw gets an aerobic workout in a Murder Trial, and after twenty minutes he's finally holding his hands steady.

The Prosecution has the **burden of proof**. It must overcome Defendant Ted's **presumption of innocence**. A PRESUMPTION accorded every criminal Defendant as a matter of law. Accordingly, State's Attorneys get to <u>argue</u> TWICE. They have **Opening** Closing Argument and **Rebuttal** Closing Argument. Defense Counsel is allowed to argue only ONCE

Having me do the OPENING is a deliberate ploy by my Boss. Pappy wants to use me as a lightning rod for CLOSING REMARKS of Mr. High Powered, the esteemed Defense Counselor. Pappy doesn't want the *meat* of State's arguments showcased too soon. He expects the Rookie's offering to be on the *lean* side. The strategy is to limit the areas that glib, smooth, experienced, esteemed Defense Gentleman has to *pick over* when he **argues**. My designated role is to <u>deflect</u> the effectiveness of Defense Counsel, if possible. Thereafter, freeing-up Mr. District Attorney to fire a heavy barrage of *zinger* verbiage, and swing the Jury concensus to **conviction**.

The strategy isn't particularly effective. I'm not sure why Pappy ever thought it would be. Mr. High Powered is a wily fellow. He isn't about to limit his remarks to areas covered by the rookie Deputy. He'll shift his *sweating tongue* into over-drive. He's going to **argue** the whole ball of wax regardless, and using *wax* as the metaphor is done advisedly. Mr. High Powered says the Prosecution's EVIDENCE is a *house-of-wax*. When the **heat** of objective scrutiny and logical analysis is <u>turned up</u> – the HOUSE MELTS!

By the way, it's <u>not</u> alleged that Defendant Ted is a TRIGGERMAN. He's the WHEELMAN. He drives the car that gets the <u>actual</u> shooters to the Crime Scene. He's someone who facilitates the commission of the crime by an ACT of **aiding and abetting** – an ACCOMPLICE.

Esteemed Counsel for the Defense **hammers** away at the State's Case for an hour and a half. Punishing the Prosecution with withering verbal volleys. Arguing in his *inimitable* way that the Prosecution has utterly FAILED to meet its **burden of proof**. He calls the Case against his client *flimsy*. The evidence implicitly *unreliable*. Contending that charges should *never* have been filed against Ted. Counsel says its *disgraceful* that Lyon County has preferred charges against his client while granting <u>immunity</u> to an ACTUAL triggerman in return for testimony <u>bought</u> and <u>paid</u> for.

But Mr. High Powered **saves** the ARGUMENT he undoubtedly believes is his CLINCHER until last. He flashes his toothy trademark grin, swaggers along the Jury rail, returns to the lectern – seemingly deep in thought, looks up, leans forward triumphantly, and PROCLAIMS that the case <u>against</u> his client would NEVER have been brought if the **murders** had occurred in Clark County. He ARGUES that the DISTRICT ATTORNEY of Clark County, recognizing the *frivolous* nature of the ACCOMPLICE evidence, would have REFUSED to file charges against Defendant Ted.

Now is that presumptuous or what? Mr. High Powered has evidently magnified his law degree with a degree in the occult. He **reads** minds!

Defense Counsel wraps up his Final Argument, and Pappy strides resolutely to the lectern. He's obviously been *angered* by the tone and content of the Defense rhetoric. His professional stature and his sense of judgment are on the line.

The District Attorney doesn't believe in beating around the bush, nor does he believe in lengthy **rebuttal**. For <u>thirty</u> minutes he barks out the connecting evidence of the State. Speaking in short staccato bursts of rationale, he describes the Case for **conviction** point by point. He's articulate, emphatic, and sincere!

Pappy directly engages Mr. High Powered at about the <u>twenty</u> minute mark. Defendant Ted has waived his Privilege Against Self Incrimination and testifies earlier in the Trial. The D.A. highlights an **inculpatory** statement *acknowledged* by Defendant Ted during Cross Examination. He has admitted to Lyon County Sheriff's Deputies that he **did** DRIVE the <u>two</u> triggermen to the Crime site, but *believes* a non violent meeting between the principals is the <u>sole</u> purpose of the conclave. Incidentally, the charged **partner** travels in a separate vehicle to the rendevous point <u>where</u> he is to meet with his <u>two</u> **partners**. Pappy brushes off the excuse. He claims the totality of proven circumstances clearly establishes the **guilty knowledge** of the Defendant.

There is another bone of contention to be masticated. Pappy squares his shoulders, expands his rather sizable chest, and declares he's going to **set the record straight** regarding the TRANSFER of the **Trial** to Clark County. Pappy explains that he **personally** reviewed the Lyon County **Case** against Defendant Ted *before* he <u>accepted</u> it. He says there is NO WAY he would have taken on the Case if he hadn't been **personally** *convinced* of the Defendant's GUILT.

Mr. Clark County District Attorney's REBUTTAL **summation**

carries the day. The Jury retires for deliberation. They consider the case for five hours and return with a **verdict**. Defendant Ted is GUILTY of *two counts* of Murder **ONE**! A month later the Trial Judge sentences him to *concurrent* Life Sentences in the Nevada State Penitentiary with the possibility of Parole.

But the story doesn't end with conviction and sentencing. The *rest* of the story is **not** anticipated by most Courthouse pundits. Within a week after rendition of judgment, Mr. Esteemed Defense Counsel Gentleman files a MOTION to *set aside* the Verdicts. Judge Bill hears argument on the Motion and takes the matter under advisement. He apparently *advises and advises and re-advises himself.* He sits on the Motion for a month.

Finally, he **rules**. The DECISION is **stunning**. Judge Bill GRANTS the Motion. He *sets aside* the Verdicts of **guilty**. Grounds: the PROSECUTORIAL MISCONDUCT of the Clark County District Attorney!

Prosecutorial Misconduct by the District Attorney? WHEN – HOW? Well it's simple, Watson. Regarding WHEN: The Court RULES that the **misconduct** is perpetrated during REBUTTAL ARGUMENT. Regarding HOW: The Court's FINDING is that **two** instances of RHETORICAL **misconduct** are perpetrated by the District Attorney.

(One) The D.A. has **improperly** referenced evidence not sanctioned by the Court. ADMISSIONS the Court hasn't formally ruled ADMISSIBLE. Defendant Ted's *acknowledgment* to Lyon County Sheriff's Deputies that he DROVE the car transporting two triggermen to the Crime Scene is *UN-MIRANDIZED*!

Mr. High Powered believes the parties have a tacit agreement not to plumb for evidence here. Yet, the District Attorney's **Cross Examination** of Chauffeur Ted garners an *acknowledgment* he has EXPLOITED in **Rebuttal Argument** to the detriment of the *UNADVISED* Defendant.

(Two) The D.A. has **improperly** expressed his personal opinion concerning the GUILT of the Defendant. He's "**set the record straight**." He's vigorously defended the CREDIBILITY of the State's Case by telling the Jury he **personally** reviewed the Lyon County **case** before accepting it. He's said there is NO WAY he would have taken on the Case if he hadn't been **personally** *convinced* of the Defendant's GUILT.

Okay. The first Court finding of **misconduct** is a bit fuzzy, but the second is a well founded, unambiguous act of **misconduct**. No doubt about it! A Prosecutor may **not** stand before a jury and expressly declare,

"There's NO WAY I'd be prosecuting this Case if I wasn't **personally** *convinced* of the Defendant's GUILT." Especially, when he's **the** District Attorney, an <u>elected</u> representative of the people he's standing before. That–is–not–permissible! Sorry Pappy. You're clearly out of bounds on this one. Ego perhaps, a desire to validate your decision to take another County's case, and the *cleansing rush* of Rebuttal Argument have made you stub your toe.

That said, a **bright line** TRUTH remains. A <u>fixture</u> of the Criminal Justice System steadfastly shines. It's **not** a small matter for <u>a Judge</u> to **pull the plug** on a Jury Verdict! On those rare, rare occasions when it happens, HIS HONOR damn well better have a **rock-solid** LEGAL <u>and</u> FACTUAL BASIS for doing it! There is a WELL-DEFINED **bright line** *division* of responsibility in Criminal Trials, to-wit: **THE COURT** is the **trier** of the LAW and **THE JURY** is the **trier** of FACT. This RULE is a sacrosanct hallmark of the American way of bringing <u>order</u> to the Courtroom and **finality** to the prosecution of CRIMINALS. The *DIVISION* **must**, under ordinary circumstances, be **respected**. Only under <u>extraordinary</u> conditions **may** it be disregarded. Otherwise, a Court steps beyond it's constitutionally endowed authority and becomes, to use slang term phraseology, TOO BIG FOR ITS BRITCHES. The result is **disorder** in the Courtroom.

Judge Bill, with all due respect, I believe you became <u>too</u> big for your judicial britches in the Case-at-bar. Your Judicial Fiat <u>superceded</u> the considered, deliberated, gut-wrenching, unanimous decision of the TWELVE TRIED AND TRUE. Your act of *setting aside* their VERDICTS made the soul-searching agony of their judgment a **waste** of time. Your Honor, YOU stepped **across** the line of judicial propriety. YOU cavalierly tossed the Jury Verdicts aside and substituted YOUR opinion for theirs. That, Sir, is a level of **MISCONDUCT** extending well past the RHETORICAL **misdeeds** of the District Attorney. What you did is a <u>slap</u> in the face of each Juror. Sir, they solemnly raised their arms at the beginning of this case, and swore to render EQUAL AND EXACT JUSTICE. Did you take a similar oath in this case? Of course not. YOU'RE the **trier of the law**. In point of fact, that's what YOU told the Jury in YOUR instructions, isn't it. **You** also told them they **are** the **triers of fact**. Remember? Apparently you didn't mean what you said. Evidently, you think **one** Judicial mind has more astute fact-finding capabilities than **twelve** Juror minds. YOU ARE OUT OF ORDER, **Sir**!

Moreover, isn't *setting aside* JURY VERDICTS a smidgen **heavy handed** under these circumstances. No doubt about it, Prosecutors can commit grave acts of **misconduct**. A Prosecutor, so inclined – and we hope such individuals are few and far between, **is** in a position to EVISCERATE the Criminal Justice System. Making the system rotten to the core. I will elucidate several examples of **EGREGIOUS PROSECUTORIAL MISCONDUCT**.

(One) SUBORNATION OF PERJURY – What happens to the **search** for truth if some form of *bribery* or other improper witness *inducement* occurs? What if Prosecution witnesses are covertly provided *scripted* testimony? Or get their memories **expanded** by the power of *suggestion* – receiving an *earful* about **testimony** needed to plug up evidence *deficiencies*?

(Two) SUBVERSION OF PROCESS SERVICE – What happens to the Defense **power** of subpoena if they can't *find* their witnesses? If witnesses are **enticed**, by any one of a thousand means available to a disingenuous Prosecutor, to relocate or lay low or disappear or conveniently lose their memories?

(Three) SURREPTITIOUS WITNESS INTIMIDATION – What happens to the Defense **right** to call witnesses at Trial if their witnesses are **prevented** or **dissuaded** from appearing by threats, coercion, arrest, or extradition?

The MISSION of a Prosecutor is **JUSTICE**. Yet, when the People's Man aborts his mission and pursues scandalous **self-servicing** objectives, he has the wherewithal to perpetrate a nefarious **INJUSTICE**.

Nevertheless, *WORDS* uttered in Open Court before Judges imbued with the POWER to sua sponte curtail *ARGUMENT* deemed to be beyond the pale, **is NOT** typically a truly **SUBSTANTIVE** category of misconduct!

What is Judge Bill dealing with? How **serious** is the District Attorney's *rhetorical misconduct* in the Case-at-bar? Hmmm, ticky-tack comes to mind!

Basis One – for casting the JURY VERDICTS aside: The D.A. has **improperly** referenced evidence not sanctioned by the Court. ADMISSIONS the Court hasn't formally ruled admissible. Defendant Ted's *acknowledgment* to Lyon County Sheriff's Deputies that he DROVE the car transporting two triggermen to the Crime Scene is *UN-*

MIRANDIZED. Further, Mr. High Powered claims the parties had a tacit agreement **not** to plumb for evidence here.

Well, I have this to say about that. The **Admission issue** is largely **Counsel-made**. A creature finding life in the mind of Mr. High Powered because of his erroneous forecast he would *WIN* the Trial. He guessed wrong. His hands are soiled. He should have raised the Miranda issue, forcing the Court to rule on the *voluntariness* of the admission. **Not** placing reliance on some fuzzy assertion about an undocumented agreement between the parties. This issue is a throw in, a counsel-contrived effort to cover his rear end following adverse Jury Verdicts. The barrister has failed to solicit a Court Ruling that would have firmly established legal parameters for the Trial Playing Field. Why **reward** an error in judgment?

Moreover, failure to recite the Miranda litany, does **not**, necessarily, mean an ensuing statement **is** INVOLUNTARY. Sound logic and public interest suggest that *un-mirandized* statements, shown to be **voluntary** by a totality of the circumstances, are prima facie TRUSTWORTHY and should be admissible as evidence. Let–the–Trier–of–Fact–render–the–ultimate–decision– regarding– weight–to–be–given–the–admission!

Besides, assuming for the sake of argument, that Pappy's Summation reference to an *un-mirandized*, **un-litigated** admission is error, it is probably HARMLESS ERROR. The Jury has INDEPENDENT evidence in the record from which it certainly could have justly and reasonably inferred that Defendant Ted **did**, in fact, drive triggermen to the location of the Murders. So, what's all the fuss about? –– Well, there's a second weevil in the Trial mix.

Basis two – for casting the JURY VERDICTS aside: The D.A. has **improperly** expressed his personal opinion concerning the GUILT of the Defendant. He's "**set the record straight**." That's wrong. He shouldn't have said this – under ordinary circumstances! WHY would an experienced, articulate, knowledgeable, responsible practitioner like Pappy say it?

The ANSWER is clear, actually. Brothers and Sisters, Pappy is a **gentleman** first and foremost. When a **gentleman** receives an invitation he responds. Pappy has *received* an INVITATION. Mr. High Powered Gentleman has sent him a verbal, unsealed, gold embossed invitation – with a red bow. It's from Gentleman Defense Counselor to Mr. Gentleman District Attorney. Pappy *almost* has to say something.

Think about it. This **ENTIRE** issue has been choreographed by Mr. High Powered. It's a case of RHETORICAL ENTRAPMENT. **Invited error**! He has personally created the SCENARIO he uses, after adverse

Jury Verdicts, as the linchpin for a Motion to Set Aside Jury Verdicts. –– And **Judge Bill–goes–for–it**! Doesn't that beat all?

The REASON Pappy says, what he says, is a <u>reaction</u> to the **inappropriate**, PERSONAL OPINION **rhetoric** of Mr. High Powered. The sly, presumptuous, **mind-reader** fellow. The one professing Trial Lawyer skills with subsidiary expertise in *extrasensory perception.*

Defense Counsel **OPENS** the door. It is esteemed Counsel who flashes his toothy trademark grin, swaggers along the Jury rail, returns to the lectern – seemingly deep in thought, and crows triumphantly that the case <u>against</u> his client would NEVER have been brought if the **murders** had occurred in Clark County. Mr. High Powered ARGUES that the DISTRICT ATTORNEY of Clark County, recognizing the *frivolous* nature of the ACCOMPLICE evidence, would have <u>REFUSED</u> to file charges against Defendant Ted.

Mr. High Powered is playing **hard ball**! He's <u>really</u> saying the Case is piss poor – *frivolous*. There's **no** evidence against his client. The Prosecution's pitiful task is like trying to pin a phony tail on a tail-less donkey – blindfolded. They're clueless. The fact is, their case **is** a tail-less donkey. Prosecutors have proof of murders, but **no** proof Ted is **one** of the murderers. Allegorically, they **can't** find a tail for their donkey. Which is to say, they **can't** find **facts** necessary to establish proof beyond a reasonable doubt. It's all make believe. A Case consisting of smoke and mirrors, a paper tail – and a tack. A Case Mr. District Attorney would NEVER have **approved** for prosecution within Clark County's Criminal Justice system. NO WAY, NO HOW.

Objectively, <u>doesn't</u> the District Attorney have to REPLY to such CASE-DEMEANING rhetoric? ISN'T failing to REFUTE the allegation tantamount to **acquiescence**? Won't the Jury be strongly inclined to ACQUIT unless THE MAN whose mind has been read, **contradicts** the veracity of the reading?

Mr. High Powered can legitimately argue A FAILURE of proof. He can <u>fully</u> explore the factual short-comings of the Prosecution's Case. He can use ALL of the rhetoric described in the <u>second</u> paragraph above – and more. **BUT** he CANNOT, I repeat, he CANNOT, **properly**, SINGLE OUT the D.A., <u>expressly</u> CALLING HIM OUT for handling a Case he knows is UNWORTHY OF PROSECUTION, and which he would NEVER have **personally** APPROVED FOR PROSECUTION.

This line of argument by Mr. High Powered is **objectionable**. He places the Clark County District Attorney between the proverbial rock and a hard place. **If** HE objects it sounds like the Defense has hit a nerve and HE'S protesting too much. Whereas, failing to object seems like an acknowledgment that the charge is true. Judge Bill has the **power** to police his Courtroom, to maintain civility and propriety. HE should have projected himself into the fray. *Curtailing* such **argument** and *admonishing* Mr. High Powered to plow some different ground.

Sadly, the Court abdicates his responsibility. Sitting passively on the Bench like a bump on a pickle. THEREFORE, Pappy fills the vacuum. He forcefully REBUTS the **specious** MISCONDUCT of the Defense Counsel Gentleman. Hello! The INVITATION gets accepted.

Therefore, by any objective standard, **invited** error becomes HARMLESS ERROR. But **not** in Judge Bill's Courtroom. He CONDONES the **RSVP**, but CONDEMNS the **ANSWER**! It's a bit like the erratic behavior of the King of Hearts in Wonderland. (Lewis Carroll, *Alice in Wonderland*)

Further, the seriousness of **open-court Prosecutorial Misconduct** is debatable. In my view, MOST instances of RHETORICAL PROSECUTORIAL MISCONDUCT are superficial and inconsequential. **Truly damaging** infractions do **not** occur in the BRIGHT LIGHT of Public or Judicial scrutiny. **Dark deeds** are perpetrated in **dark places**. They are **secret** machinations committed away from Judicial oversight. OFFENSES of **stealth**!

In much the same way, the **dark deed** of **double murder** is a CRIME of **stealth**. Perpetrated in a lonely place with RECKLESS *disregard* of circumstance or social duty – or the lives of two Wyoming businessmen. Judge Bill is well advised to REMEMBER this somber **fact**. Where is JUSTICE for the deceased?

MURDER is the ultimate act of selfishness.

Cupid shoots mythological arrows with hearts for tips to inspire love.
O shoots murderous bullets with lead tips to puncture a trusting heart.
"Happy Valentine's Day, My Dearest – with malice!"

It seems like a marriage made in heaven. Friends think it is moonlight and roses and endless love. T believes the union will be a blissful happiness ever after. But the union of hand and heart must have two helping hands and two loving hearts. The union of O and T is two *minus* one. ONE loving trusting heart. ONE hateful suspicious heart. There is **no** union here. Only disunion! **Not** happily betrothed. **Maliciously** betrayed!

Two days before Valentine's Day, O calls T at her workplace. He proposes over the land wire. Not marriage, they're already married. But there's been a spat, an emotional estrangement. He proposes a truce, says they need to warm the chill. Let's MEET at **our** apartment off Eastern Avenue, and go out to dinner together. [His idea not hers.] It's to be a Pre-Valentine's Day affair. An evening of demure amour, says he. An opportunity to share some special time. A chance to renew our pledge of everlasting love. "Some wine as we dine and who knows? We'll let love's sweet flowering take us to whatever a night in the season of romance bequeaths."

She's thrilled! He's **not**. He's thinking, "Being wed is like being dead!" It's a sharp contrast in mind-set. There's no **connect** here. The proposal is a pretext, but–the–date–is–made.

T leaves work a little early. She hurries home, nevertheless, she must park in the dark. A cold wind is blowing, and it's a moonless evening. She braces herself, begins to walk, and approaches the corner of the building next to their apartment. There's a narrow alley here. She shivers as she reaches the opening, it's chilly – but she's inexplicably apprehensive too. Intuitive?

HE'S *waiting* in the darkness, and it's **not** to greet her with a hug and a lingering kiss. It **isn't** to wine and dine her on a dinner date. It **isn't** to renew their pledge of everlasting love. NO, it **isn't** to let love's fragile flower bloom in the ambiance of tender courtship. **HE'S** brought a peculiar prop to the rendevous site. **HE'S** *waiting* with a **gun**.

HE'S made a date. **HE** should be preparing to celebrate their life together. He ought to be filled with REMEMBRANCE! Mindful of the amazing gift she's given him. It's **not** a small thing for a bride to *give herself*, her love, her life, her trust, her destiny – to her husband. Such a pledge is **not** a small matter. It is **not** to be taken lightly – **ever!** O should be *remembering* and *cherishing* that exquisite **moment!** The **wondrous** instant when TWO vowed, *I thee wed.*

However, there's not a chance the ONE who has **laid-in-wait** with heat and ammo is contemplating the worth of a man's relationship with his wife. **HIS HEART** is full of a *murderous malignancy*. **HE** intends to *defile* the **gift** by *eradicating* the **gift**. Treating his woman like a piece of vermin.

HE jumps into her path. It's a hastily executed crime of **passion!** There is no hesitation. He **FIRES** *twice* at point blank range. BOTH lead tipped missiles of hate <u>penetrate</u> her heart. WHERE is *fidelity* to LIFE?

WHY? A man makes his bed, he's supposed to sleep in it. Where is O's sense of humanity? What has happened to the PLEDGE? Where has **love** GONE? WHY? Be a **man**. Be a mature **adult**. The unvarnished fact is: **YOU** choose your life. Renounce her. Leave her. Sever the emotional ties. Divorce her. Move to another part of the world. Live a life of promiscuity and drink and ease on an exotic South Sea island. Live your fantasies, if a single man ever can. **END** the <u>relationship</u>. BUT SIR, for heaven's sake – in the name of decency and all that is holy, <u>**do not**</u> END <u>her</u>!

TWO large caliber bullet **holes** in her heart. T drops like a rock. Cupid shoots mythological arrows with hearts for tips to inspire love. O shoots murderous bullets with lead tips to puncture a trusting heart. "Happy Valentine's Day, My Dearest –– with malice!

MURDER IS THE <u>ULTIMATE</u> ACT OF SELFISHNESS! O does a callous *hit and run*! He doesn't <u>hail</u> a neighbor to call 911. He doesn't <u>call</u> Police to report the *vile deed* of WIFE-KILLING. He doesn't render <u>assistance</u> to the ONE he once loved. He gets his sorry ass out of there. **HE** <u>races</u> into the cover of darkness, smoking gun in hand. Like an **amoral** *jackal*, without a <u>hint</u> of sentiment or remorse or humanity, **HE'S** in full-throttle FLIGHT. That's right, Sir. Run *jack* run. Turn your cowardly back on your fallen VALENTINE and your deadly *act of premeditated Murder.*

Benjamin Franklin once offered this intriguing advice: "Keep thy eyes wide open before marriage, and half shut afterwards." (*Poor Richard's Almanac,* 1738) Poor T. The sage counsel respecting marriage isn't totally applicable to her. She **should** have kept her eyes WIDE OPEN **after** marriage, particularly the fateful evening of February 12th.

But the Night has eyes and the Police are blood hounds. O <u>**can't**</u> run far enough or fast enough to avoid ACCOUNTABILITY. There <u>will</u> be a DAY of reckoning. A Final Judgment when <u>each</u> man's ACCOUNT is fully settled. Make book on it, Sir!

P.S. – before the above, a Criminal Trial will also be conducted.

Charges are filed, but Criminal Procedure isn't always a well honed, fully functioning mechanism. It's subject to human interpretation and implementation. The human element isn't perfect. O is a case in point. Charges are dismissed in Justice Court on a technicality. A Motion to reinstate is filed. It's being briefed. The matter languishes. O is back on the streets. *Justice* has lost her wheels.

The State seeks and obtains a <u>superceding</u> charge. The Justice Court log-jam is bypassed. A Clark County Grand Jury **indicts** O. *Justice* acquires a <u>new</u> set of wheels. However, O is allowed to remain out of custody on his own recognizance. Defense Counsel seeks dismissal of the **Indictment**. A Petition for Writ of Habeas Corpus is filed, the State answers, and the matter is scheduled for argument. The DA's Office prevails. The Habeas Petition is dismissed and the Writ is discharged. O's Case finally has traction.

The District Court puts the matter on its Master Calendar for Trial Setting. While I'm waiting in the Courtroom for O's Case to be called, the Accused, still at large on his own recognizance, comes over and sits by me.

I'm going to give negligible credit where it's due. Despite his dubious status, O is a charming man – and a salesman. He wants to score some points with his Prosecutor. Do a sales job. Convince me he's an innocent man, if that's possible. As for me, I won't say I'm a charmer, but **I am** friendly. I'll talk to <u>anyone</u>. Every person gets my ear if he has something to say.

Deputy Harmon is a Mormon. Defendant O knows this, and he knows enough about Mormons to know they <u>believe</u> in modern day Prophets. O offers several banal pleasantries, and then tries to generate some capital on his behalf. He says, "I wish SPENCER would come to Las Vegas." Well, SPENCER could be a hundred thousand different people. I don't have a clue <u>who</u> he's wanting to be a tourist in Sin City. So I say, "SPENCER who?"

And O says, "SPENCER KIMBALL, the **Prophet**." He's looking at me with a sly, knowing smile as he adds, "I've met SPENCER. I know him." I turn in my seat to directly face him now, thinking there's got to be a punch line coming – somewhere. Giving him my best poker face persona, I ask: "<u>Why</u> do you want SPENCER W. KIMBALL to come to Las Vegas?"

His scripted response, the anticipated punch line, is deliberately deadpan, but his eyes twinkle slightly as he delivers it. " I want him to come to Las Vegas so <u>he</u> can **tell <u>you</u>** I'M not guilty."

We both laugh quietly at the audacity of his coy quip. It's the **player** in him. Shooting from beyond the arc. Wanting to score a trifecta. Trying to <u>avoid</u> going to Trial – **not** *really* liking his chances before a Jury.

A short pause ensues. I'm searching for an appropriate rejoinder The reply of the Prosecutor to the Accused is terse, yet polite. "It's this way O, SPENCER is a very busy man. He probably can't fit a trip to Court into his itinerary. Anyhow, this is a forum of law not an evangelical event. Even a Prophet will have to be put under oath and cross examined to determine HOW well he <u>actually</u> knows you. Nice try, Sir!"

A few minutes later O's Case is called. Since he's at liberty, his Counselor asks for a Trial date in ordinary course and the parties go their respective ways.

I'll cut to the chase. Several months later O violates the terms of his own recognizance release, and he's remanded to custody. Therefore, the Defense seeks a **speedy** Trial. A request that is honored by the District Judge. Pertinent **evidence** is presented – sans SPENCER, the Parties **argue**, and the Jury **speaks** its mind. The Verdict is: GUILTY – **Murder in the <u>First</u> Degree with use of a <u>Deadly</u> Weapon**. O isn't smiling now. He's sentenced to Life <u>Without</u> the Possibility of Parole.

The Defense files a Direct Appeal to the Nevada Supreme Court. They allege that a <u>smorgasbord</u> of issues has deprived O of his right to a fair Trial. But <u>certain</u> members of the High Court hone in on a **single** issue during oral argument. The legal angst of these Jurists focuses on what is becoming their signature issue – RHETORICAL **Prosecutorial Misconduct**.

Mr. Justice Thunder, in particular, makes some very unflattering remarks about "Yours Truly"in Open Court. Calling me out **by name**, he says it is well <u>known</u> that this Deputy Prosecutor is routinely guilty of **misconduct** in Cases he handles. A reckless Judicial pronouncement I **categorically** DENY.

Lewis Carroll's character Humpty Dumpty sardonically avers: "When I use a word ...it means just what I choose it to mean––neither more nor less." (*Through The Looking Glass*, p.238) There's a good deal of wisdom in Humpty's derisive assertion. **Misconduct** IS in the mind of the accuser, Mr. Justice Thunder. When <u>you</u> use **the word** <u>you</u> wrap it around whatever <u>conduct</u> you CHOOSE to censure. Where is the logic and objectivity in such legal relativity? How many MURDER **Trials** have you Prosecuted, Sir? Where is the font of experience that makes you an expert on RHETORICAL **misconduct**? How would you know what it takes to survive in the Trial trenches. It's easy to take ignorant, baseless, defamatory pot-shots from the bleachers.

Paradoxically, my **wife** sits in the Supreme Court gallery for the only time in my career. To say she is *steamed* by the intemperate remarks of the loquacious Jurist is an understatement. She tells me her sentiment was an overwhelming urge to charge the Bench and punch the guy out. She stayed put, but her animus lingers.

Murder is the **ultimate <u>act</u>** of selfishness. My wife says the scathing verbosity of Mr. Justice Thunder was the **ultimate <u>act</u>** of public impudence.

I've deliberately abbreviated the bombast from the Bench, but it was ugly. Several members of the Defense Bar come up afterward, apologizing for the bellicose *personal* attack. Telling me they are <u>dumbfounded</u> by the reprimand!

The thunderous critique of the Prosecutor sort of *loses* sight of the enormity of the Crime being Prosecuted. Further, it manifests an abiding lack of confidence in the ability of Trial Judges to properly manage the affairs of their Courtrooms, and an abysmal lack of faith in the capacity of Jurors to objectively sift through evidence and reach **<u>just</u>** Verdicts – WITHOUT *Judicial interference*, thank you!

The Conviction **<u>is</u>** affirmed by the Nevada Supreme Court. However, the opinion is <u>laced</u> with criticism of purported RHETORICAL **Prosecutorial Misconduct** by O's Case Prosecutor –– **ME**. Mr. Justice Thunder being joined by an alter ego, the esteemed Justice S.

I show my Father the opinion, highlighting the harsh language. He's the good man who paid my tuition to get me through Law School. The good man who burned the cardinal principles of **<u>work</u>** and **<u>honor</u>** and the **<u>rule</u> of <u>law</u>** into my beans. A man of the soil, but a man of high personal integrity. Dad studiously reads the offensive language. His reaction is outrage. He **<u>can't</u>** understand the factual basis for the Court's criticism. He asks a rather pertinent question, "WHY are you being *rebuked* for doing your job? I don't understand this. These men are Judges? Where is their sense of Judgment? They've turned the world upside down. You should be praised not faulted."

The Supreme's <u>crusade</u>, against what they're *choosing* to call **Misconduct**, continues unabated. And of course, it's not just me! Other Prosecutors in all parts of the State come under the microscope. They're also criticized for their unique versions of RHETORICAL **Prosecutorial Misconduct**. Strangely, the spotlight From On High just singles out Prosecutors. It's as though PROSECUTORS are the only ones in the Adversary System pushing the *rhetoric* envelope. That's a trifle one sided, isn't it?

There's a saying in the Court Arena, "Lawyers <u>earn</u> their *living* by the **sweat of their tongues**, and THEY don't mind hard work." That's **Lawyers** in the plural. Well, DEFENSE **Counsel** Gentleman are LAWYERS <u>TOO</u>! They <u>don't</u> ever SAY things that **are** SLICK and SELF SERVING and OVER THE TOP? Yeah right, and milk cows **don't** poop neither.

The Supreme Court decides to appoint A COMMITTEE to explore the <u>vast</u>, Court-conceived parameters of RHETORICAL **Prosecutorial Misconduct**, and to come up with formal proposals for **curtailing** the demonic practice. Supreme Court Justice Y is selected to chair the august group. Other <u>notables</u> are picked from around the State. I'm one of those anointed for service on the COMMITTEE. Undoubtedly, chosen in the hope that membership on the COMMITTEE will have a *chilling effect* on the fervor of my Courtroom **summations**.

Listen, I served. But I was *NEVER* willing to be a COMMITTEE **stooge**. A PROSECUTOR'S **oath** is to JUSTICE. <u>Not</u> to myopic, Monday-morning-quarter- backing Appellate Judges, who **often** don't have a <u>clue</u> regarding the **pressures** and **pitfalls** and **priorities** of TRIAL PRACTICE! Judges who *choose* to elevate arbitrary, ill advised, *court-made* RULES OF RHETORIC **beyond** the bed-rock TRIAL VALUES of determining **TRUTH** and obtaining **JUSTICE**!

Now, my intention is **not** to **paint** ALL Appellate Judges with the same broad brush of criticism. <u>Most</u> Judges, at every tier of the Criminal Justice System, are astute, fair-minded, truth-seeking, justice-driven professionals. **BUT** there have been **exceptions**. I speak of them!

In the classic Man of La Mancha novel, Don Quixote embarks on a knight-errant quest in search of adventure. He dons an old suit of armor, selects a peasant named Sancho Panza as his squire, designates a farm girl as his ladylove, mounts a skinny, broken-down steed, and begins his quest by foolishly **attacking <u>windmills</u>** he believes are FEROCIOUS GIANTS. (Cervantes, *The Ingenious Hilalgo Don Quixote of La Mancha*)

RHETORICAL **misconduct** is a <u>specious</u> issue. It's *Judicial tilting*. The **act** of **attacking** an opponent or a mark or — a **<u>windmill</u>** for exercise or sport, or for *tinkering* with Prosecutorial SUMMATION. There are plenty of legitimate issues in Trial work without making up *imaginary* MONSTERS or BOGEYMEN.

So-called, **Rhetorical misconduct** is a palpably nonsensical creation of the Judiciary, for the most part. SUMMATION represents an **integral** feature of Trial Practice. Attempting to **strap** a wide-ranging **set** of one-size-fits-all guidelines around Prosecutorial *tongues* is counterproductive and impracticable. **Bridling** Prosecutorial *tongues*, while essential giving Defense Counsel a **free rein**, *carte blanche* green light to SAY whatever, runs a clear **risk** of upsetting argumentative BALANCE in the Adversarial System.

WHY are we emasculating the ARGUMENT of those who bear the **burden of proof**? Those Public Servants who must overcome the PRESUMPTION OF INNOCENCE and **prove their cases beyond a reasonable doubt**. I'm **not** against these venerable principles, I believe them with all my heart! I'm simply wondering WHY we're hamstringing the guys who represent the People? WHY malign what is benign? WHY penalize good preparation – good syntax – eloquence – **passion** – COMMITMENT? AREN'T Prosecutors supposed to be presenting **thoughtful**, **rousing**, **emotional**, **persuasive** ARGUMENTS as they *explain* the gravity of charges and the strength of their evidence? WHERE is *respect* for the dedication and special skills of a Professional Prosecutor?

Yet, some Judges persist in raising the chant of RHETORICAL **misconduct** ad nauseam. Whoa! **Words**, uttered before the Trial Judge and opposing Counsel during Closing Argument, are RARELY **big** producers of the type of substantive **misconduct** that FRACTURES the Criminal Justice System – by any reasonably objective standard. I'm sticking to the position I've previously articulated. **The misconduct** that truly SUBVERTS the system *is* perpetrated by **acts-of-stealth**. To say otherwise is to symbolically suggest that *little problems* like piss ants should be smashed with *big objects* like anvils. It **elevates** form over substance!

For example: A grisly discovery occurs on a cool March morning at **7:40**. It is ground zero for another victim of mindless terrorism. A Coca Cola salesman finds the body of a young woman laying on a cement pad behind Caesar's Palace. The woman is on her back. The only garments she wears are a blue gas station smock, a brown blouse, and a bra. Otherwise, her bloody body is nude. Her breasts are exposed. The bra has been torn apart between the cups. The blouse and smock have been pulled open. They simply cover her upper arms. Two dented, metal soft drink canisters are nearby. Each is stained with a blood-like substance.

An autopsy is performed at the Clark County Morgue at **3:45 p.m.**

The cause of death is multiple blunt-force trauma to the woman's head and face, manual strangulation, and aspiration of blood into her lungs. Death has been brutally violent and dreadfully agonizing.

The woman has multiple lacerations and contusions of the scalp and face. A left basal skull fracture. Multiple facial fractures and a fractured mandible. Which is the horseshoe-shaped bone forming the lower jaw. There is multiple hemorrhage in the soft tissue of the neck. Submucosal hemorrhage of the larynx, and multiple defensive contusions on both hands.

Hank is arrested for the Crime. <u>Connecting</u> CIRCUMSTANTIAL **evidence** is overwhelming. The accused exacerbates his plight by <u>shooting off</u> his mouth in the Clark County Detention Center.

A cell mate relates, "He asked me for a cigarette. He seemed dazed... He couldn't believe he...got arrested...He couldn't understand HOW. He said he...got her to come out of the booth by telling her he had some good weed and to come look at it. He said he should have robbed the place to alibi his story. He said he held her down by using a sticker, an icepick knife...He said she was pleading with him. 'Please let me go. Just let me go and I won't tell anybody.' He said HE COULDN'T LET HER GO...He didn't want to go to jail...He said *she **was** a beautiful girl. **He preferred white girls** BECAUSE <u>when</u> you get into one **she's in *your* pocket**...He said he had someone who was going to vouch for him. He said he went to his apartment, took his clothes off, and disposed of them behind the Sahara Hotel."

WHY am I abruptly discussing the **horrendous murder** of a beautiful young woman? It's SIMPLE – *really*! The referenced CASE graphically demonstrates the **irrationality** and **impracticability** and **irresponsibility** of *Judicial tilting*. The **Act** of TIPPING the scales of Justice toward the Defense. The RESTRAINT of Prosecutorial Rhetoric, predicated upon an *erroneous* Judicial premise that Prosecutive TONGUES **must** be *tamed*, in order to save Trial Jurors from *biased* Verdicts. Actually, the **premise** is *illusory* and the **perception** of PROSECUTORIAL **misconduct** is often *delusional*.

Defendant Hank is convicted of **Murder in the First Degree**. The Verdict is affirmed by the State Supreme Court on Direct Appeal. However, Mr. Justice Thunder, *knight-errant* in a <u>business</u> suit, is still promoting his quixotic agenda. His words are full of righteous indignation. Once again, PUBLICLY chastising the miscreant Prosecutor for his unprofessional **misconduct**. SOUNDS **serious**, huh?.

Well, what is the *dastardly* RHETORICAL **misfire** that has Mr. Justice Thunder bent out of shape? Brace yourselves. This is a biggie! The intrepid Deputy DA has **told the Jury** in his REBUTTAL ARGUMENT, pausing for drum roll, that ———— Defendant Hank, a **black** man, said he *"preferred white girls* BECAUSE <u>when</u> you get into one *she's in your pocket...*" That's it!

Hey, wait a minute. Is that <u>really</u> all there is? The Prosecutor is simply arguing EVIDENCE of **motive**. EVIDENCE that is clearly *IN THE RECORD*!

Mr. Justice Thunder **is** SAYING, in effect, that a Prosecutor **can't** argue relevant EVIDENCE of **motive** clearly *IN THE RECORD* because of some **unrecognized**, <u>illegitimate</u> legal doctrine of POLITICAL CORRECTNESS? Unbelievable, Sir!

That's a blast of dirty dog breath.

WHEN a Justice of the State Supreme Court tells a Prosecutor it's **improper** to ARGUE **evidence of motive** that's in the Trial Record, **HE'S** *OUT OF LINE*. Indulging in a *heavy handed* batch of Judicial Censorship! Extraneously meddling in the administration of Justice.

So, there we have it. PROOF of the **irrationality** and **impracticability** and **irresponsibility** of *Judicial tilting*. PROOF of **TIPPING** the scales of Justice toward the Defense. PROOF of the attempted **RESTRAINT** of Prosecutorial Rhetoric, predicated upon an *erroneous* Judicial premise that Prosecutive TONGUES **must** be *tamed*, in order to save Trial Jurors from *biased* Verdicts. PROOF that the **premise** is *illusory* and the **perception** of PROSECUTORIAL **misconduct** is often *delusional*.

I take swinging-from-the-hip Judicial improvisation very seriously. It's NOT a small matter to improvidently TIE THE TONGUES of Prosecutors in **Closing Argument**. Those who do it are *guilty* of JUDICIAL MISCONDUCT. They are striking *foul* blows at the very heart of the ADVERSARY SYSTEM.

I'd like to think my **Closing Arguments** have been cerebral and abdominal. Originating in my head and in my gut. Generally, an effective blend of facts, logic, eloquence, passion, and gut-speak. A Prosecutor is in HIS GLORY during SUMMATION. This, to a debater, is what makes the Profession so amazing – so unbelievably rewarding.

"All great truths begin as blasphemies." (Annajanska – 1919) Blasphemous, let us say, to disbelievers. This is the **Creed** of A Professional Prosecutor:

HE BELIEVES in the importance of his **calling**. He UNDERSTANDS he 's a SERVANT of the People. **HE BELIEVES** it's an **honor** to serve, and that *being* a PROSECUTOR is the **greatest** job in the World.

HE BELIEVES in the importance of **preparation**. There is NO substitute for diligent, thorough **preparation**. The SUCCESSFUL Prosecutor is a **well prepared** Prosecutor.

HE BELIEVES in the **Adversary** System. **HE** BELIEVES in the **legal** Presumption of Innocence. He UNDERSTANDS the importance of a Defendant's **Right to Counsel. HE** BELIEVES in treating **The Court** and **Defense Counsel** respectfully. **HE** BELIEVES a PROSECUTOR'S highest duty is the role of **dynamic advocate for justice**! HE BELIEVES in being a **seeker after truth**. There is **no** JUSTICE **without** TRUTH!

HE BELIEVES in the **Jury** System. **HE** BELIEVES when a conscientious Jury, representing a cross section of the Community retires to consider a Case, their DELIBERATIVE **process** represents the **FINEST HOUR** in American Jurisprudence.

HE BELIEVES in the **power** of Summation, particularly, the *inestimable* **value** of objective, analytical, passionate Rebuttal Argument. **HE** BELIEVES in fully employing *the sweat of his tongue*. **HE** BELIEVES in striking *hard* **verbal blows**, but not *foul* ones. **HE** DOES NOT BELIEVE in rhetorical hyperbole. He doesn't *exaggerate*. He doesn't fill in **evidentiary gaps** with non-existent, wistful-thinking evidence. He doesn't draw unreasonable inference. He doesn't stretch the truth. He sticks to the facts. The inimitable words of Dragnet's Joe Friday are pertinent: "Just the facts, Mam. Nothing but the facts."

"**Facts** are **stubborn** *things*." (Alain Rene' Le Sage, *Gil Blas* [1715-1735] Book X, Chap.1)

THE ARROGANCE OF LUST

"Many foxes grow grey, but few grow good."
(Benjamin Franklin, *Poor Richard's Almanack*, 1749)

Chapter 5

Rape is a crime of lust, arrogance, and opportunity. A one-on-one power play. **He** does it because **he** *can*. This one starts out as a surreptitious, night-time, Residential Burglary. *Initially* involving an <u>intent</u> to ransack a house and commit larceny. K is prowling solo. He pries a sliding glass patio door open, and slips cautiously *inside* the premises. The developing situation is a NIGHTMARISH, **worst** possible scenario for ANYONE sleeping soundly in blissful oblivion.

The **crimes** of Rape and Burglary share *two* <u>common</u> elements. **Both** involve **non-consensual** ENTRY, and <u>each</u> **crime** is complete the *moment* involuntary entry is achieved. Accordingly, once K steps across the threshold into the house with an <u>intent</u> to steal he's GUILTY of Residential Burglary.

The interior darkness of the house is only diminished by small, strategically placed night lights. The Burglar does **not** know, at the time of entry, if the house is occupied. **He's** a *risk-taker*. Someone <u>seizing</u> opportunities circumstance offers. **A night stalker** *searching* for <u>property</u> and <u>prey</u>. He's brought a pen *light* and some *insurance*. Instruments for illumination, self defense, and intimidation. K has a KNIFE. An evil man <u>makes</u> the circumstances.

He stealthily begins to explore the house. Flashing the pen *light* as he goes. Methodically reconnoitering from room to room. He's interested in occupancy and valuables. **He** finds **Her** in the master bedroom. **She** lives alone, and She's quietly *sleeping* <u>alone</u> tonight. Brazenly, He shines the *light* on her demure countenance. Listening attentively to the rhythmic sound of her breathing. A Sleeping Beauty – available, vulnerable, and desirable.

"A woman, of her gentle sex –– The seeming paragon;
To whom the better elements And kindly stars have given
A form so fair, that, like the air,'Tis less than earth than heaven."
(Edward Coote Pinkney, *A Health* [1825], Stanza 1)

Immediately, **He** experiences a strong urge to *have Her* – to touch **Her** and explore **Her** and to *penetrate* **Her**. Why not? He has the wherewithal. Yet, K is – <u>foremost</u>, a **thief** of chattel. Stealing is his livelihood. **Taking** the woman is secondary. <u>After</u> he's completed the business of *larceny*, he'll attend to the urgent demands of *LUST* – circumstances permitting.

He locates a linen closet, and removes several pillow cases. He'll use them to carry the booty. His callous collection of stolen largesse begins. He's rifling drawers in a storage room when J awakens.

She's unable to identify the specific cause for **her** concern. A *slight* noise in the darkness, perhaps? A *flash* of light? A *furtive* movement? An *instinctive* perception of <u>danger</u>? An *inner* prompting? A *bad* dream? But <u>suddenly</u>, she's wide eyed and fearful. Filled with foreboding. *Sensing* there's a hostile presence.

She gets up. Puts a robe on, and *listens* – NOTHING. Apprehensively, She passes into the hallway. Several steps later **she** *sees* it. The faint *beam* of a pen light. The one with <u>form so fair</u> has spunk. She has a baseball bat under her bed. Retracing her steps, she retrieves the bat, and <u>storms</u> into the storage room.

Not good. K seems to have eyes in the back of his head. He spins around, menacingly gripping the knife in his right hand. His words are peremptory and succinct, "Drop the bat, Bitch, or I'll slice your pretty face into mincemeat."

J ignores the injunction. She takes a roundhouse swing at his head – and misses. He wards off the blow and tackles her. The <u>two</u> fall in a heap to the floor. She's no match for him now. He pins her beneath him, wrests the bat away, and presses the knife against J's soft neck. A *fox* grows grey not good. (Franklin, ibid.)

Her aggression tweaks a nerve. She's tried to knock his block off. His priorities <u>change</u> in a heart-beat. *Larceny* is put on hold, the arrogance of *LUST* holds sway. **His** knife, **His** threats, and **His** brute strength are powerful persuaders. There is **no** further resistance. **She** silently submits to RAPE. It happens on the storage room floor. **He** does it because **he** *can*, because he's *aroused*, and because he's *angry*. BUT what he takes is **not** freely given.

K sates his sexual energy. Allowing J to get up, conditioned upon her continued docility. Afraid of being *stuck* by the knife, she agrees. She's <u>told</u> to stay next to him as he moves throughout the residence, continuing to plunder her belongings. He fills the commandeered pillow cases with foodstuff, appliances, jewelry, and miscellaneous items. Rummages through her purse. Removing ID, credits cards, a *twenty* dollar bill and change.

Then – he bids her adieu. But <u>not</u> before *reminding* J, **He** KNOWS where **She** lives and where she works. He <u>has</u> her telephone numbers and personal ID. He can come back just as easily as came. Moreover, she's *admonished* to keep her trap shut. "<u>Don't</u> tell the Cops anything. This is **Our** little secret – otherwise." The OTHERWISE **isn't** delineated. It **doesn't** have to be. She gets the drift!

Four nights later J gets a call. Oh, the *unadulterated* **arrogance** of *LUST*, and the *addle headed* **arrogance** of some character's far-out *MACHISMO*. This guy's so pumped by his rakish, Lothario-like lovemaking, He CALLS his *victim* for a DATE. Never mind that he's broken into her house as she *sleeps*, that he's terrorized and VIOLATED **Her** – **stealing** a lay and other valuables. This thieving philanderer CALLS for a DATE. Is this the <u>height</u> of shameless insolence, OR WHAT? Well, Mr. Infatuated-with-himself has pushed the bar <u>too</u> high.

She's non-committal about the DATE, and <u>very</u> frightened. Surprise! The Lady, who hasn't *yet* brought the Police into the matter, **does so** NOW! Be a jerk-off at your peril, Mr. STALKER.

Detective Dave tells her to make **the date** *if* K calls back. Police will have her house under surveillance, and they'll slap the cuffs on him as he arrives. Stay tuned. The RAPIST **is** *brazenly* persistent. K *does* call a <u>second</u> time for a DATE. The man is flat-out conceited and, shall we say, totally out-of-touch with reality. But *twice* is the charm. **She** accepts.

She tells him she'll be WAITING in the room where they met. Expectantly. She <u>doesn't</u> tell him the Coppers will be WAITING with **Her**. HELLO, *Stud*!

Hey, the *raper-dater* thing is going pretty smooth, huh? Maybe a little TOO smooth. K will mull this arrangement over. **He'll** realize what's <u>too</u>

good to be true probably **isn't** true. "The path is smooth that leadeth on to danger." (Shakespeare, *The Taming of the Shrew*) He'll be a NO-SHOW, right? Well, –– **NO**. This Laddie's brains must be in **his** nuts. **He-does-show-up**!

He drives by and parks. Detective Dave **makes** him, which is to say, he sees him well enough to be able to **identify** him. However, there's a slight hitch in the dragnet. Ironically, as K is walking toward J's house, a marked patrol car unrelated to the surveillance comes down the street. It's *really* bad timing! K is spooked. He runs in the opposite direction. Two and a half hours later, he's apprehended three blocks away in an Apartment House. WELCOME to the Criminal Justice System, *Mr. Rape-and-date*.

The Case works its way through the system. A Preliminary Hearing is held. K is bound over for Trial on Counts of **Burglary** and **Sexual Assault with use of a deadly weapon**. The Trial date arrives and we pick **the** JURY – those *twelve tried and true*. Well actually, that's most of the time.

There is no more *important* **nor** *unpredictable* stage to any Trial than the Jury Selection event! Life is FULL of choices. The selection process is an integral *fact* of daily living. Parents select names for their children. High School students select prom dates. High School seniors select colleges. Collegians select their majors. Coaches select members of their teams. People select their careers, their friends, their marital partners, their religious preference, their banks, their insurance companies –– where they shop, the books they read, vacation sites, the movies they see, etcetera!

Trial Lawyers **don't** get to select their Trial Judges, although they *wish* they could. One Courthouse wag opined – with tongue in cheek: "If I were asked what point I'd best like to have in my favor I'd say, **a deaf judge**. Or if not that, **ONE** regularly tired out." (Anthony Trollope, *Orley Farm* – emphasis added)

Judges are assigned to Cases by a system of random selection. So, Barristers don't get to choose Judges who are *deaf* or *regularly tired out*. But Trial Lawyers DO get to select their Jurors, and **no** one who has tried many Cases will minimize the significance of the **Jury Selection** procedure. Every *insightful* Practitioner in the Courtroom battlefield will express the opinion that **Jury Selection** is the *most* crucial phase of a Trial.

IF a Jury is impaneled, which *favorably* views the position of a particular party, that side is in a good position to win. Conversely, when the majority of Jurors are *unfavorably* disposed against a party, tons of evidence and oodles of rhetoric **won't** make an appreciable difference in the decision. The die is *cast* from the get-go, and the evidence and the eloquence will likely fall on *deaf* ears. There are times when a Trial Lawyer may feel comfortable with a *deaf* Judge, but he sure as hell **doesn't** ever want a DEAF Jury.

The KEY to winning is being **astute** and **lucky** during the Jury Selection process. Both sides recognize IF you don't *win* early in the Selection sweepstakes, you'll *probably* **lose** later. A PROSECUTOR looks for Jurors who possess a strong sense of responsibility to their community and are strongly predisposed to require *personal* **accountability** of Defendants who have been PROVEN guilty beyond a reasonable doubt.

A Prosecutor *wants* Jurors who *want* to serve. Persons who *believe* it's an **honor** and a **duty** to serve their community in the Jury Box. Jurors who will devote their *full* attention to the proceedings when the Court is in session. Jurors who will **base** their decisions *solely* upon the **evidence** introduced at Trial by the respective Parties and the **law** of the Case as provided by the Court. Persons who will **not** allow public opinion or media publicity or personal trepidation to influence their Verdicts. Jurors who will be as diligent and as analytical and as objective as it is *possible* for them to be *until* their service has ended. Persons who can leave the Courthouse with heads held high and with clear conscience and without regret because they have *done* their very best to achieve **just** results.

THE JURY is the **ultimate variable** in every Trial. THE JURY is the **wild card**. And when a Trial Lawyer gets to the bottom line/to the end of a Trial – **after** Evidence has been received –Legal Instructions given – Summation completed – Case Submitted to the Jury – emotional Argument and agonizing Deliberation in the Jury Room, **NOBODY** on the face of this earth is *actually* able to **predict** with any degree of *mathematical certainty* HOW the **deliberation** of a particular panel of *twelve* Jurors will END. People can make educated guesses. They may be right part of the time – even *lucky* enough to be right most of the time during phases of their careers – BUT **no one** *gazes* into a *crystal ball* that divines the future. NOT Judges, NOT Trial Lawyers, NOT Courthouse Groupies, NOT Reporters, NOT Defendants, NOT Bailiffs or Janitors –– **NOBODY!**

UNTIL the Jury Foreperson formally announces **THE JURY DECISION** in OPEN COURT, *NO ONE KNOWS* **for sure** what it will be. Interested Parties can **read** astrological *charts* or **throw** *darts* or **cast** *lots* or **rely** on Jury Selection *Consultants*, or **whatever**, but **no one** ACTUALLY **knows**!

The frame of mind of those in the Courtroom will *always* be the same at the quintessential moment of **Trial Truth**. When THE JURY RETURNS to announce its VERDICT, **everyone** *will* be sitting on the edge of his seat *wondering* – and *sweating*!

Back to the Case-at-bar. K is charged with **Burglary** and **Sexual Assault with use of a deadly weapon**, and we've picked **the JURY** – those *twelve* **not** so *tried and true* in this Case. Occasionally, the Criminal Justice System becomes a little *flaky*. This is ONE of those times. On this outing, I end up with a Jury that's flat out *flaky*. TRUST ME.

I said a few lines earlier that The KEY to winning is being **astute** and **lucky** during the Jury <u>Selection</u> process. Well, I honest believe I was reasonably **astute**. I certainly <u>knew</u> what I wanted on the Trial Jury. I've just expressed my feelings in some detail, but I need to add a caveat. You see, RAPE is <u>essentially</u> a single gender crime. There are exceptions, of course, but generally speaking –––– it's going to be a **man** *raping* a WOMAN.

Hence, though generalization is often suspect, WOMEN <u>may</u> tend to be somewhat more *empathetic* towards a **Sexual Assault** VICTIM than **MEN**. Accordingly, I'm of the MIND SET that I need a Jury in THIS CASE, pun actually intended, that's *stacked* –– with females. Frankly, I want as many <u>girls</u> on the Jury as I can possibly muster. That's the **astute** part.

Which brings me to the *Lady Luck* factor. Like Coaches, PROSECUTORS need to be **good** and they need to be **LUCKY** to win consistently! I'm **not** very **lucky** this time out. Due to a far ranging cacophony of reasons, *circumstances so arrange themselves* – this is the LUCK part, that the Prosecutor fellow who wants lots of <u>Girls</u> on his Sexual Assault Jury gets NO females. None! Zilch! Nada! What he <u>does</u> get is a Box full of Boys.

As LUCK has it, there is a disparate number of men and women on the prospective Jury Panel. Only **a third** of the Panel are females. During the <u>selection</u> process, persons are called at random to the Jury Box for voir dire. As LUCK still has it, **not** many women are called to the Box. And as LUCK further decrees, of the **few** women summoned to the Box, an <u>inordinate</u> number are either unable or unwilling to serve. Finally, as the LUCKLESS Prosecutor sits helplessly at Counsel Table, the big, bad, **astute** Defense Counselor, uses Peremptory Challenges to excuse those of the female gender who have thus far cheated *Lady Luck*. So, there you have it. **Lucky in Love**. UNLUCKY in Court – this time!

The <u>evidence</u> is presented. Matters go predictably. The *twelve* **GENTLEMAN** of the Jury sit there like bumps on a pickle as witnesses testify and exhibits are offered. Take *look* reasonably entertained.

J testifies. She is beautiful, composed, and articulate. Possibly, a little too *composed* and maybe too *articulate*. Perhaps, the *twelve* **GENTLEMEN** of the Jury are wanting to see tears, tissue being dabbed on blushing cheeks, and meek, trembling hands. But what is a Prosecutor to do? He doesn't get his witnesses out of a mail order catalog. He doesn't go to Central Casting for testimony. He takes his victims as he finds them.

J is a bright woman, a well spoken one, and very easy on the eye. She's –

"A woman, of her gentle sex –– The seeming paragon;
To whom the better elements And kindly stars have given
A form so fair, that, like the air, 'Tis less of earth than heaven."
(Edward Coote Pinkney, ibid.)

I can't resist an ad lib here. It's certainly deplorable that a **gentle** woman <u>may</u> have been taken less seriously by a *Twelve* **GENTLEMEN** Panel <u>because</u> **She** is beautiful, composed and articulate. I'd say, that's some classless **input** on the issue of credibility!

The time for SUMMATION rolls around. I *thought* **Argument** went great. My voice box never felt more muscular. My vocal cords hum on all cylinders – explaining <u>evidence</u> of the Crimes and the applicable <u>Law</u>, proclaiming that the Prosecution has met its **Burden of Proof**, emoting, imploring the Jury, exuding a profusion of *tongue sweat*.

I'm really <u>feeling</u> the *power* of words. While I stand at the Jury Rail for **Rebuttal**, dispatching, what I believe to be, a stirring string of rhetorical zingers, it appears that EVERY Juror **is** visibly nodding his head in affirmation. It seems my work is done!

I <u>tell</u> the *Twelve* **GENTLEMEN** Panel the <u>evidence</u> establishes beyond a reasonable doubt that the DEFENDANT is a RAPIST and a THIEF. Someone who has preyed on an innocent woman in the darkness of night. Breaking into her house as she sleeps, intruding upon her place of privacy, refuge, and safety. VIOLATING the *sanctity* of her **home** and her **body**!

I <u>remind</u> the *Twelve* **GENTLEMEN** Panel they were told in my OPENING STATEMENT that the evidence would **prove** the Defendant's GUILT beyond a reasonable doubt. I <u>remind</u> *The Twelve* that when they were <u>selected</u> as Jurors, they impliedly promised they would FIND the Defendant **guilty** IF **His** GUILT was established beyond a reasonable doubt. I <u>say</u>, "I've **kept** my promise! Now, I'm asking you to **keep** yours."

And sit down. Comfortable with my remarks. Pleased to be a Prosecutor. Believing the Victim is about to be vindicated. Confidently expecting a short deliberation and guilty verdicts. Cognizant still – of my lingering perception that *twelve* heads were *bobbing* in agreement.

Really, it was <u>almost</u> *twelve*. I miscounted. **Only** *eleven* were agreeing with me. Further, there have been a series of pre-trial conversations between the Jury Commissioner's Office and one of the Jurors that are totally off my radar screen. They CHANGE everything. Stacking the deck against the Prosecutor. Upping the ante on PROOF, as in PROOF **to an absolute certainty**. The upshot is this: *Not only* am I dealing with the **wild card** factor that is <u>intrinsic</u> to Juries, I'm also dealing with a Juror who is a **loose cannon**!

Panelist X has a Criminal history. However, his prior felony convictions have been expunged from the record. The Juror Commissioner's Office discovers this anomaly. They confront the prospective Juror, suggesting that the prior Felony Convictions are grounds for disqualification, and they intend to strike his name from Juror rolls.

Panelist X heatedly responds. He says he has a RIGHT to service as a Juror, and vows to litigate the matter if he is denied his right. Moreover, he insists that the expungement information **not** be passed on to the Prosecutor's Office. The Jury Commissioner backs off. Panelist X remains on the Panel and is <u>selected</u> to serve on K's Jury.

Here's the kicker. The Office of the District Attorney <u>routinely</u> checks with the Commissioner's Office for criminal histories of prospective Jurors. Panelist X is among those surveyed. However, The D.A. is **not** advised of the prior felonies expunged. In point of fact, Panelist X has been convicted of *THREE* prior **felonies**. An ominous circumstance that undoubtedly has a definite bearing on his ability to <u>render</u> **equal** and **exact** JUSTICE to <u>both</u> Parties!

So, we have a sleeper cell on the *Twelve* **GENTLEMEN** Panel. A fifth column guy, and the Bird comes to roost on the Prosecutor's shoulder. The arrogance of *LUST* mutates to the arrogance of *DISTRUST* inside the Juror Deliberation Room. The **testimony** of the Victim (DIRECT EVIDENCE of **Rape**) and the <u>testimony</u> of the Police Detective regarding **flight** (CIRCUMSTANTIAL EVIDENCE of **Rape**) become skewed, scorned, and distorted. WHAT *reasonable man* drops by for a DATE and RUNS **like a rabbit** when he sees a police presence? Huh?

Well, it's all water under the bridge now. Jeopardy has attached. The *Twelve* **GENTLEMEN** Panel retires to deliberate. They deliberate for approximately seven hours and return with TWO **Not Guilty** VERDICTS. What the heck?

The Jury **Foreman** is Panelist X. I'm advised by others on the Panel that the FIRST Juror ballot was 11-1 for **conviction**, but eventually Panelist X convinces ALL of the ELEVEN to change their votes to **Not Guilty**.

P.S. The Defendant asserted his Privilege Against Self Incrimination. He did **not** testify. NOTHING on the record **contradicts** the *sworn testimony* of the Victim. The **arrogance** of DISTRUST in the Jury Room follows close on the heels of the **arrogance** of LUST on the storage room floor. In your face, Ms. J! It seems – **gender bias** is alive and well.

I'm going to do something that's contrary to my nature now. Something that goes against the grain, that takes me out on a limb. I'm going to indulge in a bit of *second-guessing* **speculation**.

I KNOW the **evidence** that was presented to this *Twelve* **GENTLEMEN** Panel, and by any **objective standard** – I handled nearly 300 felony Trials during my career, this Case *should* have been a **lead pipe** CINCH. Therefore, I'm going to confidently surmise that the *Twelve* **GENTLEMEN** Panel went outside the record – taking liberties in their analysis. Speculating, excoriating, and saying some flippant and very unflattering things about women in general and J in particular, that THEY–WOULD–NOT–HAVE–DARED–UTTER–IF–**FEMALES**– HAD– BEEN–ON–THE–JURY! This Jury jumped the track.

Sadly, the Criminal Justice System is **far** from perfect. This **isn't** JUSTICE. This is *good ole boys* returning Verdicts **based** on GENDER. **Nor** is the Criminal Justice System being particularly SYSTEMATIC when an ALL MALE Jury is allowed to sit in **Judgement** of a **SEX** CRIME perpetrated by a MAN upon a WOMAN!

Many **foxes** in a pack grow *grey*, but few grow to *good* **judgement**! (Benjamin Franklin, ibid., adapted)

The Arson Home Invasion

"If you break your neck, if you have nothing to eat, if your house is on **fire**, then you got a problem. Everything else is inconvenience." (Robert Fulghum)

Chapter 6

Being a Prosecutor is not without risk. It comes with the nature of the Profession. A diligent Prosecutor *necessarily* <u>does</u> things and <u>says</u> things during the course of Cases that are extremely irksome to Defendants. An Accused is **not** *blind* to what is being done, **nor** does he have a set of *deaf* ears to what is being said. Prosecutors work within the context of an ADVERSARY system – i.e., The State of Nevada vs.John [or Jane] Doe. The Prosecution versus the Defense. Once a Criminal Case is approved for Prosecution, everything a Deputy DA does <u>is</u> **detrimental** to the efforts of Defendants and their Counsel to obtain Verdicts of Acquittal. The Process entails a considerable amount of **explicit** FINGER POINTING! And some Defendants have very long *memories*.

Consequently, a Prosecutor can pick up some interesting labels during his career. I'm a rather unpretentious, mild mannered sort of guy. Not the type of fellow who'd normally be a candidate for looney-house monikers, but it happened. In my case, largely because of my association with the Major Violator's Unit. Those who worked this detail quickly developed reputations of being hard nosed, prosecutorial fanatics. I'll explain.

The Major Violator's Unit arm of the Clark County District Attorney's Office begins as a two year, federally funded pilot program. Clark County is one of approximately twenty three jurisdictions selected to participate in the program. The primary aim being **reduction** of the Criminal RECIDIVISM rate in the United States. The *means* to be employed, for achieving this end, involves a drastic **reduction** in PLEA BARGAINING with respect to **repeat offenders**.

Basically, we have a ZERO **tolerance** policy for plea bargaining. **We- don't -do-it**! The **MVU** TARGET Crimes are **Residential** BURGLARY, **Armed** ROBBERY, **First Degree** KIDNAPING, **Sexual Assault**, and **Open** MURDER. If **MVU** CASES consist of multiple counts, the Prosecutorial approach is a no-holds-barred, hard ass formula, to-wit: PLEAD straight up to ALL Counts and we RESERVE the right to **argue** for MAXIMUM **punishment** at sentencing. Otherwise, brace yourselves, Defense Buddies. We're going to Trial!

The strategy takes the Defense Bar by surprise, but they think it will be all bark and no bite. Merely politics. Public posturing for media exposure. Yet at the end of the day, a transient phenomenon that **will** pass with the changing of the season. However, the Defense Bar has **misjudged** the *resolve* and the Law and Order *values* of the MVU Chief and his Deputies. THEIR Prosecutorial style has nothing to do with politics. It is grounded in public service.

ENTER: No nonsense, I've been around the horn a few times, I can plea- bargain any Case on the Planet, Defense Counselor **Ted**. He has a client whose in a heap of trouble. **He should be!** His VICTIM is a twelve year old girl.

The Mother of the Victim and a juvenile son is part of an ad hoc outreach program that encourages correspondence with Prison inmates. A humanitarian gesture that seeks to assists incarcerated felons in enhancing their self esteem and societal skills to the extent they can be reintegrated into mainstream life. A noble objective to be sure, but a quest that must be realistic and cautious!

Mom begins to correspond with a number of incarcerated felons, ostensibly with the blessing of her Husband. She writes letters to the inmates and they write to her. Describing their offenses, their aspirations, and their rehabilitative efforts. It's heady stuff. Over a several month period of *postal chitchat*, Mom bonds with one inmate in particular. I'll call him **Jesse**. He's soon eligible for Parole.

So Mom says, "Wonderful. Great. Good deal Brother. Best of Luck on the outside. It's been nice corresponding with you. Have a happy life –– **Goodbye**."

EXCUSE ME, that's what Mom should have said. Noooooooooo, she doesn't bring closure to her **inmate** outreach. Incredibly, Mom *invites* **parolee** Jesse to come to Las Vegas and LIVE with <u>her</u> family.

I know. You're saying, "Stop the crap, Harmon. You lame Writer wanna-be. No Mother would do that. Quit being melodramatic. Because what you just <u>said</u> **she said** would be freaking ridiculous. Naivete to the **max**! An open invitation for the ugly specter of dire consequence to enter her dwelling place. Like throwing the front door wide open to tragedy. Tell us what she <u>really</u> said! Okay?"

And I have to say, I-don't-know-what-she-**really**-said. I didn't read any of her letters, she didn't tell me what she said, and I'm not privy to mind reading. But **regardless** of what she *actually* said, Jesse is going to read her *words* through his skewed, institutionalized, parolee lenses and the jist of **his** interpretation will be: A <u>married</u> Mother of two juveniles is telling me she's had a *brainstorm*. I can use <u>her</u> residence as my *half-way house*. After my release, I can go LIVE with her and her family. Hey, she's got a thing for me. She <u>wants</u> to know me *better*. She wants to be a <u>very</u> special *friend*. I don't know where her old man fits into all this, but the Chick is going to cut me a lot of slack. She's giving me a *fresh* start. I'll be living in the <u>same</u> house with a twelve year old *GIRL* and her little **brother**. Sweet! They'll be like *siblings* to me. I'll get *close* to her. I'm going to like this *setup*. A day of rare opportunity is coming my way!

So, that's the context. This is the <u>point</u> of my dissertation about a parental *faux pas* and a paroled felon's **sinister** way of <u>expressing</u> <u>appreciation</u> for *family kindness*. Jesse does come to live with his **pen pal** and her family. They *open* their *doors* to a **<u>three</u> <u>timer</u>**. And he <u>repays</u> them by becoming a **FOUR <u>timer</u>**!

I guess Jesse believes in rough-housing *siblings* – <u>hard</u> <u>love</u>. Perhaps, three months after his arrival at the improvisatorial, family *half-way house*, he commits **acts** that are a radical departure from house rules. It's a nighttime offensive. Perpetrated in the bedroom of the *twelve year old*, as others in the residence are sleeping.

He begins to engage in certain *intimacies* that are rebuffed by her. This guy has an active libido, and a short fuse. He becomes enraged. Charges out of the room, *steals* money and valuables, goes to the kitchen, finds a BUTCHER <u>knife</u>, returns to the adolescent, STABS her in the upper left chest a little below her neck, runs out of the house, and **flees** into the night. He has a *bizarre* way of <u>saying</u> **thanks** for a family's effort on behalf of his rehabilitation.

The Victim stumbles from her room and alerts her brother. He summons their parents. A call is placed to 911, police and medics arrive, and she is rushed to the hospital. The *twelve year old* is fortunate. The stabbing wound <u>narrowly</u> misses a major artery, and over time, she completely recovers from the attack.

The reprobate who has chosen to **bite** the hands that feed, and **savagely assault** his "little sister," is apprehended within a week, and provided new digs in the Clark County Detention Center. Investigators of the Las Vegas Metropolitan Police Department complete their investigation, and submit a formal request for the filing of Criminal Charges to the County Prosecutor. The submission is reviewed by the Case Screening Department of the DA's Office, and volatile Jesse is charged with three felonies stemming from his **malicious actions** at his de facto *half-way house*. The Charges constitute three separate counts. They are: **Attempted Murder with use of a deadly weapon**, **Lewdness with a Minor**, and **Grand Larceny**.

The indigent status of Defendant Jesse qualifies him for Court appointed representation. The Barrister assigned to his Case is the previously documented Defense Counselor **Ted** – Mr. No nonsense, I've been around the horn a few times, I can plea-bargain any Case on the Planet **Ted**.

Defendant Jesse is a *RECIDIVIST*. His **priors**, coupled with the **nature** of his current charges, satisfy the Major Violator's Unit *case criteria*. Therefore, he becomes part of the MVU stable. It's a **mixed bag** for the child molester. On the one hand he gets the <u>experienced</u> Counselor **Ted** at <u>public</u> expense, a Lawyer who has a **knack** at *bargain basement* plea bargain deals for his clients, and on the other hand he gets the *hard ass* Chief of **MVU** at <u>public</u> expense, a Lawyer who has **kicked the habit** of plea bargain deals as a matter of Unit Policy. **Ole** Plead 'em straight up and we'll reserve the <u>Right</u> to argue for maximum punishment – Deputy **Mel**.

Defense Counselor **Ted** wants to streamline his Trial Docket, if possible. His Secretary calls. An appointment is made for him to see me about Jesse's Case. We meet a few days later for about fifteen minutes. Really, there **isn't** much to talk about. **Ted** wants a *deal* and **MVU** <u>doesn't</u> make *deals*.

He makes his pitch. He mitigates, excuses, rationalizes, and lays a sob story on me about his Client needing and never receiving love. It may all have been true, but it **isn't** pertinent to our meeting. **MVU** <u>doesn't</u> make *pre-trial deals*. If his Client wants to present these points, that's certainly his right. But don't make them to me. Go to Trial and make them to a Jury. Needless to say, Counselor **Ted** ISN'T pleased with the Trial option.

He argues that the DA's Office has **stacked** charges against his Client. He claims it's foolish to pursue all three Counts. Contending justice will be served by conviction to a **single** Offense. I tell him I disagree. However, he's certainly at liberty to go OVER my head during **argument** at Trial.

Still, Defense Counselor **Ted** is adamant. Convinced he can *plea-bargain* any Criminal Case on the Planet. He tells me we need to save the Court time and the money on this one. He says he'll plead his Client to **Battery with a Deadly Weapon**, IF the State will dismiss the Counts alleging **Lewdness with a Minor** and **Grand Larceny** – and stand *silent* at Sentencing.

Besides, Counselor **Ted** reasons, a plea-bargain will spare our *twelve year old* the emotional trauma of testifying. Intriguing, **Counselor.** This must be nice to the little lady who has been stabbed week. I'm always amazed that the Defense becomes sooooo **protective** of the Victim THEIR Client has physically and emotionally traumatized whenever they're trying to plead out a Case.

I cut to the chase. Firmly and politely responding –with tongue in cheek, "Since the Defense has so much *empathy* for the Victim, I'm going to **grant** your *wish*. This is the DEAL, **Ted**. It's a very straightforward **way** to keep the Victim off the Witness Stand. **Plead** your Client **straight up** to ALL three Counts in the Criminal Complaint, and we'll **reserve** the right to argue.

"IF we have to go to Trial, we're going to convict your Client of ALL three Counts and have the Court sentence him as a **Habitual Criminal**. It's your call!"

Defense Counselor **Ted** gets up in a slight huff, tells me he'll talk with his Client, and give me a call. A week later I receive his call. He says his Client is going to make me earn my money. He'll see me at the Preliminary Hearing. I've left him no choice. The intractable policy of MVU is regrettable. Eventually, the Matter will have to be resolved at Trial.

Several weeks later a Jailhouse Informant reports to a Corrections Officer that Defendant Jesse tells him: "When my Attorney came back from his meeting with the District Attorney's Office he said '**Harmon is a madman. I can't reason with the guy.**'" Such inmate scuttlebutt isn't likely to cause a groundswell of popularity in the Clark County Detention Center for Deputy Mel, but it probably does create a measure of mystique.

We did go to Trial. The Defendant is convicted on ALL CHARGES and is sentenced pursuant to the **Habitual** Criminal Act. Insiders <u>call</u> the Section that contains the sentencing formula for a **Major** HABITUAL Offender –– the "*BIG BITCH*." The Court lowers the boom on Defendant Jesse. He receives **consecutive** Sentences of LIFE WITHOUT PAROLE on ALL three Counts.

At least Counselor **Ted** used my name. I had a handle in Junior College that was a *parody* of my name. The oft repeated routine went something like this: "Hey **Hormone**, do you know how to make a *whore moan*? Now is that a fair question? How would a simple sod buster straight off the farm know anything about such a biochemical term? Let alone, a screeching alley cat from a **red light** district called a *whoremoan*?

I looked the terms up in my Dictionary. The Dictionary calls, "**Hormone** – a <u>regulatory</u> substance produced in an organism and transported in tissue fluids such as blood or sap to <u>stimulate</u> cells or tissues into action..." (emphasis added) I'd say that's proof enough I'm **not** a *hormone*. I'm irregular and un-stimulated. My middle initial is T. Those who knew me well used to say the T stood for *turtle*. Not surprisingly, the Dictionary didn't have anything to say about a creature called a *whoremoan*. Whorehouse, whoremonger, and whore – yes, but not a single *whoremoan*. That's strange, because these small town lads who used to taunt me <u>seemed</u> to know all about them!

My plea of ignorance was precisely the same with each teasing query, as is the punch line. I'm an easy mark."Hey **Hormone**, do you know how to make a *whore moan*?" [pause for effect] "No, I don't. But it seems like something worth knowing. How do **you** make a *whore moan*?" [pause for greater effect] "<u>Don't</u> **pay** <u>her</u>." Followed by peals of raucous laughter.

That's what I'm saying. My salacious pals with the coarse sense of humor seemed to know all about *moaning whores*. Of course, the farm kid had a tad more sophistication than he acknowledged, and the smarts to figure out the punch line after the first fifteen times or so. But I continued to play dumb – to the delight of my hecklers. Frankly, I've **always** believed in getting along with people!

However, I became a **Prosecutor**, and he's **not** able to please everybody. We moved to Las Vegas on January 21, 1968. Lived for the first year in an apartment, resided in a small home we purchased in north town for four and a half years, and then bought a house in *Paradise*. We lived there for twenty five years.

It's <u>great</u> living in *Paradise* – most of the time. Through the years as we made new acquaintances, I liked to playfully brag about the domicile angle. I'd ask where they lived, and they'd say Plano, Texas or Rock Springs, Wyoming or Barstow, California or wherever. Then I'd bide my time until I sensed I'd get the biggest jaw-dropping payoff, and say in a matter of fact way: "We live in Paradise." The reaction was always about the same. My announcement is greeted with considerable good natured incredulity.

"You're kidding. That's funny. Where do you actually live?" And mustering my best dead-pan expression, I'd say again – with emphasis: "No, <u>it's</u> **true**. We– live–in–Paradise!" Allowing such an unlikely scenario to float for a few seconds, before adding: "A fact that may seem a bit paradoxical to the uninitiated, since *Paradise* is **<u>in</u>** Sin City – Las Vegas, Nevada. –– Well to clarify, I'm **not** speaking of that destination of blessed souls in the hereafter, I'm talking about **Paradise <u>Township</u>**. It's just east of the south end of the Las Vegas Strip. So come and see us sometime. It's a *great* place to live – if you can <u>stand</u> the **heat**!"

PARADISE certainly got too **hot** in early summer – less than a year after we'd moved there. I realize this will sound a little odd, but even inhabitants of *Paradise* take vacation trips occasionally. We took a trip to the Gulf States, where there's too much summer <u>humidity</u> for the environment to be very paradisaic. My wife is from Louisiana, and she's quite anxious to visit with extended family and childhood friends. So, we load up the family car, pin our ears back, chug away from **Paradise**, and head to the Southeast.

The trip is glorious. The *camaraderie* with family and friends; the *scenery* – rivers and bayous, pine forests and pelting rainstorms, a sea of green in every direction with mowed medians and road shoulders – from freeways to country roads; the *food* – from down-home roast beef, mashed potatoes, and fried chicken, to catfish, hickory smoked barbeque, slaw, hush puppies, pinto beans, and green tomato relish – and Louisiana hot sauce seasoned Cajun cuisine; the *culture* – the presence of hundreds of impressive Churches throughout cities and towns of the so-called Bible Belt, evangelical revival meetings and fiery sermons, alligators, armadillos, fire flies, and dozens of other creatures, the Southern hospitality and charm, the friendliness and soft Southern accent, and the good ole boy country conservatism; combine to offer many <u>sharp</u> contrasts to life in the Silver State.

The thing of it is – vacations end. Though in retrospect, I'm thinking this one lasted <u>one</u> day too long. Then again, perhaps it's <u>best</u> we were gone. We traveled from Albuquerque to Las Vegas on the sixteenth day. A long jaunt at the tail end, and guaranteed to put us in *Paradise* pretty late.

We pull into the cul-de-sac around 12:30 a.m. Neighbors are milling around in the street. My initial comment suggests they must be having a party. WRONG! A couple of home invaders have had a party at our expense, and they've been playing with matches.

When I stop the car at the curb in front of the house, my mother-in-law exclaims, "There's <u>been</u> a **fire**!" But my eyes haven't adjusted to reality. What she's said is incomprehensible – and chilling. My thoughts shift into a defense mode. Hey, stop it Grandma. I don't want to hear something like that. We're dead dog tired. Anxious to unload and get some shut-eye.

Irrespective of our circumstances, <u>she's</u> **right**! Not that there would ever be a propitious time for a home fire. The neighbors quickly confirm the solemn truth. They tell us the fire fighters have just left. Three engines were at the scene. Upon closer inspection, a heavy pall of soot and smoke still envelopes the house.

The front door is open. We walk inside to witness the nightmare. The fire and smoke damage is severe. Water employed in fighting the infernal has also taken a fearful toll. We won't be unloading tonight and the shut-eye will be in short supply. The setting is ghastly. Ineffable. Words can't possibly describe the shock, the inner turmoil, the disbelief, the feelings of helplessness and despair on this late-night, sixteenth day of our vacation. It's a hellish home coming.

Realistically, we won't be having a **home coming** for a month. We pull away from the house with heavy hearts. The wreath of smoke still encircling our property is a sober testament to the evil in some men's hearts.

There are many tourists and lots of no vacancy signs in Las Vegas on this gloomy night. Eventually, we find a room in a little flea bag motel on the north end of the Strip. The three adults in our party sleep very little. Each of us is sick over our *homeless* status and fearful someone will *break* into the car. Stealing our clothing and vacation gear.

Finally, one of the worst nights of our lives ends. I call our homeowners insurance to report the claim. We meet claims representatives at the house. They survey the damage and document their findings. Afterward, our family leaves for a motel site with more suitable accommodations. We check in and try to cope with the emotional trauma implicit in our situation.

Police report the **point of entry** and the **extent of damage**. Entry has been made by means of a trellis leading to the small second floor balcony just off the master bedroom. The trellis serves as vertical support for honeysuckle branches climbing from the ground to the second floor. Carelessly, our house isn't equipped with dead bolt locks. When the burglars get to the balcony they simply punch out a section of glass from the french door – and walk inside. Presto, an insidious **home invasion** is accomplished!

As I've mentioned, this is the evening of the <u>sixteenth</u> day of our trip. The air conditioner has been off the entire time. There's no doubt the duo know <u>the</u> **moment** of entry the inhabitants have been gone for days and they have the time to indulge in <u>whatever</u> acts of mischief and larceny they desire to perpetrate.

The Modus Operandi of the onerous intrusion takes shape. The callous duo, bereft of respect for the sanctity of home and private property, begin to rifle through drawers and search rooms for valuables. But they've miscalculated. I'm employed at the public trough, not a collector of priceless jewels. There isn't really anything valuable to foot patrol bandits on the premises. Only kitchen appliances, inexpensive furniture, low budget television sets, cheap clothing, and costume jewelry. So much energy expended and so little compensation to show for the break in. It's got to be damned frustrating to a couple of carpetbagging thieves.

Still, they make a DISCOVERY which is of more than passing interest. They **find** a BADGE inside the top drawer of a dresser in the master bedroom! And **not** just any badge. This **BADGE** <u>is</u> a *BADGE of the enemy* – of a Courtroom Enforcer. It–is–the–**BADGE**–of–a–Chief–Deputy–District–Attorney. It seems these characters have <u>hit</u> the JACKPOT after all.

Immediately, malicious wheels turn inside the delusional heads of the meth freaks. There is a twisted *remembrance* of the relentless finger pointing by a long list of Prosecutorial bullies. Two <u>miscreants</u> in *Paradise* <u>plotting</u>, r**esenting** – RESOLVING, with drug induced malevolence, to strike a symbolic conflagration <u>against</u> an entire Profession. Their sinister MO: *TORCH* the guy's **house**. Impose a fiery **REVENGE** against him in particular and against his colleagues in general.

Give these denizens of the Courthouse something to smolder over.

Thus, the focus of the criminal trespass changes its objective. Taking on an ominous new dimension –**ARSON**. The **amoral** Duo go to the ground floor, collect whatever combustibles are available, and prepare FOUR spots for bonfires. Using their cigarette lighters to **ignite FOUR** <u>separate</u>, late-night-*fires* inside an absentee Prosecutor's home.

My wife and I both play the piano, but we remained piano-less for twelve years of marriage. Several months before the Arson Home Invasion, we had finally purchased a beautiful Sohmer piano. It is easily the most cherished personal property we have in our home. Unfortunately, it's located on the opposite side of a wall to the walk-in staircase closet where the largest fire occurs.

Then, the treacherous Duo scamper away like fire-intoxicated jackrabbits. Swallowed up by the dark vortex of the Las Vegas night. Their actions are –– sneaky, creepy, and unconscionable!

Our home in *Paradise* would probably have burned to the ground except for the presence of a <u>single</u> percipient WITNESS in the neighborhood. What a **huge** <u>difference</u> ONE *responsible* person can make in the lives of others. How blessed we are that this good man is being vigilant – doing his job.

Our subdivision is terraced. The Harmon home is situated on the south side of the upper level. Due to a building recession only <u>ten</u> homes have been finished. These houses are all located along the Drive that leads to the upper level, and around the cul-de-sac at the top.

Fortuitously, a new developer has recently begun to build additional homes at the lower level. Several of the houses under construction are located directly below the south side of our home. A **security guard** is <u>posted</u> in this area. A night *watchman* to keep the construction sites secure from theft and vandalism, but also in a position to see untoward acts occurring outside the construction zone. That is, if he's awake. **HE IS!** That is, if he's <u>isn't</u> daydreaming, **or** so distracted by the twinkle of celestial bodies in the sky, that he doesn't spot a problem much more urgent to the Harmon Family than astrological signs. **HE <u>ISN'T</u>!**

We haven't had any contact with him to this point, but he's <u>our</u> *guardian angel* in a sense. Our watchman in *Paradise* – and we don't have him on retainer. What he does is gratuitous. Thank you, Mike. We're in your debt. Have a great life, man! Every neighborhood needs good Samaritans like you.

Mike <u>sees</u> FLAMES coming out the livingroom window. But he doesn't have the means to call 911. That is **<u>not</u>** an impediment. He leaves his <u>post</u>. Hurrying down the street and dashing up the Drive to the cul-de-sac. Frantically, knocking on the door of the house closest to the home in peril.

Our neighbors have gone to bed. They're startled by the loud banging on their front door, and consider just hunkering down until this character goes away. But after several moments of indecision, they receive an impression that the summons needs to be heeded. Roger opens the door. He's greeted by a short, stocky, slightly scruffy, rather hysterical gentleman who says the house on the other side of the vacant lot is on FIRE. Please call the Fire Department ASAP! The call is made. Quickly, three engines roll to the front of the house that is ablaze with four separate *set fires*.

Efficiently and expertly the firefighters knock down the fires. Salvaging our home, due to their quick response and the watchful eyes of <u>our</u> *guardian angel*. Kudos to the Clark County Fire Department and a night watchman. Security Officer Mike may be short of stature, but he **stands <u>tall</u>** in *Paradise Township*.

Three days later the insurance company relocates us to a loaner house about a mile from our fire ravaged residence. Still in *Paradise*, yet – **not** Paradise. We remain there for thirty days. The stay is pleasant, nevertheless, we want to kiss the front door stoop on that marvelous day when we're privileged to enter the sweet, companionable, memorable confines of our **home** again. *Paradise* is <u>more</u> than a **place**, it's also a **state of mind** and **heart**!

There was little structural damage to the house, though fire and water and smoke cause approximately $20,000.00 worth of destruction to the interior. Those repairs have been made. There is also significant impairment to personal property. For example, every item of clothing in the house has to be cleaned and purged of the stench of smoke. Further, the impact of fire, heat, and soot upon our prized piano is disheartening. The damage to this wonderful instrument is severe.

We're given the option of replacement or restoration. Pre-warned that the artisans working on the instrument will employ their best skills, but the tone of certain keys *may* be permanently desecrated, that some permanent staining of the keyboard is *likely*, and that the color of the console *will* probably darken. For sentimental reasons, we roll the dice. We <u>choose</u> restoration. Thousands of dollars and six months later, our defiled piano **is** remarkably restored to a reasonable facsimile of its original grandeur. The tones of the keys are true, though slight staining remains on the keyboard, and the beautiful cherry wood veneer of the console has taken on a darker hue.

We still have our Sohmer piano and our grim memories of **arson**. We lived for twenty four additional years in **Paradise**. Enjoying our piano and the <u>mostly</u> *joyful* roller coaster ride of life and family and home. But dealing with a *faint* aroma of smoke in a <u>few</u> parts of the house that stubbornly refuses to be harnessed by a cornucopia of fumigating sprays – and <u>never</u> completely dissipates. My musings now, often take me back to the tender *remembrance* of those paradisaic years of trial and growth and enduring love.

The insurance company <u>isn't</u> very happy about the money they've been required to sink into the devastation of <u>our</u> home fire. The Company's always pleased to accept <u>premiums</u>, but **doesn't** ordinarily find the COMPENSATORY **obligation** imposed by the terms of a homeowner's policy nearly as heartwarming.

Three months after we've returned to our home, we receive a letter from The Company **terminating** our homeowner's coverage and informing us we'll need to acquire protection from some other provider. The Company reminds us that the Fire Department has responded to our property on <u>three</u> separate occasions within a nine month time span. They say that is unreasonable. It suggests we're a risky investment.

Well, the news is surprising and heavy handed. Like a sucker punch to the solar plexis. From our point of view, The Company is <u>acting</u> like a spoiled brat. Enthusiastically collecting premiums, but shedding any semblance of altruism when asked to satisfy a contractual burden.

It **is** a fact there have been <u>three</u> Fire Department responses to our humble abode within nine months. So what? Why hasn't The Company bothered to research the circumstances? Homeowner coverage is crucial to a family. The issue is more than a silly NUMBERS GAME. Peel back the layers of statistical mumbo jumbo and look at the **facts** unique to this situation. *Nothing* establishes we're a risky investment, UNLESS it's the policy of a major insurance company that homes of PROSECUTING ATTORNEYS <u>are</u> **uninsurable**!

I call The Company – seeking reinstatement. Speak with various low level representatives who express regret, but say they're bound by The Company policy. **Three strikes** within a nine month time frame <u>and</u> YOU'RE OUT, I'm told.

However, **an insured** *unrighteously scorned* can be <u>full</u> of fury – and tenacious. I work my way up the corporate ladder to a Regional Claims Manager. Initially, I get the same song and dance from him. But to his credit, he's willing to listen. We peel back the layers of statistical mumbo jumbo and examine the **nature** of the three responses.

#1 – About 9:00 p.m. my wife and I think we detect the smell of wood burning. Naturally, we're both alarmed. I hurry upstairs with a step ladder to check the attic. I'm unable to detect any sign of fire. Our two children are playfully splashing water in a nearby tub and are, obviously, totally oblivious to any odor of smoke. But the smell persists. Ten minutes later my wife says we should call the Fire Department. I tend to agree, instruct her to call, but to ask The Department to just send a Fire Marshall over to check things out on the Q.T. I want to keep this thing low key. There's no point in making mountains out of simmering molehills, it seems to me. The call is made.

Not two minutes later, we hear the siren wail of engines in the distance. The Department doesn't take chances. They have no interest in keeping the situation low key. There won't be a single Fire Marshall in a sedan, they're dispatching a full regalia of firefighting capability. **Two** FIRE ENGINES roll into the cul-de-sac with lights flashing, sirens blowing, and a bevy of firefighters on board.

They quickly alight from their engines, rush inside with water hoses and hatchets drawn, and fan out through the house. Incidently, the children are totally undaunted by the melee. They continue to splash in the tub as though the firemen are invisible and they have no care in the world. Their nonchalance is curious.

Five minutes later The Department reports its findings. There is **no** fire, but there is an <u>experiment</u> in urban henhouse nesting underway. The Engine Chief in charge suggests we firmly admonish the kids to cease and desist any further biddy hatching activity, and that we might want to consider taking them behind the woodshed, so to speak, for a bit of memory enhancement after the lecture.

Our children have fashioned a homemade **incubator**. A simple apparatus really. The component parts are <u>four</u> *unfertilized* eggs, a shoe box for nesting, an extension cord for power, and a light bulb for heat. The children have decided they'd like some chicks for Easter. But Dad and Mom have already said no, so they've taken matters into their own hands.

Ah hah! Things are coming into focus now. The children have placed their self-styled *incubator* under the bed in our son's room. The heat from the light bulb hasn't achieved an <u>immaculate</u> conception by hatching chicks from *unfertilized* eggs, but it has succeeded in burning a hole about twelve inches in diameter through the carpet. Singing a wooden beam that is part of the underpinning for the floor. Hence, the smell of burning wood – and a better understanding of why the children are so cavalier regarding the threat of fire.

The Department leaves. The children get their tongue lashing – **plus**, and manage to survive another Easter holiday without **chicks**. The point is: it's a *childhood prank* – one that is **never** repeated. Spare the rod and spoil the child!

Query, Mr. Regional Claims Manager: Where's the **risk**? The children who like biddies have experienced an appropriate **attitude adjustment**. Does having children make a family dwelling *uninsurable*?

#2 – About 9:30 p.m. we think we smell smoke. Once again I check the attic and every room. I also look **under** each BED this time –– nothing! Yet, the aroma becomes stronger. It's a warm evening with little breeze, and the air conditioner is on. I run outside to check the roof, but <u>no</u> smoke is detected in the darkness. My re-entry only heightens the mystery. A palpable odor of smoke now permeates the house. We're left with no alternative. Mrs. Harmon calls the Fire Department.

The previous scenario is repeated. The shrill sound of sirens, two engines, a full regalia of firefighting capability, boots, helmets, fire resistant outfits, hoses, hatchets – these guys are professionals. When firemen get to a site they're all business. They're quickly dispatched to every room checking for hot spots. The attic is explored, but the result is a big negatory. There is no fire in the attic, leaving only one other possibility. <u>So</u>, it's up on the housetop click – click – click. And the culprit isn't a berserk, fire breathing Reindeer, it's an **air conditioning** UNIT.

There are two units on the roof, and one of the units has <u>spontaneously</u> caught fire. Perhaps, a short has caused a small blaze or maybe it's elves or an act of God. Nobody knows. The Department doesn't know the precise ignition factor. They only know the unit is still smoldering and, prior to being knocked out of commission by fire, the engaged unit is responsible for disseminating a scent of smoke throughout the house. But little risk to the house ever existed. The absence of significant external wind currents has confined burning to the unit and made it highly unlikely a small flame <u>could</u> have spread to the shake roofing.

The offending air conditioning unit is <u>promptly</u> replaced within a week. After all, the full brunt of summer heat is right around the corner. *Paradise* won't be very paradisaic without air conditioning.

Query, Mr. Regional Claims Manager: Where's the **risk**? The Unit has been operational for less than a year. It's still under warranty. Does formerly having a **factory**-defective air conditioning unit on the roof make a family dwelling *uninsurable* into perpetuity? The bad unit is history, Sir. What is it about a **self-igniting** air conditioning unit, now relegated to some Sanitation Department landfill, that makes a specific family dwelling a risky insurance investment?

#3 – ARSON. An act <u>totally</u> beyond the control of the insured. A criminal malediction – a fiery supervening consequence. An absentee Prosecuting Attorney, whose taken an oath to sustain the Constitution in his pursuit of **Justice** and public **Service,** has two hooligans break into his home and TORCH his family dwelling **because** of his Profession. What say ye, Mr. Regional Claims Manager: Where's the *legally cognizable* risk? Is The Company making a blanket policy statement that the family dwellings of PROSECUTING ATTORNEYS are *uninsurable*? You might want to rethink the **public relations** ramification of such an edict. Further, this is the United States of America. This Country doesn't permit systematic, discriminatory practices against particular categories of citizens. Such CONDUCT violates the Equal Protection Clause of the United States Constitution.

Savvy, Ke-mo Sahbee. He *did* understand. The Notice of Termination is *rescinded*. The Company *decides* family dwellings that <u>house</u> **Children** and **Prosecuting Attorneys** and **roofs** <u>supporting</u> factory defective **air conditioning units** under warranty, *are* INSURABLE! Well, *all* praise to the self-serving beneficence of The Company.

It's another summer, another vacation trip, and for a few moments at least, it appears to be another family crisis in *Paradise*. We pull up to the curb in front of our home after two and a half weeks on the road. Grandma hasn't made the trip this time. She's chosen to hold down the home front instead. However, the chore must have been a lonely vigil. Evidently, she's missed us <u>so</u> much, and is <u>so</u> excited over our return, she can't bear to take the time to go through the front door to greet us.

The moment we park *there's* **Grandma** – <u>climbing</u> out the front window. A window, by the way, that leads from her room. It's an odd sight. An eighty year old elects to exit by window rather than through a door. What's up with that?

Her legs are a little too short. The result is impalement on the window sill. I hurriedly stride over to assist her. When I get closer I see the anxiety on her face. Almost as if she's seen a ghost. Which she hasn't, I **know** that. There aren't any ghosts in *Paradise*. It wouldn't be Paradise if there were.

As I take her hand to help her out, Grandma exclaims: "There's SOMEONE **in** the house. I'm hearing *popping* <u>sounds</u> coming from the kitchen. That's <u>where</u> **he is**. I didn't know what to do. I just <u>knew</u> I had to get out of the house."

Well, it's a message guaranteed to jolt the serenity of a guy's homecoming. I blink, swallow hard, and escort my Mother-in-Law to the car. Informing my wife that **her** Mother says **someone** is in the house. Would <u>she</u> go check it out!

No, not really. That's what I wanted to do. She's braver than me. Besides, when we *smell smoke* at the house she calls the Fire Department. So ya know, there is a certain pecking order in such matters. But precedent doesn't hold sway in this circumstance. I'm the MAN of the house!

I get drafted to confront *whatever* or whomever is <u>inside</u> our **kitchen**. Square your shoulders Laddie, and <u>try</u> not to *trip* as you walk to the front door. I fumble slightly with the key chain as I insert the front door key, and quietly swing the door open. Attempting to make a subtle entry. Counting on the element of surprise to enable a wimp like me to get the upper hand.

Then – I'm inside. Full of trepidation. Heart pounding. Thinking this is a hell of way to end a vacation. I'm scheduled to start a Murder Trial the following Monday and some two-bit Burglar is probably going to BLOW me away as I walk into the **kitchen** of my own home.

But **not** to worry, Hormone. I'm practically to the **kitchen** when I hear it – POP –– POP, just as Grandma described. However, I'm not being fired upon. **No** one is sliding a magazine into a pistol butt and cranking a shell into the chamber. Grandma **hasn't** been hearing a person. There's NOBODY in the house – but ME! Suddenly, I SEE a puddle of fizzy, dark brown fluid on the **kitchen** floor – and the **danger** passes. The **mystery** is solved. The **cloud** of apprehension lifts – and ole Mel is LAUGHING out loud to himself.

ROOT BEER! It's the damned bottles of homemade root beer **popping** their caps off. The Harmons love homemade root beer, but they've miscalculated. Being gone for two and a half weeks is apparently being gone for a <u>few</u> hours too long. Fresh *yeast* is a workaholic. Thus, the *yeast* in the recipe has been working all the time we've been playing, and the pressure is popping caps off. Right on cue another cap POPS, and more sweet, sticky, precious root beer comes streaming over the lip of the bottle. Descending to the shelf and dripping down to the growing brown puddle on the floor.

The joke's on Grandma. Nevertheless, she gets to relax while we get to clean up the gook on the pantry shelf and the kitchen floor. The Travelers have to roll up their sleeves the moment their boots hit the floor. Yet, we get to drink as much *home brew* as we can before it loses its fizz, and we're able to salvage about ten bottles that haven't flipped their lids.

It's an evening frozen in time. Every time we revisit this wonderful incident, *remembering* Grandma climbing out the front window, frantically fleeing from the scene of pop–pop–popping bottle caps, it's a moment of solid-gold merriment!

Late one somber night there was the frightful ARSON **home invasion**, but once upon a time there is also an occasion for gleeful *remembrance* – a time when *yeast* propelled, pop–pop–popping bottle caps **invade** our KITCHEN and our hearts!

Extremism In The Pursuit Of Procedure Is A Mockery Of Justice

"No man is an island entire of itself, every man is a piece of the Continent, a part of the main...any man's death diminishes me, because I am involved in mankind. And therefore, never send to know for whom the bell tolls, it tolls for thee." (John Donne, *Meditation XVII* – 1624)

Chapter 7

Darlene is a wife, a mother, and a Texan. Subject to the usual imperfections that plague humankind, yet in her totality, a decent, tender, fun-loving woman. She and her husband drive from Canyon Lake to Las Vegas for a short vacation in August, 1977. The trip is a belated celebration of her birthday. She had turned 37 on August 8th. They rent a motel room on east Fremont a few blocks from glitter gulch. Expecting several days of romance, fine cuisine, gambling, variety shows, and relaxation. However, within twenty four hours of arrival their trip to the entertainment capital loses its luster. What begins as an exciting getaway becomes a deviant debacle.

Marriage is satirically described as: "The state of condition of a community consisting of a master, a mistress, and two slaves, making in all, two." (Ambrose Bierce, *The Devil's Dictionary*, 1906) As misfortune has it, the <u>master</u> (her hubby) and the <u>mistress</u> (Darlene)quarrel. Perhaps, both are **slaves** to their perceptions of how the evening should be spent. The result is the unraveling of their relationship.

He stomps out of the room in a huff, heading west toward glitter gulch on foot. Leaving her alone with her thoughts and her frustrations. He also leaves their spiffy white Cadillac sedan parked in front of the room.

Thirty minutes pass. He's still gone. Therefore, she decides to go out on the town *alone*. She'll do her thing by herself. She takes a few minutes to gussy up. Inwardly, hoping he'll return before she leaves and intercept her solo flight. He doesn't. She takes her purse, locks the door, goes to the car, starts the engine, and heads east on Fremont.

Poor woman! She needs a watchful *guardian angel* **tonight**. She needs to have a calm, clear, reassuring voice whisper to her heart, "Don't go, Darlene. Stay in your motel room. Sulk and shed some tears of discontent, if you must, but **do not** go anywhere *alone* tonight. Leave the spiffy white Cadillac sedan parked in the lot. Wait for your Mister to return. The two of you can work things out. Don't do something foolish!

Actually, Darlene just needs her husband. Poor Roy! He hadn't expected to become a widower so soon. **If** he'd only known, there wouldn't have been a silly argument. He wouldn't have left her alone. **He'd** have taken her out dining and dancing somewhere – anywhere. He'd have paid his dues to the woman who has pledged to be his wife for life. He'd never have taken such an amazing gift for granted. Not for one night – not ever!

She turns left on Nellis Boulevard searching for a redneck bar. Drives about a mile, spots a busy honky-tonk on the west side of the street, and pulls off. It's called the Wagon Axle Bar. She gets out and goes in. Feeling unappreciated, a bit devil-may-care, and needing to dance. Finds a seat at the bar and orders a tall cold one. She sits there for about twenty minutes – listening to the jukebox, watching couples on the dance floor, exchanging friendly banter with the bartenders, and getting a little buzz – when someone taps her on the shoulder. It's **Pete**. He asks her to dance. The request seems polite and innocuous.

He's a stocky, roughly hewn, rather handsome fellow with white hair. And I'll theorize she's probably thinking, "What the hell. He looks harmless and the package comes with an engaging smile. The odds are he wouldn't hurt a flea. I came in here to do some dancing. So, I'll let him give me a whirl and show this dude how we really do the Texas Two-Step. Nothing ventured nothing gained."

But that's the catch. The coin has two sides. Nothing ventured nothing lost may also be applicable. This guy is a barracuda! However, Darlene hasn't experienced that facet of Pete's personality – **but she will**.

They dance four or five sets and separate for a time. His Two-Stepping skills are mediocre at best. While she's a smooth stepping phenom. Darlene tires of steering this lug around the dance floor, and declines his invitation to dance longer. She returns to the bar, has another beer, dances with several other gents, and mingles with the crowd.

Forty five minutes later, she's about to leave when Pete appears at her side again. Bad *timing* <u>can</u> be a precursor of evil. He wants to know if he may have the honor of another dance. She wants to say no, but she says yes. Darlene prides herself in being a lady.

It's a slow foxtrot, and the *fox* has his <u>quarry</u>. Pete pulls her toward him, snuggles in close, and encircles her with both arms. He hopes to make this an amorous belly rub to remember. The Lug's more assertive the second time around. Striving for full body touching. Wanting to feel her curves and absorb her femininity.

She'd like to push him away, but the lady's trying to avoid a scene. No point in offending him, she reasons. Better to let him grope her a little on the dance floor, and get it out of his system. Thus, she quietly submits to stranger intimacy. It's a bad strategy. Only whetting his brutish appetite. Dear Darlene, flying solo over strange turf, needs a **protector** to get her back to the motel room!

> "No beast is more savage than man when possessed with power answerable to his rage." (Plutarch, *Cicero*, p.1068)

It seems like an eternity, but the plodding dance finally ends. Darlene thanks him for his interest, then explains she must leave to keep an appointment. They part, he withdraws into the bar crowd, and she quickly hustles out the front door. She has a very bad feeling. She's wishing she'd never, never come to this place by herself, nor bumped into this lecherous, sweaty palmed dance partner. She can sense the moisture he's deposited wherever his meaty hands have touched her. She feels soiled and pawed and disheartened. Her wife's night out has been an unmitigated disaster.

She can't get back to her Caddy soon enough. Wants to break into a run, but doesn't. A strong perception of evil permeates the ambiance around the Wagon Axle parking lot. A premonition? She glances about. Sees no one, but tries to quicken her gait. The result is more of a stumbling shuffle than a quickened stride. Her extremities seem sluggish. Like she's walking in molasses. She's trying to hurry, but the weight of lager and worry partially immobilize her feet.

The parking lot is poorly lighted. Her car is practically enshrouded in a sullen darkness. Frantically, fatefully, she parts the gathering gloom. Her fear has become a brooding presence. To her thinking, she's in slow motion mode. But awkward step by step she approaches her haven of safety. Exhales a heavy sigh of relief, takes out her key, and arrives at the car. She's just placed the key in the door when heavy hands grab her from behind and spin her around. **It's Pete**!

Immediately he says something like, "You need company. A pretty thing like you shouldn't be alone. Something bad might happen, Sweetmeat." Well, it already has. Ole Lecherous, Sweaty Hands has intercepted her. The fox has caught his quarry – **again**!

She instinctively raises her knee, slams it into his groin. Momentarily, he's stunned. Sadly, he's not disabled – he's infuriated. Immediately, Pete brandishes a knife, and with a sudden thrust pierces the edge of her upper lip. She shrieks in pain, but no one's near enough to hear. He grabs the key and unlocks the car. Throws her into the backseat and shuts the door. Gets into the drivers seat, finds the ignition, and inserts the key. Starts the engine, spins out of the parking spot, crosses the lot to Nellis Boulevard, and speeds away. To the impression of the scary guy, not a soul sees the departure. He tells Darlene **if** she moves she's dead. An astute observer might ask, "Is the remark a warning or a self-fulfilling prophesy?"

Pete is familiar with the area. He lives alone a short distance away in a small trailer. He knows what he wants from Darlene and he knows where he'll take her to get it. But he isn't going to his digs, he's a roughrider. A man can be a primitive savage when he's possessed with the power to sate his lust.

He turns off Nellis and drives along a dirt road that winds through isolated desert terrain. Stops in the darkness after approximately 1500 feet, and faces Darlene with the ugly knife bared. Poor, poor Darlene. She's cowering in the backseat. The woman isn't dumb. She knows what lies ahead. He'll rape her and then –– .

Her options are grim. Her future tied to a slender reed. The deck stacked against the woman in a one-to-one with an armed lecher in heat. Yet, she has to resist him and try to escape at the most propitious moment. As if on cue, Pete exits and orders her to get out of the car. It's the *beginning* of the **end**!

Darlene's battered body is discovered in the middle of a dirt road about 30 yards west of the 2800 block of Betty Lane, .35 miles north of Carey Avenue, and .3 miles east of Nellis Boulevard. The decent, fun-loving Texas wife/mother, in town for a belated celebration of her 37th birthday, has been prematurely catapulted into the next estate. Small errors in judgment <u>and</u> association can lead to catastrophe.

The grisly discovery is made at 6:30 a.m. A mere five hours after the Two-Stepping phenom is seen departing the Wagon Axle Bar – following several hours of dancing, light drinking, and casual camaraderie. **Pete** is known by management. He's observed dancing with the victim. Several witnesses see him leave *at or near* the time of the lady's departure. Police are told where he lives.

The remains of the deceased lie grotesquely in the dirt. Her pants and underwear are off, her legs spread, her blouse and bra pulled back exposing her breasts. Her head is battered and bloody. She's been bludgeoned with a blunt force object. A bloody rock is discovered a few feet from the body. The thighs of the victim are smeared with blood. Presumably, fluid from her own body. The spiffy white Cadillac sedan has been abandoned nearby.

Investigating officers go to Pete's trailer. They find blood-smeared clothing and obtain an admission that he's had <u>an</u> <u>encounter</u> with the lady in question. It starts on the dance floor and ends in desert dirt. He says it's self defense. Though he manages to screw her and steal her one hundred dollar bill as he's defending himself. It's an unlikely scenario. Pete is arrested at 10:45 a.m.

The Chief Medical Examiner performs an autopsy at 12:15 p.m. of the same day. It's amazing and distressing. A convivial woman is alive and well, breathing and drinking and dancing. Then, abruptly her warm beating heart is stopped cold. She's accosted, kidnaped, attacked by a savagely malevolent man, and left dead in the dust. A few hours later the woman, who comes to Las Vegas with her husband for several days of gambling, and to be wined, dined, and romanced, lays lifeless and rigid on a cold slab at the morgue. Darlene has indulged the *wrong* form of <u>gambling</u> by going it alone on unfamiliar turf in a strange city. The life force is fragile. Something to be cherished, nurtured, and protected each day. Mortality often ends shockingly – suddenly!

The autopsy findings are heinous. There is a <u>gaping</u> **hole** in Darlene's head. A **chunk of skull** has been <u>knocked</u> out. The bloody rock is a grim testament to the ferocity of Pete's attack. Additionally, there are two separate skull fractures. Multiple blunt force bruises and abrasions are observed on the head, neck, chin, and upper chest of the deceased. The Pathologist notes that the victim has been stabbed on the right side just above her upper lip, and a deep **bite** **impression** is clearly visible on her abdomen.

She has also been **manually** strangled. Pete has locked his hands in a vise-like grip around her **neck** until she lays still. Suffocating his victim before he bludgeons her with the rock. The *causes of death* are manual strangulation and crushing trauma to the skull. Fractures of the voice box and the hyoid bone convincingly establish her assailant's **hand job**.

Adios Darlene, the bell tolls for thee!

THE STATE seeks the Death Penalty. Pete's Case becomes the first Capital Case tried pursuant to recently enacted legislation that became effective on July 1, 1977. He is indicted by the Clark County Grand Jury within ten days. The Accused is getting *custodial* room and board at the County Detention Center. His Deputy Public Defender invokes his right to go to Trial within 60 days. The Trial is set for the last Monday in October, 1977.

The Prosecution collates its evidence and Defense Counsel *ponders* the dilemma of a Client facing overwhelming CIRCUMSTANTIAL **evidence** of guilt. **Pete** is represented by RICK. Deputy Defender RICK isn't a greenhorn to the Profession of Criminal Lawyering just earning his legal spurs, nor is he a novice in the world of Trial Practice. It's the luck of the draw. Ole Pete has been assigned a Lawyer of pre-imminent credentials.

RICK's been one of the leading **Prosecutors** in northern Nevada for many years. He's a tall, slender, handsome man with a **BOOMING** voice. When The Man speaks, his deep, resonant voice can FILL Courtrooms and INTIMIDATE Courtroom adversaries. A **fact** well recognized by Attorney RICK and often exploited by him.

Further, he's a wily Trial tactician. Well prepared, articulate, possessing a strong law enforcement orientation, and is, perhaps, best characterized by a hard- nosed obstinance. He's had many Trials, being a veteran of nearly twenty years of Trial work. Nothing describes the effectiveness, the success, and the Trial record of this former Gentleman Prosecutor like his nickname. If Rick's assigned to a Case it's the end of the line for the miscreant. Invariably, he gets his man. His professional handle is "**The Noose**"

So, how is it that Gentleman Rick ends up in southern Nevada with the Clark County Public Defender's Office? The answer isn't complicated. The Prosecutor decides to become a politician. He runs for the Office of District Attorney in Washoe County <u>against</u> his boss. Some pundits might question the wisdom of tossing your hat in the ring under this circumstance.

Moreover, he commits a <u>couple</u> of cardinal offenses. He says some bad things about his opponent, <u>and</u> "**The Noose**" loses the race. It's a case of teetering dominoes. The Deputy with the bad manners to run against the incumbent, and the bad mouth to soundly criticize his record –– loses his job. He's an ex-prosecutor in the blink of a ballot!

Rick seeks greener more hospitable turf in the south. He attempts to get a job with the Clark County District Attorney. However, neither his handle nor his record in the north country impresses the hard-nosed, moralistic DA in Las Vegas. He's heard that Gentleman Rick has been married **nine** times. Well George H, assuming it's true, maybe that wasn't his fault. Yeah, nine times their fault? Right.

It's a major fault in the eyes of his prospective employer. The Boss-Man Prosecutor in Vegas doesn't want a high-profile womanizer on his staff. Rick is turned down. Accordingly, he walks out of the Courthouse, crosses Third Street, and ambles two-thirds of a block farther south to the <u>Public</u> Defender's Office. Aaarg, they're misnamed. But the misnomer sounds pretty good to the shunned wanna be Career Prosecutor.

Surprise! Rick's like a rooster in a coyote den at Defender Land, but he's welcomed with open arms by the equally moralistic, but more pragmatic, County Public Defender. And that's the short hand version of how "**The Noose**" becomes a <u>Public</u> Defender.

Another aside about Rick, who is one of **my** favorite characters. Down the road a distance, Defender Rick gets a Jury Summons. Lots of citizens get them, and many folks consider the notice a nuisance. Being much inclined to shirk their civic responsibility to perform Jury duty, if they can possibly avoid the call to service. NOT RICK. He's often nurtured the **fantasy** of spending some time in the Jury Box. I say <u>fantasy</u>, because the conventional wisdom of one side or the other, depending on whether they're Prosecuting Attorneys or Defense Attorneys and depending on what kind of Law the prospective Jury panelist practices, is that Lawyers **don't** make good Jurors in Criminal Trials. This is the prevailing view. The glittering generality before the Bar.

However, a GENERALITY should **always** be considered <u>suspect</u>! A factor needing to be scrutinized, researched, and only followed after thoughtful analysis. The GENERALITY in this instance being: that a

Prosecutor **shouldn't** allow a Defense Attorney to serve on his Jury. Well, we'll test the premise with a personal example.

Gentleman Defender Rick doesn't make excuses. He doesn't claim some exemption from service. He doesn't tell the Jury Commissioner's Office he's too busy representing Criminals to serve. He doesn't say it's a waste of time, that he'll be excused by peremptory challenge anyway – because of bias. Rick says, "YES, I'll serve," and ends up on a prospective Jury Panel for one of my cases. The charges are Aggravated Battery and Strong Armed Robbery.

We proceed to Jury Selection. The Panel of Twelve is seated in the box. The Court and Counsel are involved in the selection of two **alternate** Jurors. Each side will have one additional peremptory challenge in this segment of the process. A peremptory challenge, subject to certain legal restraints that aren't pertinent to my discussion here, can be exercised to excuse a prospective Juror without either Party offering an explanation. Maybe one of the Parties doesn't like the way the prospective venireman parts his hair, or his personality type, or the goofy way he's smiling at the gallery, or his middle name, or the negative vibes coming from wherever such impressions originate, and so forth – ad infinitum. NO REASON for dismissal has to be given.

The Clerk spins the drum again and removes two additional names. Name #1, who is seated in the slot of FIRST ALTERNATE, **IS** ––– the indomitable, Mr. Gentleman Rick of the Public Defender's Office. Madam Defense Counselor glances over at me with a broad, quizzical smile that stretches from ear to ear. She does have lovely teeth, and she's an engaging, friendly, all around nice person. However, the smile isn't reflective of her niceness. It's the *irony* she senses as a member of the Defense Bar is placed in the seat of **first** Alternate on our Jury. She's amused by what she believes will be my extreme discomfort at the very thought of a DEFENSE LAWYER – being within a heartbeat of The Twelve deciding the Case.

But Madam Defense Counselor is a relative newcomer to practice in Nevada. She **doesn't** know what I KNOW about Rick. She **doesn't** know he's been a Prosecutorial giant in Washoe County. She **doesn't** know Rick has served much longer as a Deputy D.A. than he's served as a Deputy P.D. The congenial, Madam Defense Counselor **doesn't** know that ole hang-em-high has been labeled "**The Noose**." Well, Gentleman Rick's history changes the dynamic in the Courtroom for me. The NO-defense-attorney-on-a-criminal-jury GENERALITY goes out the window **this time**! The general rule has an exception – **this time**!

We conduct a cursory voir dire of the two prospective alternates. They're passed for cause. Next, the Court asks the Prosecution to exercise its single peremptory challenge. Madam Defense Counselor gets a surprise. She thinks I'm going to send Deputy Public Defender Rick to the Juror recycle bin. Not so quick, Madam."THE PROSECUTION **waives** it's peremptory challenge and ACCEPTS the Jury as presently constituted!"

So, after Her Fairness has picked her smooth chin up off the floor, cupped her jaw as she slides an index finger across her smooth chin several times, flash pondered whether she's missed something or whether Deputy Mel has taken leave of his senses, and undoubtedly concluded – if we lose one of the regular Jurors in this Trial I've caught lightning in a jug; Madam Defense Counselor also <u>waives</u> her alternate Juror peremptory challenge.

Thus, the Jury and alternates are duly chosen – with Rick on board, and the Robbery/Battery Trial formally begins. Though Madam Defense Counselor hasn't caught lightning in a jug – she's caught a large clump of verdict annoyance.

The evidence is presented, argued, and submitted to the original Twelve. From my perspective, the evidence is cut and dried. I'm expecting a quick guilty verdict. But it doesn't happen. The Jury wrangles over the Evidence <u>and</u> the Law they must apply to the evidence for a day and a half. Still no verdict. It seems that deliberation is at an impasse. Something needs to happen to break the deadlock. It **does**!

One of the regular Jurors becomes ill. **Actually** sick or simply sick of Jury haggling? It's hard to say. She's not showing any symptoms except Juror fatigue. The Court and Counsel don't <u>know</u> the answer, though the timing seems a bit peculiar. The Court stalls, but the Juror remains adamant. She says she's so sick she may have to go to a hospital emergence room. The Court thinks it's a ploy. He's seen this before. Juror's feigning illness to get a Jury bailout. His Honor is undecided. Go forward as is <u>or</u> give the recalcitrant lady a pass?

Madam Defense Counselor thinks the Trial Roadmap is clear. She has no ambivalence in the matter whatever. The Court has to give "sicko" the benefit of a doubt. Of course, Madam Defense Counselor is also licking her adversarial chops. She's ecstatic about Rick becoming part of the deliberation process and firm in her belief that Harmon is going to get his comeuppance for foolishly keeping a member of the Defense Bar in the Box. As for Deputy Mel, I'm quite sure the Juror is a malingerer. However in my heart, I'm as anxious as Madam Defense Counselor to get **"The Noose"** on the Jury. Legal eagles occasionally call such an unexpected change of circumstances – an **act of God**. I feel confident Rick will break the deliberative standoff and bring home the bacon. The proper verdicts in this Case are GUILTY to those schooled in Criminal Justice. I think Rick will be a schoolmaster to the rest of the Panel.

Therefore, with the stipulation of Counsel for both Parties, His Honor discharges the complaining Juror. Seating a Deputy Public Defender in her place. Madam Defense Counselor is gleeful.

Six hours later her *grin* becomes *chagrin*. School is out. The Jury has chosen a second Foreman. Uh, that would be "**The Noose.**" The crash-course in Criminal Law is finished, and TWO counts of **Guilty as Charged** are returned by the **newly** constituted Jury.

So much for GENERALITIES. The likeable Lady of Law is stunned. She's a little wiser now – and humbled. It's silly to buy into a generality unless its been scrutinized, researched, and thoughtfully analyzed. Even then the proponent of the generality will probably be wrong. Expected the unexpected in a Criminal Trial!

So, that's the heads up on Pete's guy. His second – the man in his corner. But enough collateral kibitzing. What of poor Darlene's justice? The system seeks recompense for the man "possessed with power answerable to his rage." (Plutarch, ibid.)

Pete's Trial proceeds. It's a spirited battle between Trial combatants. All glib commentary about Rick's history aside, he's a first-rate professional and a fierce competitor. Deputy Public Defender Rick knows his sole responsibility is to his Client, and he uses his inestimable skills and experience in vigorous advocacy on behalf of the Accused. The fact that he loses is **not** for lack of effort, **nor** for strategically incorrect decisions. It's the EVIDENCE **stupid**.

Defense Counselors of integrity **don't** manufacture EVIDENCE. They **don't** *create* alibis and coerced confessions and exonerating DNA out of whole cloth. They're STUCK with the Case **evidence**. And the Case **evidence** against Pete is **not** simply proof beyond a reasonable doubt, it approaches PROOF to an **absolute certainty**. I'm saying, the unlikely Pete and Rick team had NO CHANCE – realistically.

True, it's an entirely CIRCUMSTANTIAL CASE, but that categorical description does **not** lessen the strength of the **connecting** evidence.

(**1**) Witnesses **testify** they SEE Pete dancing with Darlene the night of the Murder. (**2**) Witnesses **testify** Pete leaves the Wagon Axle Bar *at or near* the time of the Lady's departure. (**3**) Darlene has type A blood. Pete has type O blood. A Criminalist **testifies** that smears of blood type A are found **on** Pete's clothing **inside** his trailer the **morning after** the murder. (**4**) Her blood type is also found on Pete's **penis**. It's apparent he's had it out **after** he's bludgeoned her with the rock. Perverse! (**5**) Homicide Detectives **testify** Pete admits on three separate occasions that he's killed the Lady, to-wit: the morning of the Murder, and twice two days later. The third admission is on **video tape**. Pete claims self defense, but Darlene's been stabbed, sexually molested, robbed, bitten on her lower belly, manually strangled, bludgeoned in the head with a rock, and left **dead** on a dusty road. Pete is **alive**, unmarked, unfazed, and fails to report his *extreme* measures of self defense – *until* he's confronted by Homicide Detectives. (**6**) Exemplar dental **impressions** of the Defendant positively **match** bite marks on Darlene's abdomen. It's the first time in the State of Nevada such evidence has been admitted in a Criminal Trial. Pete's unrestrained **teeth** provide compelling evidence against him. "No beast is more savage than MAN when possessed with power answerable to **his rage**." (Plutarch, ibid., emphasis added)

The Jury is instructed by the Court, and after several hours of Lawyer rhetoric, the Case is submitted to the Jury. They're back in about two hours. Pete is found guilty of the Premeditated Murder of Darlene. There's a short Court-ordered hiatus, and a Penalty Hearing begins on the third day.

The Prosecution calls a single witness, but her testimony is highly relevance to punishment. She's from back east. Some years past, while walking home from school she's the victim of an attempted **rape** –– by **Pete**. He attacks her in a secluded wooded area, but she escapes and runs to safety. The young lady reports the offense and **testifies**. Pete is convicted and incarcerated.

He waives his right to make a statement of allocution during his Penalty Phase. The Jury is Instructed regarding the legal parameters of punishment, and the boys with the *sweaty tongues* begin to elucidate.

The Jury has three penalty options. They are: **Death**, Life Without the Possibility of Parole, and Life With the Possibility of Parole. A finding beyond a reasonable doubt that one or more **aggravating** circumstances exists is a prerequisite to the imposition of Capital Punishment.

The States alleges and argues five Statutory **aggravating** *circumstances*:

1. The Defendant has prior **crimes of violence**. He's been convicted of Attempted Sodomy in the First Degree and

Assault in the Second Degree of a school girl. Like the Crime at Bar, they are *sex motivated* felonies. However, there is one extraordinary difference. The school girl survives. She lives to tell her tale in Court. Darlene dies! Ole Pete doesn't make the same mistake twice! No woman in his face telling tales **again**. No woman pointing her boney finger at him from the witness stand **again**. No deja vu in Vegas!

2. The Murder involves **robbery**. Naturally, he's thinking a Texas woman out on the town in a Cadillac will have money. Pete admits he takes a <u>one</u> <u>hundred</u> dollar bill during the perpetration of Murder. He says in the video tape interview he took it from a pocketbook inside her purse. It's folded in half. **The clincher** – Question: "When did you <u>see</u> the money, at the bar, or after you, once you were in the car with her?" The chilling answer: "*When we were rolling around on the ground fighting.*"

3. The Murder involves **sexual assault**. The Crime Scene is a hideous snap shot of the perpetration of rape: spread-eagle legs, breasts and pelvis exposed, and abdominal teeth impressions. The condition of Pete's body and clothing are stark corroboration. He has smeared blood on his trousers, shorts, and thighs. The dried blood on his penis is an exclamation point.

4. The Murder involves **torture**. Darlene's assailant has used a <u>rock</u> to knock a gaping hole in her skull. Multiple <u>blunt</u> <u>force</u> injuries cover the upper half of her body. She has been subjected to <u>manual</u> strangulation. Both the voice box and hyoid bone have been fractured. The Medical Examiner testifies that such injuries "<u>won't</u> be present unless the Victim is rigid, tense, and resistant." Given the nature of the injuries, he's of the opinion to a reasonable degree of medical certainty that Darlene is "conscious for 5-6 minutes prior to dying."

5. The Murder involves **depravity of mind**. Pete has walked on her, kicked dirt on her, smashed a chunk out of her skull, strangled her, and <u>bitten</u> her. The <u>position</u> of **his** *teeth* marks amplify the brutal mind-set of depravity. Pete's *head* <u>faces</u> Darlene's pubic area *when* he bites her. The neanderthal, possessed with power <u>and</u> morbid passion answerable to his rage, has penetrated or attempted to penetrate his Victim

vaginally and orally while she is *dead or dying*. Necrophilia is
a plausible thesis.

A further prerequisite to the imposition of Capital Punishment is
a finding, that any **aggravating** circumstance or circumstances proven
beyond a reasonable doubt, **outweighs** the mitigating circumstance or
circumstances existing in a case.

The Prosecution argues a total absence of *mitigation*. (**1**) The Defendant
has **no** significant history of prior Criminal activity? Hardly, that isn't
apposite. He TERRORIZED a seventeen year old school girl. Try to
convince her what he did was *insignificant*. (**2**) The Defendant is under the
influence of *extreme* mental or emotional disturbance? What disturbance?
NOTHING in the record suggests Pete is intoxicated or emotionally
distraught. He made **no** such claim. All we have is the sniveling disclaimer
in his video tape statement: "I never really meant to hurt her – I never hurt
anybody in my life." This Crime is conceived by degeneracy. Pete's under
the **influence** of a primitive *lust* for sex and a *greed* for Darlene's money.
These factors are aggravators not mitigators. (**3**) The Victim is a participant
in the Defendant's criminal activity and **consents** to the act? Poppycock!
Darlene **doesn't** consent to being brutally murdered. Her death **isn't** a
case of suicide. She isn't so good natured she helps Pete find the rock
he uses to knock out a chunk of her skull. She **doesn't** place his sweaty
hands around her neck (**4**) The Defendant is an accomplice in a murder
committed by another and his participation is *relatively* **minor**? Now, that
premise would surely be turning the savage acts of a do-it-alone **predator**
upside down. Pete isn't the *culpable* party? It's *actually* the husband's fault
because he leaves Darlene alone in a motel room with a set of car keys and
a spiffy white Cadillac in the parking lot? The Wagon Axle bartender is at
fault because he serves up some beers? It's **her** fault because she agrees to
dance with him? She's stimulated his libido by allowing him to encircle
her with both arms during the slow foxtrot? The lady should have slapped
his face? The **knife** slides out of Pete's pocket and lands in his hand –
blade open? Her **bra** pops open on its own? The **rock** propels itself? A set
of **hands** attached to a set of **arms** does the strangulating – *not* **Pete**? The
poor fellow is simply a tragic victim of circumstance? Palpable nonsense!
(**5**) The crime is committed under **duress** or the **domination** of another?
Who? Pete is strong-armed by an *unseen* evil force? The **devil** made him
do it? Sorry fella, the *devil* has **no** standing in Eighth Judicial District
Courts. And so forth.

I remember closing the State's **Opening Penalty Argument** with these words: "The only TRULY **mitigating** circumstance in this Case would be the return of Darlene to her husband and her family – ALIVE! But as esteemed Defense Counsel tells us, 'You **can't** un-ring a bell.' How true, Sir.

"Counsel further asserts: 'The State is trying to get you to *kill* this man. They are out for blood.' LETS GET THIS STRAIGHT –– Defendant Pete <u>is</u> **the one** out for blood. The decision **not** to leave a witness THIS TIME is **His**. HE put himself here.

"It's incredible. There's a person in this Courtroom who has bludgeoned, bitten, and choked a vibrant human being to death. Sexually molesting her while she's dead or dying – **and** he continues to *smirk*. He thinks what we're doing is funny. Ladies and Gentleman of the Jury: YOU have the **power** to wipe the *smirk* off his face. YOU have the **power** of deterrence. YOU have the **power** to <u>guarantee</u> that Pete <u>never</u> – <u>ever</u> makes another woman a CORPSE! **YOU** can do something about violent crime. This is **your** chance. Let **your** voices be heard – CLEARLY –– UNMISTAKABLY!

"**August 16, 1977** – For whom did the bell toll? IT TOLLED for thirty seven year old Darlene –––. **November 4, 1977** – let it TOLL for the man who murdered her. Let the **bell** TOLL for Pete ––– !"

The Jury listens attentively, <u>and</u> they AGREE the **bell** should TOLL for the Defendant. They have no problem *deterring* Pete. They make his case a CAPITAL CASE. Two hours after the Case has been submitted to them, they return to the Courtroom with a **sentence of Death**. The Twelve are polled, and each reiterates the verdict that says in effect: Let the **bell** TOLL for the murderer of Texas Darlene. One month later the Court formally imposes a DEATH SENTENCE! A total of **ONE HUNDRED TEN DAYS** elapse from the time of the Crime to the adjudication of punishment for the Crime.

Indisputable PROOF that Criminal JUSTICE can be expeditiously rendered where there is THE WILL to do so. The secret is simple: **Keep the wheels greased** on CAPITAL CASES. **Prioritize** CAPITAL CASES. **Don't** indulge in JUDICIAL <u>ANNULMENT</u>. Capital Punishment is an expression of SOCIETY'S **sense** of *moral outrage* regarding the heinous nature of certain crimes. The People are ENTITLED to such **Judgments**. <u>Respect</u> the majority view concerning punishment. A Trial Jury is representative of a community. Honor the will of THE TWELVE. Validate JUST Jury Verdicts!

AND THEN --? When **does** PETE keep his **well earned** <u>reservation</u> at the EXECUTION CHAMBER?

Incredibly, inexplicably, unbelievably, inconceivably, unimaginably, unthinkably, preposterously, ridiculously, amazingly, implausibly, **<u>absurdly</u>** [there aren't enough descriptive words in the dictionary] – it's enough to GAG a **MAGGOT** – it takes a LONG – LONG – LONG time to get the answer.

How long is LONG – LONG – LONG? Brace yourselves, even serious skeptics of the Criminal Justice System are going <u>too</u> aim to low on this one. Is it **six months** later? **Two years** later? Some believe the <u>latter</u> time frame **IS** a REASONABLE **<u>deadline</u>** for processing an APPEAL under the integral constraints of a **prioritized, expedited** effort to RESOLVE appellate issues within a system that ACTUALLY *contemplates* the imposition of JUST EXECUTIONS! **Three years** later? **Six – eight – ten** years later? NO, **not** within the legal machinations of judicially contrived guidelines for trying, adjudicating, and appealing Capital Cases by those who have **no** WILL for **nor** STOMACH for EXECUTIONS, Baby. Of course, during the ten year interim Las Vegas has experienced the **<u>terror</u>** of some **nine hundred to a thousand <u>MURDERS ADP</u>**, i.e., after Defendant Pete. WHERE IS THE DETERRENCE if the **<u>deterring factor</u>** is NEVER employed?

Twelve years later? **Thirteen – fourteen – fifteen**? Come on now, this is a callous, cavalier, reckless, destructive way to carry out the people's business!

AND THE ANSWER IS --? Some speak of the evils of Judicial Activism. What we have in Defendant Pete's Appellate Procedure is JUDICIAL INACTION at its **WORST**! This is APPELLATE GRIDLOCK. This is over the top bull-crap. This is unreal! Louis Carroll would be flattered by the <u>imitation</u>. Regrettably, we witness a turtle-like shuffle of the Judiciary into the fantasy of LOOKING GLASS LAND – courtesy of the whimsical farce that is Pete's Appellate Process.

Would you believe **EIGHTEEN YEARS?** That's how long it took for the Appellate Procedure guys to <u>rule</u> that Defendant Pete received INEFFECTUAL representation of Counsel at his **Penalty Hearing**. It took the bright boys in Appellate Central **EIGHTEEN YEARS** to decide that "**The Noose**" – esteemed Counselor Rick – had not provided Pete a Constitutional Defense. UGH! That's handling the people's business with GLACIAL SPEED. That's EXTREMELY slow by any objective measurement. It took the TRIAL BOYS **one hundred ten days** to secure a DEATH SENTENCE, and it took the APPELLATE JUDGES **EIGHTEEN YEARS, er– SIXTY FIVE <u>HUNDRED</u> PLUS DAYS –** to set aside a DEATH SENTENCE. This would be comedic IF it wasn't true.

> "The time has come," the Walrus said, "To talk of many things:
> Of shoes–and ships–and sealing wax–Of cabbages–and kings–
> And why the sea is boiling hot–And whether pigs have wings."
> (Lewis Carroll, *Through The Looking Glass*, Tweedledee's
> recitation of a paragraph from a poem, "The Walrus and the
> Carpenter," p.204)

EIGHTEEN YEARS is a disparity of monumental proportion! I think the public deserves an explanation. I think the public **should** DEMAND an explanation. Where is JUSTICE for Darlene and her family? Where is JUSTICE for The People of the State of Nevada? JUSTICE delayed is often JUSTICE permanently **stayed**!

Hey, whose *minding* the store? Whose *tracking* this case? The Judges will say, "It's the Lawyer's <u>fault</u> stupid!" My rejoinder is: NO, it's **not** the Lawyers! **The Courts** have the <u>raw</u> POWER. They can <u>set</u> PRIORITIES if they **want** to. They can <u>keep</u> the wheels greased if they have the WILL and the STOMACH to **do** it! They can EXPEDITE appellate review for Capital Cases if they <u>really</u> **want to. EXTREMISM in the pursuit of procedure is a mockery of Justice!**

I want to clarify something I said <u>four</u> paragraphs back. The statement was: "Some speak of the evils of Judicial Activism. What we have in Defendant Pete's Appellate Procedure is JUDICIAL INACTION at its **WORST!**" <u>Why</u> is it the worst? Arguably, there is a simple **root cause**. It's JUDICIAL INACTION at its **WORST** because what is being done in <u>many</u> Capital Cases is prompted by an **ulterior** AGENDA. What is happening is sly and subtle – cynical and **deceptive**. The plain cold fact is: when the *layers of subterfuge* are peeled away the JUDICIAL <u>INACTION</u> **is** ACTUALLY an expression of JUDICIAL **<u>ACTIVISM</u>**. It's Courts BEING **<u>LEGISLATORS</u>** in contravention of their Constitution power. Courts obfuscating the SEPARATION between Executive, Legislative, and Judicial **<u>authority</u>** that is at the **<u>core</u>** of CONSTITUTIONS in the State of Nevada and the United States of America.

What we **<u>see</u>**, within the legal machinations <u>and</u> ENDLESS **delays** inherent in <u>judicially</u> contrived guidelines for trying, adjudicating, and appealing Capital Cases by those who have neither the WILL nor the STOMACH for **executions**, is a largely successful effort by a few *bleeding heart* **power brokers** in the Judicial System to ANNUL Capital Punishment in States within their jurisdiction! **Annul** means to make *void* or of *no effect*. It means to *abolish* and *cancel* and *abrogate*. It means to make a Judgement or a Judicial Proceeding a NULLITY!

Capital Punishment? Hell, there is **no** Capital Punishment in many Capital Convictions UNLESS a Defendant **insistently, categorically** gives up his Appeal Rights. The Courts have *strangled* the Death Penalty, and laid it to rest in many instances, just as surely as ole Pete grabbed Darlene around the neck with both bloody hands. Then choked and choked and choked until he'd laid her to rest in the Nevada *dust* where she'd fought for life until her last dying breath! Suffocating, interminable delays in Capital litigation have choked and choked and choked Death Sentences until they're as DEAD as the **murdered victims** they MEMORIALIZE.

I SHOULD **KNOW**. There was a time when **THIRTY plus** Defendants I'd been involved in Prosecuting were on **DEATH ROW.** Each of those men had received JUDGMENTS OF DEATH by Juries of their peers. JURORS who'd heard the Evidence and Court Instructions and Arguments of Counsel. JURORS who'd conscientiously deliberated the Cases and determined that respective Defendants had been proven guilty beyond a reasonable doubt. JURORS who'd sat through emotionally traumatic Penalty Hearings. JURORS who'd carefully weighed **aggravating** and **mitigating** circumstances, and concluded beyond a reasonable doubt that the appropriate punishments were **DEATH**. JURORS who'd possessed the moral certainty and strength of COMMITMENT to look these **killers** in their eyes and one by one by one – twelve times thirty + – cast their votes for **death.** CITIZEN-JURORS who'd believed **their** JUDGMENTS were **just** and **would-be-carried-out**!

Pshaw, what a pipe-dream-world they were living in! Their Verdicts have – in effect – been scrapped. Relegated to a dark shelf in a dark room away from the light of public scrutiny. Their gut-wrenching emotion and heated debate, their belief that the Criminal Justice System means NOTHING unless those who commit heinous, violent crimes **are** held ACCOUNTABLE for their despicable acts and PUNISHED accordingly, their TIME and their willingness to FULFILL their civic responsible –– *ALL* this has been WASTED in a sense. Why?

Well Sir, because the Judiciary has *nullified* their verdicts. That's a fact, the JUDICIAL INACTION that **becomes** JUDICIAL ACTIVISM **ends** up being JUDICIAL **NULLIFICATION**!! These characters don't want convicted Capital Murderers killed, so they usually succeed in KILLING the Jury Verdicts of Death – either by legal opinion or attrition.

Three paragraphs above I alluded to **THIRTY plus** Defendants I'd been involved in prosecuting being on **DEATH ROW.** What happened to those Cases? How many of those DEATH ROW INMATES have been executed? The **procedural fact** is a bitter pill for a passionate professional Prosecutor to swallow.

The ONLY **killer** I've prosecuted who went to the **Execution Chamber** is **Jesse B**. He shot and killed a young man during a botched attempted robber at a Casino Cage in Las Vegas. An errant bullet fired by the *career convict* in a standoff with Security mortally wounded a *bridegroom* on his honeymoon. Too bad the bullet didn't know it was an errant **shot**. The unfortunate victim of circumstance and Jesse's missile just happened to be in the wrong place at the wrong time. So much for *loving* marriage and *living* happily ever after.

But here's the kicker. **Jesse B.** didn't go to the **Execution Chamber** because the Appellate System put him there. **Jesse B.** put himself there. He's EXECUTED because he WAIVES his right to appeal. **Jesse B.** decides to take his punishment like a man. He says, "IF the System will cut me loose to live my life on the streets, I'll gladly – gratefully accept the offer. However, I **will not** live the rest of my life in the SLAMMER. I CHOOSE **death** over a lifetime of incarceration." Thus, **Jesse B.** categorically aborts his appellate rights, and the State of Nevada dutifully GRANTS his **death wish**.

I earnestly believe THE END RESULT of my Death Penalty efforts has been a **deplorable** debacle that graphically establishes the FUTILITY of Nevada Capital litigation – for the most part. It's simply a matter of arithmetic. Pete received his DEATH VERDICT **11/4/77**. I RETIRED **11/1/96**. Through nineteen years of Capital Litigation + thirteen years of retirement, incredibly, most of my Cases are still in the **system**.

Some intrepid wags might argue **The System** isn't very SYSTEMATIC. The antitheses of systematic is chaotic. Really, the system that takes **eighteen years** to DECIDE a **DEATH ROW inmate** wasn't *effectively* represented at his Penalty Hearing **isn't** in a systematic mode. The operative WORDS are **cavalier chaos**! How can such a DELAY in cracking the code of **alleged attorney misconduct** be justified? ——— And the unfathomable appellate delays characterize the other **TWENTY EIGHT plus** Capital Convictions **too**! [I'm excluding **Jesse B.**]

How are THE PEOPLE served by such chicanery? This kind of JUDICIAL EQUIVOCATION destroys any **causal connection** between the **Juror-decreed** punishment and **The Crime**. Society's legitimate expression of moral outrage **is** MUTED. Any possibility of DETERRENCE is shot down. The message of DETERRENCE resonates **only** when PUNISHMENT is **swift** AND **severe**!

I'm not taking a per se position FOR or AGAINST Capital Punishment. What **I'm saying** is that the WILL of The People through their Legislature **must** be respected. The Judicial Branch has NO right to trump **Codified Law**. JUSTICE occurs when Prosecutors and Jurors –– and Judges follow the mandate of LAW.

I remember the scene well. It's 8:45 a.m. I'm present for a *single case*. The District Attorney's Office has been formally notified **Pete's** Death Sentence has been OVERTURNED after **a decade plus eight**.. His Case has been remanded to District Court for further proceedings.

The Presiding Judge is about to hear his Criminal Master Calendar. The in-custody Defendants, chained together in a cheerless line, are ushered into the Courtroom by Corrections Officers and placed in the Jury Box. **Pete** isn't part of the chain-gang. However, the door to the Courtroom remains open, and I'm guessing **Pete** still waits in the wings. A short pause ensues. Suddenly, **Pete** crosses the threshold into the room. What I see is a sight for sore eyes. A space cadet who'd just dropped in from a faraway galaxy would've thought he'd touched down in a Medical Ward instead of a Courthouse.

The years haven't been kind to **Pete** – except in the ultimate sense. HE'S– STILL–BREATHING. Unlike his VICTIM, he's not lying under the ground in an advanced state of **putrefaction**. Actually, the effect of the passing years hasn't been kind to the Prosecution neither. They NO LONGER have a viable **Death Penalty Case**. Like DARLENE, the Prosecution's Capital Case has **putrefied**.

Pete DOESN'T **walk** into the Courtroom, he's **wheeled** into the Courtroom. EIGHTEEN years later – HE'S a little wizened, bent-over curmudgeon in a wheelchair. Destined to live at TAXPAYER **expense** for the rest of his mangy life. I recognize this REALITY in an instant. There's NO reason to have another Penalty hearing scheduled. A Jury will think we've *lost our minds* if we try. The notion of a second Penalty Hearing has been stripped of any vestige of credibility!

The *years* – the *change* in **Pete's** persona – the *disconnect* between that horrible night and now – the *loss* of witnesses and will – the mind boggling *frustration* of each passing year– the utter sense of *futility* – ARE in combination the COUP D'ETAT! A Legal Opinion and attrition win. The ABSURDITY of stultifying legal machinations and ENDLESS **delays** inherent in <u>judicially</u> contrived guidelines by those who have neither the WILL nor the STOMACH for executions – **WIN.** While in my view, J-U-S-T-I-C-E – **LOSES.**

Repeating the query: "When **does** PETE keep his **well deserved** <u>reservation</u> at the EXECUTION CHAMBER?" ––– **The Answer** is – NEVER.

A Courthouse bugler should be playing *taps* for J-U-S-T-I-C-E!

A Bible And A Jar Of Petroleum Jelly

"**Jealousy** [has] a *human* face; **Terror** the *human* form divine, And **Secrecy** the *human* dress." (Adapted from William Blake, *A Divine Image, Stanza I*)

Chapter 8

Francie and **Georgie** are married, but it doesn't appear to be a match made in heaven. Few celestial qualities brighten the marital landscape. The glow of fresh love has dissipated. The blush is gone from her cheeks. Their relationship, at least through Francie's lenses, has become too predictable – too pedestrian. Her pledge to her wedding vows is tenuous. She yearns for the adrenalin rush of extramarital romance. However, her pining is tempered somewhat by three children. The youngest is a son, the issue of her union with George.

Francie's a beautiful blonde. A curvaceous flirtatious cutie. George is a decent man at heart. He loves his wife and wants a successful relationship. But he's the proprietor of a small constellation of service stations, and believes a man's primary duty lies in the operation of his businesses. Homage to marriage and continued courtship of his spouse finish a distant second to pumping gas. He's gone a lot, yet he's a traditionalist. George expects his bride to be an apron toting domestic gal – a stay-at-home homemaker. He's not home much, but when he is he expects his wife and the children to be there too! It's **not** a good mix. It **isn't** her nature to be what he wants her to be. Square pegs don't fit in round holes.

So, while George runs his El Paso service stations Francie runs around. He's got a small collection of businesses, and she's got a burgeoning collection of male suitors. George doesn't bring her flowers anymore. Not a problem for Francie, she gathers plenty of flowers in other ways. The saga of Georgie and Francie becomes a tempestuous, one-sided relationship.

She has a history. A wrestler of some renown resides in town. *Rumor* has it that he and Francie have been an item. That Gorgeous G. got close enough to put her in some intriguing un-wife-like head locks. *Rumor* has it that Francie has been a regular on the bar-hopping scene. That she formerly worked some seductive shifts as a pleasure-seeking barmaid, and had an exotic way of collecting her tips. Sliding an empty bar cup between her sizeable cleavage and having customers drop their gratuities into the strategically positioned receptacle. The daring decolletage presented to ogling admirers is a win-win situation. They get an eyeful and she gets a cupful. An epicurean life-style seems ingrained in Francie's nature.

El Paso is a fairly large city, but it isn't huge. **Certain** people begin to talk. Some of the gossip probably stems from envy. Other chirping may be motivated by a sense of moral decency, and a spate of gutter verbiage likely takes the form of verbal poison darts launched by those who resent the distraction Francie presents to husbands or boyfriends. Who can really say why gossiping tongues wag?

The point is: George starts to **hear** things over a course of time. Not surprisingly, George is **not** happy about what he **hears**. He confronts Francie with allegations that have come to his attention. She stonewalls him. Accordingly, George has several employees conduct clandestine surveillance of Francie while she's enjoying her down-time from wifely responsibilities.

Their report isn't flattering. Francie has strayed, they say. She has a collection of inamoratos. Neither marriage nor motherhood is **deterring** an appetite to go extramarital. His suspicions are fact, they tell him. She's been involved in a series of erogenous trysts. He may be the only man in her life not smiling.

George is outraged. Francie is given an ultimatum. Cease and desist. Act like a mother and a wife or face the consequences. Meaning: he'll cut off her allowance and take her wheels away. The effect will be tantamount to house arrest.

She's unrepentant. Wants to severe the bonds of marriage. Alas, those ties haven't been very restricting anyhow. She gathers essential belongings and they pack the car. Francie and the children are gone by noon the following day. Slipping away right under George's nose, they begin a one-way 823 mile trip to Las Vegas for a quickie divorce and a fresh start.

"Francie and Georgie <u>were</u> lovers. Oh lordy, how they <u>once</u> loved. **Swore** to be true to each other, just as true –– as the stars above. She <u>was</u> his woman, but she done him wrong. She **<u>was</u>** his woman, **<u>yet</u>** she done him wrong." (Adapted from *Frankie and Johnny*, traditional American popular song lyrics)

George's sense of betrayal nearly consumes him. The sudden rupture of his family is emotionally devastating. He hopes Francie will have a change of heart. That she'll call or write. Asking him to wire money, so a prodigal, I've-seen-the-light wife can come back home. But she's **still** a square peg that won't fit in a round hole. Determined to find her destiny in Sin City. There is <u>no</u> call – <u>no</u> wire – <u>no</u> letter. Not a peep. NOTHING.

After a week, he's so distraught he can't eat or sleep nor effectively operate his service stations. George is a physical wreck. Missing his son. Bowled over by a two-timing wife, but still smitten by the beauty and charm he's taken for granted, but which, with her departure, now seem integral to his existence. The absence of Francie and the boy is eating him up. He <u>can't</u> get them out of his thoughts. Vivid recollections of their life together are constantly on his mind. His heart aches. He longs for news.

Thinking the worst, he imagines Francie's fallen victim to craven seducers in Vegas. Selling her body to survive. Possibly beaten, raped, and murdered. George is sick at heart. He's a pilot, and owns an airplane. Desperately, needing to know something about the status and whereabouts of his family, he flies to Vegas. His mission is simple: **Find Francie** and the children.

He doesn't locate them after twenty four hours. The trail is cold and Vegas is a big place. But **George** doesn't back off, he returns to El Paso with deadly resolve to track down his family at any cost. Needing boots on the ground in Sin City, he decides to dispatch an <u>employee</u> to be his eyes and ears and enforcer. An ex-felon named **Lee** is chosen for the task.

It's a **bad** decision – for <u>both</u> men! I understand the pathos, George. But Man – let it <u>go</u>. Give her up. Move on. There are **too** many charming, beautiful women in this world to get *done in* by a **single** headstrong, self centered, libidinous wife! Take some sleeping pills. Eat a healthy breakfast. Swallow a sedative. Go back to work. Get serious about *networking* single women, Sir.

And George, after your head's on straight contact your Lawyer. Get him serious about networking some good Nevada Attorneys. Get cracking within the parameters of the **Legal System** to obtain __custody__ of your son. Do things the legal way – which is *always* the RIGHT way!

Lee travels in a car George rents for about thirteen hours to get to the glitzy neon world of Lost Wages. Ultimately, he's going to loose more than wages on this fool's mission. George's Man treks up and down Glitter Gulch and the Las Vegas Strip– constantly looking and enquiring. He finds her, eventually. Francie is dining at a Strip coffee shop on Las Vegas Boulevard South. She's **not** alone!

Nor does she seem to be pining away for the Spouse she's abandoned. Francie is cuddling up to a lanky dark haired gentleman, perhaps fifteen years her senior. A __father__-__figure__ or a __paramour__? Their location, a booth in a remote corner of the spacious restaurant and Francie's manner, her head's on his shoulder – suggests the latter. Lee's perceptions about *what they're up to* will be crucial in the matter. His conclusions will make a tragic difference in the lives of certain principals. He slyly bides his time.

Francie and her Pal finish *whatever* they're doing. He pays the check and __they__ leave – **together**. Lee follows them to the parking lot. They depart the lot **together** in a tan vehicle. Mr. Tall and Lanky is driving the car. George's Man jumps in his car and follows. Some distance off the Las Vegas Strip, the vehicle being surveilled turns on to Maroney and stops in front of a house . Francie and the father-figure/paramour enter the dwelling – **together**. Lee records the address and heads to a pay telephone.

His report to George is gloomy. The spurned spouse is highly __displeased__. Locked into a state of mind that __isn't__ conducive to rational analysis. His thoughts are **sinister**. He wants to know **if** his wife is screwing this guy. Lee says he can't be positive, but tells George the Vegas odds are even money she is. Lee reiterates the lunch tete-a-tete. Then quips, they just walked into a house together and closed the door. The chances are good she's getting laid as we speak. George tells Lee to sit tight in Las Vegas. Says, he'll fly back, and **both** of them will go to the Maroney address to *personally* scope out the situation.

George arrives the following day, he meets Lee, and they travel in tandem to Maroney Street. It is **February 15.**They locate the house number Lee's recorded. The door isn't locked. Wanting to exploit the element of surprise **if** Francie, the children, and Mr. Tall and Lanky are there, they don't bother to ring the door bell or knock. They just barge in. Surprise guys, Lee has written down the __wrong__ number. Neither Francie, her male friend, nor the children is present. It's the WRONG house. Only **Bill** is inside. Never mind such a small detail. The two run from room to room until they're personally satisfied the persons of interest aren't present.

To say he's startled by the uninvited entry of two strange acting Texans is putting things mildly. But Billy's a laid-back sort of fellow who rolls with the punches. He wants to know if they're DEA, and if so, "Show me the search warrant." When he's told they aren't The Heat, Vegas Billy is **really** curious. He wants to know what the hell they're doing in his house.

Introductions are made and the three sit down. Ergo, George proceeds to *air out* a forty five minute sob story about being a husband scorned, and he doesn't paint a pretty picture of the woman whose done him wrong. Bill's sympathetic. He asks for and gets a description of the "two-timing bitch." It turns out the Texas boys have *narrowly* missed the mark. Vegas Bill says a woman fitting the description is living **next** door. She and three children moved in three days ago, and a lanky dark haired gentleman at least ten years her senior has been around a lot. He might be living there too.

Right on! Vegas Billy **isn't** a licensed Private Investigator and he doesn't know beans about being a *private eye*, but he's a **handy**-man. He lives in the neighborhood. In **no** way shape or form is Vegas Bill a professional investigator, he's merely a conversational stiff who happens to be strategically located next door to the quarry. Notwithstanding the aforementioned, during the course of the next hour George approaches him about doing some **eye-balling** and **fact-finding** to get the full skinny on his wife and his son. Bill's told he'll be paid handsomely for his efforts. Though the precise nature of his role is **not** formalized. It simply *evolves* over the next two and a half weeks.

There is no retainer agreement signed. No specific discussion of the amount of **green** Billy gets for his efforts. It's all unstructured, but Billy says he'll do it. If there's dirt to be found, he's happy to do the digging. Go figure, it seems George and Lee have stumble-bummed their way into a **three way**. They now have a Vegas connection. **Lee** is free to return to El Paso, and placate his wife.

The next day **Francie** learns from a friend in El Paso that George has traveled to Las Vegas. It is **February 16**. She hides at Tall and Lanky's house until she believes George is gone.

On **February 20** Vegas Billy initiates contact with the *persons of interest*. He meets **Francie** in front of her house on Maroney. She's helping Mr. Tall and Lanky start his car. He has an actual moniker. Francie's friend is named **Gordon**. Billy asks if Gordon is her husband. The reaction: "No, he's my Good Samaritan."

She tells the ad hoc inquisitor she's working at the Lady Luck Casino.

The Good Samaritan drives George's wife home from work on **February 21**. Further, he fixes her coffee and is about to go with George's son for hamburgers –– when **George** suddenly walks inside the house and snaps a photograph of the <u>threesome</u>. **Francie's** two daughters aren't in the picture. One's in her bedroom and the older girl is away from the house.

Francie grabs the telephone intending to call the Police. Right on cue, Mr. Private Eye pushes the front door open and walks into the house. Query: does being a next door neighbor the lady has briefly met the previous day **and** her scorned husband's flunky, give Vegas Bill the moral or legal authority to enter Francie's home without permission? I'd say the answer is implicit in the circumstances. She's attempting to summon help. Who is Bill there to help? Is it the legitimate occupant of the house or the <u>other</u> trespasser?

Well, there's strength in numbers for the **intruders**. George **threatens** Francie with bodily harm if she uses the telephone. Does Billy intervene on behalf of his new acquaintance. **No** –– he backs up his man George. The wayward wife backs off. She places the phone on the cradle. There is no 911 call to Police.

George tells her there's a CONTRACT on her life and the life of her boyfriend. Gordon sits in his car, waiting in the driveway. Vegas Billy throws in his two-bits worth. He tells Francie that Tall and Lanky is a bad influence. George and Francie and Billy walk outside. She darts away from George and tries to run off. The <u>two</u> men catch and restrain her. George warns, "You'd better stay here if you know what is good for you."

George walks closer to where Gordon sits waiting in his car. He exclaims, "Beat it Mister." Then as Tall and Lanky backs slowly out of the driveway, he shouts: "If you **ever** come around MY WIFE, **IF** you **ever** see her again, YOU– ARE–DEAD." Does Vegas Billy tell George to put a lid on that kind of talk? Hardly, he's chosen sides. He says ominously, "Let me handle things **my way**."

The three go back inside. George asks where Gordon was going to take his son. Francie explains that they were going for hamburgers. And Francie's pushy new acquaintance, the one who has initiated their meeting – quizzing her only <u>yesterday</u> in front of her house, and who has brazenly entered her house sans invitation <u>today</u>, now presumes to play the role of marriage counselor. He urges Francie to go back to her husband. "You had better think it over good. You had better think real hard about going back to George for the good of yourself and everyone concerned," he declares.

George tells the younger daughter that Gordon is a doper. That she has until tomorrow to make up her mind. He's got to know where she stands. The older daughter comes home, and she leaves with her step-father to get hamburgers. Later, George and Vegas Bill <u>leave</u> – but not before they've learned that power for Francie's house is in Gordon's name.

Immediately, **Francie** <u>calls</u> the police. They respond, and wait across the street until she's packed. Then, Francie and her three children *temporarily* depart for a more hospitable environment. The Police involvement <u>spooks</u> George. He returns to El Paso.

February 24 she speaks briefly over the phone with Tall and Lanky. He tells her he's frightened. His intention is to advise the police of George's threat and buy a gun. He also expresses concern for her welfare.

Time passes. Vegas Bill takes his quest for *dirt* seriously. The enthusiastic **ad hoc fact-finder** calls George four times per day for the next two weeks. Phone records establish that a total of **fifty six** calls were made from Bill's residential telephone in Vegas to El Paso telephones listed in George's name. There's **no** word from Francie to George, but a steady diet of accusatory sightings from Billy to George that reportedly document a daily *tandem itinerary* involving Francie and Lanky. Every call is received with a rising crescendo of pithy expletives from the spouse spurned.

Vegas Bill says he talks with her, and she **continues** to claim Tall and Lanky is only a friend –just a Good Samaritan helping her get settled in Las Vegas. However, Bill <u>believes</u> that's a large ration of bull sh–t. They practically live together, and he <u>thinks</u> they sleep together. This liaison is between two lovers, he asserts. They're like two peas in a pod. What's going on between their sheets is **not** merely patty-cake time.

The ugly green bile of *suspicion* oozes into the deep creases of George 's heart, shutting down any semblance of objectivity. **Malignant dark** thoughts surge into his brain. He's contemplating a **murderous act**. The thinking is irrational – stupid. **Murder** NEVER makes sense! But the enterprise George is poised to pursue is a *dead bang* **absurdity**!

Consider the circumstances. He's been driven to the brink of total goofiness by TWO PERSONS. <u>His</u> **wife** and a <u>complete</u> **stranger**. George *knows* <u>nothing</u> about Tall and Lanky except the <u>inferential</u> scuttlebutt he's gotten from his employee and his improvisatorial dirt collector. Neither

Lee nor Vegas Bill has caught them **in the act.** Billy <u>hasn't</u> seen them *in flagrante delicto.* He's only guessing. She's told him the man is only a friend – a Good Samaritan. Suppose the relationship **is** purely platonic? How <u>logical</u> is the course of conduct George has decided to take then? Or, <u>suppose</u> they HAVE been doing the *dirty deed*, <u>every</u> day in <u>every</u> imaginable position since the day they met, does that make it <u>logical</u> to eradicate <u>the</u> **stranger?** The *casual* interloper in this scenario? Mr. Tall and Lanky <u>hasn't</u> entered into any sort of fiducial relationship with George. He's not violating a position of trust with the husband. He's only a man acting in the manner of many men. Opportunistic, doing <u>it</u> because he can – assuming he **is** doing it.

However, **the** WIFE is a mare of a different color. Francie <u>does</u> have a fiducial relationship with her husband. She has exchanged solemn **wedding** VOWS with George. <u>These</u> two have the relationship of trust. **SHE is the one** who made PROMISES to him. **She's the one** whose spurned her man. "Francie and Georgie <u>were</u> lovers. Oh lordy, how they <u>once</u> loved. **Swore** to be true to each other, just as true –– as the stars above...She **was** HIS WOMAN, <u>yet</u> SHE done him wrong." (*Frankie and Johnny*, ibid)

There's a disconnect in all this. **Murder** NEVER makes sense! But **if** a husband's beef is going to be carried to the ultimacy in **murky** extremism, SHE'S probably a <u>less</u> **ignoble** choice than Mr. Tall and Lanky. Yet, notwithstanding reasonable criteria to the contrary, George is hell-bent on eliminating the interloper. He'll **not** condone ANYONE laying their hands on the recalcitrant OBJECT of <u>his</u> **affection. –––**

George, DON'T–DO–IT for heaven's sake! You're talking about human life here. You're about to unleash an evil genie that will tip you upside down. Let it go, Man. Give up on her. Move on. *DO–**NOT**–sacrifice everything* in a <u>wild</u> <u>hare</u> <u>scheme</u> to get your wife back! There are **greener** more congenial pastures. The world is full of beautiful, eligible, decent, fun-loving women. DON'T let a fish, who doesn't want to be in your net, drag you into the SLAMMER. <u>Unhook</u> Francie. **Let her go!** <u>Focus</u> on being a decent father to your son. Save yourself a lot of grief and expense. Spare yourself the ignominy of life in the Big House, Sir. FORGET you ever heard of Gordon B. and Vegas Bill. Put your ex-con back to work doing lube jobs or wheel alignments or something else that's constructive. ABORT **his** <u>mission</u>!

But as the world turns, it's unlikely anyone made such a speech to George. They should have, but they probably didn't. Whatever, it's doubtful he'd have listened anyway. He's obsessing over the Francie issue. George is a husband scorned, and he's going to make somebody pay. Even IF it means putting out a MURDER FOR HIRE **contract** for a passing *ship in the night* acquaintance of his absentee wife.

Twenty four hours later, GEORGE'S FOLLY has **Lee** on the road again. He has an *itchy* trigger finger. A .38 caliber revolver and a box of ammo in the car. A PLAN to rendevous in Sin City <u>with</u> Vegas Bill, and a stern CHARGE from his Boss to **kill** the <u>shill</u> he believes has enticed Francie into a life of debauchery. They're to waylay the **target** when he's alone. Francie is to be privy to nothing.

The big-shot **hit man** with the little gun travels straight through to Las Vegas again. When **Lee** arrives he rendezvouses with **Vegas Bill**. A more unlikely accomplice would be hard to find. He didn't know anything about Georgie's tale of broken vows until **<u>sixteen</u>** days ago. An INADVERTENT ACT sucks him into a web of intrigue, kidnap, and murder in the sage brush.

It's chilling to contemplate the ad lib beginning of this sinister consortium. Lee writes down the wrong house number. George and Lee barge inside by mistake and accidentally meet Billy boy. He's **<u>neither</u>** a professional *hit man*, **nor** a professional *investigator*, **nor** anything professional. Bill's only the *handyman*. He's in the catbird seat. Someone living next door to George's beloved. Who has been befriended by the **star-crossed** Mr. Tall and Lanky.

It's incredible. Vegas Bill's nonchalant, willful slide from spectator to fact-finder to corpse-maker defies logic. **Nor** is the Francie/Gordon B. situation a bone Lee <u>has</u> to pick. He can <u>throw</u> his **.38** into the desert. He can <u>tell</u> his Boss to take this job and shove it. He can pump gas somewhere else.

But does the disconnect give these two <u>pause</u>? NO! <u>They</u> already have their marching orders. This is leap year. Maybe the stars have made them crazy.

They'll do it the following morning. Vegas Bill has learned where Tall and Lanky lives, and he's been monitoring his schedule. Billy is reasonably certain Gordon will be at his house prior to twelve noon. Lee checks into a motel and awaits the dawning of the fateful day. I'm wondering how two men with murderous hearts sleep the night before. Fitfully? Like babies? Stone cold? Profusely sweating? Battling insomnia? Besieged by fuzzy images of playing pinball machines? Nightmares? Dreaming of jailhouse blues?

Morning comes. Lee goes to Billy's place. <u>They</u> converse – plotting their modus operandi. Each man gulps down a cup of black coffee, spiked with a shot of whiskey. <u>They</u> go together to Tall and Lanky's abode. Vegas Bill knocks. Lee stands away from the door – out of sight. Billy lures the target outside, and Itchy Fingers puts the heat on him. <u>They</u> take him to the car and travel a distance of less than half a mile to an outlying, unpopulated desert area. Francie's Pal is ordered out of the car at gunpoint. <u>They</u> walk him about fifty feet from the car. It's a **death march**, but Francie's Pal doesn't recognize the gravity of the situation, at first. He has no clue regarding the animus that prompts the gig. He asks what this is all about. Lee tells him to <u>shut</u> his mouth and <u>get</u> on his knees. Then he cocks the gun. The tapping sound is a wake-up call for Gordon B. Reveille, a call to move his feet.

He jumps up and tries to bolt away. Sadly, a man doesn't outrun a bullet.

Lee squeezes the trigger. Discharging a **bullet** into Gordon's upper back, between his shoulder blades. The bullet path is through and through. The Victim falls on his stomach, and **Lee** stoically *fires* a **round** into the back of his HEAD. The **contract** is executed. The **horrendous deed** is done. GEORGE'S FOLLY has wheels.

Did it get Francie back into Georgie's arms? Hell No! Did it get all three of the Principals into deep shit? Hell Yes! A TERRIBLE CRIME, having **no** basis in fact as an act of *punishment* and **no** basis in love-grown-cold as a means of *reconciliation* for two spouses, has – nevertheless – been perpetrated. The conspiratorial MURDER FOR HIRE makes **no** sense. It's moronic. A very bad case of **felony stupid**!

Moreover, the **Actus Reus** *isn't* a <u>work</u> <u>of</u> <u>art</u> neither. These Birds leave the body on top of the ground. Then, Vegas Billy goes home to sleep it off, and Lee goes back to Texas to return and report. George is pleased that **his** CHARGE has been carried out. **Not** pleased that the body is left in **plain view** for buzzard bait and police detection.

Guess what? The ACT OF OMISSION means **Lee** gets to make a <u>third</u> trip to Vegas. He'll be taking a **shovel** instead of a firearm this time, and a **pick** to blast through pockets of cliche might also be helpful. Further, he's got some big time EXPLAINING to do on the home front. <u>His</u> **wife** likes to be kept informed. She's been left with only vague ("It's-a-job-George-wants-me-to-do.") excuses to this point. BUT a **third** trip to Las Vegas within *three weeks*? The deal is beginning to sound VERY *fishy* to Diane. She's a suspicious woman by nature. Sudden waves of trips to Vegas have become too much for her to fathom.

She **issues** her own ULTIMATUM. "Either tell me what's REALLY going on in Las Vegas or TAKE ME with you! Otherwise, it's been nice knowing you, Buddy. I'll be gone when you get back." Diane's playing hardball, wanna-be good hubby Lee is between a rock and a hard place.

There's a saying that's applicable to accomplices in a Criminal endeavor: "**Three** may keep a secret, IF **two** of them are DEAD." (Benjamin Franklin, *Poor Richard's Almanack*, 1735 – emphasis added) These droll remarks are certainly apropos to George's folly. IF the benighted husband wants the job done right he's got to do it himself, and it's DITTO if he wants to avoid detection. *Outsourcing* a **MURDER** makes it hard to KEEP it **secret**.

The bubble bursts at **Lee's** place. It happens because a skeptical wife has to be placated. **Lee** shares the **secret** with Diane, bringing a **fourth** person into the scheme. He tells her he's killed a man in Las Vegas – SHOT him to death. That he's done it for George. The man is insane with jealousy, and he's taken care of a guy sleeping with George's wife. Lee says he didn't want to do it, but his job was on the line. He tells Diane that George is good with ultimatums too. That George told him to "Take care of the Vegas business or find yourself another line of work."

Lee tells Diane that George has a Vegas connection, a character named Billy. That he and Bill abduct the victim from his front door stoop. Take the man to a nearby desert area and gun him down.

Then **Lee** explains **trip three** to Las Vegas. "Billy and I were so hyper, so anxious to get away from the body, we FORGOT to cover the guy up. I'm going back to Vegas to BURY the body. If I want it done right, I've got to do it myself. This will be straight up and straight back, Turtledove"

Two hours later he's headed down the road *alone*. Traveling toward the spot where Mr. Tall and Lanky lies in a crumpled heap for all the world to see.

However, the world doesn't *see* the **MURDER** VICTIM. He still slumbers in plain view when **Lee** arrives – shovel in hand. The ground is hard, the digging is laborious, and the grave is shallow. But Lee gets him under the ground. His sense of relief is instantaneous. The corpus delicti of homicide is buried. The Crime is concealed, hidden from the World. The Coppers have NO body. The malicious conspiracy has been pulled off without a hitch. Their deed is secreted!

Well, not actually. The information deposited inside the heads of certain people IS **above** ground, Lee! "Other sins only speak; **murder shrieks** out." (John Webster: *Duchess of Malfi* [1623], Act IV, Sc.2)

Perhaps, if **Lee** had spoken of other sins, Diane would have let those sins quietly lie. But Lee spoke of the **"M" word**. The dreadful WORD is mind-numbing to Diane. Lee's told her he SHOT a man to death. The admission is a dagger in the heart. It tips her relationship totally out of kilter. She can't sleep. She can't eat. She can't stop thinking about Lee's words. The sin of **murder** SHRIEKS into her soul. **Lee's** return will only exacerbate her agony. She knows what she has to do. Someone has to shed light on the matter. A HUMAN BEING has been tracked down, abducted, and **murdered**.

The return of the Texas gunslinger is delayed. Lee has an automobile accident on his **third** return trip to El Paso. He overshoots a curve in the highway. Hurrying back to Diane too fast? Trying to remove himself too quickly from the scene of his coverup? Imprudently attempting to distance his thoughts from the spilled blood too – with a pint of bourbon? He's not hurt, but the car is totaled. George flies to the closest town to retrieve his hired assassin. However, **Lee** doesn't get home soon enough to retrieve his wife. He confided in Diane to keep her around, but she's gone anyway when he comes back around.

Lee's Turtledove calls Las Vegas Law Enforcement, and spills her guts. She loses a husband in the process, but she obtains peace of mind. "**Three** may keep a secret, IF **two** of them are DEAD." (Benjamin Franklin, ibid.) Vegas Bill and Lee aren't dead so the *exception* **isn't** applicable, right?

Lee cops to his wife and **Diane** cops to Police. Tomfoolery comes out of the closet. **Diane's** words have a domino effect. **Lee** is arrested. He SHOWS the Police where the BODY is buried, and gives a statement to Law Enforcement implicating George and Vegas Bill. First, **Billy** is arrested. AND THEN – GEORGE is arrested in El Paso, and Nevada submits a formal Request for Extradition to the State of Texas. Not surprisingly, GEORGE **isn't** too keen about leaving his Asylum State to face a Murder Rap in Nevada. The request for EXTRADITION is opposed.

Meanwhile, the Justice System lumbers forward in its Vegas venue. **Lee** makes a deal with Nevada Authorities. He will plead guilty to a **Second Degree Murder** of Tall and Lanky with a stipulated sentence of fifteen years – conditioned on his turning **State's Witness** against GEORGE and Vegas Bill. TRUTHFULLY testifying at **all** proceedings involving his Co-Conspirators.

The Prosecution wants leverage in the matter. Initially, the Office of the District Attorney insists that Lee *fully* **carry out** his part of the bargain before he's permitted to plead to Murder Two. This approach makes sense. Inmates **don't** like to be sent to the Slammer wearing a snitch jacket. State's Witnesses have a rough go of it in the Big House. A *snitch* is persona non grata! He's got a bull's-eye on his back. Lee knows this, and he doesn't have a single altruistic soft spot in his body. He's not a philanthropist. He's **not** made a deal to grease the Criminal Justice System. Lee's made a deal to further his own interest. Namely, *minimizing* his hard time in the State Penitentiary. His sole objective is to lubricate his trek to parole. That's why he's willing to wear THE JACKET. –– Period. End of story.

The Prosecution does a *dress rehearsal* with its **killer** witness. He testifies at Vegas Bill's Preliminary Hearing. Everything seems to go according to Hoyle. The sworn testimony correctly, exactly follows the script Lee has proffered in his recorded statements to Police. Presumably, his testimony is a truthful rendition of **fact**. The Prosecutive efforts are predicated upon that slender premise.

However, ONLY the **three** conspirators *actually* know if this is a Murder-For-Hire, and ONLY Lee and Vegas Bill *actually* know if The Murder operandi has been **correctly** described by the testifying Accomplice. The ensuing words of Sir Walter Scott are highly pertinent.

"I cannot tell how the truth may be; I say the tale as 'twas said to me."
(*The Lay of the Last Minstrel, Canto II, Stanza 22*)

At the Preliminary Hearing of Vegas Bill and thereafter in Trial Proceedings involving Billy, The PROSECUTION **doesn't** *actually* know how the **truth** may be. The PROSECUTION **only** knows the **tale** as 'twas said by their witness. And of course, it really goes without saying –– that is the STATE OF AFFAIRS in **every** Criminal Case. Unless the Prosecutor is a PERCIPIENT **witness** to the FACTS in controversy, and he'd be a witness **not** a Prosecutor if that circumstance existed, he CAN'T *possibly* know what the **truth may be**. IF you **didn't** SEE it happen or HEAR it happen or SMELL it or TASTE it or TOUCH it as it happens –– you **don't** really – really KNOW the **facts!** A Prosecutor knows **what** he *reads* in the File, **what** he *hears* from the Witness Stand, and **what** *reasonable inferences* he acquires from admitted Exhibits. A Prosecutor's TRUTH is Case TRUTH! **His factual knowledge** is directly proportional to the VERACITY of his Direct and Circumstantial Evidence.

Vegas Bill is held to answer as an Accomplice in the Murder of Mr. Tall and Lanky, and bound over to the District Court. His Trial begins approximately four months later. Another Deputy DA and myself are assigned to Prosecute the Case. Our first names rhyme. So, I'll dub the Prosecutive effort the *Dell and Mel* Show. The Defense Counselors are Devoe and Doug. So, I'll make them the *Double D* Show. Both men are worthy adversaries – and true gentlemen. The Judge runs a tight ship. He's a veteran Jurist, a legal scholar, and a stern advocate of strict Trial decorum. I'll call His Honor-ship, Judge General. It's a well deserved derivative of *Generalissimo*. Things are done The General's way in Judge General's Courtroom.

The Jury is empaneled, sworn, and briefly oriented regarding trial procedure.

Judge General peers down at Counsel tables, sizes up the <u>four</u> Barristers seated before him [They look rather small and insignificant from where he's enthroned.], and declares in deliberately measured tones, "State, —— your Opening remarks."

I'll pause to mention the obvious. Tandem Prosecution requires a **division** of responsibilities. The *Dell and Mel* Show **is** a tandem trial sojourn. But as the world revolves in such matters, PARTICULARS sometimes get lost in the big picture spin. Judge General is asking us to deliver our OPENING STATEMENT to the Jury. The problem is: **ONE** of us has *forgotten* whose giving it!

Well, it's my buddy Dell. We've <u>agreed</u> he's to deliver the Opening remarks, but he's evidently suffering from some short-term memory loss. SO ———— **we** just sit there all warm and fuzzy, not batting an eye, nor moving a muscle, or clearing out throats to get the verbal engines humming. Both <u>waiting</u> for the other to spring into action and act **lawyer-like**. Meaning: to start earning our Prosecutorial salaries by making our *tongues sweat*.

Ten – fifteen – twenty seconds pass. Judge General becomes restive. He's thinking these bozos are taking a hell of a long time to collect their thoughts. However, he takes Judicial *cognizance* of whom he's dealing with. His Honor-ship <u>grants</u> the muted duo another ten seconds.

The extra time doesn't summon any movement nor sound from the *Dell and Mel* Show. Hence, Judge General does something he's very good at. He fixes an intensely **stern** STARE upon the two DA boys, and <u>ratchets</u>

up the volume of his injunction in case we're hard of hearing. "**State, –––– your Opening remarks!**"

There's an edginess to his politeness now. He wants to say, "Gentleman, start your engines. I want to hear some rhetoric. Tell us about this case. Share what you intend to prove. Show me some *tongue sweat*. Get this damn show on the road."

Nothing changes for a few seconds. We're still sitting there like two bumps on a pickle – blissfully clueless. Each waiting for the other to rise to the occasion, and spit out an OPENING STATEMENT. Then a dawning occurs, pretty much simultaneously. A subtle recognition in both members of the team that the other **isn't** going to stand up. I turn my head to look at *Dell* in perfect sync with his head rubbernecking to gape at me.

We're both sporting quizzical expressions. Each principal in the *Dell and Mel* Show wondering why the other has lead in his feet. Each becoming rather chagrined at the *dead time* that's becoming an embarrassment. Our eyes meet. His brown and my green lock together in momentary incredulity. Those in the gallery may have thought we were doing a Prosecutorial *chant*. In a rare showing of one-mindedness we concurrently mumble, "Court's indulgence."

He whispers first. Whispering because the Court's in session. Whispering because Judge General doesn't appreciate indecision. *Dell* is whispering because he doesn't want the Jury to become aware of any Prosecutorial *confusion*. They might pose a cogent query , "If these bastards can't get it right at the gate how can we trust them to be credible at the finish line?"

Dell says, "**Get up**. You're giving the OPENING STATEMENT." I whisper my demur, "**You get up**. You agreed to give the OPENING STATEMENT. So, shake a leg."

The part of *Dell's* anatomy that moves isn't his leg. He shakes his head in disagreement, and replies: "I don't remember it being that way. I thought you were doing the OPENING. I don't have an outline prepared." "That's a **ditto** on this end," I say. "Obviously, I wouldn't have an outline for an OPENING STATEMENT, *Dell*. I'm CROSS EXAMINING the Defendant, **if** he takes the witness stand. I'll be preparing an outline for CROSS. The **agreement** is you do OPENING and I do CROSS!" The last sentence of my utterance is an exclamation, that is, **if** a Prosecutor can do an exclamation point while he's whispering.

We're at loggerheads. The whispering stops, and we just **stare** intently at one another. Neither wanting to budge. Both wanting to do it his way.

Judge General quashes the logjam. It's abundantly clear we've tried his patience to the breaking point. The DA boys are hovering on the brink of a CONTEMPT **order**.

The General says frostily, "**Gentlemen**, <u>do</u> your OPENING STATEMENT **now** or forever hold your peace. Any **failure** by ONE of you to start speaking within the next FIVE SECONDS, will be construed by the Court to be an IMPLIED WAIVER of your right to deliver an OPENING STATEMENT. Do we <u>understand</u> each other?"

A <u>second</u> showing of one-mindedness occurs. The Prosecutors are doing their *chanting* thing again. It's only three words, "YES, YOUR HONOR."

Then my good **friend** and **mentor**, who taught me how to Shepardize – the <u>senior</u> **partner** in this joint Prosecutive enterprise, pushes his rangy frame away from Counsel table without further comment, rises to his feet, strides to the lectern, looks around – a bit like a lean deer caught in the headlights, scratches his throat, apologizes for the delay, and proceeds to deliver an **excellent**, albeit impromptu OPENING STATEMENT. *Dell*, I gotta love ya, Man.

The Trial proceeds. The first Officers on the Scene, a Deputy Coroner, and the Medical Examiner have testified. The Murder Site has been identified, and the RECOVERY of the body described. The **cause of death** established, to-wit: it's a **criminal** agency perpetrated by **two** small caliber gunshot wounds. The Case against Vegas Bill has reached a pivotal phase. The *Dell and Mel* Show hopes it will be a HIGH mark in their Case. They're wrong. What happens is the <u>LOWEST</u> point in their presentation. Naturally, what is high and what is low is very different from the Defense perspective. The STATE'S <u>LOWEST</u> point makes the *Double D* Show want to do cartwheels.

Lee's on the witness stand. The problem is the State's LOST its leverage! The Defense has found a FOOL in the Office of the District Attorney, and has skillfully **PLAYED** him. I don't recall a name, but it **isn't** either of the principals in the *Dell and Mel* Show. Obviously, it's a management-type-person with enormous gullibility. A few weeks after his Preliminary Hearing <u>testimony</u>, accomplice-witness Lee begins to **whine**.

He says he's concerned about **not** getting credit for ALL the dead time he'll be serving in the Clark County Jail prior to Vegas Bill's Trial, <u>and</u> the protracted time-lapse implicit in Indictment challenges, lengthy Extradition procedures, and dilatory Trial scheduling orchestrated by

FRANK, the alleged *mastermind* of the interstate **Murder-For-Hire**. The fellow purported to have an extremely long arm extending from El Paso to Las Vegas, and a team of influential Lawyers who will slow his Prosecution to a *snail's crawl*.

Lee wants the DA's Office to cut him some slack. Allowing him to enter a Plea to Second Degree Murder and having his stipulated fifteen year sentence imposed PRIOR to the Trials of **both** Frank and Vegas Billy. That way he can be housed in the State Penitentiary, and guaranteed FULL credit for good time served.   Swell, but will the Prosecution get FULL **testimony** from their Witness under this scenario? There is resistance to **Lee's** proposal by the powers that be – for awhile. Another month passes. The **whining** persists and the Witness becomes **surly**. His Lawyer argues that he's becoming so stressed he **won't** be worth a hill of beans to ANYONE unless something is done ASAP.

Gullibility blinks. Resistance withers inside management central. A trap has been laid, but naivete is the order of the day. Thanks a bunch! **Lee** gets his DEAL consummated before he's satisfied his OBLIGATION to *truthfully* **testify** at the Trials of Billy and Frankie. The DA has specifically performed, but will **Lee** provide SPECIFIC PERFORMANCE?

Empowered by a Prosecutorial cave-in, the Killer Witness is about to be a head liner in **two** separate Courtroom dramas. He'll be Dr. Jekyll morphed into *Mr. Hyde*. The killer who has perpetrated a **monstrous** crime is about to perpetrate **fraud** in the Courthouse. His deal's in his pocket. He's **not** going to be a Courtroom informant NOW. The SNITCH JACKET **won't** fit him NOW. He'll renege. Gullibility has fashioned a sullen, glaring, uncommunicative, subversive, uncooperative, unmanageable MONSTER with a bad memory for Witness duty. Prematurely executing Lee's *bargain* **is** snake-eyes to the Trial boys.

Lee's Direct Examination proceeds predictably through Francie's exodus to Sin City and the subsequent surveillance of Mr. Tall and Lanky by **Vegas Bill** and himself. Though the Prosecution recognizes their accomplice witness is a loose cannon. We're apprehensive going into this segment of the Trial. But Dell's been casually exhaling carbon dioxide gas as his stress subsides and I've slumped back into a more relaxed posture in my chair. We're about ten minutes into *itchy finger's* testimony, and there's an undeclared sense between Dell and me that our high-level trepidation regarding **Lee's** witnessing **performance** may have been exaggerated. It

hasn't. Mr. Itchy Fingers is simply lulling us into a false feeling of security. The trap is set and it's about to be sprung!

Testimony continues to the fateful morning of the Murder. **Lee's** still on track. He testifies he goes to Billy's place and **they** converse. However, there is a subtle deviation in his proffer to the Jury. *He says nothing about plotting their modus operandi.* I'm examining. The omission is noted, but I don't see the **red flag** –YET. **Lee** testifies **they** gulp down cups of black coffee spiked with shots of whiskey. [Okay, right on dude.] **Lee** testifies **they** go the front door, and ––– [He pauses momentarily. Possibly, for effect.] Then Mr. Itchy Fingers locks a tense gaze upon me and exclaims: " AFTER THAT I LEFT, walked to my car, got in and drove to The Guy's apartment." Hey, he **isn't** speaking of a TWOSOME, that's SINGULAR! Where's the JOINT **performance**, Mister?

There's **nothing** *subtle* about the deviation from script this time! But I'm wanting to look on the bright side. Wanting the Accomplice/ Witness to be cooperative. Thinking the explicit deviation may have been *inadvertently* explicit. I rein in the Witness and steer him back to Vegas Billy's apartment. We'll try again.

Question: "You said the two of you walked to the front door, is that correct?

Answer: "Yes, Sir. We went to the front door of his apartment." Question: "What happened then?" Answer: "Well, we finished talking. Gulped down our cups of black coffee, and ––– **I** LEFT."

And I'm thinking, "Hell fires –this isn't cool," but wanting to stay upbeat I plow forward. Question: "What about [Billy], what did he do?" Answer: "Our business was complete. He stayed in his apartment. Went back to bed for all I know. I LEFT **ALONE**." Ping! Lee activates the trap spring. Gotcha, DA boys.

It's a classic instance of Prosecutors being *turned around* by a **killer** Star Witness. The head liner in Courtroom drama #1 is giving the Prosecution the shaft. Ouch, it stings! Mr. Itchy Fingers has so much to TELL, and he's been bought and paid for. Yet, he's decided to shuck his **snitch jacket. HE** has FULL complicity in a Murder, but he's refusing to SELL the Jury what he's agreed to TELL about the culpability of his PARTNERS.

The *Dell and Mel* Show is traumatized. Shaken to it's core. What's just happened may be a SHOWSTOPPER. –– We ASK *for the Court's indulgence.* Judge General grants the request. He wears an exceptionally pensive, almost sympathetic, expression on his usually dour countenance.

He's been a DA. He knows the score. Presently, it's Lions ONE – Christians ZERO. The *Double-D* Show is ecstatic!

Dell and I speak in muffled tones. Trying to maintain some degree of dignity and professional decorum as we discuss our dilemma. Thereafter, we ASK *to approach the Bench.* A hasty **five-way** conversation follows. The Trial is recessed and the Jury excused. But they aren't total dummies. They've been <u>percipient</u> witnesses to a high-stakes drama. They've *seen* it and they've *felt* it. **Tension** is palpable on the Prosecutor side of the Courtroom, while **exuberance** is palpable on the other side.

The *Dell and Mel* Show is back the next day with a NEW game plan. It has <u>two</u> phases. The Parties meet in Chambers. The Prosecutors <u>propose</u> their course of action. It's argued on the record, and His Honor-ship rules for the State. Sweet! The disingenuous treachery of Mr. Itchy Fingers **doesn't** stop the show. The Trial moves ahead.

PHASE ONE – **Lee** is **called** back to the Witness Stand and allowed to play the knave. He **tries** to SELL *a story* to the Trial Jury that has him acting as a LONE WOLF. He does it out of spite. **Not** out of love for Vegas Bill nor George, but out of deep-seeded DISDAIN for Law Enforcement. And he <u>does</u> it because he can. He's got his DEAL in his pocket.

PHASE TWO – **Lee** is **confronted** with every PRIOR <u>inconsistent</u> statement he's made describing the Murder of Tall and Lanky as a **Tale** of THREE WOLVES.(1) The declarations made by Lee to his wife *justifying* a third trip to Las Vegas. (2) The informal verbal comments made at the time Lee is *picked* up by Police. (3) An *audio* taped interview by Lee with Homicide Detectives. (4) A *video* taped interview by Lee with Homicide Detectives. (5) An *affidavit* attached as an exhibit to Requisition papers sent to Texas (6) Lee's <u>sworn</u> *testimony* at the Preliminary Hearing of Vegas Billy.

ALL are statements made BEFORE *gullibility blinks.* The simplistic act of specifically performing the State's obligation <u>before</u> their ACCOMPLICE witness has satisfied his obligation to them. The State's Rep got his wires crossed. You **don't** make a deal with the devil and expect the devil to honor his deal – without LEVERAGE!

The appearance of **Diane** is memorable. She's split from the apartment she shared with Lee, and agrees to travel from her new Texas digs to <u>testify</u>. She's a linchpin in the Prosecution"s strategy to overcome the **fraudulent** testimony of her husband. She's able to describe confidential *admissions* made by her husband within the framework of their marriage. **Lee** has NO discernable reason to mislead his wife about a *murder* he's ADMITTING he committed.

Further, his disclosure **isn't** a spontaneous declaration. Her **ultimatum** triggers his words. It's been necessary for **Diane**, in a manner of speaking, to PRY the words out of Lee that IMPLICATE him and his confederates.

She agrees to come, but her trip to Las Vegas is filled with apprehension. It's neither easy nor pleasant to be a witness in a Murder Trial. Particularly, when your husband **is** the actual **killer**, and you're being called upon to *impeach* his **perjurious** testimony. Not surprisingly, she's as nervous as "a worm in hot ashes," yet her hands are cold as ice. She's dreaded her appearance from the moment her subpoena was delivered. **Diane's** never been a witness in a Court of Law before, and she isn't thrilled about having her resume' enhanced by the experience.

Moreover, when her *hour of anxiety* arrives she's been waiting to testify in the hallway outside the Courtroom for **three** days. **Lee's** repudiation of Billy and Frankie's culpability, legal arguments spawned by the dramatic evidence swing, the resulting change in witness sequence, and other material factors – have combined to substantially slow the progress of the Trial.

And there's a curious **irony** in construction of the *access* doorways of Judge General's Courtroom that is also disquieting to **Diane**. Both doors are graced, or cursed as the case may be, with a *glass* pane that permits persons in the hallway to SEE from the outside what's happening inside. Of course, **Diane** has been one of those persons for **three** Court days worth of seemingly endless drama. So, while she's been cooling her heels in the hallway, each lingering, heart-palpitating stare into the bowels of the Courtroom has heightened her emotional despair. By the time **Diane** is summoned into the Courtroom by the Bailiff, she's bewildered, physically exhausted, and brings a brain to the Witness Stand, which if subjected to a cat-scan, would probably have resembled a bowl of mush. The Lady is a train wreck about to happen. The Defense couldn't have choreographed a better way to **freeze** an integral State's Witness if they'd tried. She's been *fouled* by circumstances beyond her control, but she won't be making her free throws.

Diane walks stiffly into the room, self consciously glancing from side to side at the gaggle of spectators. Tensely raises her right arm and swears in tremulous tones to tell the truth. When she sits down she almost missed the witness chair, and her hands shake as the Bailiff adjusts the microphone. It's too much, the chore at hand weighs heavily upon her. Persons who haven't walked in Diane's shoes don't fully appreciate the inner toughness required for Courtroom testimony. The glare of the lighting, Judge General – resplendent in his judicial robe, the Court Reporter thumping away at her stenotype machine, the Clerk, the Corrections Officers, the skeptical scrutiny of Defense Lawyers, the Courtroom gallery, the fear of the unknown, and *him*. A man accused of abetting murder in cold blood sits a few feet away –– scowling.

Lee's wife sees only one friendly face. **Her** courtroom lawyer and protector. Her sole acquaintance. She's met him twice during pretrial conferences. **Diane** zeros in on a Prosecutor, and keeps her quivering expression glued to <u>me</u> for the precious few minutes she favors us with her presence. She sees me as her anchor in these turbid judicial waters. Nevertheless, hovering inside her subconscious is an ominous suspicion, that at any moment, the bad guy will come charging to the witness box and throttle her senseless. Not a realistic fear perhaps, but strange things do happen in Courts of Law. And even stranger things pop into the minds of those pressed into the act of witnessing.

My Direct Examination begins. Question: "Madam Witness, are you acquainted with Lee –– ?" **Diane's** response is so faint, the Court Reporter asks her to repeat her answer. The Witness squeezes out a timid, "Y–es." Question: "How do you have occasion to know him?" Diane shifts nervously in her chair, glances down at her feet, sticks her flustered eyes to my face again, and pauses. Answer: "I –– I'm married to him."

Diane's Direct Exam is resembling a trip to a chicken coop. Getting answers from her is like pulling hen's teeth. The situation **isn't** going to measurably improve right away neither. No Sir.–– Rather, the situation is going to escalate in volatility. Expect the unexpected, Dell and Mel!

I take a deep breath, and continue with my business-as-usual tone. Question: "How long have the two of you been married?" **Diane** struggles to find words to frame her answer. She ricochets a glance off the ceiling. Like a doe caught in a pair of headlights, she helplessly gawps wide-eyed at her Prosecutor, and mumbles: "Mel, I can't do it."

Then without further warning, **Diane** jumps up from the Witness Chair, bolting past me – and a shocked Jury. Standing in front of Counsel Table, immediately to the right of the speedster's path, I *remember* <u>one</u> of a plethora of thoughts scooting across my mind at the time of Diane's dash being: **she's <u>your</u> witness** – *intercept* her egress. Grab her or trip her as she flashes past. But a Prosecutor's prudence being the better part of getting spun around like a wood chime in a microburst, I decide to be a gentleman and grant **her** the right of way.

She doesn't ask leave of the Court to make her hasty exit. She doesn't say, "Excuse me," as she charges by the Jury Rail. She doesn't offer her friendly Prosecutors an apologetic, "Goodbye, boys." Lee's wife simply turns jackrabbit, and runs like hell down the left aisle of the Courtroom. The sound of impact resembles a cannon-shot as she smacks the back door, and barges into the hallway.

Clearly, her abrupt departure catches the Judge off guard. Initially, he just sits, motionless and soundless on the bench, doing his generalissimo mimicry of a dummy with a black robe in a display window. Let's say more respectfully, a *stout* mannequin with a black robe in a display window. His Honor isn't alone. The Bailiff, that anointed guardian of formal Courtroom decorum, seems to have his derriere nailed to a soft chair too. Nobody else moves either – **all** of the others are immobilized. Polite chaos is running its course inside Courtroom Five.

However, disorder in Judge General's Court is rare and it's fleeting. He's a stalwart protagonist of **order** and stern **discipline**. He steers a *tight ship*, as I've previously mentioned. The loud BAM from **Diane** hurling herself against the back door stirs His Honor into action.

He doesn't move much, of course. Only his mouth moves. He does what Judges do best, His Judgeship issues **an order**. He shouts, "Bailiff, **stop** that woman!' And his Bailiff, still riveted to his soft chair and not wanting to spring into strenuous action just yet, imitates his Judge. He says to no one in particular, "Somebody, **stop** that woman!" It seems there's an echo in Department Five. It makes me smile as I think about it now.

NOBODY moves. The Bailiff is forgetting something. He has NO authority to issue orders. **Orders** come from the Bench. It's a truth that quickly dawns on the man. He's out of order – firing verbal blanks. A moment later the Bailiff launches his listless body into the fray. Leaving his comfort zone, he races down the right aisle of the Courtroom, and hits the other back door with a loud bang!

It's pandemonium in the Clark County Courthouse. TWO sets of feet can be heard running down the hall away from Court Five. The high-pitched shrieking of the runaway witness can clearly be heard above the din. "I **can't** do it, I **can't** do it! Let me **go**, let me me **go**, *pleeeease*!" So, now she's becoming polite. Casual bystanders observing the melee will likely suggest **Diane's** politeness has been a little tardy in surfacing. But some Witnesses have a propensity to do desperate things under desperate circumstances.

Other Court Officers enter the skirmish. They chase her into the Courthouse lobby. There, four burly Bailiffs succeed in subduing the wiry, reluctant Witness. Fifteen minutes later, a tearful – repentant **Diane** is escorted back inside Courtroom Five. She's shaking again, this time uncontrollably. Albeit, the focus of her fear has undergone a slight metamorphosis. She's heard some things about Judge General. Now she fears Judicial wrath more than the wrath of those accused. His Honor-ship can be terrible in his wrath, and unforgiving toward those who blithely transgress rules of orderliness and respect in his Courtroom.

Frankly, Del and I fear the worst for our flighty witness. It's not only conceivable to us, but highly probable that **Diane's** behavior will earn her a little free room and board at the County Jail. That her budding track star career will have to be put on hold, while she cools her heels in a twenty four hour custodial hiatus for *Contempt of Court*. To our pleasant surprise, we're wrong.

Given the way he handles things, Judge General could have been her uncle. He's like a big ole gentle teddy-bear on this one. We see a soft side to Judge General that isn't often displayed publicly in his Courtroom. He's stern, but his sternness is restrained. The Man in the Robe has seen the witness glancing furtively into the Courtroom for three days. He understands she's a bundle of nerves. He senses her lack of Courtroom sophistication. His Honor does **not** view **Diane's** sprint from the Courtroom as contemptuous. Rather, he sees it is as an impulsive act of desperation by a high-strung woman who has crumbled after three days in a pressure cooker. He has compassion for her.

Judge General lectures the Lady. Extracts a promise that she'll take off her track shoes and be a good girl on the witness stand. Then the Court **promises**, in effect, that he'll be her protector as she testifies. Having re-established the ground rules, he reconvenes proceedings in the presence of the Jury.

When the Jury returns **Diane** sits once again in the Witness Box. She's still timid, and her answers are halting. But the second time's the charm. This time she is able to complete her examination. Testifying about her husbands UNUSUAL trips to Las Vegas, Nevada, and fully explaining the reason he gives her for his **third trip**. He went to finish the job. He had to BURY the corpse!

What a terrible price **Gordon** pays for a husband's unrequited love.

"**Jealousy** [has] a *human* face; **Terror** the *human* form divine, And **Secrecy** the *human* dress." (Adapted from William Blake, ibid.)

The Trial settles into a more manageable mode in the aftermath of **Lee's** obstinance and **Diane's** meltdown. Proceedings become <u>less</u> exciting but more productive. Crime Lab technicians, a Criminalist, and a Firearms Expert testify. <u>No</u> gun is recovered. The Shooter says he's tossed it into Lake Mead. However, <u>one</u> projectile is discovered inside Gordon's head. The Firearms witness has examined the slug. He says it's a small caliber bullet and does not exclude **.38** caliber.

An arresting officer, two Homicide Detectives, and a Justice Court Clerk authenticate **Lee's** PRIOR statements that contradict his Trial Testimony. <u>All</u> the INCONSISTENT statements are admitted by the Court as **substantive evidence**. Which simply means: they can be considered by the Trier of Fact on the issue of guilt or innocence.

Evidence is also introduced regarding MONEY paid hand to hand by George to Billy at Francie's house on **February 21** and MONEY ORDERS sent from the conspiratorial husband to Vegas Bill on **March 3** – within <u>twenty four</u> hours of Gordon's demise.

The Trial ends. The question that looms before Jurors **isn't** complex, but it is tantalizing. Resolving the Case-at-Bar is **not** a matter of choosing between the Crime Stories of different witnesses. The gravamen of this Case is deciding WHEN to believe the **same** witness. When is Lee TRUTHFUL, after the deal is struck <u>or</u> after the deal is done?

The Jury deliberates over two days. They <u>choose</u> the **first** option. The Twelve Tried And True opt for **homicidal** culpability. Their decision: Vegas Billy is GUILTY of being an accomplice to Murder in the First Degree! In the course of **sixteen** days the catbird seat *handyman* has WILLFULLY plummeted into deep do-do. He's gone from spectator to fact-finder to **convicted** corpse-maker.

It's freaking ridiculous! He's **basically** done it for sport and pocket change. CONVICTED because he consorted with a **killer** whose a **blabbermouth**. First spilling his guts to his <u>wife</u> and then to the <u>Police</u>.

But not to fret, Billy Boy. You've got an *ally* in high places. The Nevada Supreme Court will bail you out. It's a run-a-way train ride – from conviction's deep depths of depression to the refreshing exhilaration of judicial reprieve.

Vegas Bill's **conviction** for Murder in the First Degree is appealed.

Appellate Briefs are submitted, oral argument is presented, and the High Court takes the matter under advisement. Soon, a decision of **reversal** is rendered. It's done in the form of a *Per Curiam* Opinion.

Interesting. We don't often witness the State Supreme Court issuing *Per Curiam* Opinions that REVERSE **First Degree Murder CONVICTIONS**! Generally, the High Court is a bit more deferential toward the Trial Court result in such crimes. With all due respect, the manner employed in dispatching this case is troublesome to me.

So, what is a *Per Curiam* Opinion? It's a medieval Latin phrase that refers to an opinion of the Court as a single body. My vintage 1957 version of Black's Law Dictionary calls *Per Curiam*, "A phrase used in the reports to distinguish an opinion of the whole court from an opinion written by any one judge..." Most appellate *decisions on the merits* are signed by individual Justices. Even when such signed opinions are *unanimous*, they aren't termed "per curiam." Courts usually limit *Per Curiam* decisions to issues they view as relatively non-controversial.

Well catch a whiff of dirty dog breath, Vegas Billy's case certainly seemed **contentious** and CONTROVERSIAL while we were trying it. Legal wrangling by the Parties was a distinctive feature of the proceedings. And Judge General is hardly a brash newcomer to the Trial world. He's a knowledgeable, hard-nosed, experienced Trial Judge. Further, he has considered and REJECTED the precise *issue* the Reviewing Court uses to **reverse** the FIRST DEGREE MURDER **conviction** obtained after TWO weeks of Trial and TWO days of Jury deliberation

Notwithstanding the **nature of the controversy** before the High Court, they see fit – in their infinite wisdom – to REVERSE with a ONE page **Per Curiam** Opinion. A terse brush off that explains its rationale in FOUR paragraphs . But whose counting?

Paragraph #1 – identifies the **only** issue the Court believes it needs to address. It is: "...whether any SUBSTANTIAL evidence corroborates the original accusation of appellant." (emphasis added) They're speaking about corroboration of **Lee's** original accusation of Vegas Billy. Fine, but the *standard* for corroboration of Accomplice testimony is being **misstated.** Paragraph One is contradicted by Paragraph Three, which is the **correct** *legal standard* in Nevada for corroborating an Accomplice Witness.

Paragraph #2 – offers a "**factual**"context for the *Per Curiam* and a statement of the Court's conclusion. Actually, the paragraph is full of **conclusions**, each *substituting* the view of the Court for the FINDINGS of the Jury. Frankly, it takes a certain degree of smugness for an Appellate

Court to presume it possesses the perspicacity to second-guess the Trier of Fact on issues of FACT. Giving due respect to the astuteness of the esteemed members of the Court, I'm still wondering how the Judiciary is capable of <u>independently</u> *divining* facts. Don't you have to be there? Don't you have to <u>hear</u> the testimony and <u>observe</u> the demeanor of those testifying? Don't you have to put evidence in its PROPER **context**? Why is a reviewing Court reshaping and reinterpreting and revising facts?

Paragraph #2 begins with this sentence: "In his **capacity** as a *paid private investigator*, it appears that a number of days before *her paramour* was murdered, appellant and *his client* talked to *his client's wife*, urging her to return to *the client...*" (emphasis added)

Whoa!! If the Trial Jury had it right, that sentence is a pitiful REVISION of history. The *Per Curiam* recitation pretty much cuts and pastes and labels from whole cloth. **Unlike** the author of the Opinion and the five members of the Court who ratified the language in the sentence, I <u>WAS</u> THERE. I'm one of the Trial Lawyers! Under the circumstances of this case, If Vegas Bill is a *paid private investigator* in a LEGITIMATE sense, I'll **eat** an eighty five pound bail of hay – and I won't use a jug of water to wash the green stuff down neither.

Also, did it make the Court's task of <u>reversing</u> a FIRST MURDER CONVICTION <u>easier</u> to **disparage** the VICTIM? Repeating in part, "...it appears that a number of days [**nine days**] before *her paramour* was murdered..."(emphasis added again)The Dictionary defines <u>paramour</u> as "An illicit lover, especially of a married person." Is this kind of gratuitous, demeaning verbiage REALLY necessary in the *Per Curiam*? Does it somehow elevate the stature of an Appellate Court to speak so presumptuously of a **dead man**? Here's the problem, the lady in question ALWAYS **denied** having sexual relations with the Victim – out of Court <u>and</u> under OATH. She consistently describes him as **only** a Good Samaritan.

Moreover, despite the suspicions of some [Primarily, a HUSBAND jilted by a wife hell-bent on going to Vegas, DUH!] there were **no** *in flagrante delicto* sightings. Sooooooo, why does the Court choose to speculate?

Later in paragraph #2the *Per Curiam* declares: "We have determined that, in light of the *acknowledged nature* of appellant's employment, and *other* facts of record, *such conduct* cannot be deemed to corroborate adequately the killer's original accusation of appellant..." (emphasis added)

What "**other facts**" of record? What "**<u>acknowledged nature</u>**" of Appellant's employment? – <u>Please</u>! WHO made the acknowledgment?

Vegas Bill – the fellow on Trial? His Counselors at Law? Well, they're the <u>only</u> plausible proponents of the notion that Bill is *a paid private investigator.* That question is the seminal issue of the Trial. I guarantee neither Trial Prosecutor made any such concession. Further, by their GUILTY Verdict for MURDER ONE the Trial Jury **expressly rejected** the argument that Vegas Bill was <u>merely</u> *a paid private investigator.* They held him accountable as an aider and abetter in a MURDER FOR HIRE. Billy got PAID alright. He received **MONEY ORDERS** from the spurned husband/ PRINCIPAL on **March 3**. Two hired .38 caliber bullets had catapulted poor Gordon into the next estate on **March 2**.

FOUR **times** in paragraph #2 the Court's *Per Curiam* labels the **convicted murderer** George's <u>CLIENT</u>. Now, is that turning the Jury Verdict on its ears or what? My venerable, vintage edition of Black's Law Dictionary provides the <u>more</u> traditional view of the word <u>CLIENT</u>: "A person who employs or retains an attorney, or counselor, to appear for him in courts, advise, assist, and defend him in legal proceedings, and to act for him in any legal business. McCreary v. Hoopes, 25 Miss. 428; McFarland v. Crary, 6 Wend., N.Y., 297; Cross v. Riggins, 50 Mo. 335. It should include one who disclosed confidential matters to attorney while seeking professional aid, whether attorney was employed or not. Sitton v. Peyree, 117 Or. 107, 241 P. 62,64."

Plain and simply stated, the repetitious use of <u>CLIENT</u> in paragraph #2 of the *Per Curiam* misses the mark. It's rhetorical sugar-coating. A literary sleight-of-hand reinterpreting facts. A clumsy ploy by the author of the Opinion to smooth over and justify a ruling of reversal by trying to elevate the stature of the Appellant. Calling George Bill's <u>CLIENT</u> makes it sound like Bill is in charge. GEORGE– had–Gordon–killed! Whatever Bill did he did pursuant to the biding of GEORGE. Applying the CLIENT/PROFESSIONAL P.I. rationale to Billy is like putting a flak jacket on a panhandler and calling him a Marine. It's flat-out ridiculous.

Paragraph #3 of the *Per Curiam* recites the Court's Finding: "We therefore find NO 'evidence which in itself, and without the aid of the testimony of the accomplice, **tends to connect** the defendant with the commission of the offense.' NRS 175.291(1); cf. Eckert v. State, 91 Nev. 183, 533 P.2d 468 (1975)." (emphasis added)

NO evidence independent of the accomplice testimony **tending** to connect the Defendant with the commission of the offense? Yet, **nine days** before Gordon is Murdered, the Opinion acknowledges: (a) George and Bill spoke to George's wife – "**urging** her to return" to her husband.

(b) Bill said such things as, "You had better think it over good. You had better think real hard about going back to... [George]...for the good of yourself and **everyone** concerned." (c) "Appellant [Bill] also helped **restrain**...[Francie] when she attempted to depart." (emphasis added to each quotation)

To which I'm constrained to point out in the interest of accuracy, the confrontation referenced in (a) and (b) occurs INSIDE the Las Vegas **house** Francie is renting <u>and</u> after George and Bill have **barged** inside her house. Factors relating to the basis for reversal the Prosecutor in me considers very consequential. Moreover, the brevity of the *Per Curiam* misses several nuances in (c) that arguably have a direct bearing on the issue of evidence independent of accomplice testimony that **tends** to connect the Defendant with the commission of the offense, to-wit: Bill HELPS George **restrain** his wife after the three have EXITED the house and she's TRYING to **run** for help! The unvarnished fact is: AFTER Bill and George leave Francie DOES call the Police. These omissions may be inadvertent, but measured by any meaningful contextual standard, the *Per Curiam's* abbreviated phrase that "Appellant also helped restrain...[Francie] when she attempted to depart..." –– is language that DOWNPLAYS and UNDERSTATES the significance of crucial action by the Defendant.

And as I've previously written, Billy DID get **money orders** from George the DAY–after–Gordon–was–Murdered. Isn't it plausible to say this is the **quid pro quo** of Murder for hire? Isn't this evidence which, independently of the Accomplice testimony, does **tend** to connect Billy to the Crime?

The poet Fitzgerald says, "A Hair perhaps divides the False and True– " (Edward Fitzgerald, *Rubaiyat of Omar Khayyam of Naishapur*) Likewise, decisions construing the nebulous concept of "evidence **tending** to connect" would seem to involve a good deal of hair sifting. A subtle process that predetermines whether the Court goes this way or that way. The People can only hope the Judgment is true!

A one page **Per Curiam** OPINION that **reverses** a First Degree Murder Conviction? Scrolling to the bottom line, it's <u>not</u> the decision so much, reasonable minds can disagree about the application and interpretation of rules of law, and the sufficiency of evidence. My <u>main</u> picking bones are the use of a *Per Curiam* and the use of inappropriate *language* in the *Per Curiam*. The MANNER of consigning this Conviction to oblivion appears to be a slough-off.

I recognize the heavy appellate case load that imposes time constraints upon the High Court. However, MURDER APPEALS must be prioritized. They must be given due deference and thorough scrutiny on review. **If** this Case is representative, that doesn't happen in *Per Curiam* Opinions.

How our Judicial System handles the review of Murder Convictions **defines** us as a society. It **identifies** our fundamental values. Do we take proper cognizance of the sanctity of human life and devastating family loss or do we venerate money damage, contractual, corporate, and procedural cases – et al? Obviously, every Case that goes to the State Supreme Court is important, but at the end of the day, we must choose LIFE. Cases dealing with the **premeditated** destruction of LIFE are the Cases of paramount importance.

THOU SHALT NOT KILL! **Murder** is not only a Crime, it is a serious moral and spiritual transgression.

A one page **Per Curiam** OPINION that **reverses** a First Degree Murder Conviction? What causes members of a reviewing Court to become so casually convinced of the righteousness of their Opinion? So, smugly certain of the truth of their words? How does the pantheon five acquire such olympian perception? What enables these products of the Socratic method, these persons elevated to lofty positions of legal scholarship and moral judgment – these purported denizens of objectivity – trained in the craft of seeing both sides of an argument, WHAT thought process **causes** Judges to treat a deliberate **execution-Murder** CONVICTION so cavalierly? Where is the justification for shit-canning two weeks of Trial with a *Per Curiam* opinion? Why produce an opinion so superficial – so condescendingly judgmental – so intellectually barren? What of the twelve decent men and women who returned the VERDICT, convinced beyond a reasonable doubt that the Defendant has been proven guilty? What respect are they being shown? Where is the reverence for life? Sensitivity for the suffocating emptiness and grievous suffering of those who must cope with the loss of a loved one? Where is justice for family and friends of the Murdered Victim?

Is it possible for a Court to become **jaded** to First Degree Murder? Some people swear they can find WATER in the desert with a *water witch*. I'm wondering –do certain members of the Judiciary have an *EXONERATION witch*?

A member of the United States Supreme Court once declared, "We're not final because we're infallible. We're infallible because we're final." A realistic assessment that is arguably applicable at the State level as well.

Fallibility becomes *infallibility* by virtue of *finality*. Vegas Billy's Case did go away – permanently!

But then there's GEORGE. Eventually, he **is** extradited from Texas. I vividly remember my trip to El Paso with Big Al the Homicide Detective for a key extradition hearing. More precisely, **not** the *hearing* itself – that was quite routine, actually. The appearances of the lead Homicide Detective and the lead Deputy District Attorney assigned to the Case are a sufficient demonstration of Nevada's resolve to get George to Nevada for Murder Proceedings to *dry up* whatever juice the suspect has in El Paso, and persuade Texas authorities to order his extradition. It's our **presence** more than anything we do or say that <u>greases</u> the extradition wheels. What I remember <u>most</u> is the *flight* to El Paso. The *flight* isn't non-stop, we have a scheduled touch-down in route. The **night** before the hearing in El Paso our plane lands in Albuquerque in the midst of a volatile electrical storm. The lightning flashes illuminate the Albuquerque skyline <u>and</u> the silver outline of the passenger liner. That's a white-knuckle scenario for Big Al and me. Neither of us is a frequent flier. We don't like to fly in airplanes, since neither the Detective nor the Deputy feels comfortable getting over ten feet off the ground. Consequently, every time a bright flash of lightning occurs, which is often, Big Al flinches so dramatically, but for his seat belt restraint, I think he'd have been sitting on my lap. With each brilliant flash, he'd tell me again how much he hated to fly in airplanes – particularly airplanes that are flying through electrical storms. And I share his trepidation, though I'm not as vocal. We're sweating lightning bolts. Silently saying our prayers. Thinking each moment might be our last. That the flimsy craft will yield to nature's fury and plummet into the New Mexico turf with us on board –– but miraculously, it seemed to us, we survive to ply our respective trades another day.

Eventually, George **does** go to Trial. The inestimable Judge Howard presides. He is a man of impeccable manners and flawless judicial demeanor. Born to be a Judge, I'll say. He maintains a steady and respectful grip over the Proceedings. I have an extremely capable partner at the Prosecution controls – Larry, my good friend and colleague. **George** is flanked by two Lawyers at his Trial. Is three a crowd at the Defense table?

Benjamin Franklin wryly observes, "A country man between **two** Lawyers is like a Fish between **two** Cats." (*Poor Richard's Almanack*, emphasis added)

George has Texas Joe on his <u>left</u> and folksy, Mr. High Powered Defense

Counsel Gentleman on his <u>right</u>. Appropriately seated in regards to their Client, as the Trial will establish. The out of state Lawyer must associate with a member of the Nevada State Bar, and the judgment of Mr. High Powered Defense Counsel Gentleman certainly proves to be truer than his colleague on the left.

Lee and **Vegas Bill** are transported from the Slammer to the Trial Venue. The procedure is an exercise in futility. During hearings conducted OUTSIDE the presence of the Jury, <u>both</u> gentlemen take the Fifth, that is, they **invoke** their Constitutional privilege NOT to testify. **Lee** has no surprises left in his arsenal, he's sprung his trap. He's disinclined to repeat the RETRACTIONS that characterized his testimony during Bill's Trial. He recognizes the potential persuasive power of PRIOR **inconsistent** statements and testimony. This is the **second** Courtroom drama where he's been a headliner. He remembers the **first** very well. The Defendant he tries to exculpate <u>is</u> inculpated with Lee's PRIOR finger pointing by those slick Prosecution boys. Then – CONVICTED by the Twelve Tried and True. There will be NOTHING to impeach the second time around. NO reprise of his Dr. Jekyll/Mr. Hyde act. BOTH he and Bill tell the Judge they will remain MUTE on the Witness Stand. They're excused and never seen by **George's** Jury, though a Judicial INSTRUCTION discreetly explains their absence.

The <u>key</u> witness in **George's** Trial is the woman who *had* been the <u>key</u> relationship in his life – HIS WIFE. She's been <u>used</u> by **George** as the trigger to a horrendous Crime. **Francie** describes an unhappy marriage and her flight with the children to Las Vegas for a quickie divorce. She describes meeting Gordon and the friendship that ensues. However, she vehemently contends their relationship was always strictly platonic. Says she obtained employment at the Lady Luck Casino and rented a house on Maroney Street.

She speaks of the meeting with Vegas Bill on **February 20**. An encounter initiated by him. She details the tense circumstances that occur on **February 21**. **Gordon** has driven her home from work and he's preparing her a cup of coffee. He and George's son plan to go for hamburgers. Suddenly, George barges in with a camera and begins to take pictures. She grabs the telephone intending to call the Police. Then **Bill** pushes the door open and walks into the house. She's restrained by **George**. Threatened with bodily harm if she calls 911.

Gordon is ordered out of the house, and the *tandem trespassers* bombard her with rhetoric and persuasion and <u>threats</u> regarding her "unsavory relationship" with **Gordon**. Urging her to come back to **George** – or else!

George tells **Francie** there's a CONTRACT on her life and the life of "her boyfriend." **George** and **Bill** escort **Francie** outside the house. **Gordon** is waiting in the driveway inside his car. **Francie** darts away from **George** and tries to run for help. **George** and **Bill** catch her and <u>restrain</u> her.

George walks close to **Gordon's** car and exclaims, "Beat it Mister." And as **Gordon** backs out of the driveway **George** screams: "If you **ever** come around MY WIFE , **IF** you **ever** *see* her again, YOU–ARE–DEAD."

George and **Bill** and **Francie** reenter the house. More heavy handed words and inferential threats are directed at **Francie** and her "boyfriend." Specifically, **Bill** tells **Francie**: "You had better think it over good. You had better think real hard about going back to **George** for your own good and <u>everyone</u> else concerned."

CROSS EXAMINATION is curious. It's conducted by the guy on the left of the Defendant, the irascible – Texas Joe. Evidently, he and Mr. High Powered Defense Counsel Gentleman **haven't** invested much time in consultation regarding the content of CROSS EXAM. Moreover, Texas Joe **doesn't** seem to believe in adherence to the time-honored *benchmark* of astute CROSS EXAMINATION: "If you <u>don't</u> know – more or less – what the answer will be to a question, **DON'T ASK** the question."

Well, Texas Joe elects to ask **Francie** a plethora of questions though he has **no** clue HOW the questions will be answered. He's taken copious notes that document interviews with his Client, and he uses **George's** view of the nature of things as a spring-board for lengthy CROSS EXAMINATION of **Georgie's ex-wife**. Unhappily for the peerless three, *His view is not shared by Her*. The disparity is stunning! She's **not** of a mind set to do her vigilante ex-hubby any favors.

What emerges from the dubious strategy is **not** pretty for the Defense. It's tactically disastrous. The threesome self-immolates. **George** is gratuitously <u>further</u> INCRIMINATED. Mr. High Powered Defense Counsel Gentleman is exasperated, and Texas Joe is lucky he's not strangled senseless by his Client as he tediously pursues Cross Examination. As for The State, they can't get enough of Texas Joe's free-wheeling CROSS. They get a nice evidentiary boost from an unexpected source. It's a little like expecting the house salad and being served a Fillet Mignon.

We sail into FINAL ARGUMENT. Deputy Larry offers the

OPENING SUMMATION. Texas Joe and Mr. High Powered Defense Counsel Gentleman split the Defense time – in that order. I present the State's REBUTTAL. What an amazing Profession! Three esteemed, experienced, imminently capable Lawyers argue before me, but they get **no** second bite of the apple. Larry and Joe and Mr. High Powered are DONE. What a heady experience – what a rush – what a power surge – what a lift – what a motivator – what an **advantage** it is to **speak** LAST. An opportunity afforded The Prosecution because it carries the **burden** of proof.

These occasions are to be savored by a dedicated Deputy District Attorney. They are experiences of a lifetime – exhilarating, productive, and memorable. A Courtroom Cop like me knows he may not win, VERDICTS are returned by Jurors not by Prosecutors. But a Deputy District Attorney KNOWS this: **the– LIPS–of– the–other–side–are– SEALED** while he argues his REBUTTAL. He gets the LAST SAY! Oh, the Defense can wheeze out a few objections, shake their heads in disbelief, roll their eyes, gaze incredulously at the speaker, twiddle their thumbs, stare at the ceiling, fall asleep, and indulge in a variety of tactics calculated to distract, BUT they **won't** get a crack at **sur-rebuttal**! Their ARGUMENTS are already a matter of record. So, each time I rise to deliver a REBUTTAL **argument** I'm going to be saying to myself, "Make this the very best you're capable of doing, Buddy. These are quintessential occasions in your career. Keep this in mind, under what other circumstance will you ever be guaranteed the FINAL WORD in a heated matter of controversy? Go for it, Pal. Don't leave anything important unsaid, and say it with **energy** and **passion** and **conviction**."

A dynamic advocate for Justice must leave it ALL at the lectern on REBUTTAL! He needs to prime the Juror pump with an **emotional** recitation of **evidentiary** POINTS that connect the Accused to the Crime. He has to **empty** his rhetorical tank. Dynamically launching the zingers he's reserved for REBUTTAL. Exploiting the privilege of SPEAKING LAST – of SUMMING UP with a series of exclamation points!

"The Bird of Time has but a little way to flutter––and the Bird is on the Wing." [Edward Fitzgerald, *Rubaiyat of Omar Khayyam of Naishapur*] The time-table that bookends GORDON'S MURDER is sinister and inculpatory: **February 3, 1972** – Francie leaves El Paso with her children – bound for the quickie divorce capital of the world. **Gordon** will be **dead** in 28 days! **February 5, 1972** – Francie and children arrive in Las Vegas.

The clock is ticking. **Gordon** will be **dead** in 26 days and he doesn't have a clue. On or about **February 12, 1972** – George wants boots on the ground, he sends Lee to Vegas to locate Francie and his son. Tick-tick -tick-tick. **Gordon** will be **dead** in 19 days! **February 14, 1972** – Lee finds Francie and a male friend. He follows them to her house on Maroney. Lee reports his impressions to George. Happy Valentine's Day, ya'll. **Gordon** will be **dead** in 17 days! **February 15, 1972** – Tick-tick-tick. George flies to southern Nevada. He and Lee inadvertently enter the wrong house. They meet Vegas Bill and he's enlisted as a foot soldier. **Gordon** will be **dead** in 16 days! **February 20, 1972** – Bill initiates contact with the *person of interest*. He meets Francie in front of her house. She's helping Gordon start his car. Billy asks if he's her husband. She replies, "No, he's my Good Samaritan." Nevertheless, **Gordon** will be **dead** in 11 days! **February 21, 1972** – Tick-tick-tick. The Good Samaritan drives Francie home from work, fixes her coffee, and is about to go for hamburgers with George's son. Suddenly, sans door bell or knocking, George strides into the house and snaps photographs of the threesome. It's 10 days and counting. The spiteful Bird of Time is on the Wing. Francie grabs the telephone intending to call the Police. Right on cue, Mr. Private Eye pushes the front door open and walks inside the house too. There **is** strength in numbers. George threatens Francie with bodily harm if she uses the telephone, and Gordon is ordered to wait outside.. She puts the phone down. Gordon goes to his car and waits. Then Georgie tells Francie there is a CONTRACT on her life and the life of **her boyfriend.** Vegas Bill tells Francie that Gordon is a bad influence. They walk outside. She darts away and tries to run for help. The two men catch her and restrain her. Tick-tick-tick. George warns, "You'd better stay here if you know what is good for you." George walks closer to Gordon, tells him to beat it, and shouts as he backs up: "If you **ever** come around MY WIFE, **If** you **ever** see her again, YOU–ARE–DEAD." It's a *self fulfilling prophesy*. **Gordon** WILL be **dead** in 10 days! During **the two weeks following** George and Lee's chance connect with Vegas Bill [February 15] – **fifty six** telephone calls are made from Bill's residential phone in Vegas to El Paso telephones listed in George's name. Clearly, the Bird of Time is airborne – and closing fast! On or about leap year day [**February 29, 1972**] – Lee is on the road again. He has a .38 caliber revolver, a box of ammunition, an *itchy* trigger finger, and a malignant heart as he steers the car toward Las Vegas. He's to rendevous with Bill, and they are to waylay the *target* while he's alone. Francie is to be privy to nothing. Tick-tick-tick. **Each** mile Lee travels brings Gordon closer to a trip beyond the veil. **Each** passing hour brings Gordon closer to a grisly life-ending experience. **Gordon** will be **dead** in TWO DAYS. **March 2, 1972** at **9:00 a.m.** – Tick-tick-tick. They'll–do– it–today! Bill has learned where Gordon lives. He's monitored his day-to-day schedule. He knows **the Prey** will be at his house prior to twelve noon. They begin their *murderous mission.* Gordon is lured outside. Abducted at gunpoint, taken to a makeshift hearse, and transported a half mile to his dusty cemetery. He still doesn't have a clue what this is all about. Tick– tick––––tick! Actually, it's *cold, calculated* **grim reaper** business. Carried out by two surrogates. The REAPER is a Texan from El Paso. Gordon is removed from the car and GUNNED **down** in the desert. **March 2, 1972** at **9:20 a.m.** – Time's blood-thirsty Buzzard comes home to roost. **Gordon is** a DEAD MAN! Shot down like a dog. Abduction and Murder in cold blood take only twenty minutes. The Shoe has dropped in one fell swoop!

"Done in by two characters who are STRANGERS. Two men **without** a MOTIVE. Two men who CAN'T **possibly** have a *personal* bone to pick with him. WHY would Lee drive 13 hours and 863 miles to shoot a man? Texas is a big state. If he's just *itching* to kill somebody for sport, WHY **doesn't** he *target practice* in the Lone Star State? And his spat of trips to Las Vegas make absolutely NO sense if he's a one man circus. Likewise, WHY would Vegas Bill hook up with a *killing partner* he's **only** seen ONCE before? Lee and Bill have NOTHING in **common.** But they DO have a THIRD party nexus.

"The COMMON DENOMINATOR between them **is** GEORGE! Lee works for George. He's an extension **of** George! He's George's *hired* **assassin.** However, George needs a set of eyes and boots on the ground in Vegas. He needs a *ground zero* **connection.** Bill's his Vegas Guy. He's been hired as an ad hoc *private eye* and *killing venue* trail boss **by** GEORGE. Bill's simply a long distance phone call freak? WHY does the man living **next** door to Francie suddenly make **fifty six** telephone calls to GEORGE within a two week time frame – just before Gordon's demise? Bill enjoys paying large phone bills?

"WHOSE **gig** is this? [The Trial Judge has allowed Diane to testify regarding Lee's *explanation* for making a third trip to Nevada. Judge Howard has ruled that the statements have been made in furtherance of a Conspiracy, and were admitted at George's Trial pursuant to the Conspiracy declaration exception to the Hearsay Rule.] Lee **tells** his wife it's GEORGE'S beef. That he's killed a man in Las Vegas, and has to return to bury the body. That he **didn't** even KNOW the guy. GEORGE had him kill the man whose been sleeping with his wife.

"**Jealousy** has a human face, and the jealous face in this **plot** is GEORGIE'S face – the face of a husband scorned! What DUDE has been dumped by his wife? WHOSE the Jealous Nelly who thinks his wife is playing footsie with Gordon? WHO IS the Father deprived of companionship with a young son because of his wife's precipitous action? WHO is bankrolling this caper? WHO IS paying the **green** for MURDER by **hire**? Let's trace the cash flow. Is it from Bill to Lee? Or Lee to Bill? Or from Lee and Bill to George? NOOOOO –––**The cash flow** – the PAYOFF is from GEORGE to *them*. BOTH OF THEM. The **money orders** come from GEORGE! The Bone he's picking may be fictional, but he sure as hell thinks it's REAL. GEORGE sends **money orders** to BILL on **March 3, 1972** – within twenty four <u>hours</u> of **the hit**! GEORGE sends **money orders** to LEE within ten <u>days</u> of **the hit**! GEORGE is a businessman who believes in paying his bills promptly. This **Murder** is GEORGE'S FOLLY. **But for** GEORGE, there–is–NO– Murder, and Gordon **isn't** smacked by The Bird of Time. He's *granted* a **reprieve**."

> "O threats of hell and Hopes of Paradise! One thing at least is certain,–
> This life flies; One thing is certain and the rest is Lies; The Flower
> that once has blown for ever dies." (Edward Fizgerald, ibid.)

"The OPERATIVE word in the Trial at this time is **accountability**! The PREMEDITATED **Murder** of Gordon is a heinous Crime. IF the Criminal Justice System means anything, it MEANS that a man who puts out a CONTRACT for the **Murder** of another human being MUST be held **personally** ACCOUNTABLE for his **deed.** When the Prosecution presented its Opening Statement we PROMISED you that the evidence would prove the Defendant's GUILT beyond a reasonable doubt. When EACH of you was **selected** you promised to *base* your verdict solely upon the <u>law</u> and <u>facts</u> of the Case. When EACH of you was **sworn** you impliedly promised that you *would* find the Defendant GUILTY if he'd been proven guilty beyond a reasonable doubt. We've **kept** our PROMISE and we ask you now to **keep** YOURS! **Hold** the **murderous** Defendant ACCOUNTABLE for his **Murder**!"

Thanks to the totality of CIRCUMSTANTIAL **evidence** introduced, the inner toughness of **George's** ex-spouse, the tenacity of a Lady who puts the lid on a temptation to sprint from the Courtroom again, a whopping assist from Texas Joe, and emotional Summation by the good guys, **George's** Trial Jury **doesn't** need accomplice testimony to be persuaded. Hearing from Itchy Fingers and Vegas Billy isn't the prerequisite to a hard-nosed Verdict. The Jury holds **George** ACCOUNTABLE!

It's two for two. The first Jury has convicted **Billy**, now the second Jury convicts **George.** He stands *unrepentant* before Judge Howard for Sentencing, still smarting from the sting of rejection by his Wife and his Jury.

A sentence of Life in the Nevada State Penitentiary WITH the possibility of parole is imposed by the Court.

Judge Howard: "Mr. Defendant – Sir, do you have any request of the Court prior to being remanded for transportation to the State Prison?"

Defendant **George**: "If your Honor – please, I'll be fine. All I need is **my** BIBLE and a **jar** of VASELINE."

Judge Howard: "Very good – Sir, you are remanded."

P.S. –– The second Jury's VERDICT has much smoother reception at the State Supreme Court than the first Jury's VERDICT. **George's** verdict **is** affirmed.

Moreover, LEE is subsequently prosecuted for **perjury** in the Eighth Judicial District Court based upon testimony he's proffered at BILL'S Trial. He **is** CONVICTED and sentenced to Life WITHOUT Parole under Habitual Criminal guidelines.

CLUES IN A BLOOD SPLATTERED ROOM

"Double, double toil and trouble; Fire burn and cauldron bubble...
Eye of newt, and toe of frog; Wool of bat, and tongue of dog...
By the pricking of ...[HIS] thumbs, Something wicked this way
comes. Open, locks, Whoever knocks!" (William Shakespeare,
Macbeth, Act IV, Sc. 1, Lines 10, 14, 30, 44)

Chapter 9

Paula A. is the tour coordinator for a junket trip from the Twin Cities to Las Vegas. Born and raised in Minnesota, she is heart and soul a product of the emerald beauty that is the Land of Ten Thousand Lakes. Country bred and countrified, she is an issue of the prairies and rolling hills and dairy farms. Where Holsteins graze hungrily on lush pastures in Summertime and huddle closely inside enclosed barns in Wintertime – away from the drifting snow that piles high on frozen tundra. Perky Paula is one of the, so called, *frozen chosen*.

She's been to Vegas on prior junkets, but has a sense *this one* will be special. The charter flight to the gaming capital will have every seat filled with enthusiastic Minnesotans looking forward to <u>four</u> days of gambling and fun on the Las Vegas Strip. The junket tour business is her job. However, she recognizes from past experience, that traveling to Las Vegas on a junket will involve much more than tour coordination chores. She expects plenty of down time as well. A trip to Vegas is an occasion when junketeers don't want to be encumbered by a tight leash. They seek private playtime. Accordingly, Paula A. envisions plenty of pool side sunning, dining, spinning roulette wheels, lounge acts, and *personal* escape time.

The junket trip from Minneapolis-St. Paul arrives in Neon Central at 11:50 p.m. on Friday, March 29, 1974. Sadly, the trip to Las Vegas will **not** live up to its advance billing for the tour coordinator. The spring thaw escape in Vegas for the frozen-chosen lady from Minnesota **isn't** going to be special – nor pleasant! There is very little play-time for Paula. She'll be DEAD on Sunday morning. The Las Vegas slogan, "What happens in Vegas stays in Vegas," doesn't contemplate a fate so literal. Vivacious, pretty, dark-haired Paula's LAST **breath** is in a Las Vegas Strip hotel room. The ambiance that touts itself as a place to escape from reality, does not provide safe-haven for <u>her</u>. She **cannot** escape the dreadful reality of a knife wielding PREDATOR!

Being tour coordinator has its privileges. OR DOES IT? She is the <u>sole</u> occupant of a room assigned to her on the eleventh floor. It has a fantastic view of the famed Las Vegas Strip, but it fails to provide a view <u>inside</u> the malignant heart that lurks nearby.

> "Double, double toil and trouble; Fire burn and cauldron bubble...
> Eye of newt, and toe of frog; Wool of bat, and tongue of dog...
> By the pricking of...[HIS] thumbs, **Something wicked** this way
> comes..." (William Shakespeare, ibid.)

We don't know where HE *sees* her first. Probably somewhere on the hotel property. Presumably, it's sometime – somewhere on Saturday, March 30. Is it at a breakfast buffet? A chance encounter inside a gift shop? Do his lusting eyes spy her at pool side? Riding an elevator? While she sits at a bar having a strawberry daiquiri? When he's peering at pretty girls in the hotel lobby? On the casino floor at the black jack tables? During an evening Lounge Act? As she feeds quarters into a one armed bandit? This guy is cruising for chicks. Once HE *sees* her, he begins to shadow her. Paula becomes an unwitting *two-some* without any sense of her impending dilemma. She'll have to choose between giving up her virtue or her life. This lecherous *two-armed* bandit wants MORE than quarters. HE wants close up, in your face, one–on–one sexual contact. HE'S a beast in heat stalking his prey.

Tony S. is an egregious ass. <u>Outwardly</u> smiling, cordial, and conversant; <u>inwardly</u> conniving, self absorbed, and sadistic. Fantasies of rape are HIS turn-on. Having consensual sex **isn't** enough, Tony S. wants forceful entry. HE wants to be in the drivers seat. HIS elixir is the **power surge** that comes from control and debauchery. HE stealthily follows Paula to her room to learn where she's staying. Then, HE slyly repeats HIS quest until HE'S convinced she's ALONE in the room.

On several occasions, he brazenly engages in light banter on the elevator with the object of HIS fancy. Too bad for Paula. **She's** DOOMED! The prurient deviant decides he <u>will</u> have her.

It's 8:45Sunday morning – March 31. Go fishing on the Sabbath, if you're a compulsive fisherman. Some *swear* fishing is always better on Sunday. Go for a *drive* to Mr. Charleston for hiking and picnicking with the family, if Church isn't on your agenda. *Go* out to eat. *Go* to a movie. *Read* a book – the Bible would be nice. But damn it to hell Man, DON'T take an elevator to the eleventh floor with a *seven*-inch switch blade knife in your pocket for the purpose of **violent**, non-consensual sex with a guileless young woman on the Sabbath Day. Come to your senses, Tony. CEASE and RESIST!

But Tony is of a mind to persist. Knife in hand, he's at the door now – KNOCKING. "The time and...[HIS] intents are savage-wild, More fierce and more inexorable far Than [an] empty tiger..." on the prowl! (William Shakespeare, *Romeo and Juliet*, Act V, Sc. 3, Line 37)

Tony's breathing hard. HIS heart pounds. Heat builds in HIS temples. HIS eyes acquire a menacing gleam. HE'S an *empty* tiger seeking gratification. The intent is savage-wild, as fierce anticipation of illicit coitus rages. HE clutches the switchblade in a vise-like grip. The adrenalin rush **drives** HIM – **empowers** HIM.

Paula has retired very late on Saturday night, she doesn't get to bed until 3:00 a.m. She is sleeping lightly when Tony S. comes calling. She's awakened by the KNOCKING on her door. Through the morning haze of initial cognizance, she's wondering, "WHO could that be, room service?" IF ONLY it had been!

Paula is about to have a daytime nightmare with her brown eyes wide open. "By the pricking of...[HIS] thumbs, Something wicked this way comes. Open, locks, **Whoever knocks**!" (Shakespeare, *Macbeth*, ibid., emphasis added)

Poor Paula is discovered by a hotel maid who hears moans as she wallks by in the hallway. The pretty junket coordinator **won't** be doing anymore coordinating – ever. She'll never again, with mortal eyes, see the emerald beauty of the Land of Ten Thousand Lakes. She's found, SAVAGELY **stabbed**, lying in the doorway of her hotel room about 9 o'clock on Sunday morning, March 31, 1974.

Paula DIES within 20 minutes after the crime is detected. Her **blood-splattered** room provides valuable clues. A number of *identifiable* LATENT PRINTS are lifted from surfaces inside the room. The *identifiable* prints include THREE **bloody** latents deposited on the ROOM TELEPHONE. The PHONE has been forcibly detached from the wall. One of the TELEPHONE **latents** is expeditiously eliminated by Crime Scene Investigators. It is a right THUMB PRINT of **Paula A.** Left on the phone AFTER the bloody attack [It's a **bloody print.**], but a phone obviously wrenched from her grasp by the **malevolent perpetrator** BEFORE she can call for help. [The other two **bloody** prints are **MATCHING prints.**] Neither the KNIFE nor the ASSAILANT is recovered at the **Crime Scene**. The obsessive *thief* of life has fled in an attempt to save his hide!

Sometimes, low-life stupidity causes Criminals who RUN to come undone. The first *law of flight* is to keep a low profile. **Tony** shouldn't indulge in idiotic acts that attract Police scrutiny. Perhaps, **Tony** doesn't know about the first *law of flight.* He's in another State, perhaps he thinks he's fallen completely off the radar screen. That his brutal homicide has been forgotten. That he won't be tracked. A case of out of sight being out of mind. ––– Indubitably INCORRECT, Sir. Your despicable deed weighs heavily on the minds of Vegas Homicide Cops. They're looking for you **Tony**, and the criminal dragnet has a way of crossing Ts and connecting Dots for punks like you!

FIVE days later at approximately 2:30 a.m., Police Officers in Colorado Springs, Colorado are dispatched to a local bar. The owner has called the Department regarding a Burglary *in progress*. The first Officer to the scene observes **Tony S.** standing on an old water heater just outside the rear door of the bar. A louver to the door has been removed, and **Tony** is attempting to enter the building. He's doing a hell of a job self spotlighting. Putting himself front and center on Police Radar. Akin to shouting, "Here I am. Come and get me Coppers."

Tony is detained. Back-up Officers question him about his dubious efforts to enter the business. The Detainee tells Officers he'd been drinking inside the bar, that he'd arranged to meet with ONE of the *bar maids* after the bar closed, that she failed to keep her promise, [SMART GIRL!] and he'd returned to recover the *money* he'd given her. Thereafter, the bar owner declines to press charges, [Sounds like he's aware some of the girls are doing some **moonlight** HOOKING.] but asks that **Tony** be instructed to leave the premises. The Back-up Officers advise their Detainee accordingly and, feeling the matter is closed, <u>two</u> of them leave.

But <u>ONE</u> STAYS. Fortunately, Officer W. is more circumspect. He's a credit to his profession. A top of the line Peace Officer. He <u>walks</u> **Tony** to his car. A *simple* procedure that enables him to better take the pulse of this cat <u>and</u> guarantee the early morning skulker actually leaves. Near the rear door to the bar, the vigilant Officer makes an intriguing discovery. He notices an automatic weapon lying partially exposed under the detached louver. Officer W. picks up the PISTOL and asks **Tony** if it belongs to him. He acknowledges it **is** his. Officer W. decides to HANDCUFF **Tony** as a protective measure during <u>further</u> *investigatory detention* and radios the other two Back-up Officers to return to the scene. Subsequently, Officer W. looks into **Tony's** car. He observes credit cards lying on the console between the two front seats. The Officer examines the cards. They bare the surnames *Gilner* and *Simmons*. **Tony** offers a half-ass explanation. He says he purchased the **gun** and the **credit cards** from "a hippie." Yeah, sure you did, Pal. **Tony** is transported to the Station House.

Police scour pertinent records. They learn that **Tony S.** is a federal parole *violator*, he's driving a *stolen* vehicle, and he's been *staying* at a motel in Colorado Springs for several days. **Tony** is <u>formally</u> ARRESTED. He asks for permission to go to the motel to recover his belongings. Permission is denied without proper escort. However, the Colorado Springs gendarmes tell him they'll **accompany** him to his room to retrieve his property. BUT, there's a slight technicality. Officers explain that they <u>can't</u> enter his motel room without a *search warrant* <u>or</u> a *consent to search* **signed** by him, and since he's under arrest, he <u>can't</u> enter the room by himself [WILL TONY TAKE THE BAIT?]

<u>Yes</u> he does! He's <u>shined</u> the *spotlight* on himself by getting himself busted. Now, instead of letting sleeping dogs lie, he *shines* the *spotlight* on his digs. **Tony S.** is either very complacent – or very naive. THANKS a bunch, Killer! He **SIGNS** a CONSENT to search his ROOM.

Tony and Officers go to the motel room. He's in handcuffs, but tells Police the room key is in his jacket pocket. The key is removed and given to **Tony**. He places the key in the lock and opens the door. The Arrestee and the Officers enter the room. In the process of gathering **Tony's** personal effects, Officers find a 4-inch switch blade knife and two books. They are entitled, "Astrological Sex Murders" and "Brothels of Nevada."

They return to the Police Station and **Tony** is booked. During the BOOKING procedure, Officer W. **thoroughly** searches the <u>contents</u> of

Tony's WALLET. He finds a *scrap of paper* bearing the name and telephone number of a local resident named John Store. The *scrap of paper* is like a needle in a haystack. Yet, Officer W. checks out the information. Store **is** CONTACTED! The **act** is a buzzer-beater. A dedicated Law Enforcement Officer leaves no needle unturned. Regardless of how trivial it lays in the stack. The Officer **is** a CRIME BUSTER in this instance.

Officer W. learns that Store and his wife had met **Tony S.** in LAS VEGAS, NEVADA several weeks earlier, and invite him to visit them if he ever comes to Colorado Springs. Also, Officer W. learns that **Tony S.** has called them on APRIL 1, stating that he will be driving through Colorado Springs and will stop by to say hello. Moreover, He tells Store HE had been out the previous evening with a girl WHO had been **reported** MURDERED *the morning* of his telephone call!

This information is immediately reported to authorities in Las Vegas. Later, **Tony's** FINGERPRINT exemplars are rolled in Colorado Springs, and forwarded to Las Vegas. BINGO! **Identical** MATCHING prints are found on numerous surfaces inside the victim's hotel room! The matching prints include the TWO **bloody** fingerprints lifted from the room phone wrenched from PAULA'S GRASP by the **malevolent miscreant** who MURDERS *her*!

It's been said in substance, that by small and simple acts are great things brought to pass. The paradox is impressively validated by Officer W. of the Colorado Springs P.D. To recap the germination of the investigation: **Tony** has some truly BAD LUCK, though he's instrumental in triggering the bad luck. We start with a nondescript **kook** *loosening* a louver on the rear door to a bar at 2:30 a.m., because he claims he wants to settle a score with a barmaid he's **paid** some *cold cash* in response to an alluring smile and a promise of some risque, late night companionship. She stiffs him, of course. And never mind the *lateness* of the hour, that he doesn't have *a receipt*, and that the bar in question is *closed*, it ALL seems to make perfect sense to the mischief maker. I guess **Tony** thinks this chick sleeps where she works.

Police are summoned by the owner, but he hears the *alibi* and decides not to press charges. Maybe his barmaid has been *unjustly enriched*. The scoundrel is about to be released. Other officers depart, but ONE chap drags his feet. His cop sense is astute. Officer W. chooses to subject **Tony**, the late-night kook, to a little closer scrutiny. There's something creepy about this character. Perhaps Officer W. is thinking, "There's more to this guy than meets the eye." Well, that's **true** Mr. Policeman. **Tony** has some serious baggage in tow. He's a Federal Parole violator driving a stolen car, and ――― there's that dreadful matter on the eleventh floor of a Las Vegas Strip hotel. "A **Hair** perhaps divides the False and True–– " (Edward Fitzgerald, *Rubaiyat of Omar Khayyam of Naishapur*) Officer W. is the slender threadlike strand dividing falsehood and truth in this investigation. His devotion to duty cracks the case!

The Officer, who has a penchant for crossing Ts and connecting Dots, elects to WALK **Tony** to his car. And it isn't just a casual stroll in the moonlight, Officer W. has keen sight. He finds the automatic hand gun on the ground and sees credit cards on the console. He <u>rescinds</u> the initial decision that would have allowed a murderer to slip through Police fingers. His action gets **Tony** to the Police Station, results in the discovery of his parole violator <u>status</u> and his possession of a <u>stolen</u> car, leads to the search of his motel room, the recovery of a switch blade knife and the kinky books. His attention to detail during booking produces the <u>scrap</u> of paper that bears the NAME and TELEPHONE NUMBER of **John Store**. Which leads, of course, to **Tony's** connection to **Las Vegas** and **Murder** and **matching bloody fingerprints**.

BUT FOR the diligence of Officer W., <u>none</u> of this would have happened in Colorado Springs –– within a week of the Homicide. Instead, it is quite likely a psychopathic killer would have been anonymously wallowed up in the shadowy under belly of society and Paula's grisly stabbing would have been relegated to COLD CASE oblivion. By small and simple acts are great things brought to pass! The People are in your debt, Sir.

Tony S. is returned to Las Vegas for Criminal Proceedings. He qualifies for Public Defender representation. The Attorney he's assigned has already been introduced in an earlier chapter. It is none other than "**The Noose**", that Lawyer of preeminent credentials – the esteemed Counselor Rick. He's the fierce competitor with the **booming**, deep, resonant voice that fills Courtrooms with a persona he hopes will INTIMIDATE opponents. The Prosecutor turned Defender. I know from the get-go that Rick will provide his usual brand of vigorous advocacy on behalf of his Client. But that's okay, I'm hyped for this one. Bring it on, Rick! Give it your best shot, Counselor.

The Trial has <u>several</u> crucial stages that are etched into my memory. They stand out thirty five years later as though they happened yesterday.

The Case against **Tony** is largely *CIRCUMSTANTIAL* – with **one** notable variation. There is one facet of the evidence which, by its **timing** and **proximity** to the Offense, I'm going to dub a *circumstantial hybrid*. Committing heinous Murder high in the sky on the Las Vegas Strip has some drawbacks, not least of which is GETTING DOWN. After the clown has done it, he has to <u>extricate</u> himself from the bloodbath he leaves behind. As it happens, **Tony's** *flight* from the scene of his horrendous Crime does **not** go unobserved. He takes a hotel <u>service</u> <u>elevator</u> to get from floor eleven to ground level on Sunday – March 31. He's playing the law of averages. Believing his chances to avoid being sighted are better if he's **not** riding a guest elevator conveyance.

It's ALL <u>clear</u> when **Tony** steps surreptitiously into the <u>service</u> <u>elevator</u> on the eleventh floor. However, something happens to the *fleeing felon*, who **desperately** <u>wants</u> to fly solo, as he distances himself from his deed. The elevator makes an unscheduled stop on the <u>ninth</u> floor. Serves you right, **Tony**. Don't expect a smooth *flight* down, when up there you've defiled the Sabbath day with savage debauchery. Expect a bumpy descent, Fella.

Enter **Mabel**. She works in housekeeping. A late thirties black woman on her way to the basement. She's mildly surprised to <u>see</u> **Tony S** on the <u>service</u> <u>elevator,</u> and is intuitively wary. He's *disgruntled*, to say the least, by her companionship. He'd hoped to catch an express to the basement level. For an instant, a strong urge to poke her eyes out and stab her silly sweeps across his carnal mind. But he's already **disposed** of the bloody, *seven*-inch switch blade knife, and her cheerful "Good Morning" has a calming influence. Her Sabbath Day salutation soothes the beast in him, and possibly saves her from grievous injury. **Tony** sullenly nods at his fellow passenger.

The two face each other from opposite sides of the elevator. A killer and a maid. Locked in a *thirty second* chance meeting. His eyes are cast down, while she quizzically stares. And she's thinking, **not** dressed like an employee and going to the basement? Perspiring and breathing hard. Avoiding eye contact. <u>Both</u> hands in his pockets. Has he been working out? Is he sick? Or is it nerves? Do **I** make him nervous? His demeanor is that of a man who wants to be left alone. Who'd prefer **not** to be seen. Someone who <u>wants</u> to be invisible. It's curious! But there's an expression that curiosity killed the cat. She doesn't try to engage him in small talk. They ride the nine floors to the basement in silence.

The elevator door opens. He leaves first. Darting to the right. She goes left. The encounter ends without incident. But it impresses her.

Thirty minutes later the shocking news swoops like a tidal wave through the corridors of the hotel. A young woman's been MURDERED on the eleventh floor! Ingress an egress to the building have been sealed off. Employees and guests are in a high state of alarm. Has the killer left the premises, or does the monster still lurk somewhere inside? Those with possible information are encouraged to go to the lobby and speak with Police.

In fact, the escape hatch has been closed fifteen minutes too late. **Tony** is GONE. Speeding out of Sin City in his stolen car with his lurid memories. As for **Mabel**, she's gone to the lobby to report her elevator encounter. Given a statement form, and is briefly writing about the man she's seen. –– It's one of many. Law Enforcement garners fifty to sixty handwritten statements. **Mabel** is put on the back burner. Lost in the paperwork shuffle.

Inexplicably, notwithstanding its **timing** and **proximity** to the Offense, there is still **no** followup by the Coppers after the suspect is IDENTIFIED. I suppose **no** one bothered to re-read the Crime Scene statements. There is **no** in-depth recorded and typewritten statement added to the file. **No** photographs viewed. **No** physical lineup conducted? Really, **no** perceptible interest in the housekeeping lady by investigating officers that is tangibly manifest. Perhaps, the Homicide Boys feel the **fingerprints** are sufficient.

However, to a Prosecutor – the guy who is the followup *Courtroom Cop* – there can **never** be TOO much evidence. A Prosecutor knows that nothing can be taken for granted with Jurors. He NEVER knows what he has is sufficient until the Jury Foreperson reads a GUILTY **verdict** into the record. He NEVER knows when he has enough. It ain't over until it's over!

Reshuffle and re-read the pile of witness statements. Leave **no** handwritten statement unturned – unread! Being thorough often pays big dividends. I read and re-read and ponder **Mabel's** statement. She's subpoenaed. A Pretrial Conference is conducted, and – by and by – she's waiting outside the second story Courtroom for her turn to testify. Intently observing those who pass by as she waits. Wondering if it's possible she'll see the man she saw in the service elevator.

Afternoon sessions for Trials in the **three** courtrooms on this level are about to begin. Court personnel, Lawyers, Police Officers, Witnesses, spectators, out-of-custody Defendants and in-custody Defendants being escorted to Court by Corrections Officers are congregating. Some immediately enter a Courtroom, while others remain outside studying notes, mingling, and conversing.

Mabel is to be the first witness for the 1:30 p.m. session of **Tony's** Trial. I check with her to confirm that she's ready to go just before I enter the Courtroom. She is ready! Primed for her witness time. Moreover, Mabel tells me **she's** SEEN *HIM*. Who? The–**Guy**–in–the–<u>service</u>–<u>elevator</u>. Describe the Man you saw? She offers a <u>description</u> that **does** sound like **Tony S.**, but I have NO way of knowing for sure whom she's describing.

She's understandably nervous. Testifying in a Murder Trial is a high-stakes, tension filled runaway cable car ride. I tell her to relax. That she'll be fine. To get comfortable on the Witness chair, to be polite to the Court and Counsel, to speak slowly and distinctly – the Jury won't remember testimony they can't hear, and to be sure every question is understood before it's answered. All we're asking is that she *does her best* to tell the Jury **<u>exactly</u>** what she remembers about her one-to-one encounter with a man in the <u>service</u> <u>elevator</u> on the morning of the Crime. She's the only person on the planet who knows WHAT Man she sees! While she's testifying, she'll need to look around to determine if the SAME **<u>man</u>** is in the Courtroom.

We're poised for an intriguing Courtroom Drama. I **<u>don't</u>** have a clue *what* her decision will be *when* she sees the Defendant in the Courtroom. A Murder Trial is a series of events that are <u>never</u> completely **predictable**!

It's 1:35 p.m. – high noon, so to speak – the Bailiff summons **Mabel** into the Courtroom. Her right arm flinches slightly as she raises it for the Witness Oath. She **<u>swears</u>** to tell the truth, sits down, adjusts her position to be comfortable, clears her throat, and LOOKS around. It's time for **Direct Examination** – round <u>one</u> of her testimony. Will the Bell toll for **Tony S.**?

The Witness is guided through her description of a <u>peculiar</u> sighting which, by its **timing** and **proximity** to the Offense, I've dubbed a *circumstantial hybrid*. I'll briefly explain. As this treatise has previously documented, there are TWO great branches of evidence in The Law. They are: **Direct** and **<u>Circumstantial</u> Evidence.** DIRECT EVIDENCE is whatever a person **perceives** with <u>any</u> of her physical senses <u>at the time the Crime is</u> BEING <u>perpetrated</u>! CIRCUMSTANTIAL EVIDENCE is *everything else*. Obviously, **Mabel** does **<u>not</u>** see the Crime BEING perpetrated. What she **sees** occurs AFTER the commission. Therefore, assuming the Man she **sees** is the killer, he is in the act of FLEEING the scene of his odious Offense. That makes it **<u>Circumstantial</u> <u>Evidence</u>** –– technically.

BUT the **timing** and **proximity** of this SIGHTING cause it, in a sense, to *almost* be an EXTENSION of the Crime. **Paula** is discovered, savagely stabbed, lying in the doorway of her hotel room at about 9:00 a.m. It would seem that she has attempted to FLEE the scene of her knife wielding **assailant's** onslaught, but collapses at the door. According to **Mabel**, TWO floors down and DIRECTLY below the Crime Scene she enters a <u>service</u> <u>elevator</u> at ABOUT 9:00 a.m. The single occupant is a NON-employee MAN who is *sweating* and *breathing hard* and has *both hands* in his pockets. He *averts* her gaze, and they ride nine floors to the basement in *silence*. And the Gent <u>isn't</u> a gentleman, he leaves the elevator FIRST. Darting *quickly* to the right – and out of sight. Accordingly, I'm saying **Mabel's** testimony is a *circumstantial hybrid*.

However, irrespective of the semantical nit-picking –this much is CERTAIN, her **testimony** is of ENORMOUS **importance** to BOTH parties. And – it all hinges on HOW **Mabel** reacts when she *sees* **Tony**. IS HE or ISN'T HE the cat she's **seen**?

She glances several times at the Defendant during her **Direct Examination**, but her expression provides no hint regarding her state of mind. Frankly, I'm stuck on the horns of a dilemma. It's apparent to me that **Mabel's** *thirty second* chance encounter on the elevator **is** with the killer. Yet, six months have passed since the day of the Murder. Will she be able to make an <u>identification</u>? This character has committed an atrocious crime, will **Mabel** have the gumption to <u>identify</u> even if she is able to identify? And what will be the effect upon the lay-person Jury **IF** I ask the Witness whether the Man she <u>**saw**</u> is in the Courtroom – and she says NO?

I have a strong predilection <u>against</u> asking CRUCIAL questions unless I'm reasonably confident of the answers. I'm **not** confident at this time. So, the career Prosecutor makes a command decision. He chooses to go conservative, electing to err on the side of caution. Deciding to indulge in a <u>wait</u> <u>and</u> <u>see</u> strategy. The *description* the Witness has made in her testimony is certainly consistent with the Defendant, <u>perhaps</u> the members of the Jury will make the connection on their own. Also, I know that Esteemed Counselor Rick is an aggressive advocate. Someone who likes to take the bull by the horns. <u>Perhaps</u>, my failure to ask will **lure** Rick into the breach. He <u>may</u> assume she **can't** identify because I <u>didn't</u> ask for an identification.

Perhaps? Maybe? Possibly? It's all conjecture. **Not** asking **Mabel** to IDENTIFY during **Direct** IS a glaring omission. A gamble. A roll of the dice. – Is the Deputy's verdict true? Only time will complete the rumble in the Trial jungle. Not unlike Jury deliberation, the **examination** of a witness isn't over until its over. The point is: the Bell **doesn't** toll for **Tony S.** during the first round of **Mabel's** testimony.

ROUND TWO – **Cross Examination**. Rick's a pugilist. He's got to somehow overcome the *presumption of guilt* **Tony's** BLOODY **fingerprints** will raise. He concludes he'll swing from the hip early. Seize the advantage at the outset he believes is his to exploit. Convinced the Prosecutor has not asked the seminal question because he knows the answer will be NO, Rick charges across the ring, in a manner of speaking, and goes for a KNOCKOUT.

Gentleman Rick starts his **Cross** dramatically. Throwing caution to the wind. Confident the Prosecution's ploy has given him an opportunity to snatch victory from the jaws of defeat. Utilizing his booming voice to full affect, he directs the attention of the Witness to his Client. Tells her to look intently at him, and then to tell the Men and Women of Jury if **Tony S.** *is* the Man on the Elevator.

Mabel follows her instructions to the letter. She pivots slightly in the Witness Chair, looks directly at the Defendant, takes his measure for about *thirty seconds* [Probably about the same length of time she has **seen** him on the service elevator.]and says: "The Man I'm looking at **certainly** LOOKS like the Man I saw on the Elevator, but he's sitting down. I **can't** tell how TALL he is. I need to know if he's the SAME **height**. [Pointing to **Tony S.**] Will you have **this Man** stand up so I can tell how big he is?"

Folks, I wish you could have seen the look on ole Rick's face. The scenario is his creation. He's TRAPPED. He has no other option available, he **has** to ask **Tony S.** to stand up. On occasion, adrenalin-charged Attorney's **do** rush in where angels fear to tread. The Prosecution *inadvertently* sets a land mine and Rick's just been asked to have his Client step on it.

It-is-flat-out-impossible-to imagine-a-Prosecution-Witness-reacting-any-better-than-**Mabel**-does-in-this-instance!! And I've had the shifting-sand challenge of shepherding between seven and ten thousand through the System. Her intuitive conduct could **not** have been better had it been scripted – and it WASN'T. JUSTICE is **not** served when Witnesses are **told** what to say. Witness tampering has **never** been my modus operandi. My sole objective has been dynamic advocacy for Justice. A Verdict not predicated upon **Truth** can't be JUST. There was NO *willfully* subverted Justice on my watch – ever!

Esteemed Counselor Rick takes his hemlock. Dutifully telling **Tony** boy to stand up. The Client senses things aren't going particularly well at the moment. He sighs, then reluctantly stands – though the posture he assumes is *clearly* a slouch.

Mabel doesn't miss a beat. She turns her attention to Rick. Saying: "Mr. Lawyer, tell your Man to stand straight."Poor Rick. He continues to squirm in the pickle juice he's concocted. He pirouettes toward his Client and barks, "Tony – stand tall." **Tony** hesitates, sighs again, and with great effort, it seems –lifts himself slightly. The Witness focuses on the Defendant once more. She eyeballs him for about *ten seconds* this time. Then leans forward and announces in a very excited tone, "**THAT'S HIM**! I'M **POSITIVE** THAT'S HIM!

Hey Tony, the–bell–is–tolling! Esteemed Counselor Rick continues his Cross Examination, but the starch has come out of his questions. He probes and parries and rolls his eyes in feigned disbelief for a spell. There are no breakdowns. **Mabel** hangs tough, and a chastened Rick meekly passes the Witness.

As for the Prosecution's REDIRECT, knowing it's advisable to quit while you're ahead. It's **not** going to get any better than it already is – that **isn't** possible. I say emphatically, "NO FURTHER QUESTIONS."

> "Double, double toil and trouble; Fire burn and cauldron bubble... Eye of newt, and toe of frog; Wool of bat, and tongue of dog... By the pricking of...[HIS] thumbs, Something wicked this way comes..." (Shakespeare, *Macbeth*, ibid.)

Tony S. has some explaining to do. After the Prosecution finishes its Case, he *waives* his privilege against self incrimination and takes the Witness Stand. It's ALL on the line for the Eleventh Floor Bad Boy. What are you going to say, Tony, "I **wasn't** there – but it was SELF DEFENSE?" Not really! The **PRINTS** and the **WITNESS** inferentially **put-him-there**.

The ROOM PHONE **didn't** disconnect itself from the wall, catch an elevator to the lobby where Tony is checking out chicks ––– and hop into his lap. The PHONE **didn't** secrete the **bloody prints** from its own private pores. The BLOOD **didn't** spontaneously generate itself out of thin air! The BLOODY PRINTS – to return to Thoreau's expression concerning *circumstantial evidence*, constitute a proverbial TROUT **in the milk**. Excuse me, they constitute a small SCHOOL of TROUT **in the milk.** Now, the Jury didn't *see* **Tony S.** inside the ROOM, nor *hear* him pull the PHONE out of the wall, nor *sense* **Paula's** fear as the hideous assault occurs, nor *smell* the foul body heat of **Tony's** adrenalin rush or of his profuse sweating aura as he commits his loathsome deed – BUT **they** KNOW **he** **did** **it** just as surely as percipient witnesses would know.

Actually, the convincing factor is stronger. "Some *circumstantial evidence* is **very** strong..." (Henry David Thoreau, ibid., emphasis added.)The **bloody** **prints** tell the story conclusively and they **don't** **lie**! MATCHING prints are **never** *biased*. Neither are they subject to *sensory* limitation. Those that are in the VICTIM'S **blood** are **not** *hard* of hearing or seeing or smelling or touching. They are simply cold, dry, inanimate STAINS that immutably connect **Tony S.** To MURDER IN COLD BLOOD!

And the JURY will have to fly away on wings of fancy to say it's a Case of Self Defense. THEY'D have to be insane. They don't <u>look</u> like lunatics, Tony! After all, you **didn't** wait around for a roll call. You **didn't** call 911. You **didn't** provide a Police Dispatcher with your name, rank, serial number, and criminal history. You **didn't** offer medical assistance to the fallen woman. NOT YOU **TONY**, you took a *cowardly*, hasty hike to the <u>service</u> <u>elevator</u> and went down – and far AWAY.

Esteemed Counselor Rick tells his client the same thing. Accordingly, **Tony S.** ADMITS he's **inside** The Room. – The **dispute** is over HOW he's managed to get PRINTS in various places in The Room and, specifically, WHY his right *thumb* and right *index* finger PRINTS IN BLOOD are on The Telephone inside **Paula's Room.**"Some circumstantial evidence is very strong, as when you find a [school of] trout in the milk."(Henry David Thoreau, ibid.)

It's truly a dilemma for **Tony** – a bucket of worms. Enough to make a killer have nightmares. Maybe scratch his head until he's almost bald. A case of "Oh bother" – worry, worry, worry.

WHY – WHY – WHY – are your prints in the room of the **murdered** woman, **Tony S.**? Well, this is the Defendant's best effort at explaining such a salient <u>fact</u>. During **Direct Examination**, he tells the Jury he's innocently on the Eleventh Floor of the Hotel on Sunday morning – March 31st. As he walks down a hallway, he hears sounds of distress coming from a guest room. The door is ajar, so he pushes the door open and walks inside. He says the scene he *sees* in the room is stunning. There is **blood** **spatter** everywhere, and a woman covered with blood is writhing on the floor. He says he quickly *walks* to the Room Phone, *picks* it up, and *tries* unsuccessfully to call the Front Desk. Then belatedly realizes The Phone cord has been <u>pulled</u> from the wall. **Tony** says he's simply <u>attempting</u> to get *help* for the injured Victim, an Ordinary Joe just doing his civic duty. After that he *leaves* The Room in a *panic*, fearful Police <u>will</u> think he's the perpetrator due to his presence in The Room, and *rides* a <u>service</u> <u>elevator</u> to the basement with a black woman who gets on at the ninth floor. Not a very plausible scenario, but **Tony** tries to touch all the bases that need to be covered.

What incredibly bad timing for the poor fellow. His luck in being at that specific spot, as opposed to ALL the other places he could have been in Las Vegas at that particular time, is abysmally bad. Right? But that's **Tony's** *story* and he's sticking to it. The PRINTS **don't** lie. What choice does he have – really?

Moreover, a Defendant who *waives* his Privilege Against Self Incrimination by taking the Witness Stand knows the Prosecution will get a crack at him too. An adversarial **Cross Examination** is definitely in your future, **Tony** – and the thesis you've posited will be fertile terrain to explore! He did some perspiring at the scene of his **Murder**, and he's doing some big-time *sweating* in the Courtroom. Well founded *sweat*, I'd say.

Tony has constructed a house of cards during **Direct**. A house of cards is flimsy. It easily falls down. The explanation of his PRESENCE in The Room begs the second question. *Innocently* on the eleventh floor Sunday morning between 8 o'clock and 9:00 a.m., Sir? For what purpose is <u>Your Innocence</u> there? Freelancing the delivery of escort service flyers? A heathen searching for an early morning high-rise worship service? A window washer without a shammy? Not likely.

The **mystery** remains –– WHAT **is** an unregistered drifter <u>doing</u> *prowling* an eleventh story hallway of a Las Vegas Strip Hotel on Sunday morning – or any morning? He's guilty of misdemeanor <u>loitering</u> unless he can provide a legitimate reason for his presence. Were you, psychic, **Tony**? You had a premonition something awful was going to happen so you hurried up to eleven? Arriving just in time to be too late. THE FACT IS: **Tony** offers **no** coherent reason for being AT **or** NEAR the Crime Scene. That's because he gets a trifle nonplused on the Witness Stand when he tries to *deal* with The Telephone.

It's in evidence of course. The **blood stained** PHONE with the <u>detached</u> cord is a haunting EXHIBIT. An awesome visual aid. The People's Man has ONE simple question for **Tony S.** regarding THE TELE. Three cheers for the penetrating barb of Cross. Legal scholars have hailed the power of **Cross Examination** for centuries.

"Cross-examination is the greatest legal engine ever invented for the discovery of truth. You can do anything with a bayonet except sit on it. A lawyer can do anything with cross-examination if he is skillful enough not to impale his own cause upon it." (John Henry Wigmore)

The Prosecution has been hammering away at **Tony's** story for about twenty minutes. **Tony's** doing his best to fend off the Prosecutive parries, but a Defendant can't sit on a bayonet. He's nervously twisting on the Witness Stand, eyes darting back and forth between Esteemed Counselor Rick and myself. IT'S TIME. Lights – camera – action!

Tony *doesn't* know what's coming. Adversaries in Courts of Law **don't** *telegraph* their questions. A Defendant **isn't** provided a Legal Brief that previews the People's Cross. We don't do dress rehearsals outside the presence of the Jury. THE KEY to successful Cross is the <u>element</u> of surprise. A testifying **killer** <u>never</u> knows when the thrust of the bayonet is on its way or what form it will assume.

I request the indulgence of the Court, approach the Clerk, and ask her to pass me the bayonet – I mean, the **blood** **stained** TELEPHONE with the <u>detached</u> cord. The Clerk hands me The Exhibit, and I walk resolutely toward the Witness Stand. **Tony** *SEES* what I have in my grasp, blinks twice, and swallows hard. He **can't** think of anything coming from the impending confrontation that will be favorable to him. He'd like to high-tail it out of here and hop a freight train. He'd love to be on sunny Las Vegas Boulevard South leering at the Babes. However, the Court Services Officer is a very big guy – and agile.

Trial Terrain doesn't grace its participants with money-back guarantees. We're dealing with variables here, not unchanging verities. As the renowned Mr. Wigmore warns, Prosecutors <u>can</u> get *impaled* on their own questions if their inquisition **isn't** skillfully employed. I'm aware of the risk, but extremely confident. It's <u>not</u> complicated, and **Mister Tony** has no clue what I intend to do with THE TELEPHONE. I don't really believe there's any <u>reasonable</u> likelihood he'll be able to <u>avoid</u> **the trap** –– and **impalement** of THE BLOODY PHONE.

I'm standing before him now with THE TELEPHONE. He's **not** looking at his Prosecutor's face anymore, his EYES are glued to the Prosecutor's hands. It's like **Tony S.** is mesmerized and <u>can't</u> stop staring at THE PHONE. Beguiled by the apparatus that's been his undoing. Spellbound. Wondering – what's next!

Well, what's next – is THE QUESTION. The–ONE–simple–question– about **The Telephone!** The Defendant is squirming and THE QUESTION is on the tip of my tongue. Which doesn't happen to be *sweating* much at the moment. Seventeen words are strung together in carefully modulated tones. Each spoken distinctly and deliberately, "**Where–did–you–place–your–HANDS–when–you–picked–up– the–telephone– intending–to–call–for–assistance?**"

I hadn't in my wildest dreams hoped for a reaction as good as I got. It's as though the Defendant's *eyes* instantly glaze over, and he experiences a sudden *brain freeze*. CONSCIOUSNESS of *guilt* is scribbled all over his face. He just sits there like a bump on a pickle for – say – thirty seconds. The quarry has clearly lost his focus. Maybe **Tony S.** has *slipped* into another dimension. Bemused and pondering: "*Why* is this short fellow standing in front of me with a telephone that has a detached cord and *WHO* are these other **fourteen** people in The Box, [The regular Jurors and two alternates.] and *WHY* are they staring at me like this?"

When the haze parts and **Tony** returns from his *fugue* state, he tries to buy a little more time with this lame repartee, "Would you repeat the question?" I'm certainly willing to oblige. It protracts and enhances his discomfort. "**Where–did– you–place–your–HANDS–when–you–picked–up–the–telephone–intending–to– call–for–assistance?**" And it's deja vu. He just sits there like a bump on a pickle again – staring at THE PHONE.

We're at an impasse. The Prosecutor has to take the offensive to break the gridlock. There are only so many Courtroom hours in a day. "**Mr. S.** – since you **don't** seem anxious to answer the question––"

Mr. Esteemed Counselor Rick – employing his BOOMING voice to full disadvantage. The inflection merely spotlights the dilemma of the guilty bastard who is twisting in the wind, so to speak: "OBJECTION, the form of the question is argumentative!"

The Court: "Sustained."

The Prosecutor – shifting gears slightly, moving ahead to THE POINT he always intended to get to anyway: "**Mr. S.** – since it's apparently hard for you to **explain** where you placed your hands on the telephone, I'll **pass** THE PHONE to you and **you–SHOW–us–where–you–put–your–hands.**"

Tony continues to hunker down like an armadillo caught in the high voltage **beam** of a Flying Saucer. Obviously, he's not going to say yea nor nay to my proposal. I say, "Your Honor – may I approach the Witness?"

The Court: "You may, Counsel."

I walk to the Witness stand, extending my arms to pass him THE EXHIBIT. He hesitates. He doesn't take THE TELEPHONE at first. It's incredible. **Tony** isn't liking this. I'm pretty damn sure at this precise moment, **Tony S.** is wishing he **didn't** have *any* hands. That way he could AVOID the demonstration. BUT **Tony** <u>does</u> have hands. They are the *same* pair of **malignant** HANDS that inflicted the horrendous butchering of **Paula A.**

<u>Finally</u> in a mind set of *cold sweat* indecision, **Tony** reaches for THE TELEPHONE. By his tentative manner, one might have presumed he is being asked to hold a *rattlesnake*. And perhaps, given his predicament, THE EXHIBIT **is** as lethal as a *Diamondback*. He's heard the testimony regarding **the Prints**. He KNOWS he has to explain <u>away</u> the <u>powerful</u> *INCULPATORY* effect **his** right *THUMB* and right *INDEX* finger PRINTS in **blood** on THE TELEPHONE have produced.

The **root** problem is this: He knows he has to place his HANDS on THE PHONE in a manner <u>CONSISTENT</u> with the location, direction, angle. stain pattern, and associated **matching** prints. Otherwise, his testimony **won't** be – **can't** be feasible. It's a daunting task. The hideous tapestry that is a <u>chilling</u>, <u>inanimate</u> TESTAMENT to **Murder** is intricate in its detail and subtle in the interlocking relationship of its respect parts. Further, **Tony's** problem is magnified because he's trying to construct his Defense from whole cloth. He's MAKING UP this whole business about picking up THE PHONE to call for *assistance*. He **is** the high altitude assailant on the eleventh floor. **HE–IS–THE–KILLER!**

It's **Paula A.** who grabs THE PHONE to cry for assistance. **Her** PRINTS are *also* on THE TELEPHONE. It's <u>her</u> **BLOOD TYPE** that **stains** THE EXHIBIT and <u>now</u> –– *CRIES* out for **Justice**! This is the *numbing* Case Truth!

"...Eye of newt, and toe of frog; Wool of bat, and tongue of dog...By the pricking of...[His] thumbs, Something wicked this way comes. Open, locks, Whoever knocks!" (William Shakespeare, *Macbeth*, ibid.)

Had the tete-a-tete between the Witness and the Prosecutor simply been a bit of Broadway, slapstick comedy would have been the ruling of the day. However, the head-to-head **is not** a thespian exercise. It's deadly earnest. All the marbles are on the table for the **Jury** to *see* – and **Tony** knows it. Still, he <u>can't</u> decide how to grasp THE EXHIBIT. He cups HIS HANDS together and extends them to within inches of THE PHONE, then rapidly changes his approach to this way or that way. Moving HIS

HANDS in fidgety haste – reaching, reconsidering, pulling back, adjusting his angle, evaluating –– *sweating*.

BUT notwithstanding his personal angst, the flat-out flustered Defendant **does** EVENTUALLY **choose** a grip. He gets THE PHONE in his hands. And – **Justice wins!** His **choice** is WRONG, of course. He gets it all WRONG. The **position** he selects is a farce. NOTHING coincides with the location, direction, angle, stain pattern, and associated **matching** prints on the EXHIBIT. **Paula's** DEAD and **Tony's** DEAD–IN–THE–WATER *inconsistent* with the PHYSICAL EVIDENCE. Obviously, **The Jury** *sees* his DUPLICITY in an instant.

Moreover, there's the matter of **John Store's** TESTIMONY. Remember him? He and his wife have an encounter with **Tony** in Las Vegas several weeks prior to the Murder. They hit it off and the Stores invite him to visit them if he ever comes to Colorado Springs. John testifies to the intriguing telephone call they receive from **Tony** on Monday morning, April 1, 1974. Yeah, April 1st, but the words imparted by **Tony Boy** aren't an *April Fools* joke. He's in full-throttle flight from the macabre scene of Murder in Cold Blood, and curiously – beset with some sort of inner compulsion to allude to The Offense during his conversation. To pass along a cryptic, out-of-the-blue Sin City *news bite*. Possibly wanting to do a little esoteric venting to someone. What kind of warped sense of gratification causes a **killer** to make an obscure reference to his *hideous* crime, during a long distance call, to a man who is practically a stranger?

We **don't** know WHY he said it. However, thanks to the cooperation of the Witness, we **do** know WHAT he said. And it's very sporting of **Tony** to have said it. He tells the Stores he's driving though Colorado Springs and will stop by to say hello. Then **Tony** tosses in his gratuity – an enigmatic gem. HE SAYS **he** had been out the *previous* evening with a girl WHO had been **reported** MURDERED *the morning* of his telephone call.

Tony's feeling rather smug at this point. Thinks he's out of harm's way. That he's committed a perfect crime. That he's above the Law. WRONG, **Tony.** You're a killer on the lam whose infected with foot-in-mouth disease, and the big foot in your mouth is going to give you much more than aching gums.

It's great how things come together. **Tony** has this slick plan at Trial about how he'll explain away **prints in blood**. He's simply a Good Samaritan guy wanting to assist a maiden in distress. However, ole Tony says **nothing** about his *altruistic action* when he confides in John Store. NOTHING. A glaring omission to be sure. *Gotcha*, Tony!

Another anomaly occurs. The 4-inch switch blade knife Colorado Springs Officers find in **Tony's** motel room is NOT the Murder Weapon. The Medical Examiner testifies, to a reasonable degree of medical certainty, that in his opinion the **BLADE** used by the Killer is *at least* **six** inches long. He bases his opinion upon the depth of certain penetrating wounds. So, presumably the ACTUAL knife was never placed in evidence for Juror consideration. But is there a *SIGHTING*?

The Parties have ARGUED and the Jury is sequestered in deliberation. They've been going at it for five or six hours when **a note** is passed to the Bailiff. The Jury has a request. They want to inspect the Crime Scene. It's not the same, naturally. The room has been rented out many times since the *Homicide* – and I doubt the Hotel has done any *full disclosure* to occupying guests regarding the grisly event of March 31, 1974.

No one knows WHY the Jury wants to view the room. Their **note** isn't enlightening. Perhaps, it's a flash of inspiration, or they just want a high-rise elevator ride, or a nice view of The Strip, or a chance to clear the air. Deliberation gets heated on occasion. Nevertheless, Judges like to accommodate Jurors when they can. The request is granted. The following morning the Jury is appropriately instructed about *changes* in the Crime Scene, informed they will **not** be taking additional *evidence* [The evidence has already been submitted.], and a Judicial *hiatus* is declared on further deliberation until after their field trip is completed. This exercise is merely an effort to aid the deliberative process after it's resumed.

Accordingly, we take a bus ride down Las Vegas Boulevard South and the Court reconvenes in a hallway adjacent to the eleventh floor crime-scene room. The Judge, Court personnel, Counsel for both Parties, the twelve regular Jurors and two Alternates are present. **Tony S.** is the odd man out. He doesn't get chauffeured to the Las Vegas Strip. He gets more jail time. Get used to it **Tony**, there's a lot more lock-up time on the way.

The Judge makes a preliminary record, and the Jury is allowed to inspect the Crime Scene. The Judge and Counsel follow from a respectable distance. We do not intermingle with the Jurors during this procedure. Great caution is employed to avoid any type of interaction that would be legal basis for a **mistrial**.

I have only ONE **specific** recollection of the Jury viewing, but **it's** burned into my psyche for perpetuity. I went through this procedure with some degree of regularity during my career, but ALL the **other** Juror visits to Crime Scenes have simply meshed into an indiscernible dark memory gap – except for this ONE.

While a Juror is gazing out a window at the Crime Scene, he *sees* an **object** on a LANDING about two stories down. Surprisingly, it <u>looks</u> like a **switch blade** *knife*. Therefore, the Jury Foreperson has an additional request. Climbing through the window will provide a much more definitive perspective of the **object**, and the building is constructed in a manner that will permit a clearer observation to be safely accomplished. Hence, the Foreperson asks that Jurors be allowed to climb through the window in question, so they may scrutinize the object below from a better vantage point.

His Honor sizes up the situation, receives input from Counsel on the subject, and enters an **order** permitting the requested jury-viewing from the <u>other</u> side of the window. The event is really quite extraordinary. The Bailiff is posted at the window, and – one by one in the sequence that follows – he assists the regular and alternate Jurors, the Judge, and Counsel for both Parties, through the window for an eagle-eye view of what certainly appears to be an abandoned, six inch plus **switch blade** *knife*!

Is it possible this is the <u>missing</u> *knife*? That the Murder Weapon was lying two stories down, right under the noses of Crime Scene Investigators as they processed The Room? Overlooked by those trained **not** to miss anything? That the MYSTERY of the absentee **switch blade** has been solved by an observant Juror? A Layperson. We can't tell from our height if the blade is **blood** *stained*, but such a condition <u>can't</u> be visually eliminated.

However, it's a moot point legally. Simply a curiosity. The evidentiary phase of the Trial is complete. The object isn't a tree, there's **no** carbon dating process for precisely determining how long the *knife* has been reposing on the landing. It may have been tossed there last night by a hotel guest or inadvertently dropped years ago by a cleaning crew. Still, the presence of the *knife* is fuel for speculation

The Jurors are returned to the Courthouse for further **deliberation** without additional incident – though *The Knife* may have been a bell ringer to them. They return in <u>forty five</u> minutes with a VERDICT. **Not** good news for **Tony S**. It's GUILTY – MURDER ONE! The punishment subsequently imposed by the Judge – LIFE **in the Slammer** WITHOUT **the Possibility** of PAROLE! The Predator has stalked his last Chick.

"...toe of frog; Wool of bat, and tongue of dog...

By the pricking of...[HIS] thumbs, **Something wicked** this way comes. Open, locks, <u>Whoever knocks</u>...?" (William Shakespeare, *Macbeth*, ibid., emphasis added)

A Bowl Of Chicken Soup
Before We Part M'lady?

> "Affliction is enamour'd of thy parts,
> And thou art wedded to calamity."
> (William Shakespeare, *Romeo and Juliet*,
> Act III, Sc.3, Line 1)

Chapter 10

I guess Walter doesn't like chickens. His wife is **no** chicken, but she's on the *crazy* side of forty, a tough little bird whose as stubborn as a nail. The fellow who **isn't** a chicken lover is on the *crazy* side of sixty – and not especially fond of **her** neither!

Marriage has been called "...the union of hand and heart."(Bishop Jeremy Taylor) However, the merger of Walter and Si Son has descended to daily *disunion*. It's a bond characterized by an absence of helping hands and loving hearts. Their marital relationship has settled into a sort of cultural war. She's an Asian. He's a German – and set in his ways. More than twenty years older than she. The two hail from different races and different generations. They argue incessantly over a wide range of issues. For example, she insists on having a small flock of chickens, and they aren't confined to the coop. She treats them like pets. Meaning: they have full access to the house. No, not the hen house. These foul friends have full clucking rights to Walter and Si Son's domicile. Scampering and scratching and pooping in the yard and on the floor. Such a circumstance is, to borrow a word with Germanic origin, verboten to him.

He's demanded she keep her chickens out of the parlor, but she's ignored him. He says it's apparent she'd rather play house with her feathered friends than her husband. Poor, nostalgic Si Son – no disrespect intended, she's just reliving the quaint ways of her youth in the old country.

When marital vows have become empty promises and the partners have stopped partnering, <u>divorce</u> is often considered a viable option. Walter and Si Son have discussed a breakup, but they're at loggerheads over the terms of <u>divorce</u> proceedings as well. He says she's greedy, that she *only* cares about the **dollar bill**. He's willing to give her half, but she *wants* <u>everything</u>! She says –– . Actually, we're **not** privy to what she says. Si Son isn't around anymore.

The abrupt disappearance of Si Son <u>is</u> a **mystery**. Sometime between July 2, 1985 and July 20, 1985 – she seems to fall off the edge of the earth. Her adult children **<u>aren't</u>** apprised of her departure. Her car and her chickens and all her personal effects are **<u>left</u>** behind. She **doesn't** leave a note explaining her intentions, **<u>nor</u>** any forwarding address. There are **no** post cards or letters or telephone calls. **Si Son** simply vanishes into thin air! The wife who **<u>wants</u>** EVERYTHING, according to her husband, has left with NOTHING.

Walter <u>isn't</u> helpful. His comments are cryptic and inconsistent. Days pass. Si Son's three children press him for information. His reaction is essentially that of stonewalling the circumstances. He says he **<u>doesn't</u>** know where she's gone. Shrugging off her absence. Making smug disclaimers – he's claims to be as baffled as they are. Figuratively, throwing up his hands in disbelief.

Eventually, he avoids family members. When the children come to see him, he locks the door to the house. When they call, he hangs up the telephone. Factual data **isn't** forthcoming from the Air Force retiree about his wife.

Police get involved. **Walter** <u>originally</u> tells Detective D. on July 20 that his wife left on July 4th. He comes home and she's gone. She hasn't left a note, nor a shred of information concerning her whereabouts. <u>Later</u>, He tells Detective D. she went to California. Detective D. quizzes him regarding the apparent contradiction, "**Why** did you say earlier you didn't know where she went?" Walter counters, "A few days <u>before</u> she said she was going to California."

<u>Six</u> <u>months</u> later **Si Son** surfaces. No, she doesn't wash up on a California beach. She's not doing itinerant labor in Orange County strawberry fields. A hiker and his three dogs find her partial *remains* cohabiting with Nevada sage brush. It's early Sunday afternoon on January

26, 1986. The dogs target an area where there is freshly moved dirt and a slight odor of chlorine. The dog owner <u>sees</u> several bones at the site he believes are human. He takes them to the Las Vegas Metropolitan Police Department for confirmation. They **are** human *remains*.

CSI responds to the area where *remains* of 25-30% of a **human body** are discovered. The **human** parts include "a bit less than half of the skull." The grave site is located in a remote desert area near Nevada State Road 160 east of Pahrump, about thirty feet off Mule Spring Road and just west of Mountain Springs Pass.

The Coroner-Medical Examiner's Office has a twofold responsibility. They must <u>identify</u> the *remains* and <u>determine</u> the *cause of death* – if such findings are possible under the grisly circumstances. **<u>Both</u>** tasks are accomplished. A Forensic Pathologist examines the skull. He concludes that the *teeth* have distinctive Mongoloid (Oriental) characteristics – called "shovel incisers."Also, the recovered bone structure is "small and delicate," consistent with the female gender. One of the existing bones is a <u>tibia</u> bone, the inner and usually larger of two bones extending from the knee to the ankle. Utilizing a general formula applicable to all races, the height of the Victim is estimated to be in the range of 5'1" – 5'2". The *time of death* is believed to be 6-12 months prior to discovery.

The **<u>children</u>** have formally reported their mother as a missing person on July 20, 1985. The anatomical findings of the Forensic Pathologist are consistent with the description of **Si Son.** Therefore, her dental records are subpoenaed from a Las Vegas Dental Group. The Dental Charts reflect eleven visits with six dentists from May 10, 1983 – April 18, 1984.The charts include **dental x-rays** of a *fixed* **<u>stainless</u> <u>steel</u>** *bridge* of the upper jaw.

The upper jaw *remains* of the deceased and a duplicate of the Dental *records* of **Si Son** are released by the Coroner-Medical Examiner's Office to a Forensic Odontologist for comparison. He takes **x-rays** of the upper jaw *remains* and blows up frames of the upper jaw **<u>stainless</u> <u>steel</u>** *bridgework* from the Dental Group **x-rays**. Dr. R. makes a positive identification. The upper jaw *remains* MATCH the *bridgework* depicted in the Dental Records of **Si Son.** He testifies there is NO doubt whatever. He's POSITIVE of the identification. No additional teeth are necessary to achieve <u>certainty</u>. Further, according to the children *hair* strands and a *red* thumbnail recovered from the burial scene are similar to their mother's hair color and a commonly used nail polish. *Stripped* fabric at the grave site is also similar to a shirt their mother often wore.

Moreover, <u>determining</u> the *cause of death* <u>**isn't**</u> a problem. The Medical Examiner has been to the grave site. He eliminates natural disease, suicide, and accident as proximate causes of death. NO evidence of these factors is detected in **Si Son's** *remains*. He wryly observes that it's very difficult for a deceased person to *bury* HERSELF. The cause of death <u>**is**</u> HOMICIDAL, to-wit: **Death** at the hands of another person.

The findings are succinct and gruesome: "There is <u>massive</u> blunt trauma to the head. <u>Multiple</u> fractures are seen. **Si Son's** skull has been <u>struck repeatedly</u> with a blunt object. FIFTEEN <u>separate</u> skull fragments have been recovered. The skull is badly fractured. Characterized by <u>many</u> fracture lines. TREMENDOUS <u>damage</u> to the head exists, and the blunt force trauma is ALL localized. Confined to the head, except for a <u>single</u> fracture of the left forearm – which is probably a wound inflicted as the Victim attempts to defend herself.

"There is NO evidence of <u>animal</u> damage to the skull. The elements **haven't** impacted the condition of the skeletal remains to any significant degree. Natural elements have little effect upon BONE up to <u>one</u> year after burial."

But WHAT is the **blunt object** the KILLER has used to **pummel** the head of his Victim? The ANSWER comes from a curious source. The KILLER who has obviously done a <u>blind side</u> number on his wife gets <u>blind sided</u> himself – from a totally unexpected source. Walter's eighty six year old MOTHER does something mothers **don't** generally do. She's asked Walter what REALLY happened to **Si Son**, and he's told her. She hasn't wanted to believe his words. However, when the body is discovered she <u>**is**</u> seriously conflicted. Wrestling with her dilemma for over a week. Her conscience tells her to fess up to Law Enforcement, but the thought of doing <u>**it**</u> is an emotional blockbuster. It breaks her heart.

With grave misgiving, she takes the Police into her confidence after a week plus and RATS on her boy. Walter's MOTHER *tearfully* provides the **bottom line** skinny on HOW it happened and WHY it happened.

The chickens are the trigger! The clucking is <u>too</u> obnoxious – the smell <u>too</u> onerous – the droppings <u>too</u> ubiquitous – the mess <u>too</u> pervasive. A flock of hens and a rooster aren't going to win any *good housekeeping awards*. Walter has **no** further forbearance with **insider** CHICKENS. He's **ordered** her to keep them out of the house, but his repeated demands have fallen on deaf ears.

The charade happens with monotonous regularity. Whenever Walter leaves by the front door to run his errands, the back door to his domain swings open, a doorstop is strategically placed against the screen door as a standing invitation for full feathered entry, and the gaggle of foul comes scuttling inside. Occasionally, snoopy cluckers find their way into the den. Roosting on his leather recliner. Bringing their filth and feathers to his inner sanctum. The aftermath is enough to gag a maggot – let alone a husband whose a tidiness freak!

Walter returns on the fateful day in July of '85 to the unseemly spectacle of scratches on the seat of his recliner. CHICKEN CLAWS! He immediately goes ballistic. Husband and Wife engage in a shouting match. Each trying to batter the other into submission and contrition with an ever increasing crescendo of scathing epithets. Neither party to the union of wedded discord backs down. The intensity of the screeching reaches a fever pitch. Hateful, hurtful words spew in a torrent from the mouth of Si Son – in broken English and in her native tongue. **Walter** SNAPS.

People SAY **things** and DO **things** in a *fit of anger* they ordinarily would not say nor do. Excessive anger is a form of temporary insanity. A *relationship* **killer** – metaphorically and literally! A destructive barrage of **non communication.** A tornado of toxic noise that can be a morbid soundtrack for Murder.

Walter has become obsessive over the *chicken thing.* **Si Son's** vehement verbiage stokes an ember of malignant feeling he's suppressed to this point. Abruptly, the faint glow of enmity erupts into a raging inferno of hostility. He cannot countenance Si Son's unwillingness to show proper respect to the titular head of their household. ENOUGH. *NO MORE.* **NEVER AGAIN!** He's Air Force, and a true proponent of a regimented domestic lifestyle. The wife does as she's told – OR ELSE! Accordingly, **Walter** does something totally inconsistent with his character. He is **not** a violent man by nature.

The **non-violent** man turns his back on the vile tirade of his wife and walks stiffly to the hallway closet. He's a big baseball fan. His favorite batter is the fabulous hitting "Splendid Splinter" of the Boston Red Sox. A Louisville Slugger reposes peacefully among **Walter's** *memorabilia.* Yet, THE BAT is about to be employed in a **most** unpeaceful manner.

It's deplorable that The Two have come to this kind of final chapter. These Two once stood at the altar and mutually pledged their *love* and mutual *respect* until "death do we part." Now, **Walter** is assuming the role of the grim reaper. These Two have exchanged vows of *fidelity*, each committing to a lifetime together – through sickness or health, during good times and bad times, for better or for worse.

What an amazing agreement! Two human beings offering the *incalculable* **gift** of a <u>loving</u> life – he to her and she to him. Consider the WONDER of two people *giving* themselves, their **love**, their **life**, their **trust**, their **destiny** to each other. Such an OATH is **not** a small matter. It is NOT to be taken lightly – **ever!** Marriage is a voluntary act. Marital companions are free agents. No one is forced to stay together in times of discord. Couples must **never – never** take each other for granted. **Walter** and **Si Son** should have *treasured* **The Gift**. *Remembered* **The Moment**. That <u>marvelous</u> **Day** when EACH <u>vowed</u>, *I thee wed*.

But the **promises** to **stick** regardless of circumstance were <u>Once</u> Upon A Time, now it's come to this ––– . What's happened to your <u>pledge</u> of *love* and mutual *respect*, Walter? Where is your <u>covenant</u> of *fidelity* today, Walter? Fidelity is attachment, loyalty, faithfulness, and <u>strict</u> conformity to promises made. Explain the role *fidelity* plays in an **Act** of **Murder**, Walter?

The man isn't thinking straight. He's lost his way. He's punched the *off switch* on his conscience. ANGER has carried Walter to the unholy realm of interim <u>insanity</u>. **Impulsively** he reaches for the Louisville Slugger. **Impulsively** he clenches it tight in his right hand. **Impulsively** he lowers the bat to his side and strides back to the living room where **Si Son** stands in defiant belligerence – still screaming. **Impulsively**, blinded and desensitized by <u>rage</u>, HE reaches **Si Son** and begins to **swing** THE BAT.

A Louisville Slugger is <u>supposed</u> to hit baseballs. It's **not** designed to strike a human head. **Not** mass produced as an <u>object</u> for the savage release of an irate husband's reservoir of resentment towards his spouse. When a baseball player swings a bat he doesn't want to have the umpire ring him up for strike three. But society wants Walter to abort his cruel sport – to stop, to desist. Society prays that Walter will strike out when he swings at Si Son!

However, his AIM is on the mark at **least** <u>fifteen</u> times. After all, the findings of the Medical Examiner establish that he took lots of swings. Whaling away at the woman who ONCE was the object of his affection. Bludgeoning her into mortal oblivion. It's a **shameful** DEBACLE. Your Prosecutor grieves for you and for her, Walter. What a **cruel** <u>payoff</u> for marriage. Dying is inevitable, Walter – but being an expediter is **not** part of a husband's job description. Complicity in your wife's death is <u>not</u> condoned, Sir.

Walter's MOTHER compounds her cooperation with Police by appearing before the Grand Jury. She shares admissions made by **Walter** to her with the Grand Jurors. They learn of a troubled marriage complicated by *unrestrained* chickens, a baseball bat that is used to *swat* **Si Son's** head rather than baseballs, and a **wife** buried in the desert without the benefit of a properly memorialized interment. The evidence is convincing to the Grand Jury, they return a True Bill. **Walter** is indicted for the Murder of **Si Son**.

A *closed* Hearing is more conducive to cooperative sworn testimony from a witness aligned by blood to the Target of the probe, but the Prosecution does **not** perpetuate ex-parte testimony by choosing a Grand Jury proceeding. Whereas, **all** Witnesses are subject to cross examination when the road to Trial includes an adversarial pit stop in Justice Court for a Preliminary Hearing. In this instance, the approach taken will prove to be a significant **misstep** for the Office of the District Attorney in the matter of Walter and Si Son. Walter's Mother has testified, but she has **not** been CROSS EXAMINED. Further, she continues to agonize over her decision to pass along **Walter's** admissions to the Police and the Grand Jury.

The Trial begins about five months later. MOM is subpoenaed and penciled in for Trial Testimony. I use *penciled in* advisedly. It's one thing for a Mother to provide inculpatory information prior to Trial, BUT it's a mare of a different hue to ask an eighty six year old woman for *personal* TRIAL involvement in sending **her** SON to the slammer. The gentle lady's reaction in the Trial Court is unforeseeable. However, the farm boy Prosecutor **isn't** betting the farm that incriminating words will pass through MOM'S lips.

The day of decision arrives. Mr. Bailiff is asked to summon **Walter's** MOTHER into the Courtroom. She enters with her head down, walks slowly along the aisle, casts a lingering look at Walter as she employs her cane to ease between Counsel Tables, and solemnly trudges to The BENCH. That's right, the prospective witness moves away from the Bailiff before he gets her in place to be administered the Witness Oath by the Clerk, and approaches the BENCH. She does so with obvious trepidation. But a Mother **often** does what a Mother HAS to do – though this MOTHER does it belatedly.

Through trembling lips, the elderly woman appeals to His Honor for a *pardon* from the gut wrenching <u>burden</u> she faces. "Your Honor, I **can't** do it. He's **my** SON. –– May I leave the Courtroom?"

She **doesn't** bolt from the Courtroom as *Diane* **does** during the Trial I have documented in Chapter 8. The <u>age</u> and <u>nature</u> of **Walter's** MOTHER militate against such impulsive behavior. She **doesn't** raise her cane and resoundingly WHACK it across the BENCH. She's too <u>polite</u> to be so unladylike. She **doesn't** drop to her knees and beg. **Walter's** MOTHER is too <u>proud</u> to indulge in such pious histrionics. What she **has** done is unequivocally **declare** her mind set and **ask** for permission to leave. The *unsworn* prospective Witness **looks** imploringly at the Judge as she awaits his response.

His Honor stares sympathetically at the distraught little woman. However, a serious problem **is** implicit in her request. There is NO legally cognizable family privilege that will allow a Mother to REFUSE to testify at her son's Trial! Perhaps, such a privilege <u>should</u> be part of existing statutory and case law. **It isn't**, at least, not in the considered opinion of Judge Paul. Of course, this would all have been a moot point had the MOTHER in question **not** provided inculpatory information to the Police and inculpatory testimony to the Clark County Grand Jury. Her maternal back bone is a bit tardy getting bowed. Sometimes SILENCE is golden!

Accordingly, His Honor says in a very measured tone, "I'm not at liberty to grant your request, Ma'am. Clerk, swear the Witness." Yet, the Witness seems uncomprehending. Her mournful plea for a *reprieve* is repeated and embellished, "Your Honor, I **can't** do it. PLEASE understand. He's **my** SON. I'm **not** going to answer any questions. –– May I leave the Courtroom now?"

Judge Paul: "I'm sorry Ma'am. You <u>have</u> to testify. You have NO legal right **not** to testify. If you refuse to answer questions, I'll have no alternative but to find you in CONTEMPT of Court. Do you understand, Ma'am?"

This time it sinks in. However, the MOTHER'S neck is <u>now</u> tenaciously bowed. She squares her shoulders to the extent an eighty six year old is physically capable. Then says softly and with dignity, "I **can't**, Your Honor. I **won't**, Your Honor. He's **my** SON." And about now I'm thinking, "Oh boy! Taking this MOTHER before the Grand Jury was a miscalculation. We needed to have her **cross examined**! This evidence proffer isn't going to turn out very well for the guys in white hats."

A short aside is appropriate. The State Legislature in its infinite wisdom has foreseen this type of scenario, and provided an escape hatch for Parties dealing with recalcitrant witnesses. Thus, the Evidence Code will permit introduction of the <u>prior</u> **testimony** of a witness who stubbornly persists in a refusal to testify at Trial, despite being repeatedly ordered to do so by the Trial Judge, <u>IF</u> the previous **testimony** has been subjected to CROSS EXAMINATION by the adversarial party to the proceeding. The rationale being that HEARSAY EVIDENCE, i.e., out of Court declarations, are **inadmissible** <u>absent</u> strong assurances of accuracy. And that CROSS EXAMINATION – that "greatest legal engine ever invented for the discovery of truth," (John Henry Wigmore) provides the **necessary** <u>predicate</u> for accuracy.

A Grand Jury hearing is **not** an adversarial proceeding. The person under investigation is **not** represented by Counsel. Therefore, the possibility for Cross Examination is **nonexistent** in a <u>typical</u> Grand Jury appearance. A Preliminary Hearing **is** an adversarial proceeding. Prosecutors, Defense Counsel, and Defendants **are** present. A Justice of the Peace presides and oversees the admission of evidence – which includes *both* **Direct** and CROSS EXAMINATION.

The Judge has to take the bull by the horns. He orders **Walter's** MOTHER to submit to the Witness Oath. Which she does. The Bailiff then assists her to the Witness Stand and she is seated. The Court says, "Madam, though I sympathize with your situation, you have NO legal right **not** to answer questions. Therefore, I am **ordering** you to testify, and I must inform you that a refusal to answer questions on your part, WILL result in your being held in CONTEMPT of COURT. **If** that happens you will be remanded to the Clark County Jail, where you will **remain** in custody until you change your mind and AGREE to testify! Do you understand the consequences of a failure to answer questions?"

Walter's MOTHER: "Yes, Your Honor. But I will **not** testify. I **can't**. I **won't**. He's **my** SON. Do what you have to do, Judge. But I'm still going to do what I <u>have</u> TO DO too."

And she did! **Walter's** MOTHER wouldn't budge from her *protective* mode. She stood by **her** BOY – even though he'd told her he killed her daughter-in-law with a baseball bat, and the Court stood by the LAW.

The MOTHER is remanded to custody, and with the assistance of her cane and the Bailiff – the eighty six year old toddled <u>OUT</u> of the Courtroom to Jail. Which is exactly what she wanted to do all along, minus The Jail part. The BOND between Mother and Son unbroken. A woman's **maternal** *instinct* and **blood** *relationship* trumping the so called Rule of Law.

These legal machinations happen late in the Trial. The matter is submitted to the Jury for deliberation within two hours of the aforementioned head-butting between a Judge bound by his oath to uphold THE LAW and a Mother bound by her heart to uphold HER SON!

It's a poignant event to me, and an occasion I'll never forget. So, what happens to the Little Woman who submits to incarceration, rather than speak incriminating words about a Son on trial for Murder? Well, the penalty imposed is tempered by a modicum of Judicial Compassion. Afterward, I learn from an impeccable source that the Bailiff sits with The Witness in the Clark County Jail holding tank until the Case is submitted to the Jury, and then released –– pursuant to Court Order.

The Prosecution secures its conviction in **spite** of the side show that deprives them of evidence of the Crime Catalyst and the Crime Instrumentality. I speak of THE CHICKENS <u>and</u> THE BASEBALL BAT. Even without them the Jury finds certain un-rebutted facts persuasive.

A bowl of chicken soup before we part M'lady? Realistically, **Walter** <u>didn't</u> offer **Si Son** a bowl of chicken soup before he checked her out of their digs. She <u>didn't</u> like chicken soup anyway. Chickens were her pets.

HE had the soup! –– **After** her violent departure, the chickens were the sad **recipients** of further violence. **Si Son's** little flock became victims of a form of reprisal *genocide* – one chicken and one bowl of soup at a time! But **Walter** didn't use a bat. He rung their necks.

"Affliction is enamour'd of thy parts, And thou... [**Si Son** were wed] to calamity." (William Shakespeare, *Romeo and Juliet*, ibid.)

It's a case of RECKLESS DISREGARD of **consequence** and **social duty**!

1. **Cause of Death** – <u>Massive</u> blunt trauma to the head. A petite woman repeatedly struck with a blunt object by Walter.
2. **Concealment of the Crime** – A wife unceremoniously buried in a sagebrush- pocked desert. An odd <u>sendoff</u> for the woman who'd given Walter her best adult years. Her disappearance <u>stonewalled</u> by him. Leaving her bewildered children in a state of torment.
3. **Blood stained carpet** – Blood <u>residue</u> consistent with the blood type of Si Son is found on the living room carpet. A

2 ½' x 3 ½' throw rug has been placed over the spot on or after July 2th. A family friend testifies the rug was definitely **not** lying at this location on July 1st. Walter's explanations are inconsistent. Initially, he says he <u>doesn't</u> know HOW it got there. Later, he says his wife spilled some <u>hair dye</u> on the carpet and tried to clean it up.

4. **Unconcerned over disappearance** – Where's the LOVE, Walter? The children say he is totally indifferent to Si Son's absence. Rather than discuss the reasons she has gone missing, Walter prefers to stress the <u>negative</u> aspects of his wife's personality. It's a bizarre reaction that suggests *guilty knowledge*!

5. **Statements against interest** – A daughter says Walter <u>spoke</u> of her MOTHER in the past tense. Others say he's *evasive*. Looking down at the floor. Refusing to look interrogators in the eye. Walter's demeanor is curious. He seems to be angry and exhausted. His eyes are bloodshot and cloudy. The Defendant's actions graphically put his wife in the <u>past tense</u>. She's completely out of the picture. Obviously, permanently gone! He tells her son he can have her *car*. He tells a daughter to take any of her mother's *clothes* that fit. What is Si Son going to drive, her bicycle? What will she wear, her birthday suit?

While conversing with a daughter over the telephone three months after the disappearance – Walter says cryptically, "Well, ya know, I'm not a *natural born killer* –– <u>your</u> MOTHER <u>brought</u> **it** **on** <u>herself</u>.. She could've shaped up and seen things **my way** and we could've had a good life." That's right Walter. Killing isn't in your genes, you jettisoned your wife in a *fit of pique*!

The Defendant calls Si Son's son to tell him he has mail at the house. The son asks him to shed some more light on the disappearance and death of his ex wife <u>and</u> the mother of his children. Walter declares succinctly, "What happened – **happened in <u>self defense</u>**." The son's take on the comment, "I thought it was very significant. I <u>never</u> forgot it!"

"O threats of Hell and Hopes of Paradise! One thing at least is certain, –– *This* Life flies..." (Edward Fitzgerald, *Rubaiyat of Omar Khayyam of Naishapur*)

Poor **Si Son**! One thing is certain and the rest is lies. When a killer strikes his victim dies – suddenly, <u>prematurely</u>. A killer puts the inevitable on fast track – as though the precious gift of mortal life needs a boost to the finish line.

"It's shameless, **Walter**! There's a **wife-killer** in the Courtroom who doesn't believe in divorce, but has no qualm about MURDER. Who has callously ripped a mother from the arms of three loving children, and is so miserly and uncaring he won't hire a mortician to assist with interment of the dead! JUDGMENT DAY has come to the Courtroom –– and the THREAT OF HELL looms ahead, Sir."

Before leaving the debacle of offensive chickens and a Louisville Slugger, I offer a brief addendum on the subject of well-meaning mothers who inadvertently get themselves intertwined with the Criminal Justice System. The subject of family members becoming Prosecution Witnesses in felony cases that pertain to <u>other</u> family members is a topic regularly discussed by my good friend Chief Deputy Dan and myself in our respective offices. By *regularly*, I mean as often as the topic became pertinent to Cases we were handling.

The subject is revisited because the two Deputies have a core disagreement concerning *familial* involvement in Criminal Matters. We personalize the issue. Discussing what **we'd** do if confronted with situations similar to that of witnesses who elect to venture into waters **not** family friendly.

I'm going to give credit where credit is due, Dan is a Prosecutor from the top of his head to the sole of his shoes. He sees crime stuff in black and white. Regardless of the participants, whether family or non family, Dan remains a hard ass. If you do the Crime, prepare to do the time – irrespective of WHO you are! He consistently takes the position that he'd have NO **compunction** testifying for the Prosecution against an immediately family member, if a serious crime of violence had been committed by that individual.

As for me, I draw the line before I get there. I'm NOT going there! I firmly believe *all* who commit serious crimes of violence, regardless of their relationship to me, **should** be held personally responsible for their acts. However, I'd *refuse* to be personally involved as a WITNESS providing **substantive** inculpatory evidence <u>against</u> an immediate family member. I'm speaking of a spouse or child or sibling or parent. It would be contrary to my most sacred moral values to rupture family relationships with adversarial testimony in Court! "Never say never" is considered a sophisticated point of view. BUT ——— I'm–saying– **NEVER**! I'd **never** darken a Courtroom door to testify <u>against</u> an immediate family member. That would be off-limits. Inconceivable! A betrayal of trust that trumps my commitment to the Criminal Justice System. Nor would Judicial <u>contempt</u> citations sway my position.

I believe The Family is ordained of God. I believe The Family is central to **The Father's** plan for the eternal destiny of His Children. I believe a man's greatest successes and greatest failures <u>can</u> occur within the walls of his own home. Therefore, maintaining family unity and harmonious family relationships is of paramount importance to me. Obviously, family unity and harmonious family relationships are **not** enhanced by Courtroom *finger pointing*.

The unvarnished, bottom-line fact is that acquisition of material things in this world won't have lasting value. They're all trinkets. Not one person will take a single dollar to the next estate. Moreover, the transient pleasures of this world won't make us genuinely happy. Secular fame or power or fortune provide nothing but momentary, fleeting diversions. At days end, at the end of mortal life, after all that can be experienced —— in moments of quiet reflection and bitter sweet *remembrance*, comes recognition of this eternal truth: fully functional vertical [Deity] and horizontal [Human] RELATIONSHIPS are the riches of inestimable worth!

Personally, I'd **never** jeopardize tender family relationships by sharing <u>confidential</u> communications with Police and Grand Jurors. Law Enforcement would have to get it's convictions the old fashioned way – by HARD WORK. Sans assistance from me.

Likewise, **Walter's** MOTHER could have bypassed her legal consternation by simply keeping her lips zipped. There would have been **no** subpoenas **nor** contempt citation if she hadn't initially *snitched off* her son.

As for **Walter**, he ultimately gets his <u>payback</u> without any boost by his Mom. The wife-killer earns this gratuity, however, he doesn't have to share his prison cell with clucking chickens!

Terror Has A Human Face

"He was not born to shame: Upon his brow shame is ashamed to sit."
(William Shakespeare, *Romeo and Juliet*, Act III, Sc. 2, Line 91)

Chapter 11

They are an unlikely couple. One a petite Native American woman, the other a massive African American man. One a placid person steeped in the traditions of her tribe and life on the reservation. Possessing an innocence that approaches naivete. She is twenty seven. The other an assertive personality steeped in the primal brutality of ghetto living and stints in the Joint. He is street smart – with a cockiness that approaches insolence. He is thirty two and amoral.

They meet in an Indian Casino where she works as a change girl. He's lonely and broke – she's curious. They rendevous at a bar after her shift, and speak casually into the wee hours. She's immediately attracted to his smile, his blackness, and his imposing masculinity. They make love at her place, and he moves in.

The two have little in common, but she brings a small dowry of savings to their union. He desperately wants to hit the open road. Foolish maiden, two days later she quits her job and they leave Bellingham, Washington in a Greyhound – for parts unknown. It's a star-crossed relationship and an ill-fated trip. She doesn't know her fellow traveler, nor what kind of entanglement lies ahead. The date is Tuesday, April 19, 1971. He will be perpetrating unspeakable acts upon <u>four</u> human beings in six days.

Punctuated by layovers, the couple bus-hop across Oregon and California – though **Barnell** isn't interested in long term sight seeing and

Christina's companionship is a matter of convenience. She's merely the means to an end. Her funds have been a jump start for getting him out of Bellingham. However, her modest bankroll dwindles steadily.

They push on to Vegas. He hopes for success at the crap tables and she wants bright lights and romance. Neither party will get his wish. The twosome check into the Queens on Glitter Gulch. The date is April 23 – TGIF. Well, not really. The weekend doesn't have a propitious start. Friday night isn't a bit productive, it's a disaster. He loses heavily in the Queens Casino, which makes him angry. They return to their room, where the view is not the splendor of Fremont Street's glitzy neon lights, it's an alley and a gloomy parking garage. Under his existing frame of mind, the setting isn't conducive to romance. So, his loss at the Tables translates into her loss under the Covers.

And things don't get any better on Saturday. Barnell loses most of what's left of Christine's money on a Queens roulette wheel. Round and round and round goes the whirling wheel. Plunk, plunk, plunk goes the pretty ball on it's merry spins – monotonously landing in slots that aren't wins. The bad luck of Christine's casino dandy is freaking ridiculous on Saturday. The House picks his pocket clean. The two are left with a serious short fall. They need cash badly. Staying at the Queens through the weekend is now <u>beyond</u> their means. His mind strays to a contingency plan. If *legal* gambling isn't the answer, perhaps *illegal* gambling will be more fortuitous! He'll replenish their nest egg by force, and it won't be his first venture into the world of random violence.

Desperation is often the predicate for dysfunctional acts. A **day** of depravity looms in Sunday's early morning darkness. "O, what may man within him hide, Though angel on the outward side!" (William Shakespeare, *Measure for Measure*, Act III, Sc. 2, Line 293) And to what extent will naivete and infatuation cause a woman to tolerate the unthinkable?

April 25, 1971 is a murky, melancholy day. A good time to be a shut-in or a choirboy or a parishioner doing penance at a local church. However, Christine's squeeze is neither choirboy nor parishioner, and a man needing bucks can't be a Sunday shut-in. Though he'll have grave need for absolution at day's end.

He leaves her in the room. She's told he's leaving to make some money. She wants to know how he'll do it, and gets this acerbic answer: "I'll say please. Then, I'll use my blue steel intimidator. It's broad daylight, so I'll have to be rough." That said, he straps on a 9-millimeter semiautomatic.

The lithe Indian maiden hadn't previously known he was armed. She's shocked, but *says* <u>nothing</u> to him nor to anyone else. It's about 10:30 a.m. He's gone for six portentous hours.

Apparently, there is <u>no</u> limit for the **depth** of depravity to which an amoral man will sink. When a man has <u>no</u> conscience, <u>no</u> moral boundaries, <u>no</u> compass to self restraint, <u>no</u> inner recognition of the inherent dignity of other humans, <u>no</u> twinge of remorse for despicable acts perpetrated, **not** shamed by shameful acts – he's a ticking time bomb when he needs the green! The immorality of bad acts does not compute in his brain! He exists to advance his personal self interest – period.

Barnell begins with a stroll down Fremont Street. Between Sixth and Seventh Streets he snatches a hooker's purse and runs into an alley. She screams pithy epithets at the streaking thief. But evidently her day is just beginning, only the equivalent of soda money – a one dollar bill and change is discovered inside her handbag. He finds an unlocked door to an apartment, and is about to cross that threshold, when he sees a motorcycle cop cruising slowly up the street. The intent to burgle is aborted. He crosses Fremont and goes west to Las Vegas Boulevard, hangs a left and proceeds south – alert to any opportunity to cash in.

He observes a Mexican Restaurant that seems ripe for robbing. With a hand on his intimidater, he stealthily walks into the building. The Eatery is preparing to open, but a gaggle of employees seem to divine his larcenous purpose. He's intercepted on his way in and chased back to the street.

Barnell is frustrated. Where's the green? His foul mood is exacerbated by the futility of his enterprise to this point. It's slim pickings on Sunday at mid-day. A dark resentful fury fills his psyche. Eventually, The Man who is unashamed of shameful acts walks east on East Charleston Boulevard.

He is about three quarters of a mile from the Queens. It is 1:30 p.m. as he approaches a business called Pantrell Cleaners. The place obviously isn't open for customers, but two cars are parked in back. Barnell surmises that company people may be on the premises. He's also thinking that a safe <u>will</u> likely be somewhere inside. Company people will have a key to the safe. Possibly, monies from the past week are locked down – awaiting a Monday morning deposit at a nearby bank. He turns the nob on the back door. Fatefully, it opens.

Good fortune does **not** rest upon those inside. If they've said their morning prayers, and asked for God's protecting influence this day, there's been a short in the heavenly switchboard. **No** act of Divine intervention will occur. On the other hand, someone has said that prayer is 98 % perspiration and 2% inspiration. Which is to say, those praying can usually do a lot to make their petition happen. Sadly, the Pantrell Cleaners people have made a slight mistake in judgment, and small errors of omission can lead to catastrophe. Those inside needed to *ask* the Lord for protection and –– they needed to **help** the Lord by *remembering* to lockup. It's the DOOR. The DOOR is the key to security.

IF the back DOOR had been locked –if––if–––if only entry had been denied to the ticking time bomb in desperate need of green, he would have taken his dark resentful fury on down the road. And the mortality of those inside would have been given a reprieve. They didn't come to the business thinking this day would be their last – but it will be for three of the four. On this **black** Sunday, those inside are incredibly vulnerable **if** the back DOOR is left unlocked!

The Leonardos and their fourteen year old son have been to morning mass, and the three have enjoyed Sunday brunch at a Strip Hotel. They're on the premises of their business to do the usual weekend book keeping and sanitizing. Even an establishment that does cleaning has to be kept clean. Their janitor is also present. Jake has been a mainstay with the Leonardos for fifteen years. While the owners work the books, he and their son are doing the housekeeping. The foursome are totally unprepared for the uninvited guest with the blue steel intimidater. The intruder's sudden appearance turns their world upside down.

The gun **does** intimidate. Barnell rounds up the foursome, and herds his hostages into the office at gunpoint. He demands that the cash register be opened. Mr. Leonardo complies, and the assailant scoops up the small amount of cash that's in the till. It's NOT nearly enough. The dark resentful fury of the man with the gun is close to meltdown.

His sullen interrogatory, ["Where is the SAFE?"] – more closely resembles a snarl than a question. But they get the drift. The aura of the place is rife with tension. Four hearts are pounding in unison. Mrs. Leonardo whimpers, "Please Sir, don't hurt us." The boy is shaking. Yet, to the person, the foursome are convinced that *fully* cooperating with the demands of the gunman will secure them the safety the unlocked door has denied them. They think he will spare them if they are compliant. That he will have compassion on them. However, they **don't** know Barnell. He is **past** feeling. He is a man devoid of compassion – cold and hard, insensitive and offensive.

But there's another factor that will trump pity anyhow,

they–have–SEEN– him! Barnell exists to advance HIS self interest. This guy's got a rap sheet. He's done time in the slammer. He doesn't want to be convicted. He knows the damage eyewitnesses can inflict in Court. He knows, **DEAD PEOPLE** don't tell tales! NO witnesses means: NO subpoenas, NO testimony, NO in court identifications, NO   h a r d time!

It's a floor safe behind the counter. Mr. Leonardo reluctantly tells the gunman where the safe is located. Barnell orders him to produce the key, open the safe, and remove the valuables. What choice does Mr. Leonardo have? He's looking into the barrel of a 9-millimeter. The lid to the safe is opened. BINGO! The brazen robber's *illegal* gambling instantly pays off, sharply contrasting with his blackjack table and roulette wheel failures. The Leonardos have over $5,000.00 in cold cash and checks stashed inside the SAFE.

A **bank** **bag** is also stored in the safe. Mr. Leonardo is directed to stuff the money into the bag. He does as he's told, and hands the bag of currency to Barnell. –– The ruthless assailant will have a brutal way of expressing thanks. The money he's stealing will be **BLOOD MONEY**. No, more egregious than that. It will be a self styled **IMMOLATION!** A monstrous escalation of Burglary and Kidnaping and Robbery –– to **ARSON MURDER**.

The **victims** are roughly shepherded from the office to the dry cleaning area. They're told to do exactly what the gunman says. If there's any goofy stuff he'll blow their heads off. Do they get the picture now? Are they sensing the impending debacle? Irrespective of their thoughts, the foursome go like sacrificial lambs to the slaughter. They need a Priest to administer last rites. Quickly!

The foursome are directed to sit on the floor. They meekly comply. Then, inexplicably, Barnell goes berserk. There is **no** provocation. They are striving to soothe their antagonist in a vain endeavor to save themselves. Yet, the crushing frustration of his failed life suddenly explodes into a maniacal tirade against the helpless four, and the scenario becomes a creepy exercise in the **infliction** of *pain for sport*. The heartless man with the big gun becomes the human embodiment of Twain's stern indictment uttered forty seven years earlier. He's a fiendish worst nightmare. Terror has a human face!

"Of all the creatures that were made he [man] is the most detestable. Of the entire brood he is the only one –– the solitary one –– that possesses malice...He is the only creature that inflicts pain for sport, knowing it to *be* pain..." (Mark Twain, *Autobiography* [1924], Vol. II, Page 7)

The heartless robber begins to systematically clobber the four with the heavy butt of his 9-millimeter. The gratuitous pummeling to the skulls and faces and shoulders of the cowering victims triggers shockwaves of excruciating pain and blood spatter. They are cruelly beaten until they lay whimpering and spasmodic. Where is the humanity? Are you man or beast, Sir? Or is there any difference in your case?

Revisiting the sober critique of Mark Twain: "The fact that man knows right from wrong proves his *intellectual* superiority to the other creatures; but the fact that he can *do* wrong proves his *moral* inferiority to any creature that *cannot.*" (*What Is Man?* [1906]. Chap.6)

Nor is Barnell done. He finds a roll of cotton cord and cuts it into strips. **Tying** the hands and ankles of the Leonardos, their boy, and the janitor; arranging the four elbow to elbow in a hideous row on the floor. He's paranoid – and in a diabolic frenzy. Wanting to ignite an infernal. Thinking cremation. Hell bent on eliminating all trace of his victims, and of any inculpatory evidence. Deliberately wanting to make Pantrell Cleaners a chamber of horror. Orchestrating incalculable suffering – in reckless disregard of consequence and social duty.

He gathers up combustibles. Carrying rack after rack of garments to ground zero. Covering four innocent human beings – battered and bloodied but alive – with mounds of clothing. Moreover, he wants a flame accelerant. The stone heart invader of a dry cleaning company searches and locates jars of cleaning solvent. Then pours copious amounts of the inflammatory liquid on the pile of combustibles that covers the prone, bound, pleading, screaming quartet. Have you **no** soul, Mister? Do **not** *defile* Sunday with such MADNESS!

But Barnell's mind is set. He is establishing a benchmark for depravity. The amoralist with <u>no</u> conscience, <u>no</u> compass to self restraint, <u>no</u> sense for the intrinsic dignity of humankind, continues to pursue his shameful objective.

The tinderbox is ready. How <u>inconvenient</u> for his hostages, he's a smoker. A small box of matches is in a pants pocket. Methodically, deliberately – maliciously he clutches the matchbox and removes a match. THEN the morally *deficient* wretch STRIKES **the match** and cavalierly tosses the flickering flame into the incendiary heap he's created –– and runs like a rabbit.

IGNITION is **instantaneous**! An explosive orange fireball fans across the stacks of clothing. Triggering pitiful cries of agony from the helpless foursome engulfed in white-hot fire and plumes of noxious smoke. Terror has a human face, human hands, and a human heart!

Can anyone imagine the pain – the malevolence – the stupefying selfishness that produces such horror? It's incomprehensible. Barbaric. Unreal! What of kindness and brotherhood? Of properly thanking the Leonardo"s for the <u>cash</u> with an ad hoc <u>pardon</u> at the execution scene? Of repudiating a vile, primitive, base adherence to the thesis that *four* DEAD people **don't** tell tales? Of taking your chances? Of a course adjustment – they're tied up, just scoot? Of allowing justice to take its course? Of putting the Coppers and Prosecutors to the test? Of requiring them to do the grunt work of meeting their burden of Proof, if <u>they</u> can? Of accepting your punishment like a <u>real</u> man, if YOU can?

Barnell hasn't been observed entering Pantrell Cleaners, nor is he detected leaving the crime scene premises. But the rabbit with the bank bag stash doesn't stop running until he's three blocks away. Only then does he dare stop in an alley to catch his breath. He inhales deeply. Relieved, elated, and empowered. Then he casually makes his way back to the Queens and to Christine. Daddy's bringing home the bacon and he wants to party. They do room service and love making.

However, Barnell's caper isn't a *perfect crime* – though it seemed that way at the time. There are three slight problems. Each solid indicia of an *imperfect crime*. (1) **The Indian woman**: His party-time includes booze and obtuse JAWBONING about the day's affairs. A successful killer needs to have lockjaw. (2) **The Bank Bag**: His fiery infernal incinerator doesn't destroy all the inculpatory evidence. One piece of <u>bright</u> <u>line</u> evidence isn't a component of the bonfire. It's the MONEY POUCH, stupid. It came from the floor safe that's missing $5,000.00, and the words "Pantrell Cleaners"<u>are</u> written on the bag. He takes it with him to the Queens, but he FORGETS to take it with him when he and his ladylove <u>leave</u> the Queens two days later. Damn it to hell! Occasionally leaving toothbrushes, razors, jackets, change, tic tacs, and a potpourri of other items in hotel rooms can be expected, but FORGETTING–the Bank–Bag **is** BRAIN DEAD. (3) **The Survivor**: Surprise, LITTLE big man! Your self-styled IMMOLATION doesn't kill everyone, at least – not at first! Jake the Janitor lives for thirty days. Witnesses from across the street in a Safeway parking lot must deal with an horrendous sight Sunday afternoon just before 3:00 o'clock.

It begins with obvious screams of anguish. A figure can be seen waving his arms in the air as he crosses the sidewalk, and lurches toward the shoulder of the roadway. East Charleston is a busy thoroughfare, but this fellow's intention is to jaywalk. He's making a beeline toward the Store. Willing to buck the traffic rather than walk a short distance east to the crosswalk and a traffic light. Hoping, as spectators soon learn, to find safety, medical assistance, and a chance to share his ghastly story at Safeway. Continually calling for help as he does a discombobulated version of trotting, stumbling, and hopping.

Then, witnesses notice something extraordinary. The man is smoking. No, not puffing on a cigarette. The guy's **body is smoking**. He's so hot he's steaming. Smoke is rising from his clothes, his shoes, and his flesh! Unimaginably, as his movements take him into the street, while motor vehicles swerve, tires squeal, and horns blare, he deposits burnt clumps of shoe leather on the pavement – and smoldering pieces of flesh and fabric fall off his body with every successive step. Leaving a grisly trail of singed debris in his wake.

The man slumps to the asphalt when he's half way across the street. Emitting a repulsive aroma –– and quivering. Witnesses are stunned, and unsure at first: *Is what we're seeing real or apparitional?* The scene is a macabre introduction to the massacre that has occurred in Pantrell Cleaners on this appalling afternoon.

Citizens rush to the street. The vile deeds perpetrated inside the Cleaners represent a man at his most **repugnant**. The instinctive reaction of citizens, who rush into the street to aid a fallen brother, is a manifestation of human beings at their most **sublime**. Some direct traffic around the stricken janitor, while others gather around him – offering encouragement and assistance. Oblivious to the personal risk of traffic and the emotional trauma implicit in exposure to such a dreadful circumstance.

The poor man is *de profundis*. Uttering a spate of chilling words from the depths of unfathomable agony and sorrow: "The big black man came in with a big gun.[gasping] It was terrible. He wanted money. Robbed the floor safe. Treated the four of us like cattle.[sobbing] Herded us into the dry cleaning room. Told us to sit down. [wheezing] Beat us mercilessly with the butt of his gun. Tied us up. Covered us with clothing. Set us on fire.[moaning] He's a devil. I'll never forget his face. A man without a conscience!"

But the Police have no leads – until **The Indian Woman** surfaces <u>five</u> days after the carnage. I'll fiddle with Franklin's classic comment which I've already referenced in Chapter 8. "...[**Two**] <u>may</u> keep a secret, IF...[**one**] of them...<u>is</u> DEAD." (Benjamin Franklin, *Poor Richard's Almanack*, 1735 – tinkering and emphasis added) Don't have a traveling buddy when you commit a serious criminal offense. And keep your lips zipped if you do. When he talks <u>she'll</u> talk!

Christine telephones from Bellingham. She's separated from the man without a conscience now. However, **her** *conscience* **is** intact and there are things she needs to tell the Police –– about Sunday and Vegas and Barnell B. The Lady carries a hideous secret inside a tender heart. It's made her physically ill. She can't eat nor sleep. What's inside is consuming her. It's like a swelling, toxic abscess. The torment has to end, but she needs disclosure before she can obtain closure.

Las Vegas Police fly to the Emerald State and get a formal statement from Christine. Her information is a *case maker*. The breakthrough the coppers need. The Monday after, Christine reads in a Las Vegas newspaper about the arson deaths of **three** people, and the grievous burns inflicted upon a **fourth** man at a cleaning establishment on East Charleston Boulevard. She believes a correlation exists between the time of the Crime and the absence of Barnell Sunday afternoon. It's odd. He leaves without money and comes back to the room with lots of money – **greenbacks** in a **money pouch**. Moreover, Barnell seems to be experiencing a peculiar adrenalin rush, and his clothes smell like smoke when he returns.

Also, he reads the paper too and <u>says</u> things to her. Quips like: "Well, I had to get cash someway...G–damn! I can't believe the janitor guy got out of the place... Everybody was supposed to go up in smoke!"

Christine describes her bad boy paramour. The police are able to retrieve Barnell's rap sheet from the personal data provided, and she identifies a mug photo.

Further, she remembers their Queens' room number. The Crime Lab is notified and they respond to the hotel. The date is Saturday – May 1.

The guest register for the past weekend confirms the veracity of the Lady's memory. Curiously, Barnell has eschewed the use of an alias. So, it doesn't appear that **arson-murder** is originally on anyone's itinerary. Moreover, there's a bonus. Although The Room has been rented to <u>two</u>

separate parties during the three night span following the departure of the suspect and his lady friend, Barnell's left palm print is lifted from the top of a chest of drawers. Not a tribute to the diligence of housekeeping perhaps, but a testament to the skill of the **print** people. Hence, connecting **The Killer** to The Room is <u>not</u> a problem.

Though there <u>is</u> a problem connecting the **Bank Bag** to The Room. CSI meticulously processes The Room, but the Crime Scene Investigators come up empty with respect to the <u>money pouch</u>.

Possibly, the Technician who searches The Sofa is moonlighting as a housekeeping rep at the Queens. A **lack** of painstaking thoroughness comes to mind. But <u>not</u> to worry! The lead Homicide Detective assigned to the Case does a *second* search several days later. **He** FINDS the <u>bag</u>! It <u>is</u> underneath a SOFA PILLOW – wedged against an armrest support. So –– Barnell **is** connected to the ROOM and contents of the ROOM connect him to **the <u>Murder</u>**.

It's a domino effect. Christine puts the <u>spotlight</u> on her paramour. She gives the Police a NAME and a FACE. Which leads to the Room at the Queens shared by the Twosome – and, eventually, to the Pantrell Cleaners' **Bank Bag** in the SOFA. Moreover, **The Survivor** <u>still</u> lives. Against all odds, Jake the Janitor clings to life. The percipient witness has SEEN the <u>diabolical</u> **killer** at the epicenter, and <u>he</u> gives the Police a Statement describing the Offenses. His morbid memorialization of the horrific Crimes will be admitted into evidence at Trial as a *dying declaration*. Statements made when a declarant believes <u>his</u> death is imminent is a longstanding exception to the Hearsay Rule. Further, Jake is shown the FACE of the suspect. Police assemble a photographic lineup that includes Barnell's PICTURE. The <u>lineup procedure</u> is videotaped and **The Survivor** IDENTIFIES Barnell's PHOTO! It is a pivotal moment in the investigation, and a profile in courage. Two and a half weeks later he's a DEADMAN.

A warrant is issued for Barnell's arrest. He is captured a week later and formally charged with **Burglary, First Degree Arson**, four counts of **First Degree Kidnaping**, four counts of **Robbery**, and four counts of **Open Murder**. A man like Barnell B. isn't born to shame, "Upon his brow shame is ashamed to sit." (William Shakespeare, *Romeo and Juliet*, ibid.)

Six months later the Defendant goes to Trial. I'm teamed up with the District Attorney, and the most honorable Judge Howard presides. The Trial lasts a month. We call **eighty three** witnesses and the Defense settles for **three**. Sounds like a landslide, right? Well —— No! Numbers don't decide the outcome of Criminal Trials. **Evidence** decides Trials. The Defense has NO **burden**! The Prosecution bears the BURDEN OF PROOF.

Naturally, Prosecutors do not shrink from THEIR **burden**. It is entirely appropriate that the entity bringing Criminal Charges should shoulder the responsibility of going forward with the evidentiary proof! Theoretically, three witnesses *can* be sufficient to create a reasonable doubt. That's ALL the Defense ever needs. Accordingly, the Deputy and the County's Chief Law Enforcement Officer won't be taking anything for granted. I'll deliver the OPENING SUMMATION and he'll present the REBUTTAL. Mr. District Attorney insists on doing **two** things in every Trial he works. He Cross Examines the Defendant and he gives the Rebuttal Argument. However, Roy gets a pass on his first proviso this time. The man without a conscience, un-shamed by shameful acts [Setting a fourteen year old kid on fire, Barnell?] – ducks Cross Examination. His butt doesn't budge from his chair at Counsel Table. Obviously, Barnell B. has no desire to waive his privilege against self incrimination and be subjected to Cross Examination. He's got bravado when he's packing heat, but he's firing blanks in the Courtroom.

Nevertheless, a Prosecutor always has REBUTTAL – the plum pudding of his profession. And irrespective of order, we'll both be leaving it all at the lectern.

Listing **the connecting evidence** that forges the *links* of the **Defendant's chain of guilt**. Arguing **the points,** pursuant to the demands of Justice, *link by link* until he's toast, After all, this is a **quadruple murder** Case.

"Some circumstantial evidence is very strong, as when you find a trout in the milk." (Henry David Thoreau, *Journal. November 11, 1854*)

State vs. Barnell B. is a classic circumstantial case. The evidence is totally circumstantial, notwithstanding Jake's survival for thirty days following the crimes. Remember the distinction between the two great branches of evidence in Criminal Cases. Whatever a person perceives with any of his physical senses, *as the Crime happens*, is **direct evidence**. EVERYTHING ELSE is **circumstantial**!

The Leonard's are percipient witnesses, however, they died at the Crime Scene. Their lips were sealed. The Janitor is a percipient witness, but he didn't live long enough to testify in Court. His *dying declarations,* i.e., his <u>statement</u> describing the offenses and his photographic lineup <u>identification</u> of the Defendant are admitted into evidence as <u>exceptions</u> to the Hearsay Rule. They are NOT **direct evidence**, and if they're NOT **direct** they've got to be CIRCUMSTANTIAL!

Christine **isn't** present at the commission of the Crimes. She DOESN'T <u>perceive</u> the perpetration with any of her physical senses. Her evidence **isn't** direct evidence. The BANK BAG is inanimate. It neither perceives nor testifies, therefore it's also CIRCUMSTANTIAL.

Actually, *the bank bag in the sofa* <u>is</u> the proverbial **Trout in the Milk** in this case. Nobody saw Barnell B. carry the **Pantrell Cleaner's bank bag** from the premises to the hotel, but we can be absolutely **positive** he did. Why? Because the natural habitat of **The Bank Bag** sporting the words *Pantrell Cleaners* is a floor safe – NOT a sofa in a room at the Queens. Because **The Bag** didn't sprout little legs and get itself to a room at the Queens. Because **The Janitor** puts Barnell at the Crime Scene and **The Indian Woman** puts Barnell at the Room.

Hence, Thoreau's astute observation of record applies with full force to the Case-at-Bar. We didn't SEE the Defendant put **The Bank Bag** in the Sofa, but the circumstances are so compelling we **know** it DID happen! The <u>empty</u> **Bank Bag** secreted in the Sofa inside Barnell's Room at the Queens is **irrefutable** evidence of his GUILT!

Thomas Carlyle said, "Man makes the circumstances." The <u>responsibility</u> of the Trial Jury is discharged within the framework of the Court's **instructions** and the Case **evidence**. The sole task of the Jury is deciding **WHAT MAN <u>*made*</u>** these ***criminal circumstances***! Following a lengthy deliberation, The Jury presents its findings: Barnell Bishop <u>is</u> **The Man** who MADE the circumstances.

I said the Jury reached verdicts after "a lengthy deliberation." The Jury is the ultimate variable in a Criminal Trial, and the duration of their deliberation may or may not reflect the strength of the evidence. In this instance, the amount of Juror discussion has more to do with a <u>single</u> constituent of the Jury than the nature of Trial evidence. The Barnell B. Jury has a wild card. The **Queen of Hearts**? I have it on good authority that after deliberating forty five minutes the Jury is 11-1 for conviction on *all* counts.

Juror Q of H had joined The Panel by default. She is summoned to the Jury Box after the Prosecution has exercised its eighth and <u>last</u> peremptory challenge. Lousy timing, I'd say, for the guys in white hats. For reasons I will not amplify, she is unacceptable as a Juror. A strong inference of bias immediately surfaces. However, there is <u>no</u> **legal** predicate to challenge her for cause. She is seated as Trier of Fact # twelve.

As the Trial progresses, quirky Courtroom demeanor of Juror Q of H becomes very troublesome to Prosecutors. Despite the heinous nature of charges against him, she seems perversely enamored of the Defendant. Constantly striving to make eye contact with Barnell B. while the Court is in session, shaking her head in apparent disbelief as incriminating evidence is introduced, and smiling at The Accused as he enters and exits the Courtroom – etcetera. Moreover, these are not simply conclusions of the DA boys, a half dozen or so persons in the gallery report similar observations. Inexplicably, some type of surreal emotional bonding occurs between Juror # Twelve and the Defendant in full view of everyone in the room.

Prosecutors react by asking His Most Honorable Howard to excuse Juror Q of H. A hearing is conducted outside the presence of The Jury and the issue is thoroughly analyzed. The Trial is at a critical juncture. The Court is fearful of building error into the record, not surprisingly, he chooses to retain Juror # twelve. Thus, she is part of The Panel retiring to deliberate the fate of the alleged **quadruple** ARSON **murderer**.

Though –– reportedly, she <u>refuses</u> to engage in meaningful deliberation. Declaring at the outset that Barnell B. is being framed and that she believes he is Not Guilty. Then she moves to a corner of the Jury room during this and ensuing deliberative sessions, turns her back on the other eleven, and stoically lapses into total silence – for **days**.

But the stand-off is eventually resolved. A heart to heart occurs – something like, "The State has gone way beyond the burden imposed by law. The evidence submitted by them has proven this Defendant guilty <u>beyond</u> ANY doubt, and we're going to find him guilty if we have to sit here until hell freezes over. So, you'd better get off your high horse and *dispassionately* weigh the evidence."

Juror Q of H has her ears on. She leaves her post in the corner, <u>rejoins</u> the eleven, and starts talking again. Finally, the recalcitrant Juror **changes** her vote and a hung Jury is averted.

Barnell B. is convicted on all counts. The Department of Parole and Probation submits a Pre-sentence Report, Counsel for the respective parties argue their positions on punishment, and **severe** judgment is imposed by the Court. Do the Crimes do the hard Time stuff. The Defendant is

maxed out by Judge Howard. He is sentenced to LIFE WITHOUT the possibility of parole for each of the **four** counts of Murder in the First Degree – to run **consecutively**. He is sentenced to LIFE WITHOUT the possibility of parole for each of the **four** counts of Kidnaping in the First Degree with substantial bodily harm – to run **consecutively**. He is sentenced to imprisonment for FIFTEEN YEARS in the State Penitentiary for each of the **four** counts of Robbery – to run **consecutively**. He is sentenced to FIFTEEN YEARS in the State Prison for Arson in the First Degree and to TEN YEARS in the State Prison for Burglary. Further, as an emphatic expression of the Court's contempt for these hideous crimes and their perpetrator, **EACH** of the **FOURTEEN** counts are to **run wild!**

Which is to say, Barnell B. must COMPLETE serving his time on **EACH COUNT**, *one through fourteen*, BEFORE he begins to serve time on the next count.

Needless to say, the Defendant is somewhat subdued by the stark news from The Bench. The cockiness is gone. The reality of life behind bars is a brooding presence. His Most Honorable stares intently at the prisoner standing before him. Then, ever The Gentleman – ever The Consummate Jurist, The Court asks in a deliberately solemn tone: "Mr. Bishop, do you have any request of the Court BEFORE you are remanded to the custody of The Warden to begin serving YOUR TIME on the JUDGMENT imposed?"

Barnell B. stands silently before The Judge for a brief time. Pondering perhaps, whether he should remind His Honor of the implausibility of **His Judgment**. He opts to vent his thoughts. Maybe the guy with the black robe needs some remedial tutoring in basic arithmetic. "Your Honor, you've sentenced me to EIGHT terms of LIFE **WITHOUT** the Possibility of Parole, FOUR fifteen year terms, ONE ten year term – and you've made them ALL **run wild**. I think you've forgotten something, Judge. I won't live long enough to complete the terms of imprisonment you've given me."

The moment is still vivid in my memory. His Honor smiles sympathetically and says, "I understand the dilemma you face, Sir, *just do the BEST you can.*"

It's a fitting exclamation point to the **Bench** JUSTICE fashioned for a *CONVICTED* **quadruple** ARSON **murderer!** Anyone sufficiently diabolical to beat and tie up victims, cover them with combustible materials and drench them with cleaning solvent, *then* cruelly set fire to FOUR helpless human beings during the commission of Robbery, **one** being a <u>fourteen</u> year old child, MUST be isolated from society interminably!

"What is JUSTICE, but for <u>every</u> man to receive his **due**."(Aristotle) Is it any wonder I found my career satisfying – and yes, with JUST **guilty verdicts** and JUSTIFIED **sentencing** – EXHILARATING! This character "...was not born to shame. Upon his brow shame is ashamed to sit." (William Shakespeare, *Romeo and Juliet*, ibid.)

A Learning Experience

"The next thing most like **living** one's life over again seems to be a **recollection** of that life, and to make that recollection as *durable* as possible by putting it down in **writing**." (Benjamin Franklin, *Autobiography*, [1793 – 1868] Chap. I – emphasis added)

Chapter 12

A Prosecutor needs to have good judgment, but levelheadedness isn't an attribute that's easy to **get a handle on**. A Criminal Case isn't a fungible. Every Case is unique, possessing its own set of facts and issues and witnesses. Therefore, JUDGMENT is relative. What's good in Case A may be lousy in Case B. Strategies must be reinvented for each Trial outing, and fine tuned each day of the Trial –– sometimes after every witness. A Prosecutor must be astute, adaptive, and adroit. Turning on a dime as circumstances require a shift in tactics. And TIME is always a crucial factor. There's never enough of it! Trial Practice by its nature is a race against time. A ton of planning, preparation, and performance has to be crowded into each day.

As for JUDGMENT, consistent with the Court's gentle admonition to Barnell B. at his Sentencing Hearing, I've **tried to do** *the best I can* in prosecuting Cases assigned to me. Though exercising good judgment is an elusive commodity on occasion. Even with the best of intention, things can go to hell in a hat basket. A Deputy DA charts his Case Course with imperfect judgment.

SO ———————— what are a **few** other factors I've learned during twenty nine years of *Prosecution* in the Clark County Courthouse?

1. PROSECUTING IS *ALL* ABOUT **PEOPLE**.

My father often said in his later years, "It takes all kinds of people to make a world." I've come to appreciate his simple phrase. It's actually rather profound. A *recognition* of <u>inherent</u> **value** in the various human races and cultures, an *expression* of **tolerance** for the <u>differences</u> people exhibit, and an *acceptance* of the NEED to <u>peacefully</u> **interact** and **cooperate** with others.

This book has been about people. A Trial Lawyer works with ALL KINDS of people, that's a given. The key to having some degree of success is recognizing the congenital value of each person – good or bad, becoming indulgent of their human variables, cultivating the social and legal skills necessary to **convince** witnesses to <u>impart</u> their evidence to you, and then to <u>disclose</u> it under oath from the Witness Stand. A two-pronged approach has worked well for me: <u>Be</u> **friendly** to everyone and <u>treat</u> everyone with **respect**! And I do mean EVERYONE. Victims, Families of Victims, Judges, Counsel, Defendants, Court Personnel, Witnesses, Spectators, Reporters – everyone. Give them all capital letter status, empathy, and dignity. Each person is a brother or sister trekking along life's oftentimes troublesome trail. IT'S ALL ABOUT **RELATIONSHIPS** in Mortality – including the Courtroom!

2. PROPER **ATTITUDE** EMPOWERS.

The great Psychologist and Pragmatist William James once said: "The greatest discovery of my generation is that you can change your circumstances by changing your attitudes of mind."

I'm a firm proponent of that principle. *Attitudes of mind* <u>**do**</u> CHANGE *circumstances*! The Dictionary calls **attitude** a settled opinion or way of thinking. Once I was a farm boy, but over time I acquired a **settled opinion** about excessive sweat – especially when I had a shovel in my hands on steamy summer afternoons. In my case, the plowboy became a Prosecutor because he decided farmers have to sweat too much. Prosecutors have to work hard too, but it's not a pore secretion triggered by <u>physical</u> labor. Their sweat is largely metaphorical.

But those who become Prosecutors aren't automatically <u>effective</u>. Being an **effective Prosecutor**, <u>a</u> <u>dynamic</u> <u>advocate</u> <u>for</u> <u>justice</u>, is a **way of thinking**. A way of approaching the job. An orientation. A point of view – a *belief* that the calling of Prosecuting Attorney carries *special* public responsibilities. Some practitioners <u>never</u> become effective advocates. Some highly intelligent, highly qualified persons <u>never</u> realize their potential – <u>never</u> really capture the <u>Spirit of Prosecution</u>. Why? Because the indomitable spirit that makes a practitioner of criminal law an **effective Prosecutor** *comes from inside*! It comes from the Prosecutor's gut. It comes from the heart and core values –– from focus and deliberate prioritization. It's who the Prosecutor wants to become! Is it a matter of garnering a little courtroom experience while passing through the system or is it a career? A passionate enterprise of the soul?

The <u>Spirit of Prosecution</u> is a burning *desire* to serve one's community. It's a fervent *commitment* to achieve justice in every case the Prosecutor handles – truly being a *servant of justice*. It's a steadfast *empathy* for victims and victim's families. A *recognition* of the tragedy that lies in lives prematurely and senselessly catapulted beyond the veil. It's taking <u>every</u> case seriously <u>and</u> *personally*.. Taking complete *responsibility* for being defacto counsel of the departed – those whose lips are sealed by murder. In a sense, it's *making* **Prosecution** our *life*! It's *acquiring* a sober appreciation for the nobility of our Profession. It's having *an abiding conviction* that <u>our</u> <u>cause</u> <u>is</u> <u>righteous</u>. This is the **attitude** that CHANGES **circumstances** and WINS the cases which *should* be won

3. **PREPARATION** IS THE GREAT EQUALIZER.

Most prospective Attorneys hear it in Law School. I did. Well–it's–true! "The law <u>is</u> a jealous mistress." The legal profession demands earnest and energetic devotion from those who want to excel. To which I am compelled to add: **each** *Murder Case* a Deputy DA handles <u>is</u> SURELY a jealous mistress. During every journey through the *Trial Arena* the task at hand requires singled minded <u>fidelity</u> as a precondition to winning. Trial practice demands constant courtship. JUST VERDICTS <u>will</u> <u>not</u> <u>be</u> <u>won</u> by trifling effort – only by lavish respect for the cause. Winning isn't an accident. **Hard** **work** makes winners!

A Prosecutor doesn't have to be the smartest or the handsomest, nor a particular gender, or a specific color, nor married or single, nor a Republican or a Democrat –– BUT he does have to be the BEST PREPARED! That is the litmus test for first rate performance in the Courtroom and the solemn **duty** <u>every</u> Prosecutor owes his community.

There is **no** substitute for being *thoroughly* **prepared**. Phillip's Case is illustrative of the need for rigorous preparation if Justice is to prevail. This is a six week Murder Trial. It involves a SET **fire** on the eleventh story of the Las Vegas Hilton Hotel. Phillip is an employee of the Hilton. The Prosecution has charged him with deliberately using a match or cigarette lighter to ignite shear curtains in an eleventh story lobby. The blaze rapidly spreads – with catastrophic consequences. Eight persons are killed in guest elevators while attempting to flee the fire, heat, and suffocating smoke that permeates various floors of the hotel. Others are seriously injured in the melee. However, **the eight decedents** climbed into elevators that were death traps.

An <u>Object</u> lesson, it seems. Ya get caught in a hotel fire – *remember* the Las Vegas Hilton ARSONIST'S **deadly** legacy, and think twice before boarding an elevator. It might be a very short flight. Experts testify that the cause of death in each instance is smoke inhalation. They also suggest it isn't prudent to use elevators for descent to the ground floor when fire rages in close proximity. Use stairways and emergency outside ladders for egress from fire zones.

Yet, the greater <u>Case</u> lesson lies in its affirmation of exhaustive **preparation**.

The Prosecutor <u>must</u> know his evidence and his issues. It's imperative for an **effective Prosecutor** to have *relentlessly* studied and *absorbed the* FACTS of his Case before he delivers <u>Summation</u>. The predicate of every **Closing Argument** must be thoughtful, methodical, meaningful <u>preparation</u>.

I'm teamed up with the inestimable gentleman Prosecutor, Chief Deputy Ray J. He will do the honors on **Rebuttal** and I will present the **Opening** Summation. It's tough coalescing the testimony and physical evidence of a six week trial into a cogent outline. A lengthy <u>Murder</u> Trial represents a very large pile of daily transcripts, exhibits, and notes to review. The process takes TIME – lots of it. Only a profusion of *brain power* and *finger sweat* will suffice as the prelude to a persuasive *sweating tongue* before the Jury. Now is not the occasion to catch one's breath nor to coast into **Final** Argument. There **aren't** any shortcuts to victory. **No** down time. This **is** STUDY time. Put your petal to the metal and let it roar time!

Many Case Scenarios *readily* give up their secrets. The evidentiary truths of these cases are apparent. Straightforward. Jumping right out at an Advocate. On the other hand, it seems like some Case Plots are *begrudgingly* coughed up. Such Cases test the mettle of their Prosecutors. Presenting facets of evidentiary <u>mystery</u> that are difficult to master. Factual enigma where the full meaning and impact on the outcome may be subtle and practically indiscernible. It will be impossible to properly fit a piece of such evidence into the larger Case Mosaic without *perception*. <u>Absent</u> tremendous energy and focus, earnest commitment and unabated – meticulous study, the *insight* **<u>won't</u>** come. The evidentiary code **<u>won't</u>** be cracked. The puzzle will remain UNSOLVED! *Perception* is the product of the **knowledge** indefatigable study brings.

I'll digress momentarily. Phillip is an employee , but he is a lower echelon worker for The Hilton. Though he's ambitious. Possibly, looking for a gimmick to boost his upward mobility in the Hilton organization. Curiously, it is Phillip who *allegedly* <u>discovers</u> the fire and reports it to Hotel Security. Coincidental?

Immediately, there are wags who say a **<u>fire</u>** on the eleventh floor reported by Phillip may <u>not</u> be coincidental. The whole thing strikes them as being a little **too** convenient to be credible.

THREE **<u>riddles</u>** cast a heavy shadow over the Hilton Fire Case. They are WHO – WHY – WHEN? Somebody has torched a large area of a major Las Vegas Strip Hotel. **Whodunit? What's the motive? ––– When did Phillip REPORT the fire?** NO, I'm not speaking of TIME. Hotel Security has a recording of the *report*. They know <u>precisely</u>, to the very second, when Phillip called in the fire. I'm alluding to WHEN he says there's a FIRE with respect to **WHEN** THE FIRE actually *STARTS*! The answer to WHO lies in **WHEN**.

A rather large number of hotel guests have provided witness statements to the Police. TWO of these have caused me a degree of consternation throughout my Case Preparation – before, during, and after the evidentiary phase of the Trial. I kept having a *recurring IMPRESSION* that I **<u>wasn't</u>** *perceiving* a crucial aspect of their evidentiary **message**. They're both handwritten documents. One penned by a German man and the second by an American. These two gentleman tourists were <u>among</u> the first to detect the flame .OR **were–they–the–FIRST?** I'll say it again, I believe it's impossible to properly fit an enigmatic piece of evidence into the larger Case Mosaic without *perception*. <u>Absent</u> tremendous energy and focus, earnest commitment and unabated – meticulous study, the *insight* **<u>won't</u>** come. **It–takes–TIME–to–get–<u>perception</u>.**

My recollection **is** that the statements of both these men, for whatever reason, were admitted into evidence. Thus, they are part of the small mountain of Exhibits and Trial Transcripts to be considered by the Lawyers during their preparation and, subsequently, by the Jury in its deliberation.

I went through the whole pile. However, I paid <u>extra</u> attention to The STATEMENTS of the two referenced in the second paragraph above. While working on my CLOSING ARGUMENT I'm still trying to crack the metaphorical Rubik's cube that is the **pivotal** <u>**mystery**</u> of the Las Vegas Hilton fire. WHEN Phillip calls in the FIRE is he *reporting* a FIRE <u>**before**</u> or <u>**after**</u> the FIRE *starts?*

I'm thinking the answer lies in The STATEMENTS, and I'm determined to get closure. I <u>methodically</u> *read and reread* the TWO STATEMENTS. There **aren't** any shortcuts to victory. This is for all the marbles. And I must have gone over The STATEMENTS *at least* **twenty five** <u>**times**</u> before the light bulb finally came ON. I *relentlessly* studied and, eventually, *absorbed* the **defining TRUTH** of the Case. The **KEY** that unlocks the treasure chest where Phillip's incriminatory skeleton lies. It's the CHRONOLOGY. A <u>**time**</u> CONUNDRUM for Phillip. He's put the cart <u>before</u> the horse. The **call** <u>before</u> the **fire.**

There are those times when an Advocate <u>doesn't</u> readily take *cognizance* of **TRUTHS** right under his nose. Maybe they're too obvious. Possibly, they represent a *state of facts* totally **unanticipated** that clouds his *insight.* Be that as it is, MURDER **does** <u>**not**</u> stay hidden!

> "Truth will come to light; murder cannot be hid long." (William Shakespeare, *Merchant of Venice*, Act II, Sc. 2, line 86)

It's been *subtly* <u>expressed</u> in The STATEMENTS from the beginning, but I'd never really got a handle on it <u>until</u> six weeks of Trial were a matter of record, much serious reflection logged, and **twenty five**, or was it **one hundred twenty five** <u>**readings.**</u> FINALLY – the T's are crossed, the dots connected, the haze dissipates, dogged study reaps its reward, and the **time line** *enigma* is resolved. PERTINENT FACTS: The German and American tourists *see* the initial **flickering flames** in shear curtains of an eleventh floor foyer, that instantly spread as if whipped by hot wind in zero % humidity, *at least* <u>**THREE**</u> MINUTES <u>**after**</u> Phillip *reports* a blaze on the eleventh floor. **The jig's up,** SIR.

ARSON <u>**isn't**</u> a very shrewd way to achieve upward mobility in the corporate hierarchy. As for **MOTIVE**, Phillip has previously shed some light by flapping his lips to a co-worker. "A fools mouth is his destruction." (*Holy Bible*, Proverbs 18:7) Perhaps, it's merely puffing. Foolish braggadocio to a cohort. But Phillip says he **SET** the fire in the hope of becoming a *cause celebre* and *collecting* a handsome reward by being the one to **REPORT** the fire. A Case of wanting to create a circumstance that will make him famous.

Studious Juries are successful Juries. Success being measured by their ability to reach JUST **verdicts**. That involves investing the necessary amount of time and energy into determining what the evidence is. Then going where that evidence and the Court's instructions *take* them. Juries take notes during the introduction of evidence and the introduction of Argument. Six days into Deliberation their tireless study facilitates a break though. A shaft of light – of *insight*. The light bulb goes ON in the Jury Room – and they *perceive* the **Deliberation-changing TRUTH** for themselves. Phillip has reported a fire BEFORE there is a fire! And that FACT breaks the deadlock.

It's precisely like *A Trout In The Milk*. Nobody saw the dairy farmer dip his milk can into the stream of water, but we're **absolutely** POSITIVE he did. Why? Because the natural habitat of a cutthroat trout is **not** a can of milk. Because FISH **don't** spawn in a can of warm milk, and FISH **don't** hatch in that environment neither! The FISH in the milk has HIM **hooked**!

Likewise, **No** amount of reading tea leaves is going to **empower** a Hilton Hotel employee to acquire the CLAIRVOYANCE necessary to know there's going to be a fire BEFORE there **is** a fire, UNLESS –––– **he's–going–to–set–the–FIRE!** Phillip is **not** endowed with the *spirit of prophesy*. IF he calls in a fire WHEN there **isn't** a fire, then **WHEN** tells us **WHO** –––– PHILLIP *SETS* *The* FIRE!!

The Trial Jury announces it has **Verdicts**, and returns GUILTY VERDICTS for ARSON and **eight** counts of MURDER IN THE FIRST DEGREE.

Preparation is the great equalizer. It compensates for scores of shortcomings. If a Prosecutor isn't charismatic or charming or glib – nor brilliant or skilled in the dramatic arts – it **doesn't** matter. ALL **isn't** lost. **Effective preparation** WILL level the playing field! Giving a GRUNT like me a chance. In my case, a strong work ethic, reaching deep – the

GRUNT mentality, harks back to my ancestral tree and years of laboring by the *sweat of my brow* on The Farm.

4. <u>**PASSIONATELY**</u> REPRESENT YOUR VICTIMS.

Passion comes from a powerful sense of connection to those who have *suffered* **loss** of property, dignity, and life. It's a major aspect of the <u>Spirit</u> of <u>Prosecution</u>. Reverting to prior language, it's having a steadfast *empathy* for victims and victim's families. A *recognition* of the tragedy that lies in lives prematurely and senselessly catapulted beyond the veil. **Passionate** Representation is taking COMPLETE **responsibility** for being defacto counsel of those deprived of property and dignity, of life – and loved ones.

Oh –– blessed, wondrous, miraculous, incredible LIFE! Consider the glory of being alive: of having a living Spirit, a beating Heart, and the recurring twinge of conscience – of having thoughts and taste and tears and sight and hearing – and hope. LIFE is everything. Without LIFE we are <u>nothing</u>. We have no being. There is no meaning to anything – only **darkness**. Those who fail to *reverence* **life** are out of touch with sacred realities.

The RIGHT to <u>live</u> is the paramount value. We begin reciting the *Declaration of Independence* and the *Bill of Rights* as grade school children. They remain <u>viable</u> throughout our lives. Particularly to a Prosecutor!

"We hold **these** <u>**truths**</u> to be self-evident, that ALL men are *created* **equal**, that they are endowed by their Creator with certain unalienable rights, that among these are LIFE, liberty, and the pursuit of happiness. That, to secure these *RIGHTS*, governments are instituted among men, deriving their <u>just</u> powers from the consent of the governed."(*The Declaration of Independence*, July 4, 1776 – emphasis added)

"...nor shall ANY PERSON...be *deprived* of LIFE, liberty, or property, <u>without</u> **due process of law**..." (Fifth Amendment of the United States Constitution – emphasis added)

"...**No State** shall make or enforce any law which shall abridge the *privileges* or *immunities* of citizens of the United States...<u>**nor deny**</u> to ANY person within its jurisdiction the **EQUAL protection** of the LAWS."

(Fourteenth Amendment, Section 1.of the United States Constitution – emphasis added)

MURDER is **heinous**! Barbaric. Blind to the *Rule of Law*. This **is** the bedrock **truth** for a <u>Homicide</u> Prosecutor: NO **life** is more valuable than another! The **blood** runs RED in Murder –– REGARDLESS of race or nationality, of religious or moral values, of language or occupation, of gender or age, of education or wealth or social status! <u>Every</u> VICTIM of Murder **must** be given the same type of pull-out-all-the-stops, 110% **representation.**

Accordingly, a Prosecutor is **not** discriminatory of his Murder Victims. **All–Victims–are–alike–unto–the–Homicide–Prosecutor!** This <u>principle</u> is the *guiding light*. The <u>inspiration</u>. The <u>mind-set</u> capstone. Socrates said, "All learning is remembering."A Homicide Prosecutor must always *remember* the <u>canon</u> of VICTIM **equality!** Never forgetting it while he's in Murder Trials – even for a moment.

<u>Whether</u> it's a **stabbing** victim in a crowd at Freedom Park during a Sunday evening blowout of binge drinking and folk music, or <u>whether</u> it's two Wyoming businessmen **gunned** down in a remote area of Lyon County pursuant to a contract murder; <u>whether</u> it's a wife **ambushed** by her husband in a hail of bullets two days before Valentine's Day – [Cupid shoots mythological arrows with hearts for tips to inspire love. T's husband shoots murderous bullets with lead tips to puncture a trusting heart. "Happy Valentine's Day, My Dearest – with malice!"], or <u>whether</u> it's a Texas wife and mother whose solo act – [She argues with her husband and unwisely seeks solace at a redneck bar in a strange city.] leads to **brutal** demise at the hands of a savage stranger – making her a bloody statistic in the dust of a dirt road off Nellis Boulevard; <u>whether</u> it's a Good Samaritan/ paramour kidnaped, **shot** at point-blank range, and buried – [A one-man welcoming committee for a woman wanting a quickie dissolution of her marriage in Sin City.] the unwitting target of a Murder for Hire by the spurned husband in El Paso, or <u>whether</u> it's the sickening switchblade **stabbing** of a pretty young Minnesota tour coordinator on the eleventh floor of a Strip Hotel – silenced in her blood splattered room by a predatory, <u>obsessive</u> *thief* of life; <u>whether</u> it's an Asian wife **battered** into deadly submission by a husband wielding a baseball bat – purportedly motivated by marital discord fueled by parlor privileges the Lady affords her chickens [He says she'd rather play house with her feathered friends than play house with him. Poor Si Son – no disrespect intended, she's just reliving the

quaint ways of her youth in the old country.], or <u>whether</u> it's an industrious, devout Italian family of three [The boy is only fourteen. Terror has a human face. A murderous visage un-shamed by shameful acts.] and their janitor – bound, beaten, covered with combustibles, doused with cleaning solvent, and **burned alive** in their business after attending Sunday morning Mass; OR a used carlot saleswoman, kidnaped and murdered, her remains <u>never</u> found – **cause of death** unknown; OR a diminutive eighteen month old toddler – [What should a precious little girl know about **physical abuse**?] killed in a fit of anger by the mother's *live-in* boyfriend; OR a bright, brown eyed, six year old bundle of life and energy – **kidnaped** from the grounds of a Hebrew Day Care Center and <u>never</u> recovered [Where is the promise once written on Carey's gentle brow? Where lies that promise now? – And how are loving parents to cope with lingering, lonely heartache? Oh, wretched, hateful, despicable **Murder!**]; OR a retired 5'4" 156 lb 86 year old school teacher bludgeoned to death in her bed with a **tire iron**, – ruthless intruders enter her home between midnight and 3:15 a.m., then sett her house on fire in an effort to conceal their Crime – [Betrayed by a carelessly placed <u>key</u> and <u>two</u> treacherous hearts. An elderly woman's worst nightmare becomes stark reality.]; OR the **stabbing** death of an ex-girlfriend in her mobile home within hours of the jailhouse release of her former boyfriend –a <u>twice</u> convicted Domestic Battery Offender [A <u>systemic</u> breakdown and the woman dies.]; OR the young woman of hope and resolve who flies from Ft. Lauderdale to Las Vegas searching for a *new life* and is dead within ten days, **stabbed** <u>thirty</u> <u>five</u> times in her apartment by a psychotic neighbor – who later torches her digs [Drawn inexplicably back to the scene of his hideous crime during ensuing days. To gloat and eyeball his corpse? To fantasize over the taking of human life? Indifferent to elementary concepts of human dignity and the sanctity of life? To savor the carnal rush, the perverted high, the intoxicating – chilling ecstasy of his plunging blade and her screams of agony? To search, to loot, and to ransack for the spoils of murder? What *madness* a man may hide within, though angel on the outward side. (<u>preceding</u> sentence adapted from, William Shakespeare, *Measure for Measure*, Act III, Sc.2, Line 293); OR the 53 year old taxicab driver **shot** in the right temple and to the left side of his head with a .25 caliber derringer in the 1500 block of Viking Road – <u>without</u> provocation [Killed for peanuts by two <u>nuts</u>. The robbers net a paltry sum of *forty dollars* for perpetrating a depravity against humanity. Both shots are contact wounds, i.e., the muzzle of the firearm is pressed against Ken's skin.]; OR the **shooting** death of an FBI agent during a botched *bank* robbery – his courageous effort to thwart brazen criminal acts of the <u>two</u> robbers culminating in a tragic and premature termination of his stellar Law Enforcement career [A <u>bullet</u> once sent abroad, flies irrevocably.]; OR a single mother surnamed Pechpho asphyxiated by **ligature** strangulation <u>and</u> her handsome four year old son dead of **stab** wounds to his chest and back, both discovered in their bathtub – he is four and she is twenty four [The offense unconscionable. Who? Why? <u>Something</u> wicked breaks the kitchen window and crawls inside. Incredibly, the <u>something</u> is a villainous petty thief – a sobbing-in-court *sixteen* year old boy.]; OR *grandparents*, fifty eight and fifty seven years respectively, routed out of bed by <u>five</u> trespassing hooligans about 1: 00 a.m. and **shot** like stray puppies by a *<u>grandson</u>* and his co-conspirators [Thinking the unthinkable, and <u>doing</u> it. Committing a demonic double-murder – from Dale with hate and to hell with filial piety. Accomplice statement: "He grabbed his grandmother by the lower jaw, put her down on the bed, and SHOT her!"(<u>three</u> times) The step-grandfather is shot <u>seven</u> times as he runs down the stairway. The corpses are somber/gruesome *character* evidence of satanic **night stalkers**. Another accomplice statement: "If I had a choice I'd soar like a hawk, I'd search for my prey only at dark."]; OR the woman **gunned down** with a .9mm sawed off rifle (in full view of four eye-witnesses) by her ex-husband inside a transmission service garage [What's all the shooting for Dave? Got an answer – really? The unfortunate reality is that many <u>irresponsible</u> persons believe every dispute –however petty, should be settled with the barrel of a gun; nor do *shoot em up* <u>mentalities</u> care *where* or *when* they gun down the object of their displeasure.]; OR Hardung, the gentleman from Oklahoma, reclining in bed with a prostitute at a Las Vegas Strip Hotel room, **shot** in the back of his head by the guileful, gold-digging lady as she pretends to give him a back rub [The poor man needs <u>four</u> eyes, two of them in the *back* of his head. <u>Never</u> trust a hooker on your first date –– <u>nor</u> on any followup trysts. This one is also an accomplice in the fatal robbery/**shooting** of a taxidriver.]; OR the Principal of a Las Vegas High School **shot in the heart** by one of his students at 7:50 a.m. – the weapon is a fully loaded Sturm Ruger "single six" .22 LR revolver and the shooter has two boxes containing 131 live rounds in his pockets [Teacher: "Pat, would you like your seat?" Shooter: "**No**, I won't be needing it." Sets his books down, stoically takes a gun out of a holster, holds it with both hands, says: "Mr. Piggott,"(The Principal is also in the room.)aims – fires, and declares: "That takes care of that." –– Hello, is anybody in there? This is lunacy. It takes care of NOTHING!] ; OR the young couple, he is twenty eight and she is twenty nine, both **shot** in the head – lying on the floor in separate bedrooms of their home [She is tied to a bedpost and the house has been ransacked. Are the killers searching for dope and cash? The shooters are purported associates of the husband. That connection is the magnet luring two thugs to this particular address. Cocaine is a lie. It promises paradise – what it brings is hell. The devil is a white demon inside a plastic bag. And Vicky would assuredly confirm this deadly truth IF she could. Joey's wife is clean. Illicit drug free! Condolence to poor – sweet – innocent Vicky. A tragic victim of circumstance. Simply in the wrong place at the wrong time.]; OR Hilda – wealthy sixty seven year old dowager living in an exclusive gated community, *unaware* her husband has a mistress – gagged, neck deeply compressed by ligature, throat **slashed**, stabbing and cutting **wounds** of the neck, and a butcher knife protruding from her upper back [The <u>victim</u> of a quartet of hit-men and a hit-woman, but her husband isn't one of them. He's **not** a <u>conscious</u> conspirator. Though his *infidelity* sets off the chain reaction that ends with his wife's *Murder*. You see, her husband's paramour has her own squeeze and the TWO of them hatch a **six step** scheme for *unjust* enrichment. (One) **kill** Hilda. (Two) Husband **inherits** Hilda's fortune. (Three)Mistress **marries** Husband. (Four) **kill** Husband. (Five) Mistress **inherits** Husband's fortune (Six) Mistress and Squeeze **live** happily ever after! Morbid and unfeasible, but does murder ever make sense?]; OR seventeen year old blue eyed, dusky haired Sabrina – manually **strangled** by the man [Called, "An evil, heartless predator – a parent's worst nightmare," by the Trial Judge.] *promising* to <u>make</u> her a famous model or actress, but aborting his *promise* by <u>making</u> her a bloated corpse floating in the Colorado River below Hoover Dam – "Little <u>lost</u> angel of a ruined Paradise."(Percy Shelley); OR the robbery/ murders of two young female roommates in their twenties by gagging, ligature, and manual **strangulation** – [What's the *worth* of a human being? Here's a news flash, this guy thinks he has it figured out. He's improvised a formula. It's the VALUE of the *property* he steals, i.e., a red 1988 Nissan, a leather suitcase, fifty tapes of "DL" soul music, a black/ white stripe coin purse, a black snap-shut coin purse, two automatic gate/ garage door openers, a "Guns and Roses tape," and the credit remaining on various credit cards – <u>divided</u> by **two**] one of the woman is <u>disabled</u> when she's struck by a beer bottle while speaking on the telephone; OR the methodical, early morning, room by room slaughter of a forty seven year old wife, a twenty year old step-daughter, and a twelve year old step-daughter by **blunt** force trauma and manual **strangulation** – [An evil assailant stalks his prey in their bedrooms as they sleep – with a <u>claw</u> hammer, <u>suffocating</u> hands, and a <u>malicious</u> heart."Evil is easy, and has infinite forms." (Blaise Pascal, *Pensees*. Sect. VI, No. 408)] killed by a despondent husband and step-father unable to cope with family conflicts and family finances; OR the swing shift clerk of a Stop N Go Market <u>gratuitously</u> **shot** in the face by a member of the thrill-kill robbery tandem confronting her at the counter – [Mortality is fragile. "The Bird of Time has but a little way to flutter and the Bird is on the wing." (Edward Fitzgerald, *Rubaiyat of Omar Khayyam of Naishapur*)] Michelle, a twenty one year old newlywed, is found behind the sales counter in a pool of blood; OR the Asian wife **shot** with a stun gun and **stabbed** three times in the chest with a kitchen knife, while sitting behind the wheel of her Mazda in a parking lot across the street from City Hall – [Recovered from the right rear passenger floorboard next to the <u>kitchen</u> <u>knife</u> is a 5" x 7" envelope addressed to *Doreen*. It holds an anniversary card from her husband. He has written, "Doreen, here's $500.00 reasons why I love you. Forever, Ray." A green vase of red roses, carnations, babies breath and greenery lies on the middle of the back seat. Inside the attached envelope a card conveys the following handwritten message from her husband: "For the millions of reasons I love you. Much more to come. RG"] the **"much more"** takes her breath away permanently, **<u>murder</u>** is a bizarre method for *remembering* a couple's nuptial ————— ; WHOEVER – WHENEVER, *whatever the circumstances*, THEY'RE **<u>EACH</u>** entitled to their DAY IN COURT —— AND TO **<u>equal</u>** JUSTICE! Which is acknowledged in Constitutional decree, not literally perhaps, but the <u>spirit</u> of EQUALITY for **murdered victims** is enshrined in Constitutional Doctrine.(Fifth and Fourteenth Amendments, ibid.) **<u>EACH</u>** HOMICIDE VICTIM has a <u>sacred</u> RIGHT, in **<u>absentia</u>**, to DUE PROCESS OF **LAW** and EQUAL PROTECTION under **The Law**! Moreover, it's the *personal* **<u>responsibility</u>** of the Prosecutor to make this a REALITY in <u>every</u> Murder Trial.

5. PERSONAL RESPONSIBILITY IS THE EMBODIMENT OF JUSTICE.

"**<u>No</u>** man is above the law and **<u>no</u>** man is below it; **<u>nor</u>** do we ask any man's permission when we require him to obey it. **Obedience to the Law** is <u>demanded</u> as a RIGHT; **<u>not</u>** asked as a favor." (Theodore Roosevelt – emphasis added)

I agree with Roosevelt's principle of **Obedience to Law**. An effectively functioning society has a RIGHT to demand the **obedience** of it citizens. The Criminal Justice System **loses** all CREDIBILITY unless it *REQUIRES* **personal** ACCOUNTABILITY for **Disobedience to the Law**. If the Justice System means anything, it means persons committing grievous crimes must be held **specifically** RESPONSIBLE for their culpability!

While I was a schoolboy, I became acquainted with a fellow dubbed *Circumstance* Jones. I don't know his given name, but I know exactly where the nickname originated. Brother Jones came to be known as *Circumstance* because of a figure of speech he frequently employed. The phrase being: "*CIRCUMSTANCES* so **arranged** themselves." It became his signature expression. Repetitiously, his mouth spued out recitations about circumstances. How that circumstance —— or these circumstances —— or those circumstances **arranged** themselves. Thus, producing particular results that precluded his compliance with the obligation in issue. Rather convenient – is my take on the oft used maxim. With due respect to *Circumstance* Jones, his catchy slogan sounds like a method of **excusing** himself. **Do** CIRCUMSTANCES actually **arrange** themselves? It's an amusing expression, but are our RESULTS dictated by some amorphous, external, out there in the blue somewhere – **arrangement** of circumstances?

NO SIR! "MAN makes the circumstances, and spiritually as well as economically is the artificer of his own fortune." (Thomas Carlyle, *Diderot* – 1833, emphasis added)A CIRCUMSTANCE is inanimate. Impotent. The creative prowess of a circumstance is nil – a big fat goose-egg. It's just – well, *a circumstance*. An event. A happening. It does **nothing** until it's acted upon. Circumstance has to be linked to a cause and effect event. MAN being the cause, circumstance the effect. It takes a composer to write a musical score. A maestro to conduct a symphony orchestra. An author to write a book. A person to read the book. A good hitter to smack home runs. Teamwork to make good teams. People to do good deeds. A KILLER to commit **murder**.

CIRCUMSTANCES are **cognition** driven. A CIRCUMSTANCE is at the mercy of the circumstance **MAKER**. A mere circumstance is a victim of **arranged** *volitional* circumstance. Whether it's a *Higher Power* or *manpower*. **We** are CRAFTSMEN of circumstance. **Free Agents! Our** *choices* create our circumstances. Moreover, once we've made them we have to live with them and face the consequences that flow from them.

CIRCUMSTANCE doesn't commit **murder**. Greed and jealousy,

malice and the perceived self interest of PEOPLE perpetrate **murder**. A CIRCUMSTANCE has **no** properties of mobility or perception. **No** power to persuade or chastize or harm. **No** wings, **no** arms, **no** hands, **no** voice box –– **nor** brain. It **can't** commit *crimes*. **Hasn't** got a scintilla of ability to coerce and seduce, to rob and rape, to kidnap and murder.

Nor does CIRCUMSTANCE make **justice**. JUSTICE doesn't simply happen. **Dedication** and <u>tenacious</u> **effort**, buckets of **sweat** and an *effectively* administered **Criminal Justice System** <u>produce</u> specific, justifiable <u>personal</u> ACCOUNTABILITY.

> In the play *Julius Caesar* – Caius Cassius proclaims: "Men at
> some time are Masters of their Fates. The **fault**, dear Brutus,
> is NOT in our stars, But in **ourselves** that we are underlings."
> (William Shakespeare, Act I, Sc. 2, line 134 – emphasis added)

In other words, the **catalyst** for success or failure *lies* **within** us. It's **not** some external force or entity. Excuses? Typically, there is **no** viable EXCUSE defense. In a word, to excuse self is to **accuse** self.

When a <u>guilty</u> Defendant is **convicted** at Trial the <u>fault</u> is not in his **stars**. His astrology chart hasn't <u>greased</u> his slide into darkness. The <u>fault</u> isn't in his **genes**. Perhaps, he possesses a mediocre genetic blue print, but no evidence of a predilection-to-commit-murder gene has been identified! The <u>fault</u> isn't in his **childhood**. His parents did their best. He's a big boy now. He claims to have been under the influence of hard **drugs**, but dope doesn't kill – people kill! The <u>fault</u> isn't in his **firearm**. The gun didn't load itself, cock itself, aim itself, and squeeze its own trigger. The <u>fault</u> isn't in some other **dude**. [The SODDI defense, *some other dude did it*, isn't applicable here. His Lawyer argues this proposition, however, but says he doesn't know *where* the culprit is. "Ladies and Gentleman of the Jury, I've got a news flash for you. I **do** KNOW *where* Defense Counsel's other suspect is –– this transient ghoul about whom Counsel alludes. He says he doesn't know *where* he is, but says, 'I can offer some suggestions about *who* he is.' Impossible, Sir! He doesn't have a name. He doesn't have a social security number, nor a post office box number, nor a telephone number, nor a street address, nor personal references, nor employment, nor a rap sheet, nor a mug photo neither. Nevertheless, I KNOW *precisely where* he is. Counsel's other suspect is exactly *where* he's always been. The fact is, he's *inside* the Courtroom right now. We don't see him, he's invisible. But I **know** he's here anyway. Even though I have to use reading glasses to see my trial notes clearly. He's here because Defense Counsel is here. Wherever Counsel goes he goes! Why? Because the so-called '*other suspect*' is INSIDE Counsel's head. He was conceived in Counsel's head. He lives in his head. He'll die in his head – after Counsel starts his next trial. You see, there ISN'T any *other viable suspect*. He only exists in Counsel's **imagination** and in his **notes** and in his **arguments.** The *other suspect* ISN'T a *real* person. There's only ONE actual suspect. **Only one** KILLER! He's in the Courtroom too. I'm **pointing at him**. He's **right there**. He's **the Defendant!**"] The <u>fault</u> is not in his **Victim**. She's not simply a name or a statistic. Not merely a short resume' on a missing person report. *Once* she was a living, breathing, loving, responsible human being. She didn't ask to be killed. The <u>fault</u> is not in the **witnesses** who testified against him. To the man or woman, they were responding to subpoena or a sense of civic duty. The <u>fault</u> is not in the **Police** who investigated the case. They were performing duties imposed by sworn oaths to honorably serve and protect their community. "Nor is the <u>fault</u> in your **Prosecutor**. He's just part of the lunch pail crowd. Earning a living and attempting to magnify his calling as a public servant. I *don't* know you personally, and I'd *never* met any of the non-police witnesses prior to pretrial interviews I conducted. I have *no* interest in the outcome of the Trial other than an earnest hope that justice is achieved!" The <u>fault</u> is not in the **Court**. The Judge has a heavy Criminal Docket. His Honor didn't need this case to keep him busy in the Courtroom. His Criminal Calendar is already busting at the seams. For cases scheduled to go to trial in ordinary course, a defendant better have a penchant for patience in this Courtroom."Mr. Defendant, the <u>fault</u> is **person specific!** 'Cruelty has a human heart.' (William Blake) Sir –– the FAULT lies in **you!**

Yet, we live in a society where very <u>few</u> want to take the bull-by-the-horns and straight-up accept **personal** RESPONSIBILITY for **wrongdoing**. By a significant preponderance of numbers, today's marching orders seem to be **equivocation** followed by **rationalization** – if necessary. Muddy the water, hedge, obscure, confuse, dance around an issue, but **never** accept blame – <u>unless</u> solidly <u>connected</u> to the act in question. Then offer up a ration of EXCUSES for doing it. Explaining WHY there can be **no** accountability for doing the bad act. Whether the EXCUSE is the **devil** made me do it or **addiction** or **genes** or a seemingly endless list of *acronym* **disorders** or etcetera – ad nauseam.

Fortunately, despite all the knocks against it, there are **bright line** occasions when the Criminal Justice System <u>does</u> impose **specific** ACCOUNTABILITY upon those who are **Disobedient to the Law**. I'll conclude with a few additional examples:

1. **<u>Once</u> may not be enough.** It isn't an easy task to pass JUDGMENT. Hung Juries are not an infrequent occurrence. I'll offer two examples. I believe they attest to the importance of <u>persistence</u> in obtaining JUSTICE.

   a. *Colony Club Justice* – The Victim lay in a contorted heap against a blood stained, bullet riddled, glass exterior door. By **all** Trial accounts, the Accused did not testify, the Victim was fleeing from a fusillade of gunfire. Adroit and speedy and motivated, but evidently **not** quick enough.

The FIRST Trial ends with the Jury **hung** 10-2 for acquittal. Not too upbeat for the boys with white hats. A significant number of nay-sayers in the DA's Office urge me to hang up my jersey on this one. "Give it up. Move on to your next case, Buddy. Ya can't win 'em all."

Well, I certainly knew this to be a fact from personal experience. Nobody had to tell me that. However, I <u>should</u> have won this one. Rolling over will be a travesty of justice – in my view. The Victim did **not** deserve to die. <u>Nothing</u> about the *circumstances* **justified** the use of **deadly force**, and the family is grief-stricken. They're depending on <u>me</u>. I stand at the gate as a guardian against the on-rushing criminal horde.

Moreover, I remembered the Judge's disgruntled reaction when the Jury Foreman said they were hung, and the obvious *disdain* for the impasse exhibited by His Honor when he excused the Jury from further service in the Case. It wasn't so much an expression of thanks as a tongue lashing. My assessment of the Case is fortified by a perception that the Judge isn't simply unhappy with the deadlocked Jury – that happens on occasion. Rather, his biggest beef with this crew is the vote of 10-2 for **NOT** guilty.

We decide to retry the Case, and persistence pays off. <u>Once</u> didn't do it, but **twice** does. Ironically, Murder Trial *two* is a **carbon copy** of Murder Trial *one*, except for <u>one</u> salient difference. **Same** Judge. **Same** Lawyers – Harmon for the Prosecution and Miller for the Defense. **Same** Jury selection process. **Same** Opening Statements. Witnesses for both parties are identical to the *first* outing – **same** people, **same** testimony. The **same** exhibits are introduced. The Judge presents the **same** legal instructions. Closing Arguments are basically the **same**. Verbiage varies some, but theories of the case and major points argued are identical. The Jury retires to the **same** room for deliberation, and takes about the **same** amount of time to end its consideration of the Case.

However, the Opinion of Jury *two* is 300 degrees DIFFERENT than the Opinions of Jury *one*. The unanimous VERDICT returned by Jury *two* and recorded by the Court Clerk is –– **GUILTY!** So, we go from 2-10 (two Jurors short of acquittal) to 12-0 and *LIFE* in the slammer *WITHOUT* the possibility of parole for a **FIRST DEGREE MURDER CONVICTION.**

It's been a roller coaster ride, but how sweet it is! **Proof** positive that **ONE TRIAL** may not be enough, and that Jurors are a **huge** RESULT variable. We **never** know until the foreperson reads The VERDICT!

      b. *Biker Justice* – The ghastly discovery is made on a street about the length of a football field east of the Sahara Hotel. A young prostitute has been unceremoniously dumped in an intersection. She's been **stabbed** sixty nine times. Talk about overkill. There is also another object on the blacktop, the sadistic character with a fondness for sharp knives does the Police a favor. Nestled next to the deceased is a Harley-Davidson *wallet*. Obligingly, while the **killer** *deliberately* dumped the body he *accidently* dumps his wallet too. So, Police have evidence of murder at the drop site, and – possible evidence of the **murderer**. It's quite a bonanza for investigating officers. The owner's driver's license, complete with Photo Identification, is among contents gracing compartments of the *wallet*. Ooops!

I'll cut to the chase. Las Vegas Metropolitan Police Officers complete their investigation, and the *wallet's* owner does turn out to be their man. He's charged with commission of the call-girl murder and, in due course, the Cop's man goes to Trial. The Parties are introduced, the Jury picked, opening remarks presented, evidence introduced, instructions read, summations made, and the Case submitted.

Four days later the Jury is summoned to the Courtroom and the Foreperson announces a deadlock. His Honor declares a Mistrial. The Twelve Tried and True can't decide what to do. Well, let's amend the last statement. As we learned from conversation with Jurors *after* their release from service, Eleven Tried and True have decided what to do and the Other tried and true has decided too – but **not** the same way. It's 11-1 for guilty of **First Degree Murder**, but a VERDICT has to be unanimous. It's back to the Prosecutorial drawing board.

Is **Once** enough? NO! There are **EIGHTY** reasons why **Once** is not enough, to-wit: sixty nine stab wounds and the eleven Jurors voting for conviction. The Case is RETRIED. And the Verdict is ———— ?

Hey! Is the needle stuck here? It's a deja vu thing. The SAME result. Exactly the same: HUNG 11-1 for guilty of **First Degree Murder** – again!

Are we **Done** with do-overs? **Once** wasn't enough, but is **Twice** enough? Murder retrials cost bundles of bucks and the Trial Court has a busy calendar. His Honor is agonizing over this one and the DA Ladies and Gentlemen on deputy row are giving a **second retrial** mixed reviews. Deplorably, some are now saying – "It's only a hooker."

But NOT the Trial Boys. There are now **NINETY ONE** reasons why **Twice** isn't enough. Namely: the twenty two Jurors voting for conviction and the sixty nine times this *biker guy* has plunged his razor sharp blade into the BODY of a living, breathing *human being*. Disrespecting her. Hurting her in an excruciating way. Depriving her of her precious life. Killing her savagely with **each** vile wound. Carving bloody holes in her torso, stifling her cries of anguish, and silencing the beat of her heart. Pulling the plug on her thoughts and tears, her hearing, her sight, and her last ray of hope. The Victim's life style **is** IRRELEVANT to this Case. What she does for a profession is between her and Law Enforcement. The Criminal Justice System doesn't cotton to vigilantism! This *biker guy* **doesn't** get a freebie because of WHO **she** is. Nobody in The System authorized him to inflict deadly moral judgment, and Heaven doesn't employ *death angels* –– it's PRO LIFE!

The Case is RETRIED again. And the Verdict is ———— ?

Praise the Lord and the Judge and the **Third** Jury! Third time is the charm. Trial Deputy tenacity triumphs and the satisfaction is immense. A lady of the evening gets her Day in Court and a vicious killer gets his comeuppance in Court, belatedly held **personally** ACCOUNTABLE for his bloody crime – the **Third** time around. **Each** VICTIM is entitled to impartial and coequal consideration of the evidence in her Case to VERDICT.

2. **Trout in the milk evidence**. Ultimately, EVIDENCE produces **personal** RESPONSIBILITY. **All** the career *dedication*, the power of proper *attitude*, and the diligent *study*, **all** the hard

work, the *even-handedness*, and the *empathy*, **all** the sense of personal *accountability*, the astute selection of *Juries*, and the passionate *representation*, **all** the meticulously *prepared* Argument Outlines, the well crafted Court *Instructions*, and the dynamic *rhetoric*, WON'T get the job done without EVIDENCE. And the **best** evidence sometimes comes in very **small packages**! Say, a sales receipt and a pubic hair.

a.   *The Sales Receipt* – The incriminating EVIDENCE is found in a refrigerator. Not just any frig mind you, it's Richard's refrigerator. Why does that matter? Well, Richard's refrigerator is in Richard's kitchen inside Richard's house, and Richard – poor soul, lies on the kitchen floor in a puddle of blood just beyond the kitchen table. He's been **shot twice** in the chest with a large caliber pistol. The projectiles killed him approximately thirty six hours earlier. Inducement for the offense is theft of an expensive gold coin collection. The suspect, whom we'll call **Chester**, is an acquaintance of Richard. He's obviously a rascal. The Victim is sociable to him, but Chester doesn't return the civility. He steals Richard"s gold coins and his life.

Police interview Chester and learn he's been at the crime scene, but he is adamant in the assertion he was there on Thursday. Which is the day BEFORE the **Murder**. Sundry groceries picked up at a Sav-on Drug Store are the key to cracking the Case, however. The guy talks too much for his own good. He's too helpful to Police in a verbal process of trying to help himself. A flapping jaw can flap itself directly to jail.

Chester offers further enlightenment to the Cops, trying to buttress his version of events with *details* and an *inference* of cash liquidity. Ergo, wrong date and lack of motive – he already had money. Chester says he picked up treats for the two of them at mid morning on Thursday. *Mr. Too-Wordy* remembers the specific items he purchased. He lists two six packs of bottled Budweiser, a can of sardines, a large bag of pretzels, a large bag of barbecue potato chips, a medium size can of dry roasted peanuts, two small cups of strawberry yogurt, a box of toothpicks, and a container of dental floss. For a grand total of – **ten** articles.

Hey, that's too much information from a person of interest. However, the Constitution doesn't frown on admissions. Self incrimination is unconstitutional only when it's coerced. The Constitution isn't offended when a guilty man trips over a tongue he's voluntarily wagging.

A few careless words imparted to Homicide Detectives and a flawed memory can make a huge different in a Homicide Investigation. To borrow a time-tested expression, *It's just a matter of putting two and two together.* I'm referring to Chester's allegation of **Thursday** and **shopping** juxtaposed with proof of **Friday** and a **sales receipt.**

Yeah, the Crime Scene Investigators find evidence of Chester's Sav-on groceries at the Crime Scene – all **ten** of them. An unopened six pack of Bud together with a *sales receipt* inside a plastic Sav-on bag, two cups of strawberry yogurt, and a partially full can of sardines are found in the refrigerator. A Bud beer carton and six empty bottles of Bud are found in a kitchen trash basket, open bags of pretzels and barbeque potato chips, an open can of dry roasted peanuts, an open box of toothpicks, an unopened spool of dental floss, and miscellaneous pieces of pretzels, chips, and peanuts are scattered across a section of the kitchen counter. So, we know Chester was at the scene. The pivotal question is **when?**

Hel– lo, not a problem for Law Enforcement, but a definite pain-in-the-ass for Chester. There's *a trout in the milk* inside the refrigerator. Abracadabra –– the aforementioned Sav-on bag is hiding something besides an unopened six pack of Budweiser. It's a slip of paper Chester is going to wish he hadn't forgotten. One little ole measly piece of paper with **ten** items plus **date** and **time** printed on it. Why Chester forgot about the damned SALES RECEIPT when he shot off his mouth! And the SALES RECEIPT tells us that Chester bought his Sav-on merchandise at 6:10 p.m. on **Friday.**

Therefore, revisiting the principle of putting **2+2 together** –– or **guilt by associating facts.** What does juxtaposing Chester's version of **Thursday mid morning** with the Sales Receipt version of **Friday** at **6:10 p.m.** tell us about Chester? Answer: It tells us Chester is a stone-cold LIAR. He wasn't at The Scene the day BEFORE the Crime, he was at the CRIME SCENE on the DAY **of** the Crime. Further, it suggests if Chester is **lying** about being at The Scene on the DAY of the **MURDER** it's probably because he COMMITTED the **Murder** and now wishes he'd torn that SALES RECEIPT into a thousand pieces.

Pathetic murderous Chester – **done in** by a scrap of paper he heedlessly left in the Frig inside a beer bag! That-a-boy Chester, keep your *trout in the milk* fresh so it won't spoil.

b. *The Pubic Hair* – If a witness **sees** something, or **hears** something, or **smells** something, or **touches** something, or **tastes** something –– <u>as</u>–<u>the</u>–<u>Crime</u>–<u>happens</u> –– it's DIRECT EVIDENCE. *Everything* else is CIRCUMSTANTIAL. One of the last Cases I partnered before retiring from the Clark County District Attorney's Office involved **DNA** evidence.

The Criminal Act occurred at a construction site between midnight and 5:42 a.m. A carpenter arrived at the scene and made a gruesome discovery under the staircase of a framed house. His 911call is received at the later time referenced in the second preceding sentence. Clearly, the instrumentalities employed in the homicide have been spur of the moment, get whatever's handy improvisation. An early morning rendevous between assailant and victim, apparently begins with a false presumption by the killer that there will be consensual love-making. His amorous ploy is obviously rejected, but the self-centered hooligan with the hots turns a deaf ear to a married Lady's *NO thank you.*

According to Crime Scene Investigators and the Medical Examiner's Office, the Victim has been bound and gagged. A white plastic Wonder bread wrapper is stretched between the jaws and tied at the back of her head. The arms are bound at the wrists behind her back with a white plastic construction strip. The type used in automatic screw guns. Two brass screws are still attached to the strip. The young lady has been stabbed <u>eleven</u> times in the left chest and <u>once</u> in her upper back with a 6" screwdriver. Evidence of blunt force trauma is observed on her head, neck, left chest, right and left shoulders, and back – with resulting contusions and abrasions. Presumably inflicted by the bloody 2 ½ foot 2X4 situated a few feet from the body. Defensive wounds are also present on both upper arms.

Sexual Assault and Serology kits are collected. They include combed and pulled *pubic hair* from the Victim.

It's a crime of stealth and malicious self preservation. Cade does it because he's stronger. Takes what he wants against her will, and brutally kills her to silence her. Then –– he walks away.

A perfect crime? Violent deeds that leave no clues? A crass male chauvinist who eludes the Criminal Justice System? HARDLY! The best evidence can be a very small object, and the Crime Lab finds it. A <u>single</u> *foreign* **pubic hair** has been combed from the Victim's pubic region. The <u>crinkly</u> <u>little</u> <u>hair</u> becomes the *linchpin* of the Case. The heavy shoe of Justice drops a month later. Cade is arrested.

At Trial, the Jury learns the *foreign* **pubic hair** is **microscopically** *indistinguishable* from a pubic hair standard of the Defendant. **<u>Identical</u>** in color, length, tip, root, diameter, cuticle, scales, pigment, medulla, cortex, and damage. Moreover, the **DNA** obtained from the *foreign* hair and the *standard* hair is also IDENTICAL. The **frequency rate** of this particular **DNA** type is ONCE in **twenty six hundred**.

Thus, a **single** PUBIC HAIR becomes *a* figurative *trout in a can of milk* in the Murder Case. It's natural habitat is **not** the pelvic area of the young woman saying, *HELL –– no*! This is a COMBED hair not a pulled hair. A threadlike strand that grew out of the skin of someone else. And it doesn't have legs or wings, nor did it come equipped with a jet ski. It couldn't get itself into the thick of things.

The *foreign* **pubic hair** needed a set of wheels to get to the construction site. A self-centered hooligan with the hots transported the **hair** to the hard, unyielding concrete under the staircase. And it's still embedded in his groin until friction from the sexual penetration transfers it from him to her. JUSTICE has you by the short hair, Killer. – GOTCHA!

Harry S. Truman said, "I don't give people hell. I just tell them the Truth, and they think it's Hell." I earnestly hope this approach was a trademark of my career. "Facts are stubborn things." (Alain Rene Le Sage, *Gil Blas* [1715-1735] Book X, Chap.1) James Russell Lowell makes the same point. He said, "Facts are contrary 'z mules." (*Biglow Papers*, Series II [1862], No.4) I tried to maintain an unvarying persona in the Courtroom towards Defendants and their Counsel. Always be pleasant. Always be polite. Always be respectful. Always be fiercely competitive, but always be factual.

A responsible Prosecutor, someone committed to *just* results, **never** indulges in hyperbole. Stick to the facts man – nothing but the facts. Truth has a biting edge for those who are criminally culpable. When a Prosecutor's *tongue sweats* in summation he doesn't have to be disrespectful or bombastic. He doesn't have to give Defendants hell. He simply tells them the Truth – a rhetorical bottomless-pit maker for the **guilty**, and they think they're in Hell!

Justice is grounded in fact!

Well, the proverbial trout in the milk, *if I could be a Trial Lawyer anybody can*, has treaded his watered-down milk long enough. He's a bit weary, wary of circling – and slightly blinded by the frothy stuff. The finicky fellow who ONCE wore a floppy straw farm hat has stirred up sufficient Court Room eddies and splashed much of his metaphorical Milk out of the can. I genuinely hope readers have enjoyed the swim, and won't be saying as we part: *We loved the words in your text, but we're wondering if you could possibly put them in a totally different order.* If that's the view of some – I'm sorry. I've done all I could.

A man should know who he is. Be proud of his name, his ancestry, his life – and what it means. My words express a part of what I am.

Many inhabitants of this planet have an identity crisis. Though I'm riddled with ambiguity and shortcomings, a strong sense of **identity** is <u>not</u> one of my problems! I KNOW WHO I AM! I've come to terms with myself – and I'm content.

But ONCE I was a Prosecutor. ONCE upon a time I did my best to **toll the bell** for JUSTICE. *I took to the law, and the muscular strength it gave to my jaw has lasted all of my life.* (Lewis Carroll, adapted)

Sincerely,
Mel Harmon.